An Insider's Guide to Academic Writing

Academic Writing

A Brief Rhetoric

SECOND EDITION

An Insider's Guide to Academic Writing

A Brief Rhetoric

Susan Miller-Cochran

University of Arizona

Roy Stamper

North Carolina State University

Stacey Cochran

University of Arizona

 bedford/st.martin's

Macmillan Learning

Boston | New York

For Bedford/St. Martin's

Vice President, Editorial, Macmillan Learning Humanities: Edwin Hill
Executive Program Director for English: Leasa Burton
Senior Program Manager: Laura Arcari
Marketing Manager: Vivian Garcia
Director of Content Development: Jane Knetzger
Developmental Editor: Sherry Mooney
Senior Content Project Manager: Ryan Sullivan
Workflow Project Manager: Lisa McDowell
Production Supervisor: Robert Cherry
Associate Media Project Manager: Emily Brower
Media Editor: Julia Domenicucci
Editorial Services: Lumina Datamatics, Inc.
Composition: Lumina Datamatics, Inc.
Text Permissions Manager: Kalina Ingham
Text Permissions Researcher: Arthur Johnson, Lumina Datamatics, Inc.
Photo Permissions Editor: Angela Boehler
Photo Researcher: Candice Cheesman, Lumina Datamatics, Inc.
Director of Design, Content Management: Diana Blume
Text Design: Claire Seng-Niemoeller
Cover Design: William Boardman
Cover Art: Andrea Tsurumi
Printing and Binding: LSC Communications

Manufactured in the United States of America.

1 2 3 4 5 6   23 22 21 20 19 18

For information, write: Bedford/St. Martin's, 75 Arlington Street, Boston, MA 02116
ISBN   978-1-319-10404-7

Acknowledgments

Text acknowledgments and copyrights appear at the back of the book on page 354, which constitutes an extension of the copyright page. Art acknowledgments and copyrights appear on the same page as the art selections they cover.

Preface for Instructors

What is an "insider"? In all walks of life, insiders are the ones who know the territory, speak the language, have the skills, understand the codes, keep the secrets. With the second edition of *An Insider's Guide to Academic Writing*, we want to build on the success of the first edition and continue to help college students, new to the world of higher education, to learn the territory, language, skills, codes, and secrets of academic writing in disciplinary contexts. While no single book, or course, or teacher could train all students in all the details of scholarly writing in all disciplines, *An Insider's Guide* offers a flexible, rhetoric-based pedagogy that has helped our students, and students across the country, to navigate the reading and writing expectations of academic discourse communities across the curriculum. We have found that because the pedagogy is grounded in rhetorical principles and concepts, writing instructors who might otherwise be wary of teaching outside their scholarly expertise feel confident about the approach. Moreover, students quickly grasp the transferable benefits of the approach to their future courses, so their level of enthusiasm and personal investment is high. With this new edition, we are celebrating the success of this book in achieving its goal of bringing students into the academic fold, as it was adopted at more than seventy schools, spanning four-year and two-year institutions. We are also fine-tuning that approach based on feedback from the students and instructors who have trusted us to support their efforts. New to the second edition is additional foundational support on the writing process, critical reading, and reflection, to give students the tools they need to be confident writers in any discipline.

As a unique enhancement to its rhetoric-based pedagogy, *An Insider's Guide to Academic Writing* integrates, through video and print interviews, the writing advice of scholars and undergraduates from many disciplines; they speak from and about their own experiences as academic writers. (We conducted, filmed, and curated the interviews ourselves, and they are available as part of the LaunchPad package with the book.) Whether professor or student, these credible and compelling experts humanize and demystify disciplinary discourse, sharing their insider knowledge with academic novices.

An Insider's Guide to Academic Writing derives from the research and teaching that went into transitioning the first-year writing program at North Carolina State University to a writing-in-the-disciplines (WID) approach. This approach is gaining wider currency nationwide as calls for instruction in transferable college writing skills increase. At that time, more than a decade ago, faculty in the program (including the authors of this book) immersed themselves in scholarship on WID and WID pedagogy. We also began to seek supporting instructional materials, but did not find any existing textbooks that met our needs. While several texts focused, to varying degrees, on introducing students to writing in the academic disciplines, few texts employed a rhetorical approach to explore these kinds of writing. Fewer still employed a rhetorical approach to understanding the conventions of writing that characterize those disciplinary texts while also providing support for students' own production of disciplinary genres.

The book that emerged from these years of teaching and research, *An Insider's Guide to Academic Writing*, is a composition rhetoric with readings that distills much of the writing-in-the-disciplines approach that we and our colleagues have used with success for many years. This approach begins by applying rhetorical principles to the understanding of texts, and then shows those principles at work in various domains of academic inquiry, including the humanities, the social sciences, the natural sciences, and the applied fields. It does so mainly by (1) introducing students to rhetorical lenses through which they can view the genres and conventions they will be expected to read and produce in other courses, (2) providing examples of those genres and conventions to analyze and discuss, and (3) including carefully scaffolded writing activities and projects designed to help students explore and guide their production of those genres.

We believe that composition programs pursuing a WID-oriented approach to academic writing will find that *An Insider's Guide* provides a foundation of instruction in disciplinary thinking and writing that is flexible enough to accommodate the diverse teaching interests of individual instructors. Some faculty, for instance, use this approach to support themed courses; they examine how a particular topic or issue is explored by scholars across a range of disciplines. Other faculty situate principles of argument at the center of their course designs and explore disciplinary perspectives and writing in light of those principles. Still others organize their courses as step-by-step journeys through academic domains while attending to the similarities and distinctions in writing practices (rhetorical conventions and genres) of various fields.

The goal of each of these approaches is to foster students' understanding of the various academic communities they participate in as part of the typical undergraduate experience. With the support of *An Insider's Guide to Academic Writing*, these approaches can also foster a deepening rhetorical sensitivity in our students while providing opportunities for them to analyze and practice the kinds of genres they often encounter in college. The book encourages students to exercise rhetorical skills that are transferable from one writing situation to another and supports a rhetorical approach to understanding writing that should be at the core of any first-year writing experience.

A Closer Look at What's in the Book

An Insider's Guide to Academic Writing takes students inside the worlds of higher education, academic writing and research, and disciplinary writing.

- Part One, "A Guide to College and College Writing," begins by introducing students to colleges and universities, as well as to the kinds of writing expectations they will likely face in college. It introduces students to core principles of rhetoric and writing process, and reviews basic principles of argument and strategies for conducting library research.

- Part Two, "Inside Academic Writing," is an exploration of the research practices, rhetorical conventions, and genres that characterize the major academic disciplinary domains: the humanities, the social sciences, the natural sciences, as well as a number of applied fields. The first chapter in Part Two (Chapter 6) explores the role of the core principles from Part One—rhetoric, argument, and research—in the various academic disciplines. Each of the remaining chapters begins with an exploration of research practices specific to particular academic communities and employs a practical, three-part framework (SLR, or "structure, language, and reference")* for identifying and analyzing the conventions that characterize writing in each discipline.

"INSIDER" FEATURES

The chapters in this book provide a number of features that help facilitate instruction and student learning:

"Insider's View" Sidebars and Videos Linked to LaunchPad
Students hear directly from scholars in various academic fields who explore disciplinary writing expectations and reflect on their own writing practices. These unique features provide a form of personal access to the academic world that students sometimes find alien, uninviting, or intimidating. Each video is accompanied by a pair of activities within LaunchPad, one to confirm

Insider's View
Purpose and audience shape every decision
KAREN KEATON JACKSON, WRITING STUDIES

"Purpose and au[...] decision you will [...]

LaunchPad
See what writing studies instructor Moriah McCracken has to say about genres.

Sidebars and video links

*For the concept of the SLR framework, we are indebted to Patricia Linton, Robert Madigan, and Susan Johnson ("Introducing Students to Disciplinary Genres: The Role of the General Composition Course," *Language and Learning across the Disciplines*, vol. 1, no. 2, October 1994, pp. 63-78).

students' understanding of the content and the second inviting them to make larger connections and provide thoughtful written responses.

"Insider Example" reading

"Insider Example" Readings

These readings appear throughout the chapters, providing models of writing by scholars and students. Most of the readings exemplify important genres of academic and disciplinary writing; many are annotated with marginal commentary that identifies writers' rhetorical moves and/or poses questions for students' further consideration. These annotations take students "inside" the production of various disciplinary texts and, by extension, inside the academy itself.

"Inside Work" and "Writing Project" Activities

These activities appear strategically throughout the book's chapters. They are designed to provide opportunities for students to put their learning into action, to analyze and practice the skills and moves taught in the chapters, building a scaffold that supports students' mastery of skills needed to produce the various "Writing Projects" explored throughout the book, from rhetorical analyses and interpretations (in the humanities), theory response papers and literature reviews (in the social sciences), research proposals and formal observation reports (in the natural sciences), to lesson plans and memoranda (in the applied fields).

"Inside Work" and "Writing Project" activities

INSIDE WORK Drafting a Scene for a Literacy Narrative

Brainstorm a list of at least five specific scenes you could choose from that best illustrate your literacy development.

Choose one and free-write for five minutes about where the scene happened (location), how long the scene took place (ideally, between a few minutes and a few hours), who was in the scene, and how the scene helped shape your identity.

WRITING PROJECT Composing a Literacy Narrative

The purpose of the literacy narrative is for you to reflect on and tell the story of your literacy development. Effective narratives have a beginning, middle, and end, and a literacy narrative follows a series of connected scenes (perhaps three) that illustrate points regarding how you developed your skills, identity, and views of yourself and others as a literate person.

Summary "Tip Sheets" Each chapter concludes with a "Tip Sheet" that underscores critical concepts and insights for students as they move from novices to academic insiders.

Finally, the appendix, "Introduction to Documentation Styles," discusses how specific citation styles reflect disciplinary concerns and emphases while concisely explaining and exemplifying the basics of MLA, APA, and CSE documentation.

What's New in the Second Edition?

In response to instructor feedback, we have enhanced the second edition of *An Insider's Guide to Academic Writing* to include the following new features:

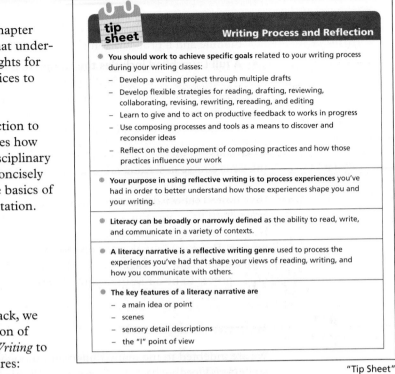

"Tip Sheet"

- **A new Chapter 2, "Writing Process and Reflection,"** introduces students more fully to process-based writing, and it prepares them for the kinds of reflection that writing research shows us will help them develop as writers in the long term. The principles and activities in Chapter 2 will help scaffold reflection throughout a course so that students develop reflective writing habits. That reflection will further enable them to translate their skills into future coursework or writing in their eventual careers.

- **New and updated examples throughout the text,** including more extensive coverage of school types and the exploration of a community college mission statement in Chapter 1, reflect a broader range of educational experiences and career goals, attending to the needs and interests of students at community colleges as well as four-year schools.

- **Expanded coverage of health fields and criminal justice** has been added to Chapter 10, "Reading and Writing in the Applied Fields," broadening the scope of student career paths covered. This material, including a new Insider video, illuminates additional professional avenues and the writing conventions within them.

- **New modules on Engineering, Media, and Information Technology** showcase additional applied fields in the LaunchPad—and are available as custom options for the print text. These brief modules address the conventions and concerns of writing in these career-focused disciplines and include key writing genres for each field, such as script pages in the Media module and a problem-solution proposal in the Engineering module.

- **A full LaunchPad includes the complete e-book,** offering the most extensive resources for teaching and learning with *An Insider's Guide to Academic Writing*. Along with the e-book, the LaunchPad includes Insider videos and activities, reading comprehension quizzes for every selection in the book, and LearningCurve adaptive quizzing.

In all walks of life, not all who are invited inside become insiders. Students taking your course in writing are there because they have accepted the invitation to higher education; they've crossed the first threshold. But to become insiders, they'll need the wisdom and counsel of other insiders. We have prepared this book, with its supporting videos and ancillary materials (detailed on p. xii), to help them learn the territory, language, skills, codes, and secrets of academic writing. But a guidebook can only do so much. Students need insiders such as yourself and your colleagues to guide their understanding. We hope our *Insider's Guide* proves to be a resource you rely on as you start them on their journeys.

Acknowledgments

We are indebted to the many skilled and thoughtful instructors who have used and offered feedback on the first edition of this book. We are truly grateful to you for supporting, through your engaging advice and encouraging criticism, our efforts to make this book the best it can possibly be. Most of all, we are grateful to the student writers who shared their work with us for inclusion in this edition of the book. We are grateful for the incredible support from our team at Bedford. First and foremost among that team is Sherry Mooney, our editor, who has helped us see this project through to completion while providing insightful suggestions that have guided our approach. We are also indebted to composition publisher Leasa Burton, who understood our goals and championed this project from the beginning. We have also received outstanding support and guidance from Ryan Sullivan, who guided the book through the production process with great care and good humor. Claire Seng-Niemoeller created the superb design of the book. We thank Vivian Garcia for her marketing and market development efforts. We remain grateful to other contributors who helped in so many ways behind the scenes, including Edwin Hill, Laura Arcari, Michael Granger, Kalina Ingham, Suzanne Chouljian, and Julia Domenicucci, as well as William Boardman, who designed the cover.

We are also indebted to the students who were willing to try this approach and, in many cases, share their writing in this book. Their examples provide essential scaffolding for the book's approach, and their honest feedback helped us refine our explanation of various genres and disciplines.

We are also grateful to our colleagues in the First-Year Writing Program at North Carolina State University and the Writing Program at the University of Arizona, who have shared their expertise and ideas about teaching writing in and about disciplines over the years. Without their support and their innovation, we would not have been able to complete this project. We are also indebted to Kate Lavia-Bagley, whose experience and success with teaching this approach is showcased in the outstanding Instructor's Manual she has written to accompany the book.

We also appreciate the outstanding comments and suggestions we received from reviewers throughout the development of this second edition: Mark Blaauw-Hara, North Central Michigan College; Grace Chen, University of Arizona; Jonathan Cook, Durham Technical Community College; Kelly Giles, McDowell Technical Community College; Anne Helms, Alamance Community College; Michelle Jarvis, Davidson County Community College; Brenda Kennedy, Rockingham Community College; Kevin Knight, Cape Fear Community College; Carey Millsap-Spears, Moraine Valley Community College; Melissa Mohlere, Rowan-Cabarrus Community College; Tim Oldakowski, Slippery Rock University; Christopher Osborne, Guilford Technical Community College; Paula Rash, Caldwell Community College & Technical Institute; Daniel Stanford, Pitt Community College; Elizabeth Terry, University of Cincinnati/Clermont; David Townsend, Richmond Community College.

As always, we remain indebted to our friends and families, who provided a great deal of support as we worked on this edition of the book.

Susan Miller-Cochran

Roy Stamper

Stacey Cochran

We're all in. As always.

Bedford/St. Martin's is as passionately committed to the discipline of English as ever, working hard to provide support and services that make it easier for you to teach your course your way.

Find **community support** at the Bedford/St. Martin's English Community (**community.macmillan.com**), where you can follow our *Bits* blog for new teaching ideas, download titles from our professional resource series, and review projects in the pipeline.

Choose **curriculum solutions** that offer flexible custom options, combining our carefully developed print and digital resources, acclaimed works from Macmillan's trade imprints, and your own course or program materials to provide the exact resources your students need. Our approach to customization makes it possible to create a customized project uniquely suited for your students and, based on your enrollment size, return money to your department and raise your institutional profile with a high-impact author visit through the Macmillan Author Program ("MAP"). *An Insider's Guide to Academic Writing* has pre-built custom modules for Engineering, Media, and Information Technology that can be added to customize the base text.

Rely on **outstanding service** from your Bedford/St. Martin's sales representative and editorial team. Contact us or visit **macmillanlearning.com** to learn more about any of the options below.

LaunchPad
macmillan learning

LAUNCHPAD FOR *AN INSIDER'S GUIDE TO ACADEMIC WRITING*: WHERE STUDENTS LEARN

LaunchPad provides engaging content and new ways to get the most out of your book. Get an interactive e-book combined with assessment tools in a fully customizable course space; then assign and mix our resources with yours.

- **Insider videos** offer insights into how experts write in various disciplinary fields.

- **Expanded coverage of the applied fields,** featuring modules on Engineering, Media, and Information Technology.

- **Diagnostics** provide opportunities to assess areas for improvement and assign additional exercises based on students' needs. Visual reports show performance by topic, class, and student as well as improvement over time.

- **Pre-built units**—including readings, videos, quizzes, and more—are easy to adapt and assign by adding your own materials and mixing them with our high-quality multimedia content and ready-made assessment options, such as **LearningCurve** adaptive quizzing and Exercise Central.

- Use LaunchPad on its own or **integrate it** with your school's learning management system so that your class is always on the same page.

LaunchPad for *An Insider's Guide to Academic Writing* can be purchased on its own or packaged with the print book at a significant discount. An activation code is required. To order LaunchPad for *An Insider's Guide to Academic Writing* with the print book, use ISBN 978-1-319-22336-6. For more information, go to **launchpadworks.com**.

CHOOSE FROM ALTERNATIVE FORMATS OF *AN INSIDER'S GUIDE TO ACADEMIC WRITING*

Bedford/St. Martin's offers a range of formats. Choose what works best for you and your students:

- **Rhetoric and Reader Edition** The full edition includes the same great content along with a four-chapter disciplinary reader. To order the full edition, use ISBN 978-1-319-10399-6. To order the full edition packaged with LaunchPad, use ISBN 978-1-319-22338-0.
- **Popular e-book formats** For details of our e-book partners, visit **macmillanlearning.com/ebooks**.

INSTRUCTOR RESOURCES

You have a lot to do in your course. We want to make it easy for you to find the support you need—and to get it quickly.

- *Resources for Teaching An Insider's Guide to Academic Writing: A Brief Rhetoric* is available as a PDF that can be downloaded from **macmillanlearning.com**. Visit the instructor resources tab for *An Insider's Guide to Academic Writing*. In addition to chapter overviews and teaching tips, the instructor's manual includes sample syllabi, context and suggested responses for questions within the book, and suggestions for expanding activities and writing projects.
- *Resources for Teaching North Carolina English 112 with An Insider's Guide to Academic Writing* is available as a PDF that can be downloaded from the Bedford/St. Martin's online catalog at **macmillanlearning.com**. This brief resource complements *Resources for Teaching An Insider's Guide to Academic Writing*, with teaching attention to specific course outcomes and transfer requirements articulated in the 2014 Comprehensive Articulation Agreement between the University of North Carolina and the North Carolina Community College System.

How This Book Supports WPA Outcomes for First-Year Composition

Note: This chart aligns with the latest WPA Outcomes Statement, ratified in July 2014.

WPA Outcomes	Relevant Features of *An Insider's Guide to Academic Writing*
Rhetorical Knowledge	
Learn and use key rhetorical concepts through analyzing and composing a variety of texts.	*An Insider's Guide to Academic Writing* is built on a foundation of rhetorical analysis and production that commences in Chapter 3, "Reading and Writing Rhetorically" (pp. 45–58), and is extended through the rest of the book. The book uses a variety of "rhetorical lenses" to help students become academic insiders who know what conventions to expect and adapt in disciplinary writing. And it brings in, via print and video, the insights of real academic professionals to help students become insiders.
Gain experience reading and composing in several genres to understand how genre conventions shape and are shaped by readers' and writers' practices and purposes.	Each of the ten chapters in Parts One and Two provide instruction in reading and composing a variety of key academic and disciplinary genres, from a rhetorical analysis (Chapter 3, "Reading and Writing Rhetorically," pp. 52–58) to a literature review (Chapter 8, "Reading and Writing in the Social Sciences," pp. 211–26) to a research proposal (Chapter 9, "Reading and Writing in the Natural Sciences," pp. 271–79).
Develop facility in responding to a variety of situations and contexts, calling for purposeful shifts in voice, tone, level of formality, design, medium, and/or structure.	*An Insider's Guide* is predicated on the practice of situational and contextual composition, where rhetorical context and attention to conventions of structure, language, and reference determine a writer's approach to material. For example, in Chapter 6, "Reading and Writing in Academic Disciplines" (pp. 122–28), an astronomer explains how he writes for different audiences, with examples of the same scientific research written up for two different audiences. The chapter introduces the "Structure/Language/Reference" heuristic.
Understand and use a variety of technologies to address a range of audiences.	The use of "Insider's View" videos, available in LaunchPad for *An Insider's Guide to Academic Writing*, models and reinforces the principle of using different technologies to communicate to a range of audiences. The videos of academics explaining how and why they write represent a different channel of explanation, to students and instructors, than the pedagogy in the print book. See astronomer Mike Brotherton's interviews (Chapter 6, "Reading and Writing in Academic Disciplines," pp. 121, 124, 128) and "Insider's View" videos, for example.
Match the capacities of different environments (e.g., print and electronic) to varying rhetorical situations.	See the previous entry, and also the various discussions of genre and genre awareness throughout the book—for example, the opening pages of Chapter 3, "Reading and Writing Rhetorically" (pp. 46–50). See also the cluster of material in Chapter 7, "Reading and Writing in the Humanities," on interpreting images (pp. 140–43) and the Dale Jacobs essay on multimodality (pp. 145–54).

WPA Outcomes	Relevant Features of *An Insider's Guide to Academic Writing*
Critical Thinking, Reading, and Composing	
Use composing and reading for inquiry, learning, thinking, and communicating in various rhetorical contexts.	All of the discipline-specific chapters include detailed information about research and inquiry in their academic domains. See Chapter 7, "Reading and Writing in the Humanities" (pp. 142–60); Chapter 8, "Reading and Writing in the Social Sciences" (pp. 185–96); Chapter 9, "Reading and Writing in the Natural Sciences" (pp. 243–52); and Chapter 10, "Reading and Writing in the Applied Fields" (pp. 294–300).
Read a diverse range of texts, attending especially to relationships between assertion and evidence, to patterns of organization, to interplay between verbal and nonverbal elements, and how these features function for different audiences and situations.	Chapter 4, "Developing Arguments" (pp. 59–80), offers instruction in identifying claims and assertions and relating them to evidence. The genres sections of all the disciplinary chapters in Part Two, "Inside Academic Writing" (Chapters 6–10), help students pay attention to patterns of organization (e.g., the IMRaD format), with particular attention to the Structure, Language, and Reference systems in play. See, for example, "Genres of Writing in the Natural Sciences" (pp. 258–90).
Locate and evaluate primary and secondary research materials, including journal articles, essays, books, databases, and informal Internet sources.	See in particular Chapter 5, "Academic Research" (pp. 81–115), where information on locating and evaluating primary and secondary research materials—including journal articles, essays, books, databases, and informal Internet sources—can be found.
Use strategies—such as interpretation, synthesis, response, critique, and design/ redesign—to compose texts that integrate the writer's ideas with those from appropriate sources.	Chapter 5, "Academic Research" (pp. 81–115), discusses working with sources. Furthermore, Chapter 7, "Reading and Writing in the Humanities" (pp. 139–82), explores textual interpretation, response, and critique; and Chapter 8, "Reading and Writing in the Social Sciences" (pp. 183–239), pays particular attention to strategies of synthesis.
Processes	
Develop a writing project through multiple drafts.	*An Insider's Guide to Academic Writing* presents a detailed overview of the writing process in Chapter 2, "Writing Process and Reflection" (pp. 19–44), and many chapters include "Inside Work" activities that ask students to build on the previous activities to develop a paper. For example, Chapter 4, "Developing Arguments," includes a sequence of such activities on pp. 61, 64, 67, 68, and 69.
Develop flexible strategies for reading, drafting, reviewing, collaboration, revising, rewriting, rereading, and editing.	See the previous entry. Additionally, the "Writing Project" activities that generally close each chapter are sequenced and scaffolded to support process writing. Throughout the book and in LaunchPad interviews, academic insiders discuss the nature of collaborative writing and working with editors.

WPA Outcomes	Relevant Features of *An Insider's Guide to Academic Writing*
Use composing processes and tools as a means to discover and reconsider ideas.	Chapter 2, "Writing Process and Reflection," includes the section "Use Composing Processes and Tools as a Means to Discover and Reconsider Ideas" (pp. 25–28). Additionally, all of the discipline-specific chapters include detailed information about research and inquiry in their academic domains, and pay attention to the notion of testing ideas with audiences. See in particular Chapter 9, "Reading and Writing in the Natural Sciences," which traces how the process of developing observation and research inevitably leads to a modification of ideas (contrast the two papers by student Kedric Lemon on pp. 260–70 and pp. 280–90).
Experience the collaborative and social aspects of writing processes.	Many of the "Inside Work" activities require collaborative work, and the ethos of collaboration comes through strongly in the chapters on social sciences (Chapter 8) and natural sciences (Chapter 9). The chapter on writing in the natural sciences explicitly discusses the importance of cooperation and collaboration in the conventions section (pp. 257–58).
Learn to give and act on productive feedback to works in progress.	See the previous rubric and Lesson 2, which includes coverage on giving and receiving productive feedback and offers a sample rough draft with a model of peer review feedback to showcase useful feedback for students.
Adapt composing processes for a variety of technologies and modalities.	*An Insider's Guide to Academic Writing*'s start-to-finish emphasis on rhetorically situated, genre-aware, and convention-informed writing underscores this point for students.
Reflect on the development of composing practices and how those practices influence their work.	Chapter 2, "Writing Process and Reflection" (pp. 19–44), introduces students to reflective writing and the benefits of considering their own processes as they develop their writing. See in particular "Reflect on the Development of Composing Practices and How Those Practices Influence Your Work" (p. 28). Additionally, many of the "Inside Work" activities throughout the book have students reflect on what they know, what they think they know, and what they learn. For example, see the "Inside Work" activities throughout Chapter 1, "Inside Colleges and Universities" (pp. 3–18), and the "Inside Work" exercise "Reflecting on Your Thought Processes" in Chapter 2 (p. 28).
Knowledge of Conventions	
Develop knowledge of linguistic structures, including grammar, punctuation, and spelling, through practice in composing and revising.	The distinctive SLR framework (Structure/Language/Reference) introduced in Part Two ("Inside Academic Writing," Chapters 6–10; see the introduction to SLR in Chapter 6, pp. 125–26) has a Language category that emphasizes the linguistic choices and conventions in disciplinary writing, and the Reference feature puts emphasis on formatting issues that include spelling and punctuation. Bedford/St. Martin's also offers a variety of writing handbooks that can be packaged inexpensively with *An Insider's Guide*. See the preface for information.

WPA Outcomes	Relevant Features of *An Insider's Guide to Academic Writing*
Understand why genre conventions for structure, paragraphing, tone, and mechanics vary.	Genre conventions across and within disciplines are emphasized throughout Part Two of the book. Beyond that, the Appendix on documentation styles (pp. 339–53) discusses disciplinary conventions in referencing, with implications for structure and mechanics.
Gain experience negotiating variations in genre conventions.	*An Insider's Guide* provides many opportunities for students to experiment and negotiate variations in disciplinary conventions. See, for example, the "Writing Projects" in Chapter 6, "Reading and Writing in Academic Disciplines," which include "Comparing Scholarly and Popular Articles" (p. 130) and "Translating a Scholarly Article for a Public Audience" (p. 134). In particular, some of the "Inside Work" activities in Chapter 10, "Reading and Writing in the Applied Fields" (pp. 304, 314, 326, 337), ask students to become professionals "for a day" and try writing important genres by extrapolating from models in the chapter.
Learn common formats and/or design features for different kinds of texts.	The design features of key genres, such as IMRaD, are highlighted (especially in Chapters 8 and 9, on the social sciences and natural sciences respectively). Chapter 5, "Academic Research," introduces different documentation formats (MLA, APA, CSE—see pp. 99–101), which is expanded upon in the Appendix on documentation styles (pp. 339–53).
Explore the concepts of intellectual property (such as fair use and copyright) that motivate documentation conventions.	The Appendix on documentation styles (MLA, APA, CSE formats) raises issues of different documentation conventions (pp. 339–53), and the discussion of plagiarism in Chapter 5, "Academic Research," raises concerns about intellectual property (pp. 98–99).
Practice applying citation conventions systematically in their own work.	The Appendix (pp. 339–53) enables students to apply citation conventions of MLA, APA, and CSE styles systematically in their own work.

Contents

LaunchPad Additional video material may be found online in LaunchPad when the ▶ icon appears.

Preface for Instructors v

| PART ONE | **A Guide to College and College Writing** 1 |

1 Inside Colleges and Universities 3

What Is Higher Education? 3

How Do Colleges and Universities Differ from One Another? 4

▪ **INSIDE WORK:** Choosing a College 5

What Is the Purpose of College? 5

▪ **INSIDE WORK:** Writing about Your School's Mission 7

▪ **INSIDE WORK:** Writing about College 7

▪ **INSIDE WORK:** Writing about Resources at Your Institution 7

What Are Academic Disciplines? 8

How Many Different Academic Disciplines Are There? 8

▪ **INSIDE WORK:** Understanding Disciplinarity 10

Why Do Academics Write? 10

▪ **INSIDE WORK:** Thinking about What Academics Write 11

▶ **INSIDER'S VIEW:** Sam Stout, Gena Lambrecht, Alexandria Woods, Students 12

How Does Writing in College Compare with Writing in Other Contexts? 12

▶ **INSIDER'S VIEW:** Karen Keaton Jackson, Writing Studies 13

▪ **INSIDE WORK:** Understanding the Goals of Your Writing Course 14

How Do Writers Learn to Write in New Contexts? 15

▪ **INSIDE WORK:** Learning about Writing in Other Contexts 15

▪ **WRITING PROJECT:** Profile of a Writer 15

Insider Example: Student Profile of a Business Professional   16

Rubbal Kumar, *First Draft of Interview Questions*   16

Rubbal Kumar, *Profile of a Writer: Benu Badhan*   16

Tip Sheet: Inside Colleges and Universities   18

2   Writing Process and Reflection   19

What Is a Writing Process?   20

Develop a Writing Project through Multiple Drafts   21

    INSIDE WORK: Reflecting on Your Drafting Process   21

Develop Flexible Writing Process Strategies   21

    INSIDE WORK: Reflecting on Flexibility   22

Learn to Give and to Act on Productive Feedback to Works in Progress   22

Insider Example: Sample Rough Draft of Student Jack Stegner's Literacy Narrative, with Peer Review Feedback from Student Nichelle Oquendo   23

Use Composing Processes and Tools as a Means to Discover and Reconsider Ideas   25

    INSIDER'S VIEW: Jonathan Morris and Jody Baumgartner, Political Science   26

    INSIDER'S VIEW: Patrick Bahls, Mathematics   27

    INSIDE WORK: Talking about Technology with a Partner   27

Reflect on the Development of Composing Practices and How Those Practices Influence Your Work   28

    INSIDE WORK: Reflecting on Your Thought Processes   28

What Is Reflective Writing?   29

What Is Literacy?   29

What Is a Literacy Narrative?   30

Characteristics of a Literacy Narrative   30

Insider Example: Professional Literacy Narrative   32

Aimee C. Mapes, *Two Vowels Together: On the Wonderfully Insufferable Experiences of Literacy*   32

    INSIDE WORK: Drafting a Scene for a Literacy Narrative   38

    WRITING PROJECT: Composing a Literacy Narrative   38

Insider Example: Student Literacy Narrative   40

Michaela Bieda, *My Journey to Writing*   40

Tip Sheet: Writing Process and Reflection   44

3 Reading and Writing Rhetorically 45

Understanding Rhetorical Context 46
- ● INSIDER'S VIEW: Karen Keaton Jackson, Writing Studies 46
- ▨ INSIDE WORK: Identifying Rhetorical Context 47

Understanding Genres 48
- ● INSIDER'S VIEW: Moriah McCracken, Writing Studies 49

Reading Rhetorically 49

Reading Visuals Rhetorically 50
- ▨ INSIDE WORK: Reading Rhetorically 50

Writing Rhetorically 50
- ▨ INSIDE WORK: Analyzing Rhetorical Context 52

Writing a Rhetorical Analysis 52
- George H. W. Bush, *Letter to Saddam Hussein* 53

  Insider Example: Student Rhetorical Analysis 55
  Sofia Lopez, *The Multiple Audiences of George H. W. Bush's Letter to Saddam Hussein* 55

- ▨ WRITING PROJECT: Writing a Rhetorical Analysis 57

Tip Sheet: Reading and Writing Rhetorically 58

4 Developing Arguments 59

Understanding Proofs and Appeals 60
- ▨ INSIDE WORK: Writing about Arguments 61

Making Claims 61
- Thesis versus Hypothesis 62

Developing Reasons 63
- ▨ INSIDE WORK: Constructing Thesis Statements 64

Supporting Reasons with Evidence 65
- ● INSIDER'S VIEW: Moriah McCracken, Writing Studies 66
- ● INSIDER'S VIEW: Michelle Richter, Criminology 66
- ▨ INSIDE WORK: Analyzing Audience Expectations 67

Understanding Assumptions 67
- ▨ INSIDE WORK: Considering Assumptions and Audience 68

Anticipating Counterarguments 68

   ○ **INSIDER'S VIEW:** Mike Brotherton, Astronomy 69

   ▓ **INSIDE WORK:** Dealing with Counterarguments 69

Analyzing Arguments 70

     Insider Example: Professional Analysis of an Advertisement 70

     Jack Solomon, Excerpt from *Masters of Desire: The Culture of American Advertising* 70

     Insider Example: Student Analysis of an Advertisement 74

     Timothy Holtzhauser, *Rhetoric of a 1943 War Bonds Ad* 74

   ▓ **WRITING PROJECT:** Composing a Rhetorical Analysis of an Advertisement 79

Tip Sheet: Developing Arguments 80

5 Academic Research 81

Conducting Research 81

  Developing a Research Question 81

   ▓ **INSIDE WORK:** Writing a Research Question 82

   ○ **INSIDER'S VIEW:** Jody Baumgartner and Jonathan Morris, Political Science 82

  Choosing Primary and Secondary Sources 82

   ○ **INSIDER'S VIEW:** Moriah McCracken, Writing Studies 83

   ▓ **INSIDE WORK:** Collecting Primary Evidence 83

   ▓ **INSIDE WORK:** Using Primary and Secondary Sources 84

  Searching for Sources 84

   ▓ **INSIDE WORK:** Generating Search Terms 87

   ▓ **INSIDE WORK:** Generating Sources from an Academic Database 91

  Evaluating Sources 92

   ○ **INSIDER'S VIEW:** Jonathan Morris, Political Science 92

   ▓ **INSIDE WORK:** Evaluating Sources 94

  Summarizing, Paraphrasing, and Quoting from Sources 94

   ▓ **INSIDE WORK:** Summarizing, Paraphrasing, and Quoting from Sources 98

  Avoiding Plagiarism 98

   ▓ **INSIDE WORK:** Understanding Plagiarism 99

   ○ **INSIDER'S VIEW:** Karen Keaton Jackson, Writing Studies 99

  Understanding Documentation Systems 99

   ▓ **WRITING PROJECT:** Writing an Annotated Bibliography 101

   ▓ **WRITING PROJECT:** Developing a Supported Argument on a Controversial Issue 102

Insider Example: **Student Argument on a Controversial Issue** 103

Jack Gomperts, *Evaluating Hydration Levels in High School Athletes* 104

Tip Sheet: Academic Research 114

| PART TWO | Inside Academic Writing 117 |

6 Reading and Writing in Academic Disciplines 119

◐ INSIDER'S VIEW: Karen Keaton Jackson, Writing Studies 120

Analyzing Genres and Identifying Conventions of Academic Writing 121

◐ INSIDER'S VIEW: Moriah McCracken, Writing Studies 122

● INSIDER'S VIEW: Mike Brotherton, Astronomy 123

Adapting to Different Rhetorical Contexts: An Academic Writer at Work 123

▨ INSIDE WORK: Reflecting on a Discipline 124

Using Rhetorical Context to Analyze Academic Writing 124

Mike Brotherton, Excerpt from *Hubble Space Telescope Spies Galaxy/Black Hole Evolution in Action* 125

◐ INSIDER'S VIEW: Mike Brotherton, Astronomy 126

▨ INSIDE WORK: Reflecting on Rhetorical Context 126

Using Structure, Language, and Reference to Analyze Genre Conventions 127

● INSIDER'S VIEW: Mike Brotherton, Astronomy 128

M. S. Brotherton, Wil van Breugel, S. A. Stanford, R. J. Smith, B. J. Boyle, Lance Miller, T. Shanks, S. M. Croom, and Alexei V. Filippenko, Excerpt from *A Spectacular Poststarburst Quasar* 129

▨ INSIDE WORK: Reflecting on an Academic Article 130

● INSIDER'S VIEW: Mike Brotherton, Astronomy 130

▨ WRITING PROJECT: Writing a Genre Analysis of an Academic Article 131

▨ WRITING PROJECT: Writing a Comparative Genre Analysis 131

▨ WRITING PROJECT: Comparing Scholarly and Popular Articles 132

Translating Scholarly Writing for Different Rhetorical Contexts 133

Insider Example: **Student Translation of a Scholarly Article** 133

Jonathan Nastasi, *Life May Be Possible on Other Planets* 133

▨ WRITING PROJECT: Translating a Scholarly Article for a Public Audience 136

Tip Sheet: Reading and Writing in Academic Disciplines 138

7 Reading and Writing in the Humanities 139

Introduction to the Humanities 139
- **INSIDER'S VIEW:** John McCurdy, History 140

Texts and Meaning 140
- **INSIDE WORK:** Thinking about Texts 141

Observation and Interpretation 141
- **INSIDE WORK:** Observing and Asking Questions 141

Research in the Humanities 142
- **INSIDER'S VIEW:** Karen Keaton Jackson, Writing Studies 142
- **INSIDE WORK:** Observing and Interpreting Images 143

The Role of Theory in the Humanities 144

Close Reading in the Humanities 144

Insider Example: Professional Close Reading 145
Dale Jacobs, *More Than Words: Comics as a Means of Teaching Multiple Literacies* 145

Strategies for Close Reading and Observation 154
Kate Chopin, Excerpt from *The Story of an Hour* 155
- **INSIDE WORK:** Annotating a Text 156
Kate Chopin, *The Story of an Hour* 157
- **INSIDE WORK:** Preparing a Content/Form-Response Grid 159

Responding to the Interpretations of Others 159
- **INSIDER'S VIEW:** Moriah McCracken, Writing Studies 159

Conventions of Writing in the Humanities 160
- **INSIDER'S VIEW:** Shelley Garrigan, Spanish Language and Literature 160

Structural Conventions 161

Developing Research Questions and Thesis Statements 161
- **INSIDER'S VIEW:** Karen Keaton Jackson, Writing Studies 161
- **INSIDE WORK:** Developing *Why, What,* and *How* Questions 163

Developing Effective Thesis Statements 163
- **INSIDE WORK:** Drafting Thesis Statements 164

Five-Paragraph Essays and Other Thesis-Driven Templates 165
- **INSIDER'S VIEW:** Karen Keaton Jackson, Writing Studies 165

Other Structural Conventions in the Humanities 166

Language Conventions in the Humanities 167

Reference Conventions in the Humanities 169

Documentation   170

   ▨ **INSIDE WORK:** Analyzing Scholarly Writing in the Humanities   171

Genres of Writing in the Humanities   172

   ● **INSIDER'S VIEW:** Shelley Garrigan, Spanish Language and Literature   172

Textual Interpretation   172

   ▨ **WRITING PROJECT:** Interpreting a Text   173

   Insider Example: Student Interpretation of a Text   173
   Sarah Ray, *Till Death Do Us Part: An Analysis of Kate Chopin's "The Story of an Hour"*   174

Artistic Texts   180

   ▨ **WRITING PROJECT:** Creating an Artistic Text   181

Tip Sheet: *Reading and Writing in the Humanities*   182

8   Reading and Writing in the Social Sciences   183

Introduction to the Social Sciences   183

   ● **INSIDER'S VIEW:** Kevin Rathunde, Social Sciences   184
   ▨ **INSIDE WORK:** Observing Behavior   184

Research in the Social Sciences   185

The Role of Theory   185

   Insider Example: Exploring Social Science Theory   186
   Kalervo Oberg, Excerpt from *Cultural Shock: Adjustments to New Cultural Environments*   186

   ▨ **INSIDE WORK:** Tracing a Theory's Development   189

Research Questions and Hypotheses   189

   ▨ **INSIDE WORK:** Developing Hypotheses   190

Methods   191

   ● **INSIDER'S VIEW:** Kevin Rathunde, Social Sciences   192
   ◗ **INSIDER'S VIEW:** Jonathan Morris, Political Science   195
   ▨ **INSIDE WORK:** Considering Research Methods   195

The IRB Process and Use of Human Subjects   196

Conventions of Writing in the Social Sciences   196

   ● **INSIDER'S VIEW:** Aya Matsuda, Linguistics   197

Structural Conventions and IMRaD Format   197

Other Structural Conventions   205

   ▨ **INSIDE WORK:** Observing Structural Features   207

Language Conventions   207
  ▓ **INSIDE WORK:** Observing Language Features   209
Reference Conventions   209
  ▓ **INSIDE WORK:** Observing Reference Features   210

Genres of Writing in the Social Sciences   211
  ● **INSIDER'S VIEW:** Aya Matsuda, Linguistics   211
The Literature Review   211

> **Insider Example: An Embedded Literature Review**   212
> **Mihaly Csikszentmihalyi and Jeremy Hunter,** Excerpt from *Happiness in Everyday Life: The Uses of Experience Sampling*   212

Writing a Literature Review   213
  ▓ **WRITING PROJECT:** Writing a Literature Review   216

> **Insider Example: Student Literature Review**   217
> **William O'Brien,** *Effects of Sleep Deprivation: A Literature Review*   218

Theory Response Essay   227
  ▓ **WRITING PROJECT:** Writing a Theory Response   228

> **Insider Example: Student Theory Response Paper**   229
> **Matt Kapadia,** *Evaluation of the Attribution Theory*   230

Tip Sheet: *Reading and Writing in the Social Sciences*   239

9 Reading and Writing in the Natural Sciences   240

Introduction to the Natural Sciences   240
  ● **INSIDER'S VIEW:** Sian Proctor, Geology   241

Research in the Natural Sciences   243
  ● **INSIDER'S VIEW:** Paige Geiger, Molecular and Integrative Physiology   243
  ▓ **INSIDE WORK:** Considering a Natural Science Topic   244
Observation and Description in the Natural Sciences   244
  ▓ **INSIDE WORK:** Thinking about Systematic Observation in the Sciences   245
Moving from Description to Speculation   245
  ▓ **INSIDE WORK:** Practicing Description and Speculation   247
  ▓ **INSIDE WORK:** Developing Research Questions and a Hypothesis   248

Designing a Research Study in the Natural Sciences   249
  ● INSIDER'S VIEW: Michelle LaRue, Conservation Biology   250
  ▶ INSIDER'S VIEW: Patrick Bahls, Mathematics   250
  ▦ INSIDE WORK: Freewriting about an Experiment   251

Conventions of Writing in the Natural Sciences   252
  ● INSIDER'S VIEW: Michelle LaRue, Conservation Biology   253

Objectivity   253
  ▦ INSIDE WORK: Looking for Conventions of Objectivity   254

Replicability   255

Recency   256
  ▶ INSIDER'S VIEW: Patrick Bahls, Mathematics   256
  ▦ INSIDE WORK: Looking for Conventions of Replicability and Recency   257

Cooperation and Collaboration   257

Genres of Writing in the Natural Sciences   258

An Observation Logbook   258
  ● INSIDER'S VIEW: Paige Geiger, Molecular and Integrative Physiology   259
  ▦ WRITING PROJECT: Keeping an Observation Logbook   259

  Insider Example: Student Observation Logbook   260
  Kedric Lemon, *Comparing the Efficiency of Various Batteries Being Used over Time*   261

Research Proposal   271
  ▦ WRITING PROJECT: Developing a Research Proposal   272

  Insider Example: Research Proposal   272
  Gary Ritchison, *Hunting Behavior, Territory Quality, and Individual Quality of American Kestrels (*Falco sparverius*)*   273

Lab Report   279
  ▦ WRITING PROJECT: Composing a Lab Report   280

  Insider Example: Student Lab Report   280
  Kedric Lemon, *Which Type of Battery Is the Most Effective When Energy Is Drawn Rapidly?*   281

Tip Sheet: *Reading and Writing in the Natural Sciences*   291

10   Reading and Writing in the Applied Fields   292

Introduction to the Applied Fields   292

What Are Applied Fields?   292

   ▩ **INSIDE WORK:** Defining and Solving Problems   293

   ▩ **INSIDE WORK:** Considering Additional Applied Fields   294

Rhetoric and the Applied Fields   294

   ▶ **INSIDER'S VIEW:** Michelle Richter, Criminology   295

Genres in Selected Applied Fields   295

Health Fields   296

   ● **INSIDER'S VIEW:** Janna Dieckmann, Nursing   297

> **Insider Example: Professional Research Report**   298
>
> **Margaret Shandor Miles, Diane Holditch-Davis, Suzanne Thoyre, and Linda Beeber,** *Rural African-American Mothers Parenting Prematurely Born Infants: An Ecological Systems Perspective*   298
>
> **Insider Example: Discharge Instructions**   301
>
> **First Hospital,** *Discharge Instructions for Heart Attack*   302
>
> ▩ **INSIDE WORK:** Nurse for a Day   304

Education   304

> **Insider Example: Student Lesson Plan**   305
>
> **Myra Moses,** *Lesson Plan*   305
>
> **Insider Example: Student IEP**   308
>
> **Myra Moses,** *IEP*   309
>
> ▩ **INSIDE WORK:** Teacher for a Day   314

Business   314

> **Insider Example: Student Memorandum**   315
>
> **James Blackwell,** *Investigative Report on Hazen and Sawyer*   316
>
> **Insider Example: Student Business Plan**   317
>
> **Daniel Chase Mills,** *The Electricity Monitor Company*   318
>
> ▩ **INSIDE WORK:** CFO for a Day   326

Criminal Justice and Law   326

   ▶ **INSIDER'S VIEW:** Michelle Richter, Criminal Justice   327

Insider Example: Professional Legal Brief   329

University of Texas at Austin, et al., *Brief for Respondents*   329

Insider Example: E-Mail Correspondence from Attorney   336

Joseph E. Miller Jr., *Sample E-Mail*   336

    ■ **INSIDE WORK:** Lawyer for a Day   337

    ■ **WRITING PROJECT:** Discovering Genres of Writing in an Applied Field   337

Tip Sheet: Reading and Writing in the Applied Fields   338

Appendix: Introduction to Documentation Styles   339

Index   355

An Insider's Guide to Academic Writing

A Brief Rhetoric

A Guide to College and College Writing

ANDREA TSURUMI

PART ONE

A Guide to College and College Writing

1

Inside Colleges and Universities 3

2

Writing Process and Reflection 19

3

Reading and Writing Rhetorically 45

4

Developing Arguments 59

5

Academic Research 81

Inside Colleges and Universities

What Is Higher Education?

This book introduces expectations about writing you'll likely encounter in college and helps you develop a set of tools to complete writing tasks successfully. To understand those expectations, you may find it helpful to understand first how colleges and universities are structured; how your other writing experiences in high school, college, and work might compare; and what expectations about writing you might encounter in your particular college or university classes. These expectations will likely differ according to the type of college or university you attend.

As you read through the chapters in this book, certain recurring features will help expand your knowledge of college writing:

- *Insider's View* boxes contain excerpts of comments by scholars and students discussing academic writing. Several of these are gleaned from video interviews that complement the instruction in this book. The videos, which are further referenced in the page margins, can be viewed for greater insight into the processes and productions of academic writers. Video content and other helpful resources are available on LaunchPad, designed to accompany this text.

- *Inside Work* activities prompt you to reflect on what you have learned while trying out new insights and techniques.

- *Writing Projects* offer sequences of activities that will help you develop your own compositions.

- *Tip Sheets* summarize key lessons of the chapters.

Before we turn to college writing, however, we ask you to read about and reflect on some of the wider contexts of higher education—in particular, your place in it.

HOW DO COLLEGES AND UNIVERSITIES DIFFER FROM ONE ANOTHER?

As we discuss the expectations you might encounter related to writing in college, you should consider the specific context of the school you're attending. What kind of school is it? What types of students does it serve? What is the school's mission? It's important to realize that different schools have differing missions and values that influence their faculty members' expectations for students.

How did you determine where to attend college? Some prospective students send out applications to multiple schools, while others know exactly where they want to start their college careers. Some students transfer from one school to another, and they do so for a variety of reasons. If you researched potential schools, you likely realized that there are many different kinds of schools in the United States (not to mention the variety of institutions of higher education elsewhere in the world). If we just focus on the range of higher education options in the United States, we find:

- **Community Colleges:** schools that typically offer associate's degrees. Some community colleges prepare students to enter careers directly following graduation; others specialize in helping students transfer to bachelor's-granting institutions after completing most of their general education requirements or an associate's degree.

- **Liberal Arts Colleges/Universities:** schools that introduce students to a broad variety of disciplines as they pursue their bachelor's degrees. Liberal arts schools generally focus on undergraduate education, although some offer graduate degrees as well.

- **Comprehensive Colleges/Universities:** schools that emphasize undergraduate education. They offer bachelor's degrees and often some master's degrees and other graduate degree options. Comprehensive schools are frequently regional public institutions, and they can range in size. Such schools usually have a dual focus on undergraduate and graduate education, but they might not emphasize research expectations for their faculty as intensely as doctoral-granting institutions do.

- **Doctoral-Granting/Research-Intensive Universities:** schools with an emphasis on research and a focus on both undergraduate and graduate education. Doctoral-granting universities, especially those that are research-intensive, can often be quite large, and they generally have higher expectations for faculty members' research activities than other types of institutions do. As a result, students may have more opportunities for collaborative research with faculty members, and graduate students might teach some undergraduate classes.

- **Schools That Serve a Specific Population:** schools that serve specific populations or prepare students for particular careers. Such schools might be single-sex institutions, historically black colleges and universities,

Hispanic-serving institutions, or religious-affiliated schools, to name a few.

- **Schools with a Specific Vocational Focus:** schools that prepare students for careers in particular professional areas. These schools might have a focus on agricultural careers, technical careers, culinary careers, or other vocations.

- **For-Profit Institutions:** schools that operate on a business model and are privately held or publicly traded companies. Some are regionally accredited institutions; many focus on meeting the needs of students whose schedules or other commitments require a different approach from what a typical non-profit college or university provides.

What kind of school is the institution that you currently attend? Knowing how your particular college or university is structured, and how it fits into the larger context of higher education, can help you understand its institutional values and the emphasis it places on particular kinds of academic preparation. If you know these important factors, you'll be able to anticipate the expectations for your academic work and understand the reasoning behind the requirements for your degree.

INSIDE WORK **Choosing a College**

Write brief responses to the following questions, and be prepared to discuss them with your classmates.

- What kind of institution do you attend? What characteristics of your school seem to match that category?
- What degree program or major are you most interested in? Why?
- Was your interest in a particular degree program or major a factor when you decided to go to college? Why or why not?
- What classes are you taking, and how did you choose them?
- What kinds of factors do you consider when choosing your classes? What guidance, requirements, or other influences help you make those choices? ▶

WHAT IS THE PURPOSE OF COLLEGE?

People's reasons for pursuing an undergraduate degree can differ, depending on the school and the individual student. Some schools and degree programs focus on preparing students for particular careers that they can pursue directly after graduation. Others focus more broadly on developing well-rounded, informed graduates who will be active in their communities regardless of which careers they pursue. Still others emphasize different, and sometimes quite specific, outcomes for their graduates. If you have never done so, consider taking a look at the mission or values statements for your university, college, or department. What do the faculty members and administrators value? What are their expectations of you as a student?

For example, the mission statement of Texas A&M University begins by stating:

> Texas A&M University is dedicated to the discovery, development, communication, and application of knowledge in a wide range of academic and professional fields.

This statement shows a broad commitment to a range of academic interests and professions; therefore, students at Texas A&M can expect to find a wide range of majors represented at the university. The mission statement also emphasizes that knowledge discovery is important at Texas A&M, highlighting the school's role as a research-intensive university.

As another example, the mission statement of Glendale Community College in California reads:

> Glendale Community College serves a diverse population of students by providing the opportunities and support to achieve their educational and career goals. We are committed to student learning and success through transfer preparation, certificates, associate degrees, career development, technical training, continuing education, and basic skills instruction.

This statement illustrates Glendale Community College's emphasis on preparing students for careers and serving a broad range of students with specific academic and professional goals.

A third example is the mission statement of Endicott College in Massachusetts, which begins by stating:

> Shaped by a bold entrepreneurial spirit, Endicott College offers students a vibrant academic environment that remains true to its founding principle of integrating professional and liberal arts with experiential learning including internship opportunities across disciplines.

Endicott's mission mentions an emphasis on "experiential" learning, which is evident through the connection of professional experiences with academics and the availability of internships for students. Students who enroll at Endicott College should expect a practical, hands-on application of their learning throughout their coursework.

Of course, different students have different goals and reasons for pursuing undergraduate degrees. Sometimes those goals match the institution's mission fairly closely, but not always. What is your purpose in attending your college or university? How do your personal and professional goals fit within the school's goals and values?

INSIDE WORK Writing about Your School's Mission

Find your college or university's mission statement (usually available on the school's website), and write a brief description that compares your goals for college to the mission statement. How does the mission of your school fit your goals? How might the characteristics and mission of your college or university help you achieve your goals? ▶

INSIDE WORK Writing about College

Read the following questions, and write a brief response to each.

- What goals do you hope to achieve by attending college?
- What steps should you take to maximize your opportunity to achieve your academic goals?
- What will you need to do while in college to achieve your goals?
- What have you already accomplished, and what do you still need to know and do?
- How do you feel about attending college?
- What concerns you the most about being in college?
- What do you like the most about being in college? ▶

Regardless of your purpose for attending college, the transition to college can be a challenging one. Vincent Tinto, a researcher interested in what helps students succeed as they make the transition to college, has identified and written extensively about three stages that students go through as they adapt to college: separation, transition, and incorporation.* At the separation stage, students might feel disconnected to prior communities and commitments, but successful students move through a transition stage and then find a way to connect themselves with new communities in college (incorporation). The separation stage can be very challenging, though, and knowing what resources you have available to you as you make the transition to college can be incredibly helpful.

INSIDE WORK Writing about Resources at Your Institution

Take a look at your institution's website and look for support services that are available to students. These might include academic, professional, and counseling services, to name a few. What resources are available at your school that might help you improve your transition to college? ▶

---

*Tinto discusses these stages in "Stages of Student Departure: Reflections on the Longitudinal Character of Student Leaving." *The Journal of Higher Education*, vol. 59, no. 4, 1988, pp. 438-55.

What Are Academic Disciplines?

An important structural feature of colleges and universities is the way they are divided into academic disciplines. Depending on the school, this might take the form of departments, divisions, colleges, or other groupings. **Academic disciplines** are, broadly defined, areas of teaching, research, and inquiry that academics pursue. Sometimes these disciplines are listed in broad categories, such as psychology, English, biology, physics, and engineering.

At other times, disciplines are listed in more specialized categories that demonstrate the diversity of areas encompassed within higher education: for example, adolescent psychology, abnormal psychology, sociolinguistics, second language acquisition, molecular biology, physiology, astrophysics, quantum mechanics, civil engineering, mechanical engineering, computer science, Victorian poetry, and medieval literature.

While the specific divisions may differ according to the institution, most college and university faculties are grouped into departments or divisions. Larger schools are typically further divided into colleges or schools-within-schools, which usually cluster together departments that are related to one another in some way. These groupings often, but not always, fall along common lines that divide departments into broader disciplinary areas of the humanities, social sciences, natural sciences, and applied fields. We describe these broad categories in more detail in the next section.

HOW MANY DIFFERENT ACADEMIC DISCIPLINES ARE THERE?

You might find that different faculty members give varying answers to the question, "How many different academic disciplines are there?" And those answers differ for good reason. Sometimes academic disciplines are seen as equivalent to departments. Faculty in the history department study history, right? But the subject of history can be divided into many different categories, too: antebellum U.S. history, Middle Eastern history, and African American history, for example. In addition, people in other departments might study and teach topics that are related to history, such as American religious history, medieval literature and culture, and ancient rhetoric. You can probably

imagine how categorizing all these different areas of study and research would be
difficult.

For the purposes of this text, we're
going to explore writing in different disciplinary areas that are grouped together
according to (1) the kinds of questions that
scholars ask in those disciplines and (2) the
research strategies, or methods of inquiry,
that they use to answer those questions. As
mentioned earlier, we've divided various academic disciplines into four broad
disciplinary categories: humanities, social
sciences, natural sciences, and applied
fields. As we talk about these four areas of
study and the disciplines associated with
them, both here and in Part Two of the
book, you'll notice some similarities and
differences within the categories:

ANDREA TSURUMI

- Scholars in the **humanities** usually ask questions about the human
  condition. To answer these questions,
  they often employ methods of inquiry
  that are based on analysis, interpretation, and speculation. Examples of
  academic disciplines that are generally
  considered part of the humanities are
  history, literature, philosophy, foreign
  languages, religious studies, and the fine arts. For examples of the kinds
  of questions humanists ask, see Chapter 7.

- Scholars in the **social sciences** usually ask questions about human behavior and society. To answer these questions, they often employ methods of
  inquiry that are based on theory building or empirical research. Examples
  of academic disciplines that are generally considered part of the social
  sciences are communication, psychology, sociology, political science, economics, and anthropology. For examples of the kinds of questions social
  scientists ask, see Chapter 8.

- Scholars in the **natural sciences** usually ask questions about the natural
  world. To answer these questions, they often employ methods of inquiry that
  are based on experimentation and quantifiable data. Examples of academic
  disciplines that are generally considered part of the natural sciences are
  chemistry, biology, physics, astronomy, and mathematics. For examples
  of the kinds of questions natural scientists ask, see Chapter 9.

- Scholars in **applied fields** might have their foundation in any one (or more) of the disciplinary categories, but their work is generally focused on practical application. Some disciplines that could fall under the category of applied fields are criminal justice, medicine, nursing, education, business, agriculture, and engineering. Each of these fields has elements that are closely aligned with the humanities, social sciences, and/or natural sciences, but each also focuses on application of that knowledge in specific contexts. For examples of the kinds of questions scholars in applied fields ask, see Chapter 10.

These categories are not perfectly distinct, though; they sometimes overlap with one another, and they are debatable. Sometimes you'll find that different institutions categorize certain classes as part of a particular disciplinary area through their General Education requirements, for example. Another institution might list a similar class as meeting a different requirement. You'll see examples of disciplinary overlap in the chapters in Part Two and in the student writing examples there. Regardless of some of these complexities, the disciplinary categories of humanities, social sciences, natural sciences, and applied fields are useful for understanding some of the distinctions in the ways academics think and do research.

INSIDE WORK **Understanding Disciplinarity**

In your own words, write a brief description of the four academic disciplines mentioned in the previous section.

- humanities

- social sciences

- natural sciences

- applied fields

Next, look at your current course schedule. How might you classify the classes you're taking in terms of these four categories? For each class, write for a few minutes about what characteristics of the class cause it to fit into the category you've chosen. Finally, compare your answers with a classmate's. ❱

WHY DO ACADEMICS WRITE?

As you think about the writing you will do in college, keep in mind that you are learning how to participate in the kinds of discussions that scholars and faculty members engage in about topics and issues of mutual interest. In other words, you're entering into academic conversations that have been going on for a while. As you are writing, you will need to think about who your audience is (other students? teachers? an audience outside of the academic setting?), who has already been participating in the conversations of interest to you (and perhaps who hasn't), and what expectations for your writing you'll need to follow in order to contribute to those conversations. (We'll have much more to say about the concept of audience in Chapter 3.)

As we explore the kinds of writing done in various disciplinary areas, you'll notice that different disciplines have different expectations for writing. In other words, faculty members in a particular discipline might expect a piece of writing to be structured in a particular way, or they might use specific kinds of language, or they might expect you to be familiar with certain research by others and refer to it in prescribed ways. Each of these expectations is an aspect of the writing conventions of a particular discipline. **Conventions** are the customs that scholars in a particular discipline follow in their writing. Sometimes those conventions take the form of repeated patterns in structure or certain choices in language use, just to name a couple.

To prepare for writing in varied academic contexts, it might be helpful to think about why academics write. Most faculty members at institutions of higher education explain their responsibilities to the institution and their discipline in terms of three categories: their teaching, their research (which generates much of their writing), and their service (what they do outside of their research and teaching that contributes both to the school and to their discipline). Many academics' writing is related to communicating the results of their research, and it might be published or shared with academic audiences or more general audiences. In fact, a scholar might conduct a research project and then find that he or she needs to communicate the results of that project to a variety of audiences.

Imagine that a physiologist who studies diabetes has discovered a new therapy that could potentially benefit diabetic individuals. The researcher might want to publish the results of her study in an academic journal so that other scientists can read about the results, perhaps replicate the study (repeat it to confirm that the results are the same), and maybe expand on the research findings. She might also want to communicate the results of her research to doctors who work with diabetic patients but who don't necessarily read academic journals in physiology. They might read medical journals, though, so in this case the researcher would need to tailor her results to an audience that is primarily interested in the application of research results to patients. In addition, she might want to report the results of her research to the general public, in which case she might write a press release so that newspapers and magazines can develop news stories about her findings. Each of these writing situations involves reporting the same research results, but to different audiences and for different purposes. The physiologist would need to tailor her writing to meet the needs of each writing situation.

INSIDE WORK **Thinking about What Academics Write**

Look for a published piece that has been written by one of the professors that you have for another class. Try to find something that you can access in full, either online or through your school's library. Some colleges and universities have lists of recent publications by faculty on their websites. Additionally, some faculty members list their publications on personal websites. You might also seek help from librarians at your institution if you aren't familiar with the library's resources. Then write your responses to the following questions.

- What does the professor write about?
- Where was that work published?
- Who is the audience for your professor's work?
- What surprised you most about your professor's published work? ▶

How Does Writing in College Compare with Writing in Other Contexts?

Many of your expectations for writing in college might be based on prior experiences, such as the writing you did in high school or in a work setting. Some students find that writing in college focuses less on personal experience and more on research than writing they've done in other contexts. Some students are surprised to find that writing instruction in college is not always paired with discussion of literature, as it often is in high school. While some colleges and universities use literature as a starting point for teaching writing, many other schools offer writing instruction that is focused on principles of **rhetoric**—the study of how language is used to communicate—apart from the study of literature. (Rhetoric will be discussed in detail in subsequent chapters throughout this book.) As you may have already experienced, many courses require you to write about different topics, in different forms, and for different audiences. Depending on your school, writing program, and instructor, the study of literature might be part of that approach, but you might also need to learn about the expectations of instructors in other disciplines.

When we compare the writing expectations in college with what you might have experienced in other contexts, we're making some general assumptions about your experience that may or may not be true. We're also making generalizations about colleges and universities that might differ from the school you're currently attending. One of the most important concepts we'll discuss in this book is the importance of context (see Chapter 3), so you'll need to balance the principles we talk about in this text with your firsthand experience of the context of your particular college or university. You might find that some of our assumptions are true to your particular experience and some are not. When possible, make note of the principles we discuss that are similar to your experience and the ones that are different. As you do so, you'll be learning about and applying these principles in a way that is much more useful than just memorizing information.

Although the approaches toward teaching writing at various colleges and universities differ, we can talk about some common expectations for college-level writing. The Council of Writing Program Administrators (CWPA), a professional organization of hundreds of writing program directors from across the country, published a list of common outcomes for first-year writing courses that has been adapted for use by many schools. The first list of common outcomes was published in 2000, and it has been revised twice since then, most recently in 2014. The purpose of the statement is to provide common expectations for what college students should be able to accomplish in terms of their writing after finishing a first-year course, but the details of those expectations are often revised to fit a specific institution's context. For example, the first outcome deals with "Rhetorical Knowledge" and emphasizes the importance of understanding how to shape your writing for different purposes and audiences. It states that:

> By the end of first-year composition, students should
>
> • Learn and use key rhetorical concepts through analyzing and composing a variety of texts

Insider's View
We're looking for students to get their own voices
KAREN KEATON JACKSON, WRITING STUDIES

"In general, the sense that I get is that in high school, writing is more focused on literature. At the college level, we're more interested in critical thinking. We're looking for students to get their own voices in place. Really getting students to think stylistically about the choices they make, really thinking about purpose and audience and the whole rhetorical context. I think that's really key at the college level. By college we're looking at the purpose, and the audience, and the style, and how all of this is determined based on the different writing situation you're in."

 LaunchPad
Get expert advice on transitioning to college writing.

- Gain experience reading and composing in several genres to understand how genre conventions shape and are shaped by readers' and writers' practices and purposes
- Develop facility in responding to a variety of situations and contexts calling for purposeful shifts in voice, tone, level of formality, design, medium, and/or structure
- Understand and use a variety of technologies to address a range of audiences
- Match the capacities of different environments (e.g., print and electronic) to varying rhetorical situations

http://wpacouncil.org/positions/outcomes.html

The statement introduces several specialized concepts and terms that we will describe in more detail throughout the book. You might also notice that the statement doesn't specify what kinds of writing students should do in their classes. It is left up to individual schools to determine what will be most helpful for their students.

Some institutions follow the guidelines from the Council of Writing Program Administrators explicitly, while others do not. Even at institutions that use these outcomes as a foundation for the writing curriculum, however, it's often possible to find many different approaches to teaching writing that help students achieve academic literacy. How do your institution's outcomes for writing compare and contrast with your experience in other English classes you have taken? How do the outcomes for writing compare and contrast with your writing experience outside of school (perhaps in work-related or personal settings)?

INSIDE WORK **Understanding the Goals of Your Writing Course**

Take a look at the goals, objectives, or outcomes listed for the writing course you are currently taking. You might look for a course description on the school's website or in a course catalog, or you might find goals or learning objectives listed in the course syllabus.

- What surprised you about the goals or objectives for your writing course?
- What is similar to or different from the writing courses you have taken before?
- What is similar to or different from the expectations you had for this course?
- How do the outcomes for the course align with your goals for writing and for college?
- What does the list of goals for your course tell you about what is valued at your institution? ❱

HOW DO WRITERS LEARN TO WRITE IN NEW CONTEXTS?

In this chapter, we have discussed the goals and expectations of writing in college and how they might differ from writing you have done in other contexts. The culminating writing project in this chapter asks you to learn from another writer, someone who has more experience in the kind of writing you will be doing in your own academic or professional career, by asking how they discovered the conventions and expectations for writing in their field.

INSIDE WORK **Learning about Writing in Other Contexts**

For this activity, you will interview one of your classmates to understand the kinds of writing they have done in school and how they have learned about writing in a new context. Choose one major writing assignment for a course other than your English class and discuss the following questions:

- What was the assignment?
- What kinds of writing instruction did the instructor give you?
- Was there a writing prompt?
- Did you receive feedback?
- Did you read student samples?
- How did you feel about the instruction and the assignment?
- What are the biggest challenges you've faced regarding writing that you've done in classes other than our English course?
- What advice would you give to students who must take a writing class in order to help them succeed? ▶

Profile of a Writer

WRITING PROJECT

For this writing project, you will develop a profile of a writer in an academic field or profession of interest to you based on an interview you conduct. Under the guidance of your instructor, identify someone who is either a professor, graduate student, or upper-level student in your major (or a major that interests you); or a professional who works in a career that you could imagine for yourself. You might choose someone with whom you already have a connection, either through taking a class, having a mutual acquaintance, or enjoying a shared interest. Ask the person if you can interview him or her, either in person or through e-mail. Consider the descriptions of different disciplinary areas in this chapter, and write a profile of the writer that addresses questions about his or her writing, such as the following.

- What kinds of writing do people do in your field?
- What is the purpose of the writing you do in your field?

- What writing conventions are specific to and important to your research or work? How did you learn those conventions?
- What kinds of writing do you do most often in your work?
- What was your experience the first time you attempted to do those kinds of writing?
- What expectations do you have for students or new professionals who are learning to write in this field?

Be sure to follow up your questions by asking for specific examples if you need more information to understand your interviewee's responses. In addition, you might ask to see an example of his or her writing to use as an illustration in your profile. Don't forget to thank the person for taking the time to respond to your questions.

A profile of a writer should do two things: (1) make a point about the person being interviewed (in this case, your point should focus on the person's writing), and (2) include details about the person's experiences that help develop the point. Incorporate the person's responses into an essay that uses the interview to make a specific point about his or her development and experience as a writer.

Insider Example
Student Profile of a Business Professional

Rubbal Kumar, a sophomore at the University of Arizona, conducted an interview with Benu Badhan, a software engineer from India. Kumar is a computer science major, and he interviewed Ms. Badhan to learn more about the expectations for writing in his future profession. Through his interview with Ms. Badhan, Kumar learned that writing is very different for a software engineer than for a computer science major, but the writing he does as a computer science major will still prepare him well for his future career.

Rubbal Kumar's First Draft of Interview Questions

1. Why did you choose this specific major?
2. What is your specific area of interest in computer science and why?
3. What different types of writing are involved in this field?
4. Is there any specific set of rules for writing in the IT field? If yes, then how is it different from college writing?
5. Did you face any difficulties in understanding writing conventions of computer science?

Rubbal Kumar's Final Profile Draft

Rubbal Kumar

ENG108

May 30, 2017

Profile of a Writer: Benu Badhan

Benu Badhan is a software engineer at Infosys, an information technology consulting company. She has been working in this field for about five years and her specialty includes software testing: manual testing and automation. She has completed her Bachelors in Technology in Computer Science from the Indian Institute of Technology, Mumbai, and completed her Masters from Delhi University, New Delhi. She worked for two different IT firms, Calsoft and Wipro, before joining Infosys.

In an in-person interview, she told me that writing expectations in an IT firm are totally different in comparison with college writing. She said, "In college, we had to write 4-5 page essays, but in the workplace there are totally different conventions." At work, software engineers are expected to write programming codes, and along with each programming code, they have to explain the function of each line using the comment feature. Comments are the description of the logic used to write the code. Commenting on the code is necessary because a programmer may inherit the features of existing code in his or her own code. Therefore, to transfer code successfully, comments are necessary. In this way, if someone else reads the code, the comments make understanding the logic far easier. She said that comments are the heart of the code because without comments another person cannot easily understand the programming code.

When I asked further about whether college had prepared her for writing comments clearly for her code, she replied that if there had been no college writing then she would have had difficulty. She also said that college writing prepares students to express things clearly and concisely, and this is one of the requirements in the IT field. She said that whether it is college writing or workplace writing, quality matters instead of quantity.

Apart from writing comments in programming code, another form of writing she engages in frequently is writing email. In order to communicate effectively with colleagues, she mentioned that it is important to have good email etiquette. She said that without good communication skills, a person cannot survive in an IT company. In addition to commenting on code and writing email, there are video conference calls and PowerPoint presentations which demand good communication skills. Sometimes she has to lead projects, so leadership qualities and clear communication with a team are also important. As an example, she described working on an idea proposal with her project group and drawing on skills she had learned through college writing. She is convinced that college writing prepares students for other writing assignments in their careers.

I learned through my conversation with Ms. Badhan that workplace writing is different from college writing in computer science, but the academic writing we do in college prepares us well for what we will be asked to do in the workplace. The workplace is competitive, so it is important to have good writing skills, communication skills, and leadership qualities, and to be a

[margin annotations]

A key point of the profile, followed by examples from the interview

Quotation that emphasizes the differences between college and IT writing

A second key point, which builds from the first one

A paragraph elaborating on the second key point with examples from the interview

The central point of the profile

good problem solver. Through my interview with Ms. Badhan, I learned that in order to be successful in writing in the workplace I must also perform well in my writing in college. While the writing conventions may change in the IT industry, the foundation built in college writing is essential.

Work Cited

Badhan, Benu. Personal Interview. 22 May 2017.

Discussion Questions

1. Read through Rubbal Kumar's interview questions of Badhan. What was his purpose in interviewing Badhan? What did he want to understand?

2. Was there anything that surprised you in the profile? If so, what was it?

3. If you were going to add a question to Kumar's interview, what would it be? Why would you add that question?

tip sheet — Inside Colleges and Universities

- **Colleges and universities are not all the same.** Different kinds of colleges and universities have varying purposes, majors, and degrees, and they appeal to a variety of potential students.

- **The institution you attend has a specific focus.** You may find it helpful to identify this focus and understand how it fits with your academic and career goals.

- **Colleges and universities are divided into disciplinary areas.** You might see these areas at your school as departments, divisions, and/or colleges. In this book, we talk about four broad disciplinary areas: humanities, social sciences, natural sciences, and applied fields.

- **Academic and professional writing follow unique conventions.** When academics and professionals write, they often follow conventions specific to their writing situations and to their disciplinary and career areas.

- **Writing in college is not always the same as writing in other contexts.** In college writing courses, we focus on principles of rhetoric, or how language is used to communicate.

Writing Process and Reflection

This chapter has two main purposes. The first purpose is to introduce and discuss the concept of a writing process. The second purpose is to support the development of your reflective writing skills in order to help you better understand the writing processes that you use. The culminating project for this chapter is a literacy narrative, a genre of reflective writing that can help you develop agency in understanding who you are, see how and why you've come to view writing the way you do (both good and bad), and discover what direction your academic and professional career might take based on what you discover about yourself. This is particularly relevant if you are trying to decide what to major in, what career to choose, or whether the major or career you're considering is the right one for you. Reflective writing emerges as a powerful tool for understanding the values and experiences that have shaped you, as well as how those values and experiences may align with the academic major you are considering.

Research study after research study across virtually every profession points to the need for excellent communication skills and development of the "whole person" in the workplace. Whether you want to become an accountant, a nurse, an attorney, an architect, or an engineer, the ability to communicate exceptionally well is a skill that supervisors look for during the hiring process and when making decisions regarding raises and promotions. Many of your communication skills are highly developed already. This chapter will help you develop your writing process and

ANDREA TSURUMI

reflective writing skills in order to better understand yourself and to develop a set of tools that you can take with you into new writing situations you may encounter in your major and profession.

What Is a Writing Process?

When you think about major writing assignments you have written in the past, how would you describe the steps you took to complete them? You've written a lot of things by the time you reach college, and when you're asked to write a new assignment for a new class, you may find it helpful to think about how you've written most successfully in the past. What works best for you? What doesn't? And how do you draw from the steps you've taken in the past when you're encountering new assignments? In short, what are the writing processes that you use to make your writing the absolute best it can be?

A **writing process** consists of all the steps you use when writing. Some common steps include brainstorming, freewriting, collecting evidence, drafting, outlining, revising, and receiving and applying feedback from others. How many revisions do you usually work through on a major assignment? Do you like to receive feedback from peers, an instructor, a parent, or a tutor as you are drafting? What types of feedback are most helpful to you? If you have to write an assignment that requires multiple days of drafting, or even weeks, what are the steps you use to maintain focus and consistency?

In Chapter 1, we discussed the Council of Writing Program Administrators' recommended goals for college writing classes, especially the goals related to rhetorical knowledge. Listed below are their recommended goals related to college students' writing processes, highlighting skills you need in order to develop an effective writing process and to succeed in college.

Council of Writing Program Administrators' Selected Goals for Writing Processes

By the end of first-year composition, students should:
- Develop a writing project through multiple drafts
- Develop flexible strategies for reading, drafting, reviewing, collaborating, revising, rewriting, rereading, and editing
- Learn to give and to act on productive feedback to works in progress
- Use composing processes and tools as a means to discover and reconsider ideas
- Reflect on the development of composing practices and how those practices influence their work

Let's consider these goals and reflect on the experiences you have had that demonstrate relevant skills.

DEVELOP A WRITING PROJECT THROUGH MULTIPLE DRAFTS

By now, drafting is a skill you have probably developed quite well. The hard part about drafting is just doing it. We live busy lives and sometimes put off work until the last minute. For some writing assignments, you might be able to get away with last-minute writing. For more complicated projects, however, you may need to develop your assignment over the course of several weeks or months. A lot of this time may be spent analyzing an assignment sheet, reading examples of the kinds of assignments you're asked to write, brainstorming topics, highlighting or annotating sources you've found to support your points, writing an outline, and drafting. These steps are all part of a well-developed writing process that will be discussed throughout this chapter. Just keep in mind that becoming a better writer takes hard work and practice, but developing a writing project through multiple drafts can take your work to a higher level.

Don't be too hard on yourself. Sometimes the expectations for what you have to write can overwhelm you or just aren't interesting to you, and the motivation to stay on task and do a little bit of work each day on an assignment can be hard to come by. The keys are to stay focused, to understand the purpose of the assignment, and to remain as open and engaged as possible.

INSIDE WORK   **Reflecting on Your Drafting Process**

Describe the most complicated writing assignment you've written prior to this course. It could be for any class, not necessarily an English class.

- What was the class, and what topic did you write about?
- What was the purpose of the assignment?
- How many revisions did you work through before turning in a final draft of the assignment?
- What writing processes did you use to maintain your focus when drafting the assignment? If you have difficulty naming steps, this might indicate just how much work you need to do to improve your drafting process. By contrast, if you're able to name several specific steps you took to maintain your focus while remaining open to improving your drafts, chances are you've developed some good drafting skills. ▶

DEVELOP FLEXIBLE WRITING PROCESS STRATEGIES

The key word in this goal is *flexible*. In a first-year college writing class, flexibility is most important in the context of reading, drafting, reviewing, collaborating, revising, rewriting, rereading, and editing. That's a long list for sure. But each of these steps is essential to improving your success in college writing.

If you had to rate which of the items in the list you're already adept at, what would you choose? Reading and revising? How about collaborating? Equally important, right?

If you are rigid, set in your ways, and unable to adapt to a variety of demands, you're going to have trouble. By contrast, if you are flexible and adaptable in your approach to collaborating, writing, and learning more broadly, you will be much more likely to succeed. Everybody brings a different set of experiences to a classroom, and your experiences have gotten you this far, so you certainly have some successful strategies already.

Nonetheless, flexibility is essential in a writing classroom and beyond.

INSIDE WORK **Reflecting on Flexibility**

1. Begin by defining what "flexibility" means to you as a personal character trait. Then, think of examples of people in your life who are inflexible. How does their inflexibility affect their relationships, work, and ability to succeed?

2. Describe a time when a situation demanded that you be flexible in your approach to a relationship, friendship, move, or work situation. How did the demand to be flexible affect you? Was it easy or stressful?

3. Reflect on your writing experiences. What teacher or assignment required that you be the most flexible? What was it about the teacher or a specific assignment that required a flexible approach on your part? ❿

LEARN TO GIVE AND TO ACT ON PRODUCTIVE FEEDBACK TO WORKS IN PROGRESS

Many of the skills that demand flexibility in writing are demonstrated in peer review activities. **Peer review** is the process of reviewing a peer's writing while a project is in a drafting phase in order to provide feedback to improve their work, or of having your own work reviewed by a peer. When you think of peer review, perhaps you think of fixing grammar, punctuation, and spelling issues—content we would refer to as surface-level improvements. While that kind of feedback is important, equally important is the more variable and flexible feedback that shapes the direction or ideas in a peer's writing. These might be called deeper-level revisions.

Essential too, and often overlooked, is the understanding that giving feedback is itself a skill that is developed in the peer review process, and it is also one that requires flexibility. Often we tend to focus only on the end product of the paper that will be graded, but the skill of giving effective feedback to peers is one that requires excellent social skills, generosity, and intellect. Furthermore, the ability to give constructive feedback to peers is a highly sought-after skill relevant to a variety of careers beyond college. To give effective feedback on someone else's writing, you must be able to read the writing from different perspectives and write comments that will be helpful to the author—this requires flexibility in both your reading and writing.

Below, you will see a draft of student Jack Stegner's literacy narrative project for a first-year composition class that has been peer-reviewed by one of his classmates, Nichelle Oquendo. We will discuss the literacy narrative in more detail later in this chapter as an example of reflective writing. As you read Jack's literacy narrative, you should pay attention to the comments Nichelle wrote. In what ways is she practicing flexibility in her reading of Jack's work and in the ways she writes her comments? How is she thinking about his writing from perspectives other than her own?

Orientation to high school was a big thing for me when I was fourteen. I was at one of the best high schools in the country getting ready to start my future life. I was excited yet nervous at the same. I came from a school where I had known kids my whole life and it was different seeing these new faces. I was afraid to talk to anyone since I felt like everyone knew each other. I got my school ID photo taken as I heard a man yelling from the crowd telling freshman to get in line. I looked over and saw this lean man with dark blonde hair and eyes as blue as the sky. As a tiny freshman I was scared to get even close to this man. That was before I realized he was one of the best teachers I would ever have.

> how did ya feel about that

> that was deep

> why were you scared of this man

The next day I walked into my fourth period classroom, and the tall lean man from yesterday was there standing in front of the class. I rolled my eyes to the back of my head saying, "Great, I have to deal with this guy the entire year." The first thing he did was assign us seats, which I wasn't used to, coming from a public school to a private school. He stood in front of the class and said his name was Mr. Alumbaugh and that he was going to be teaching us for the next school year. Then he asked us to write a paper that was due the next day discussing why we decided to go to De La Salle. I left class that day wanting to transfer out. I was already depressed as well not having many friends at the school. I came home crying to my mom saying how I didn't want to go back and

> add some description of what he was wearing, etc.

> how did your mother react when you said this

how I wanted to go to the high school all my friends were going to which was Northgate. She told me at the end of the year if you still feel the same way we can transfer you out.

make a transition from the first sentence to the second

add description of what natalie and lauren looked like and describe your friendship with lauren

A few months went by. I was still at De La Salle but still depressed from not having much of a social life. My friend Lauren wanted me to go out with her friend Natalie. We went on a few dates and we started to catch feelings for each other. Although I was her boyfriend and was friends with her friends I still didn't have many male friends. Then one day in English, Natalie was texting me during class when Mr. Alumbaugh saw. He then took my phone and started texting Natalie as my whole class was laughing at me. I was so embarrassed being called out and having everyone laugh at me. After class however, my friend till this day as well, Chris came up to me and asked if I could join him and his group for lunch. I was finally invited to something and although I was embarrassed I was happy to be made an example of to get noticed.

In the Spring, I was conditioning for football and track, had to give my girlfriend attention, and had to juggle school and social life as well. I was starting to become closer with my classmates and actually making friends. I ended up forgetting about my friends at Northgate and even not wanting to go there. I was starting to become happy and realizing that people did care about me and that they did know me. In English, Mr. Alumbaugh assigned us homework to go up in front of the class and just talk about ourselves for two minutes. At first, I laughed, saying to myself "That's too easy of an assignment." When it actually came to writing about it though, I was puzzled and had no idea what to write about. I went to Mr. Alumbaugh's room one day after class ended and asked if he could help me with the assignment. He looked at me smiled and said, "Jack I can come up with a five minute speech about you and who you are. Just write how other people perceive you."

what was the office room set up like

what was he wearing

The day of the presentation came and I was calm. It felt like I wrote a pretty good speech about myself, good enough to be confident about speaking it to the class. My name was called up and as I stood there the butterflies came out of nowhere, reminding me of the beginning of the year. I started speaking "Hello my name is . . . ." I looked down at my paper when suddenly Mr. Alumbaugh yelled "Stop! Cut!" I was startled. Mr. Alumbaugh said that he could tell I was nervous but I didn't need to look down to see what my name was. The class laughed and I laughed about it, shaking off my nerves. He then said, "Go ahead and try again." I read my speech about myself and my goals in life, and I actually got the best grade in the class.

why

Ever since that day in Mr. Alumbaugh's class, I have never been nervous to give a speech to an audience or to a class. He congratulated me personally and we had a great friendship after that year.

Discussion Questions

1. How did you feel about Nichelle's peer review feedback? Which of her comments is the most helpful to Jack and why? Where is she practicing flexibility in her comments?

2. What type of feedback do you prefer to receive when drafting your own papers?

3. What are some of the skills necessary in order to give effective peer review feedback?

One of the remarkable things about Nichelle's feedback on Jack's draft is that many of the comments she makes are description-related and idea-related. She doesn't comment much about grammar, punctuation, and spelling matters, and she often phrases her feedback in the form of questions and points to things she would like to know more about. She uses humor and seems authentic and sincere in her approach. She helps Jack see his own writing through another perspective, which will help Jack develop flexibility in his own writing. This ability to give and receive effective feedback is a skill that can be developed with practice and guidance and is relevant to many careers beyond college.

USE COMPOSING PROCESSES AND TOOLS AS A MEANS TO DISCOVER AND RECONSIDER IDEAS

A robust, well-developed writing process is critical to improving the quality of your ideas and writing. It's important, too, to know how to use the processes you've developed and the tools available to you for writing. Often the best moments for discovering new ideas come when you encounter a problem and need to draw on your composing processes to solve it. Perhaps you have a page or two of your draft completed, but then you suddenly find yourself stuck and you don't know how to continue writing. You might talk with peers, family, and teachers, or you might search for a more technological solution, such as a digital bibliography generator. It's at exactly these moments when, if you possess the skills of a complex writing process, you can navigate toward the insight and discovery of ideas that will make your work outstanding.

You might already be familiar with some of the commonly discussed steps of the writing process from other classes you've taken. Often, writing teachers talk about some variation of the following elements of the writing process:

- **Prewriting/Invention**   This is the point at which you gather ideas for your writing. There are a number of useful brainstorming strategies that students find helpful to the processes of gathering their thoughts and arranging them for writing. A few of the most widely used strategies are freewriting, listing, and idea mapping.

LaunchPad

*Find additional advice
on the writing process.*

Freewriting, as the term implies, involves writing down your thoughts in a free-flow form, typically for a set amount of time. There's no judgment or evaluation of these ideas as they occur to you. You simply write down whatever comes to mind as you consider a topic or idea. Later, of course, you revisit what you've written to see if it contains ideas or information worth examining further.

Listing is a way of quickly highlighting important information for yourself. You start with a main idea and then just list whatever comes to mind. These lists are typically done quickly the first time, but you can return to them and rework or refine them at any point in the writing process.

Idea mapping is a brainstorming technique that is a favorite among students because it allows you to represent your ideas in an easy-to-follow map. Idea mapping is sometimes referred to as cluster mapping because as you brainstorm, you use clusters of ideas and lines to keep track of the ideas and the relationships among them.

- **Research**   Sometimes research is considered a separate step in the writing process, and sometimes it is part of prewriting/invention. Of course, depending on the nature of your project, there might be a considerable amount of research or very little research involved. We explore some strategies for conducting research in more detail in Chapter 5.

- **Drafting**   At the drafting stage, you get ideas down on paper or screen. You might already realize that these stages don't happen in isolation in most cases; drafting might occur while you're doing prewriting/invention and research, and you might go back and forth between different stages as you work.

- **Peer Review**   As we discuss above, writers often benefit from seeking the feedback of others before considering a project complete. This is only one stage in your writing process, so be sure to consider the point at which it will be the most beneficial to you.

- **Revising**   At the revision stage, a writer takes another look at his or her writing and makes content-level and organizational changes.

This is different from the final step of editing/proofreading.

- **Editing/Proofreading**   Finally, the writer focuses on correcting grammatical, mechanical, stylistic, and referential problems in the text.

Depending on the rhetorical context of a writing task, these processes might shift in importance and in the order in which you do them. Imagine you get a last-minute writing assignment at work. You would progress through these stages rather quickly, and you might not have time for more than a cursory peer review. If you're writing a term paper for a class, however, you might be able to do initial prewriting, research, and drafting well before the project's deadline. As we discuss different types of scholarly writing in this text, you might also consider how the writing process for each of these types of writing can vary. For instance, when conducting an experimental study, the research stage of the process will take a significant portion of the time allocated to the project.

Increasingly, students and professionals must also learn how to use technological tools to support the writing process. No doubt you've had a great deal of experience using technologies that contribute to your writing. As you think about the more complex writing assignments you've completed, consider which technological tools have been most helpful in your writing process.

Insider's View
The finished product begins with a hundred or two hundred pages of just scribbles
PATRICK BAHLS, MATHEMATICS

"The more formally recognized genres would be research articles or expository articles or reviews of one another's work. Sometimes you'll see technical reports, depending on what area you're working in. Statisticians will frequently write technical reports for folks for whom they're doing consulting or for government work.

"But I think the day-to-day writing, to me, is much richer and often goes overlooked. When you think about the finished product of a five- or six-page research article—I'll look back over the notes that I would've written to generate the work to end up with that article. And even if you only see five or six pages of polished writing, I look back over my notes and see a hundred or two hundred pages of just scribbles here and scribbles there."

LaunchPad
Hear more about genres of writing.

INSIDE WORK   **Talking about Technology with a Partner**

Choose a partner and talk about technologies you have both used when writing or researching. Perhaps your partner has used Google Docs, PowerPoint, Google Slides, Prezi, or some other technology to improve their writing. Perhaps you have accessed articles, videos, or audio clips from a database, mobile app, or website that represents an emerging technology.

Ask each other the following questions and take notes regarding your partner's responses:

- What technologies have you found most useful in improving the quality of your writing?

- Is there a mobile app you've used or heard about that might be helpful for developing research or writing?
- What tools do you find most useful when you're trying to gather information on a topic that interests you?
- What tools do you know about that other people may not that could be helpful in the writing and research process?

After talking with your peer, what did you learn? Did your peer's discussion of technologies give you insight into tools you already use or would like to use? ◗

We'll ask you to practice different parts of your writing process throughout this book, both through the exercises you'll participate in and the larger writing assignments that you'll complete. As you work through the exercises, think about what part of the writing process you're addressing and what tools might help you to complete that stage most effectively.

REFLECT ON THE DEVELOPMENT OF COMPOSING PRACTICES AND HOW THOSE PRACTICES INFLUENCE YOUR WORK

Reflection—and reflective writing—is a powerful tool for understanding yourself, your experiences, your strengths, your weaknesses, and your unique way of seeing the world. Understanding who you are is absolutely essential to aligning with a satisfying major and career. Scholars refer to this kind of awareness and understanding of one's own thought processes as **metacognition**.

INSIDE WORK **Reflecting on Your Thought Processes**

Practice engaging in reflection by writing your responses to the following questions:

- If you could learn one thing about yourself that you don't already know, what would it be?
- Discuss a time when you realized your thought processes were different than someone else's and that their thought processes had value to you.
- Describe your personality in three to five sentences.
- Describe the personality of one person who is not related to you, but who contributed positively to who you are. What do you like about their personality and how is it different from your own?
- Discuss how your personality aligns with the career you'd like to have. If you're not sure what career you would like to have, discuss a dream job and explain how that job would make you happy. What kind of major would lead to the career you want? ◗

What Is Reflective Writing?

Reflective writing is writing based on an author's experience. It is often used to process events, relationships, or experiences in order to make sense of them. One of the best-known genres of reflective writing is the diary, but there are many other reflective writing genres such as memoir, exercise/workout journal, travel blog, research logbook, personal letters, and the literacy narrative.

One of the common purposes of these genres is to process experiences and to organize those experiences in a meaningful way. Diaries often feature sections organized by date, and the audience is usually limited to only the writer herself. Sometimes diaries do reach publication and a wide audience, such as *The Diary of Anne Frank*, but this is usually not their intended purpose.

By contrast, the memoir genre of reflective writing is usually written for publication and with a wider audience in mind. Famous examples of the memoir genre include Maya Angelou's *I Know Why the Caged Bird Sings*, Elie Wiesel's *Night*, and Jon Krakauer's *Into Thin Air: A Personal Account of the Mt. Everest Disaster*. Krakauer's memoir, for example, details the author's experience in the 1996 Mount Everest disaster, one of the deadliest expeditions in mountaineering history.

In academic writing classes, the literacy narrative is one of the most commonly used reflective genres. The purpose of the literacy narrative is to describe the events that contributed to development of literacy and how that literacy helped shape understanding of the world. We'll talk more about literacy narratives after exploring what we mean by the word *literacy*.

What Is Literacy?

Literacy is sometimes defined as the ability to read and write, but when we are talking about academic contexts, we'd like you to use a broader definition. Think of literacy not only as the ability to read and write, but also as the ability to function successfully in a specific context or contexts. When you consider your literacy development over the span of your life, it is easy to see marked improvement. When you were a small child, for example, you first learned the alphabet, how to hold a pencil or crayon, and how to make the shapes of letters that would later become words and sentences. What's harder to see are the subtle changes that take place over a shorter span of time, such as a single semester of college. Perhaps you only pick up a few skills: knowledge about when to ask a peer to review your writing, how to insert a direct quotation into a paper, or how to create a graph from data you've collected. Each of these small skills accumulates with others over time to prepare you for the kinds of writing and research that will serve you in a career beyond college.

Scholarship in writing studies suggests that the habits of mind most essential to transferring knowledge gained in one context (say this class) to another context (say a senior-level writing intensive course in your major) are metacognition and flexibility/adaptability. If you think about it for a moment, it makes sense. Metacognition is the awareness of one's own thought processes. If your awareness of how you think and process knowledge is highly developed, you'll be able to take knowledge you acquire and more readily draw from that knowledge in another instance. This is where reflective writing is especially helpful because reflective writing improves metacognition.

What Is a Literacy Narrative?

A **literacy narrative** is an essay that reflects on how someone has developed literacy over time. It is a form of reflective writing that draws on your memories and experiences, and as such it is non-fiction. The purpose of the genre is to reflect on your identity as a literate person, as someone who has or needs to develop a skill. When done well, the literacy narrative makes meaning from experience and helps you to better understand yourself, why you feel the way you do about the skill you gained, and how to chart a path forward in your life, drawing from the knowledge you have acquired.

A literacy narrative need not be confined to an academic setting. As we've begun to explore, literacy can mean much more than the ability to read and write, and the attitudes we bring to a classroom are informed by thousands of experiences that may have nothing to do with a classroom, teachers, or reading and writing directly. A literacy narrative might encompass the story of how you learned to speak and act as a softball player, YouTube celebrity, or employee at a movie theater. That kind of literacy narrative might explore the slang, codes of behavior, dress, or attitudes that others impressed upon you. Your instructor may have specific guidelines about the kinds of events she wants to see in your literacy narrative. The underlying theme, though, should be literacy (either narrowly or broadly defined), how you came to be literate, and what your feelings and attitudes about literacy are.

CHARACTERISTICS OF A LITERACY NARRATIVE

A literacy narrative almost always includes the following characteristics:

1. a main idea (or point) regarding your literacy development
2. scene writing (specific settings with a location and time)
3. use of sensory detail to describe the scenes (sight, sound, smell, touch, taste)
4. the "I" point of view

Effective narratives generally involve a struggle, obstacle, or challenge that you overcame. The struggle could be emotional (shame or anxiety, for example), or it could be physical or situational (perhaps you learned how to read with the help of a single mother who was working two jobs). All struggles appeal to emotions and as such can inspire readers to find persistence, passion, and perseverance, or to overcome challenges.

Main Idea

Probably the most important aspect of a literacy narrative is the guiding principle or main idea of your narrative. This should be something you have a sense of before you get far into the drafting phase of your essay, but it may well develop or change as you write. For some students, it takes writing a full draft of a paper to really begin to see what the main idea is and what point they are trying to make.

The main idea of your literacy narrative should be tied into your identity, how you view literacy, and how your views developed through experiences good and bad. One activity that helps to brainstorm ideas is to list five words that describe your personality.

Scenes

In a literacy narrative, a scene consists of a specific time and location. The bus stop on the morning of your first day of high school, the classroom where you took the SAT, an auditorium stage where you gave a speech, your kitchen table where an adult helped you learn to spell your name when you were four years old. These are specific scenes. They take place at a specific location over a fairly short amount of time (from a few minutes to a few hours). A literacy narrative written for a college class will usually be between four and ten pages. This affords you the space to select approximately three scenes from your life to describe.

If you had to select three scenes from your life that informed how you view reading, writing, language, and education, what would they be? Can you connect the scenes to the main idea you would like to convey about your identity as a student?

Sensory Details

So you decide on a scene. Then what? Writers rely on our five senses—sight, sound, touch, smell, and taste—to describe scenes vividly. To use sensory detail, you absolutely have to use your imagination and memory.

It's like painting. The key is to blend your sensory details to create an impression. Make use of as many senses as you can.

Rather than summarize huge chunks of time (your entire middle school experience, for example), decide on three specific scenes with short timespans and fixed locations that paint an impression of who you are, how your views of reading and writing were shaped in an instant of time, and then make use of all the sensory details you can to paint that scene.

"I" Point of View

One of the most commonly asked questions in a first-year writing course is "Can I use the 'I' point of view in my paper?" It seems that many college students arrive having been taught contradictory rules about using the "I" point of view for writing in a class. Let's try and clarify this rule for you once and for all.

Use or non-use of the "I" point of view in a paper for a class totally depends on the genre in which you are writing. When writing in the literacy narrative genre, you should make use of the "I" point of view. You are telling your story from your life, and the "I" point of view is the most appropriate point of view to use. In a scientific report, however, it might not always be helpful or appropriate to use the "I" point of view.

Insider Example
Professional Literacy Narrative

In the following scholarly article, "Two Vowels Together: On the Wonderfully Insufferable Experiences of Literacy," Aimee C. Mapes advocates for the use of reflective writing such as the literacy narrative as a form of resistance to the emphasis on standardized testing in school curricula over the past two decades. In making her case, Mapes draws on some of the stylistic conventions of the literacy narrative while introducing readers to the scholarly discourse surrounding the literacy narrative itself. Notice the ways that she develops a main idea through specific scenes in her narrative.

Two Vowels Together: On the Wonderfully Insufferable Experiences of Literacy

AIMEE C. MAPES

AIMEE MAPES

When I was four years old, I learned to write my given name using big and small letters: *A-i-m-e-e*. The problem was that I couldn't write the little *e*. For two years, every *e* turned upside down.

I could write:
I could write:
I could write:
I could write:
Twice:

Despite my Irish Catholic grandmother trying her damnedest to rehabilitate this propensity, the habit formed. Even now, using tools in

Microsoft Word to recreate an upside down *e* (twice!), I transport back in time to my grandmother's small bungalow in the north valley of California, kneeling over a mocha-stained wood coffee table, issues of the *National Enquirer* and *Readers Digest* layered on the lower level. On recycled white construction paper, my unsteady hand sketched *A*, then *i*, then *m*. My pencil moved directly left, circled down right, and then circled up to the left. Upside down. *Slap.*

My hand stinging, Grammie said, "You're doing it wrong. Do it right. Like this."

Stubby pencil in hand, I moved left, circled down to the right, and circled up, to the left. Upside down. *Slap.*

With two vowels together, I was twice wrong. *Slap. Slap.*

INSUFFERABLE HABITS

When I return to four-year-old me tracing letters, what I recall is not Slap, Slap. It is shame. Myself a teacher of writing with a four-year-old son experiencing his emergent literate practices, I'm curious about what heightened my grandmother's desire to rectify this upside-down *e* habit. Doing it wrong was failing. Doing it right, "like this," was learning. Where she observed failure, many literacy scholars would describe learning (see Goodman). There's the rub. My grandmother observed only deficits. As an instructor of first-year writing and an assistant director of a university writing program, I imagine first-year students similarly positioned as not learning. I imagine how high-stakes assessments and institutional placements attach a discourse of deficit to students as a consequence of facile narratives of learning. Anxieties over college readiness come to mind. Slap. Slap. The current sociopolitical and economic juncture—where fears about a literacy crisis, socioeconomic uncertainties, and flourishing digital and information technologies coalesce into economies of an educational crisis—is precisely when literacy narratives are necessary.

THE KIDS DON'T STAND A CHANCE

At present, teachers of English know all too well claims of a literacy crisis in education. Popular and scholarly reports lament students' reading and writing habits—texting, being distracted, the five-paragraph theme, low achievement on standardized measures. Chris Gallagher writes that standardized testing, among other neoliberal agendas, "provides fodder for a continuous, manufactured education crisis" (454). Calls for education reform construct students as failing to learn. Since the early 2000s, reports contribute to manufacturing a college student crisis. Citing a 2003 National Assessment of Adult Literacy, for instance, Emory University English professor Mark Bauerlein surmises a decline in college graduates' literacy skills in the 1990s. Based on results of numerous standardized assessments of civic learning, quantitative skills, and participation in the arts, he contends that today's college students have stark knowledge deficits, as does another notable (and contested) study by Richard Arum and Josipa Roksa in *Academically Adrift*. Grand narratives about learning circulate locally and nationally that, taken together, advance an educational crisis. Amongst circulating narratives, accountability discourses, according to Chris Gallagher, reinforce a "bureaucratic-institutional model" of assessment wherein "those closest to and most involved in the central activity of the system—teaching and learning—are accorded the least primacy and authority" (463). That is, teachers and learners function as byproducts of wider systems of institutional competition. In neoliberal accountability discourse, what follows is rote pedagogy designed to support students' achievement on high-stakes assessments—or, as my grandmother would describe, doing it right, "like this." Indeed, Yancey, Robertson, and Taczak's research in *Writing across Contexts* explains that "students do bring to college what the school culture has emphasized: a test-based writing practice keyed to creating texts with simple beginning-middle-end structures, a central claim, and some evidence, producing what is called the five-paragraph theme" (13). There is no room for upside-down *e*'s.

For me, literacy narratives in first-year writing emerge as powerful tools to disentangle these economies and interject complexly lived experiences with literacy. As a writing program administrator, I champion literacy narratives knowing the genre has been/is maligned by some in the field of composition and rhetoric (see Kara Alexander; Daniel; Hall and Minnix). For instance, literacy narratives, according to Kara Poe Alexander, reinforce dominant master narratives, as simple success stories. Some personal narratives, explains Thomas Newkirk ("Transformation"), invite "students to view their self-development as a series of pivotal moments that result in qualitative changes in their value systems or identities" (264). As a genre, literacy narratives suffer from the same pitfalls: the story is at once a celebration of writing "for self-examination" and also the burden of transformation (Newkirk, *Performance*, 23). Despite this, for over twenty years, composition scholars depict benefits of pedagogies focused on students' literacy experiences prior to college and in relation to academic literacies. Elizabeth Chiseri-Strater explains that all literate practices inform students' overall literacy. Literacy narratives, according to Mary Soliday, invite students to consider the place and communities where language is acquired. Jonathan Alexander's case study of two gamers argues for composition pedagogy built around "literacies that students are already developing outside the classroom and [that] demonstrate how they can be complemented and augmented with more 'traditional' academic literacies" (53). So, too, literacy narratives allow students to identify and carefully cultivate an awareness of sponsorship in their literate lives as Deborah Brandt's research demonstrates in *Literacy in American Lives*. For the students that I teach, the benefits of tapping these enterprises are twofold: (1) Students are in a position to acknowledge themselves as legitimate readers, writers, and producers of texts and as having a history of engaging organizations much like they will or are engaging the university, and (2) The engagement can scaffold students' recognitions of intricate webs of support over a lifespan, for narrative reflections create opportunities for relationships and meaning making. Coming from the belief that students bring personal lives into the classroom, I expect first-year writing, in particular, to draw on the multiple lifeworlds of students, and literacy narratives afford legitimate opportunities to do so.

TAKE THE POWER BACK

When I reflect on being four years old and resisting standards for drawing the letter *e*, I recall feeling shame, certainly, then anger, and finally resentment about my name. I was always twice wrong. But there is more to that story. The narrative shifts. After three years in elementary school—three years of being one of two or even three Amy's to a classroom—my perspective changed. I still resented being one of a pair of girls named Amy in my third grade class, but I experienced the spelling of my name newly. The other girls spelled their name *A-m-y* and arrived in school with well-combed hair. A-m-y wore dresses. She brought lunch in Care Bear lunchboxes, sandwiches secured in orange Tupperware. My Wonderbread peanut butter sandwiches came to school in plastic wrap inside a brown paper bag, which I subsequently discarded. On rare occasions I brushed my hair for school, and usually my mom reminded me. I wore faded jeans and jersey tees. A-i-m-e-e, as I learned, was French. It meant beloved. It was unique. Being A-i-m-e-e undercut feelings of inferiority in school where I felt shame differently, shame for being a girl who didn't comb her hair perfectly. Shame for living in a rental duplex with a kitchen absent Tupperware. Shame for having a single mother. By contrast, A-i-m-e-e meant my parents loved me. The trouble with an upside-down *e* transformed.

Whenever I encounter cyclical reports of an American literacy crisis, I'm reminded of my own literacy crisis. Current anxieties about college readiness aren't new. They are new versions of old conflicts. Composition theorists have a history of contesting literacy crisis discourse, especially as it disproportionately harms non-dominant communities (see Lamos, Fox, Trimbur). One of the most celebrated literacy narratives in our field, Mike Rose's *Lives on the Boundary* artfully details this very pattern. Almost thirty years ago, literacy scholar Geraldine Clifford (1988) explained that "cycles of concern for an integrated holistic approach to English language instruction have periodically emerged in reaction to historical forces that are essentially fragmenting in their effects" (3), but it is misleading to perceive the pattern as endlessly repeated cycles of back to the basics because over time reversals are not as extreme as they first seemed. When situated amid historic perspectives on literacy instruction, even current research in composition and rhetoric on program assessment, transfer of knowledge, and metacognition is circumscribed by discourses of accountability. As the field explores concepts like transfer and metacognition, for example, I think about how current scholarship has the potential to default into narratives of progress that fail to characterize learning as full of regressions and resistance.

EVERYTHING IS EVERYTHING

As a mother of a four-year-old and a teacher for twenty years, I am ever grateful for upside-down *e*'s. Teaching and learning, according to Gallagher, "succeed or fail on the strength of *relationships*" (463, emphasis kept) because, Robert Yagelski explains, "language and literacy are wonderfully, insufferably complex and resist control (and human beings, the more so)" (266). In the current educational crisis, curriculum should provide a counterscript to pervasive constructions of student deficits. The power to showcase literacies rests firmly in first-year writing where narrow scripts of learning can be grappled with, explored, and resisted through effortful reflections of students' cultural histories and shared literacies. Provide students opportunities to voice their stories, and you will create meaningful reflections on the wonderfully insufferable complexities of literacy.

REMIX: THE WONDERFULLY INSUFFERABLE LITERACY PLAYLIST

"Wonderful World," Sam Cooke. *Greatest Hits: Sam Cooke*. BMG Entertainment, 1997.
"Habit," Ought. *More Than Any Other Day*. Constellation Records, 2014.
"2 Vowels Together," Miss Jenny & Friends. *Phonics Time*. Jennifer Fixman Kramer, 2013.
"The Kids Don't Stand a Chance," Vampire Weekend. *Vampire Weekend*. XL Recordings, 2008.
"School," Nirvana. *Bleach*. Sub Pop Records, 1989.
"We're Going to Be Friends," The White Stripes. *White Blood Cells*. Third Man Records, 2001.
"Take the Power Back," Rage Against the Machine. *Rage Against the Machine*. Sony Music Entertainment, 1992.
"Everything Is Everything," Lauryn Hill. *The Miseducation of Lauryn Hill*. Ruffhouse Records, 1998.

WORKS CITED

Alexander, Jonathan. "Gaming, Student Literacies, and the Composition Classroom: Some Possibilities for Transformation." *College Composition and Communication*, vol. 61, no. 1, 2009, pp. 35–63.
Alexander, Kara Poe. "Success, Victims, and Prodigies: 'Master' and 'Little' Cultural Narratives in the Literacy Narrative Genre." *College Composition and Communication*, vol. 62, no. 4, 2011, pp. 608–33.
Arum, Richard, and Josipa Roksa. *Academically Adrift: Limited Learning on College Campuses*. University of Chicago Press, 2011.

Bauerlein, Mark. *The Dumbest Generation: How the Digital Age Stupefies Young Americans and Jeopardizes Our Future*. Jeremy P. Tarcher/Penguin, 2008.

Brandt, Deborah. *Literacy in American Lives*. Cambridge UP, 2001.

Chiseri-Strater, Elizabeth. *Academic Literacies: The Public and Private Discourse of University Students*. Boynton/Cook, 1991.

Clifford, Geraldine Joncich. *A Sisyphean Task: Historical Perspectives on Writing and Reading Instruction*. National Center for the Study of Writing, 1987. Technical Report, no. 7, NWP.org. National Writing Project, 1987.

Cooke, Sam. "Wonderful World." *Greatest Hits: Sam Cooke*, BMG Entertainment, 1997.

Daniel, Beth. "Narratives of Literacy: Connecting Composition to Culture." *College Composition and Communication*, vol. 50, no. 3, 1999, pp. 393–410.

Fox, Tom. *Defending Access: A Critique of Standards in Higher Education*. Boynton/Cook, 1999.

Gallagher, Chris. "Being There: (Re)Making the Assessment Scene." *College Composition and Communication*, vol. 62, no. 3, 2011, pp. 450–76.

Goodman, Yetta. "The Development of Initial Literacy." *Perspectives on Literacy*, edited by Eugene Kintgen, Barry M. Kroll, and Mike Rose, Southern Illinois University Press, 1989, pp. 312–20.

Hall, Anne-Marie, and Christopher Minnix. "Beyond the Bridge Metaphor: Rethinking the Place of the Literacy Narrative in the Basic Writing Curriculum." *Journal of Basic Writing*, vol. 31, no. 2, 2012, pp. 57–82.

Hill, Lauryn. "Everything Is Everything." *The Miseducation of Lauryn Hill*, Ruffhouse Records LP, 1998.

Lamos, Steve. "Literacy Crisis and Color-Blindness: The Problematic Racial Dynamics of Mid-1970s Language and Literacy Instruction for 'High Risk' Minority Students." *College Composition and Communication*, vol. 61, no. 2, 2009, pp. W125-W148.

Miss Jenny & Friends. "2 Vowels Together with Miss Jenny." *Phonics Time*, Jennifer Fixman Kramer, 2013.

Newkirk, Thomas. "The Dogma of Transformation." *College Composition and Communication*, vol. 56, no. 1, 2004, pp. 251–71.

-----. *The Performance of Self in Student Writing*. Boynton/Cook, 1997.

Nirvana. "Schools." *Bleach*, Sub Pop Records, 1989.

Ought. "Habit." *More Than Any Other Day*, Constellation, 2014.

Rage Against the Machine. "Take the Power Back." *Rage Against the Machine*, Sony Music Entertainment, 1992.

Rose, Mike. *Lives on the Boundary*. Penguin, 1989.

Soliday, Mary. "Translating Self and Difference through Literacy Narratives." *College English*, vol. 56, no. 5, 1994, pp. 511–26.

Trimbur, John. "Literacy and the Discourse of Crisis." *The Politics of Writing Instruction: Postsecondary*, edited by Richard Bullock, John Trimbur, and Charles Schuster, Heinemann, 1991, pp. 277–95.

Vampire Weekend. "The Kids Don't Stand a Chance." *Vampire Weekend*, XL, 2008.

The White Stripes. "We're Going to Be Friends." *White Blood Cells*, Third Man Records, 2001.

Yagelski, Robert. "Stasis and Change: English Education and the Crisis of Sustainability." *English Education*, vol. 37, no. 4, 2005, pp. 262–71.

Yancey, Kathleen Blake, Liane Robertson, and Kara Taczak. *Writing Across Contexts: Transfer, Composition, and Sites of Writing*. Utah State University Press, 2014.

Discussion Questions

1. What do you think is the main point that Mapes is making in her literacy narrative?

2. Why does Mapes says she feels "shame" when she recalls her early literacy development with her grandmother? Why shame?

3. What scenes does Mapes develop in her narrative that demonstrate that shame?

4. How does Mapes feel about Mark Bauerline's assertion that college students' literacy skills have declined? Who do you agree with and why?

5. What does Mapes mean by "curriculum should provide a counterscript to pervasive constructions of student deficits"? How might the literacy narrative be beneficial, according to Mapes?

Finally a word or two about scene length. If the scene you're envisioning takes place over more than a few hours, it likely ceases to be a scene. Your entire freshman year of high school, for example, isn't a scene. However, one specific lunch period in the cafeteria during your freshman year when you and a friend decided to ditch school would be a scene. Scenes consist of fairly short stretches of time in a specific location. The tighter the time-line and location is in your mind, the more vivid the scene will be when you write it.

INSIDE WORK   **Drafting a Scene for a Literacy Narrative**

Brainstorm a list of at least five specific scenes you could choose from that best illustrate your literacy development.

Choose one and free-write for five minutes about where the scene happened (location), how long the scene took place (ideally, between a few minutes and a few hours), who was in the scene, and how the scene helped shape your identity.

WRITING PROJECT   ## Composing a Literacy Narrative

The purpose of the literacy narrative is for you to reflect on and tell the story of your literacy development. Effective narratives have a beginning, middle, and end, and a literacy narrative follows a series of connected scenes (perhaps three) that illustrate points regarding how you developed your skills, identity, and views of yourself and others as a literate person.

Your instructor may give you more direction about how to define literacy for the purpose of this assignment, but you could focus on the following questions:

Academic Literacy

- What are your first memories of writing in school?
- How did you learn about the expectations for writing in school?
- Can you think of a time when you struggled to meet the requirements of a school writing assignment? What happened?

Technological Literacy

- What early memories do you have of using technology?
- How do you use technology now to communicate in your daily life? What technologies are most important to you for work, for school, and/or for personal commitments?

Workplace Literacy

- What writing and communication skills are expected in the occupation you aspire to when you graduate? How will you develop those skills?
- Can you think of a time when you encountered a task at work that you didn't know how to accomplish? What did you do? How did you address the challenge?

Social and/or Cultural Literacy

- Have you ever been in a social situation where you didn't know how to act? What did you do?
- What groups do you identify with, and what expectations and shared beliefs make that group cohesive?

In a narrative essay, explore the development of your own literacy. You might do this chronologically, at least as you start writing. Be specific in identifying how you define literacy and how you developed your abilities. In your narrative and analysis, provide examples from your experience, and show how they contribute to the development of that literacy. Ultimately, your narrative should be directed to a particular audience for a particular purpose, so think of a context in which you might tell this story. For example, a student who is studying to be a teacher might write about his early literacy experiences and how they led to an interest in teaching other children to read and write. Or an applicant for a job requiring specific technological ability might include a section in an application letter that discusses her development of expertise in technological areas relevant to the job. Be·imaginative if you like, but make sure that your narrative provides specific examples and makes a point about your literacy development that you believe is important.

Insider Example
Student Literacy Narrative

MICHAELA BIEDA

The following literacy narrative was written by first-year college student Michaela Bieda regarding her self-awareness that her strengths and skills did not always align well with the expectations that schools, teachers, and peers had about what a "good student" should be. In her literacy narrative, Bieda reflects on the awakening she had through learning her strengths in an academic context and how a teacher contributed to her developing self-awareness of her individuality, her strengths, and her identity. Bieda makes use of all of the aspects of the literacy narrative we've introduced so far:

1. a main idea
2. scenes (locations and a fixed period of time)
3. sensory detail to describe those scenes (sight, sound, smell, touch, taste)
4. the "I" point of view

Literacy Narrative

Michaela Bieda

My Journey to Writing

"I" point of view

As a young kid, I struggled a lot in school. I was that student who had a hard time being able to focus and maintain that focus. I was easily distracted, and my eyes and mind would wander rather than listen and watch my teacher. I even fell asleep in class at times either as a result of over-stimulation that I couldn't handle or maybe an underlying depression, knowing I just couldn't cope in a regular classroom or keep up with my fellow students who didn't seem to share my mindset. I remember many a teacher telling my parents, "Micki just doesn't apply herself. She's smart but she's lazy." I wasn't lazy, and I wasn't sure if I was smart or not. I just knew that I couldn't sit still at my desk and do what all the other kids

Michaela sets up a problem that leads to the main point.

were able to do. Nothing in school held my interest. The traditional way of presenting the three R's didn't hold my attention. I would much rather daydream, waiting to go home and work on my art projects, designing and coloring a world I created. The world of academia had already labeled me ADHD, where I thought of myself as creative. My parents were well aware of the skills I had as well as the ones I didn't have. They thought that by changing schools, I might not resent schoolwork and teachers so much. When

I was in 4th grade, I went to another school, but since it was just another private Jewish day school, nothing much was different. "Mom," I complained almost from the first day at the new school, "I've got the same books and the same schedule. All that's happened is that I have to make new friends." The change of schools didn't result in an attitude change for me or a new understanding—and possible appreciation—by my new set of teachers. As they say, "Same old, same old."

In 5th grade, I remember sitting at circular tables, waiting for the teacher to come into the classroom. The school principal walked in and announced, "Class, this is Mrs. Crincolli. Please make her feel welcome." As usual, I wasn't really paying attention to the person entering the room, but I did perk up when she had us decorate nametags and stand them up on our desks. Finally! An art project! And it had a practical application! I was thrilled. It meant so much to me to be able to perform a task I knew I could excel at. I loved my nametag, and I have kept it all these years as a tangible marker of my first school success. From that point on, I started noticing how different I felt about going to school. I had never been so excited to see what Mrs. Crincolli was going to ask us to do next. For her part as a caring teacher, she noticed my lack of success on tests yet how good my writing and art projects were. She took the time to work with me to help me find ways to understand and remember the material for tests. I was a tricky learner because, with a mind that tried to absorb a billion things at once, prioritizing one thing to concentrate on took skills I didn't innately have but had to acquire. Mrs. Crincolli helped me to believe that I could learn that skill and then apply it. I can still hear her voice in my head, encouraging me: "Give it a whirl, Micki. You can do it."

By the time I hit 8th grade, I had fallen in love with writing, whether formal essays or free-form association. Mrs. Crincolli had also introduced me to the stories and poetry of Edgar Allan Poe. His dark Gothic elements spoke to me, and I tried writing stories and poems—not just emulating him but in my own voice as well. My favorite writing in school was free thought writing. Every day in class, we students had about 10 minutes to write in our journals. We could use the teacher's prompt or just go off on a personal tangent of feeling. Thanks to Mrs. Crincolli, from 5th grade on, I grasped that writing and literature could appeal to anyone needing a creative outlet. Mrs. Crincolli had been so clever in the types of assignments she gave and the books we were assigned to read in class. I always identified something

A new scene

An important character is introduced.

Dialogue adds specific detail

in my life with what I had to write about or the characters and plots I had to follow. The lack of direction and purpose I'd felt before Mrs. Crincolli entered my school life was now replaced by the joy of expressing myself on paper . . . or a screen. I wanted to impress her and the other teachers I had in each successive grade. In each English class I had with Mrs. Crincolli, the way she presented curriculum was so different from the usual textbook approach. Everything she had us students do was interesting, encouraging, and provocative. She had us constantly thinking out of the box, which was something I never thought I could do before she became my mentor.

I became very close with Mrs. Crincolli, spending time after class to help her with her bulletin boards. Eventually during my high school years, I became her Teacher's Assistant. Throughout high school under her tutelage, I learned to appreciate English even more and felt my strength in those skills more than any other class. I remember on more than one occasion, counting pages of younger classes' writing journals. So many of those students just scribbled or wrote random words in order to get the required number of pages completed. I shook my head, sad that these youngsters hadn't yet caught on to the value of journal writing or the joy of exploring oneself through language.

When it came time to graduate from high school, I reflected on the many years I had developed a real relationship with words—using and understanding them—as well as the prize of having a friendship with Mrs. Crincolli. My school, like so many others, had the usual awards ceremony at graduation. Special to my school though was the tradition that each teacher spoke about one student who had made a real impact during high school. I was sitting far in the back of the assembly with my mom as the slide show of our senior class played. All the other students in my class and our teachers

Sensory detail — sat together, watching this heartwarming video under twinkly lights tangled in the trees. One by one, each teacher walked up to the front of the gathering. When it was Mrs. Crincolli's turn, my mom whispered to me, "I just know she'll talk about you." I wanted that to happen so badly—for her to know and share how much she meant to me and also how much I meant to her. My heart overflowed and so did my tears as she started to talk . . . about ME! She mentioned not only how I had been her student for so many years, but one of the first friends she had at the school—someone who put herself out for a teacher with the only expectation of learning as much as she could. I was so grateful that she understood just how I felt. She was the one, the pivotal one at the pivotal point in my life who made such a difference and such a contribution to me as a person as well as a writer. I don't have to wonder whether she knows how important she is to me or whether she has done her job as a teacher. We both know, and I cherish her and the confidence she gave me to celebrate a creative mind and channel it to positive and productive ends.

The main point of the narrative: Mrs. Crincolli helped Michaela identify her own strengths.

Discussion Questions

1. What would you say Michaela learned about herself by writing her literacy narrative? What evidence suggests this?

2. What is the main idea (or ideas) of her specific story? What point is she trying to make about her literacy development?

3. What kind of major and career could you see someone with Michaela's strengths going into that would make her happy?

4. How did Michaela's teacher, Mrs. Crincolli, contribute to Michaela's development?

5. What relationships or events from your own life contributed the most to how you see yourself as a student? Who contributed the most to the vision you see of yourself in a specific career one day? How did they contribute?

- **You should work to achieve specific goals** related to your writing process during your writing classes:
  - Develop a writing project through multiple drafts
  - Develop flexible strategies for reading, drafting, reviewing, collaborating, revising, rewriting, rereading, and editing
  - Learn to give and to act on productive feedback to works in progress
  - Use composing processes and tools as a means to discover and reconsider ideas
  - Reflect on the development of composing practices and how those practices influence your work

- **Your purpose in using reflective writing is to process experiences** you've had in order to better understand how those experiences shape you and your writing.

- **Literacy can be broadly or narrowly defined** as the ability to read, write, and communicate in a variety of contexts.

- **A literacy narrative is a reflective writing genre** used to process the experiences you've had that shape your views of reading, writing, and how you communicate with others.

- **The key features of a literacy narrative are**
  - a main idea or point
  - scenes
  - sensory detail descriptions
  - the "I" point of view

Reading and Writing Rhetorically

You read and write in many different situations: at school, at home, with your friends, and maybe at work. Perhaps there are other situations in which you read and write, too, likely through a variety of different media. You might read and write in a journal, on social media, in a word processor as you prepare a paper for school, in a text message, or in a note to a friend. You could probably name many other situations in which you read and write on a daily basis.

Have you ever considered how different the processes of reading and writing are in these situations? You're performing the same act (reading or writing a text) in many ways, but several features might change from one situation to another:

- the way the text looks
- the medium or technology you use
- the tone you use
- the words you use (or avoid using)
- the grammar and mechanics that are appropriate

Even within the more specific category of "academic writing" that we address in this book, some of these features might shift depending on the context. The structure, vocabulary, style, and documentation expectations differ from one discipline to another. If you've ever written a lab report for a physics class and a literary analysis for a literature class, then you've likely experienced some of those differences. The differences arise because of the specific demands of each of the differing writing situations.

ANDREA TSURUMI

Understanding Rhetorical Context

As you read and write, we want you to consider closely the specific situation for which you are writing. In other words, you should always think about the **rhetorical context** in which your writing takes place. We introduced the importance of "rhetorical knowledge" through the Council of Writing Program Administrators' outcomes statement in Chapter 1, but we want to explore in more detail what rhetorical knowledge and rhetorical context mean. In this text, we'll define rhetorical context through four elements:

- who the author is, and what background and experience he or she brings to the text
- who the intended audience is for the text
- what issue or topic the author is addressing
- what the author's purpose is for writing

Each of these elements has an impact on the way a text is written and interpreted. Consider how you might write about your last job in a text message to a friend in comparison with how you might write about it in an application letter for a new job. Even though the author is the same (you) and the topic is the same (your last job), the audience and your purpose for writing are vastly different. These differences thus affect how you characterize your job and your choice in medium for writing the message.

Sometimes writing situations call for more than one audience as well. You might address a **primary audience**, the explicitly addressed audience for the text, but you might also have a **secondary audience**, an implied audience who also might read your text or be interested in it. Imagine you wrote a job application letter as an assignment for a business writing class. Your primary audience would likely be your instructor, but you might also write the letter as a template to use when actually sending out a job application letter in the future. So your future prospective employer might be a secondary audience.

In academic settings, these elements of rhetorical context shift depending on the disciplinary context within which you're writing as well. Consider another example: Imagine a student has decided to research the last presidential election for a school assignment. If the research assignment were given in a history class, then the student might research and write about other political elections that provide a precedent for the outcome of the recent election and the events surrounding it. The student would be approaching the topic from a historical perspective, which would be appropriate for the context of the discipline and audience (a history professor). If the student were writing for an economics class, he or she might focus on the economic impact of elections and how campaign finance laws, voter identification laws, and voters' socioeconomic statuses affected the election. Even though the author, audience, topic, and purpose seem similar at first glance (they're all academic research assignments, right?), the student would focus on different questions and aspects of the topic when examining the election from different disciplinary perspectives and for different audiences. Other elements of the student's writing would likely shift, too, and we'll discuss those differences in Part Two of this book.

Why might it be important to consider the rhetorical context when reading or writing? As you read, noticing the rhetorical context of a text can help you understand choices that the author makes in writing that might at first seem confusing or inconsistent, even in academic writing. For example, writers might use the passive voice in an experimental study report ("the data were collected by . . .") but not in a reflective essay about conducting the same experimental study ("I collected the data . . ."). Or the same scholar might write in the first person in one kind of academic text (like this textbook) but not in another (perhaps a scholarly article). In all these writing situations, the author makes choices based on the rhetorical context. In this textbook, the first person ("I" or "We") and second person ("You") help to establish a personal tone that might not be appropriate for an academic journal article. We (first person) made this choice specifically because of our audience for the textbook—students (like you, second person) who are learning to navigate academic writing. We wanted the text to have a friendlier and less academically distant tone. Such a conversational tone wouldn't always be appropriate in other rhetorical contexts, though. When you write, understanding the rhetorical context can help you be more effective in achieving your purpose and communicating with your audience because you make choices that are appropriate to the situation.

As you notice the kinds of choices a writer makes, you are analyzing the rhetorical context of the writing: that is, you are taking elements of the writing apart to understand how they work together. Analyzing rhetorical context is a key strategy we'll use throughout this book to understand how different forms of writing work and what the similarities and differences are in writing across various disciplines.

INSIDE WORK Identifying Rhetorical Context

Think about a specific situation in the past that required you to write something. It could be any kind of text; it doesn't have to be something academic. Then create a map—by drawing a diagram, a chart, or some other visual image—of the rhetorical context of that piece of writing. Consider the following questions as you draw:

- What was your background and role as the author?
- Who was the audience?
- What was the topic?
- What was your purpose for writing? ▶

Understanding Genres

As you learn to analyze the rhetorical context of writing, keep in mind that much writing takes place within communities of people who are interested in similar subjects. They might use similar vocabulary, formats for writing, and grammatical and stylistic rules. In a sense, they speak the same "language." The common practices that they typically employ in their writing are called conventions, as we discussed in Chapter 1. As you read and analyze the writing of academic writers, we'll ask you to notice and comment on the conventions that different disciplines use in various rhetorical contexts. When you write, you'll want to keep those conventions in mind, paying attention to the ways you should shape your own writing to meet the expectations of the academic community you are participating in. We'll go into more detail about how to analyze the specific conventions of disciplinary writing in Part Two.

In addition to paying close attention to the conventions that writers employ, we'll ask you to consider the genre through which writers communicate their information. **Genres** are approaches to writing situations that share some common features, or conventions. You already write in many genres in your daily life: If you've sent an e-mail message to a friend to schedule an event, written a text message to verify directions to the event, and written a thank-you note for a gift, then you've written and read examples of three different genres that are all associated with personal writing. If you like to cook, you've probably noticed that recipes in cookbooks follow similar patterns by presenting the ingredients first and then providing step-by-step directions for preparation. The ingredients usually appear in a list, and the instructions generally read as directives (e.g., "Add the eggs one at a time and mix well"), often in more of a prose style. Recipes are a genre. If you've looked for an office job before, you've probably encountered at least three different genres in the job application process: job advertisements, application letters, and résumés. How well you follow the expected conventions of the latter two genres often affects whether or not you get the job.

You've also likely had experience producing academic genres. If you've ever written a business letter, an abstract, a mathematical proof, a poem, a book review, a research proposal, or a lab report, then you might have noticed that these kinds of academic writing tasks have certain conventions that make them unique. Lab reports, for example, typically have specific expectations for the organization of information and for the kind of language used to communicate that information. Throughout Part Two of the book, we offer examples of a number of other academic genres—a literature review, an interpretation of an artistic text, as well as a theory response, just to name a few.

We'll focus more on analyzing genres in Part Two. But because different writing situations, or rhetorical contexts, call for different approaches, we ask you to think about the genre, as well as associated conventions, that you might be reading or writing in any particular situation so that you understand the rhetorical context better. Our goal is not to have you identify a formula to follow for every type of academic writing, but rather to understand the expectations of a writing situation—and how much flexibility you have in meeting those expectations—so that you can make choices appropriate to the genre.

LaunchPad

See what writing studies instructor Moriah McCracken has to say about genres.

Reading Rhetorically

Since we're talking about paying attention to rhetorical context, we want to explain the difference between the reading you do with an eye toward rhetorical context and the reading you might do in other circumstances. Whenever you read during a typical day, you probably do so for a variety of reasons. You might read:

- **To Communicate:** reading a text message, a letter from a friend, an e-mail, a birthday card, or a post on Instagram
- **To Learn:** reading instructions, a textbook, street signs while you drive, dosage instructions on a medication bottle, or the instructor's comments at the end of a paper that you turned in for a class
- **To Be Entertained:** reading novels, stories, comics, a joke forwarded in e-mail, or a favorite website

The details that you pay attention to, and the level at which you notice those details, vary according to your purpose in reading.

In this text, however, we will ask you to read in a way that is different from reading just to communicate, learn, or be entertained. We want you to *read rhetorically*, paying close attention to the rhetorical context of whatever you are reading. When you read rhetorically, you make note of the different elements of rhetorical context that help to shape the text. You'll notice who the **author** is (or, if there are multiple authors, who each one is) and what background, experience, knowledge, and potential biases the author brings to the text. In addition, you'll notice who the intended **audience** is for the text. Is the author writing to a group of peers? To other scholars in the field? How much prior knowledge does that audience have, and how does the intended audience shape the author's approach in the text? Are there multiple audiences (primary and secondary)? You'll also notice what the **topic** is and how it influences the text. Does the author use a specific approach related to the topic choice?

Additionally, you'll notice the author's **purpose** for writing. Sometimes the purpose is stated explicitly, and sometimes it is implied. Why does the author choose to write about this topic at this point? What does the author hope to achieve? Finally, you'll want to notice how these four elements work together to shape the text. How is the choice of audience related to the author's background, topic, and purpose for writing?

Reading Visuals Rhetorically

We should stress that the strategies for understanding rhetorical context and for reading rhetorically are applicable to both verbal and visual texts. In fact, any rhetorical event, or any occasion that requires the production of a text, establishes a writing situation with a specific rhetorical context. Consider the places you might encounter visual advertisements, as one form of visual texts, over the course of a single day: in a magazine, on a website, in stores, on billboards, on television, and so on. Each encounter provides an opportunity to read the visual text rhetorically, or to consider how the four elements of author, audience, topic, and purpose work together to shape the text itself (in this case, an advertisement). This process is called **rhetorical analysis**.

In fact, noticing these elements when you read will help you become a careful and critical reader of all kinds of texts. When we use the term *critical*, we don't use it with any negative connotations. We use it in the way it works in the term *critical thinking*, meaning that you will begin to understand the relationships among author, audience, topic, and purpose by paying close attention to context.

INSIDE WORK   **Reading Rhetorically**

With the direction of your instructor, choose a text (either verbal or visual) to read and analyze. As you read the text, consider the elements of rhetorical context. Write about who the author is, who the intended audience is, what the topic is, and what the author's purpose is for writing or for creating the text. Finally, consider how these elements work together to influence the way the text is written or designed. Later in the chapter, we'll ask you to engage in this kind of *rhetorical analysis* in a more formal way to understand different kinds of texts. ❭

Writing Rhetorically

Writing is about choices. Writing is not a firm set of rules to follow. There are multiple choices available to you any time you take on a writing task, and the choices you make will help determine how effectively you communicate with your intended audience, about your topic, for your intended purpose. Some choices, of course, are more effective than others, based on the conventions expected for certain situations. And yet, sometimes you might break conventions in order to make a point or draw attention to what you are writing. In both cases, though, it's important to understand the expectations of the rhetorical context for which you are writing so that your choices will have the effect you intend.

When you write rhetorically, you'll analyze the four elements of rhetorical context, examining how those elements shape your text through the choices that you make as a writer. You'll think about the following elements:

- **What You, as the *Author*, Bring to the Writing Situation**   How do your background, experience, and position relative to the audience shape the way you write?

- **Who Your Intended *Audience* Is**   Should you address a specific audience? Has the audience already been determined for you (e.g., by your instructor)? What do you know about your audience? What does your audience value?

- **What Your *Topic* Is**   What are you writing about? Has the topic been determined for you, or do you have the freedom to focus your topic according to your interests? What is your relationship to the topic? What is your audience's relationship to it?

- **What Your *Purpose* Is for Writing**   Why are you writing about this topic, at this time? For example, are you writing to inform? To persuade? To entertain?

Outside of school contexts, we often write because we encounter a situation that calls for us to write. Imagine a parent who wants to write a note to thank her son's teacher for inviting her to assist in a class project. The audience is very specific, and the topic is determined by the occasion for writing. Depending on the relationship between the parent and the teacher, the note might be rather informal. But if the parent wants to commend the teacher and copy the school's principal, she might write a longer, more formal note that could be included in the teacher's personnel file. Understanding the rhetorical context would help the parent decide what choices to make in this writing situation.

For school assignments, thinking about the topic is typically the first step because students are often assigned to write about something specific. If your English professor asks you to write a literary interpretation of Toni Morrison's *Song of Solomon*, your topic choice is limited. Even in this situation, though, you have the freedom to determine what aspect of the text you'll focus on. Do you want to look at imagery in the novel? Would you like to examine Morrison's use of language? Would you like to analyze recurring themes, or perhaps interpret the text in the historical and cultural context in which it was written?

In this text, we would like you also to consider the other elements of rhetorical context—author, audience, and purpose—to see how they influence your topic. Considering your purpose in writing can often shape your audience and topic. Are you writing to communicate with a friend? If so, about what? Are you completing an assignment for a class? Are you writing to persuade someone to act on an issue that's important to you? If you are writing to argue for a change in a policy, to whom do you need to write in order to achieve your purpose? How will you reach that audience, and what would the audience's expectations be for your text? What information will you need to provide? Your understanding of the rhetorical context for writing will shape your writing and help you to communicate more effectively with your audience, about your topic, to meet your purpose.

INSIDE WORK **Analyzing Rhetorical Context**

Think back to the rhetorical situation you identified in the "Inside Work: Identifying Rhetorical Context" activity on page 47. Consider that situation more analytically now, using slightly revised versions of the questions from that activity as a guide. Write your responses to the following questions.

- As the *author*, how did your background, experience, and position relative to the audience shape the way you created your text?

- Were you addressing a specific *audience*? Was the audience already determined for you? What did you know about your audience? What did your audience value or desire?

- What was your text about? Was the *topic* determined for you, or did you have the freedom to focus your topic according to your interests? What was your relationship to the topic? What was your audience's relationship to it?

- What was your *purpose* for creating a text about that topic, at that time? For example, were you writing to inform? To persuade? To entertain? ▶

Writing a Rhetorical Analysis

When you read rhetorically, you analyze a text through a particular lens. Examining a text through the formal framework of author, audience, topic, and purpose can be a way of analyzing a text in a written assignment as well. Such an examination, called a rhetorical analysis, is a genre of writing that explores elements of a text's rhetorical context. We'll provide several opportunities for you to conduct rhetorical analyses in this book, since it is one of the ways you will begin to discover the features of writing across different academic contexts.

In a rhetorical analysis, the writer uses a rhetorical framework to understand how the context of the text helps to create meaning. One framework you might use involves walking through the different elements of rhetorical context to examine the piece of writing in detail:

Rhetorical Context

Author	What does the author bring to the writing situation?
Audience	Who is the author addressing, and what do they know or think about this topic?
Topic	What is the author writing about, and why did he or she choose it?
Purpose	Why is the author writing about this topic, at this time?

These four components of the rhetorical context function together dynamically. You might analyze the author's background and experience and how he or she develops credibility in the text. Or you could make assertions about the author's primary and secondary audiences based on the author's choices regarding style and language. But in reality, all four of the rhetorical context components function together to shape how someone writes or speaks.

The following text is a historic letter that George H. W. Bush, the forty-first president of the United States (and father of the forty-third president, George W. Bush), sent to Iraqi president Saddam Hussein on January 9, 1991, shortly before the United States, in cooperation with over thirty other countries, launched an assault to expel Iraqi forces from Kuwait. This action came in response to Iraq's invasion and annexation of Kuwait in 1990, and it became a part of the history that is now referred to as the First Gulf War. While the events that precipitated this letter occurred a long time ago, it is a helpful artifact for understanding the complicated power dynamics at play in the U.S. involvement in ongoing events in the Middle East. As you read the letter, pay close attention to the rhetorical moves that President Bush makes. Who are his primary and secondary audiences? Is his audience only Saddam Hussein? If not, then who else is his audience, and what in his letter suggests who the secondary audience is? What is the letter's purpose? Does Bush seem to think Saddam will leave Kuwait? How do you know?

Letter to Saddam Hussein

GEORGE H. W. BUSH

Mr. President,

We stand today at the brink of war between Iraq and the world. This is a war that began with your invasion of Kuwait; this is a war that can be ended only by Iraq's full and unconditional compliance with UN Security Council resolution 678.

I am writing to you now, directly, because what is at stake demands that no opportunity be lost to avoid what would be a certain calamity for the people of Iraq. I am writing, as well, because it is said by some that you do not understand just how isolated Iraq is and what Iraq faces as a result.

I am not in a position to judge whether this impression is correct; what I can do, though, is try in this letter to reinforce what Secretary of State James A. Baker told your foreign minister and eliminate any uncertainty or ambiguity that might exist in your mind about where we stand and what we are prepared to do.

The international community is united in its call for Iraq to leave all of Kuwait without condition and without further delay. This is not simply the policy of the United States; it is the position of the world community as expressed in no less than twelve Security Council resolutions.

We prefer a peaceful outcome. However, anything less than full compliance with UN Security Council resolution 678 and its predecessors is unacceptable. There can be no reward for aggression.

Nor will there be any negotiation. Principles cannot be compromised. However, by its full compliance, Iraq will gain the opportunity to rejoin the international community. More immediately, the Iraqi military establishment will escape destruction. But unless you withdraw from Kuwait completely and without condition, you will lose more than Kuwait. What is at issue here is not the future of Kuwait—it will be free, its government restored—but rather the future of Iraq. This choice is yours to make.

The United States will not be separated from its coalition partners. Twelve Security Council resolutions, twenty-eight countries providing military units to enforce them, more than one hundred governments complying with sanctions—all highlight the fact that it is not Iraq against the United States, but Iraq against the world. That most Arab and Muslim countries are arrayed against you as well should reinforce what I am saying. Iraq cannot and will not be able to hold on to Kuwait or exact a price for leaving. You may be tempted to find solace in the diversity of opinion that is American democracy. You should resist any such temptation. Diversity ought not to be confused with division. Nor should you underestimate, as others have before you, America's will.

Iraq is already feeling the effects of the sanctions mandated by the United Nations. Should war come, it will be a far greater tragedy for you and your country. Let me state, too, that the United States will not tolerate the use of chemical or biological weapons or the destruction of Kuwait's oil fields and installations. Further, you will be held directly responsible for terrorist actions against any member of the coalition. The American people would demand the strongest possible response. You and your country will pay a terrible price if you order unconscionable acts of this sort.

I write this letter not to threaten, but to inform. I do so with no sense of satisfaction, for the people of the United States have no quarrel with the people of Iraq. Mr. President, UN Security Council resolution 678 establishes the period before January 15 of this year as a "pause of good will" so that this crisis may end without further violence. Whether this pause is used as intended, or merely becomes a prelude to further violence, is in your hands, and yours alone.

I hope you weigh your choice carefully and choose wisely, for much will depend upon it.

Discussion Questions

1. For what purpose(s) does President Bush write this letter?
2. How does Bush establish his credibility, honesty, and resolve in the letter?
3. Who is the primary audience? Who are the secondary audiences?
4. What conventional features for this form of writing (genre) does Bush's letter exhibit?

Insider Example
Student Rhetorical Analysis

The following is a student rhetorical analysis of the letter written from George H. W. Bush to Saddam Hussein. As you read this analysis, consider how the student, Sofia Lopez, uses audience, topic, and purpose to construct meaning from Bush's letter. Additionally, pay attention to how Sofia uses evidence from the letter to support her assertions. These moves will become more important when we discuss using evidence to support claims in Chapter 4 (see pp. 65–67).

Sofia Lopez

Mr. Harris

English 100

January 2018

The Multiple Audiences of George H. W. Bush's Letter

to Saddam Hussein

President George H. W. Bush's 1991 letter to Saddam Hussein, then the president of Iraq, is anything but a simple piece of political rhetoric.

The introduction outlines the writer's approach to analyzing Bush's letter. Based on the introduction, what do you see as the writer's overall purpose for this rhetorical analysis?

In this paragraph, the writer outlines potential audiences for Bush's letter in more detail. Who are those audiences?

In this paragraph, the writer explores the ways Bush is able to align himself with multiple audiences. What evidence does the writer use to demonstrate Bush's associations with his various audiences?

The writer frequently refers to Bush's "complex author position." What do you think the writer means by this?

The topic of the letter is direct and confrontational. On the surface, Bush directly calls upon Hussein to withdraw from Kuwait, and he lays out the potential impact should Hussein choose not to withdraw. But when analyzed according to the rhetorical choices Bush makes in the letter, a complex rhetorical situation emerges. Bush writes to a dual audience in his letter and establishes credibility by developing a complex author position. By the conclusion of the letter, Bush accomplishes multiple purposes by creating a complex rhetorical situation.

While Bush's direct and primary audience is Saddam Hussein, Bush also calls upon a much larger secondary audience in the first sentence of the letter by identifying "the world" as the second party involved in the imminent war that the letter is written to prevent. Bush continues to write the letter directly to Hussein, using second person to address him and describe the choices before him. Bush also continues, however, to engage his secondary audience throughout the letter by referring to resolutions from the UN Security Council in five separate paragraphs (1, 4, 5, 7, and 9). The letter can even be interpreted to have tertiary audiences of the Iraqi and the American people because the letter serves to justify military action should Hussein not comply with the conditions of the letter.

Because Bush is addressing multiple audiences, he establishes a complex author position as well. He is the primary author of the letter, and he uses first person to refer to himself, arguably to emphasize the direct, personal confrontation in the letter. He constructs a more complex author position, however, by speaking for other groups in his letter and, in a sense, writing "for" them. In paragraph 4, he speaks for the international community when he writes, "The international community is united in its call for Iraq to leave all of Kuwait. . . ." He draws on the international community again in paragraph 6 and refers to his coalition partners in paragraph 7, aligning his position with the larger community. Additionally, in paragraph 7, he builds his credibility as an author by emphasizing that he is aligned with other Arab and Muslim countries in their opposition to Hussein's actions. Writing for and aligning himself with such a diverse group of political partners helps him address the multiple audiences of his letter to accomplish his purposes.

While the primary and literal purpose of the letter is to call upon Iraq to withdraw from Kuwait and to outline the consequences of noncompliance, Bush accomplishes additional purposes directly related to his additional audiences and the complex author position he has established. The primary purpose of his letter, naturally, is addressed to his primary audience, Saddam Hussein. The construction of the letter, however, including the repeated mention of UN Security Council resolutions, the invocation of support from other Arab and Muslim countries, and the reference to other coalition partners and the international community, serves to call upon the world (and specifically the United Nations) to support military action should Hussein not comply with the conditions of the letter. The construction of a letter with a complex audience and author allows Bush to address multiple purposes that support future action.

> What other elements of the rhetorical situation might the writer explore to further analyze Bush's letter?

Discussion Questions

1. What does Sofia Lopez identify as Bush's purpose? How does she support that interpretation of Bush's purpose?

2. Whom does Sofia see as Bush's audience? How does she support that reading of the letter?

3. What might you add to the analysis, from a rhetorical perspective?

Writing a Rhetorical Analysis

WRITING PROJECT

In this paper, you will analyze the rhetorical situation of a text of your choosing. You might want to choose something publicly available (already published) that represents a piece of polished writing so that you know that the author(s) has finished making revisions and has had time to think through important rhetorical choices. Alternatively, you might choose something written for an academic, personal, work, or other context. Start by reading the text carefully and rhetorically. Use the elements of rhetorical context to analyze and understand the choices the writer has made in the text.

Rhetorical Context

- author
- audience
- topic
- purpose

In addition to describing the rhetorical features of the article, you will also explore why you believe the author made certain choices. For example, if you're analyzing a blog entry on a political website, you might discuss who the author is and review his or her background. Then you could speculate about the writing choices the author has made and how his or her background might have influenced those choices.

Consider what conclusion you can draw about the text, and highlight that as an assertion you can make in the introduction to your analysis. The body of your paper should be organized around the rhetorical features you are analyzing, demonstrating how you came to your conclusion about the text.

In your conclusion, reflect on what you have found. Are there other issues still to be addressed? What other rhetorical strategies could be explored to analyze the work further? Are there surprises in the choices the writer makes that you should mention?

Keep in mind that your essential aim is to analyze, not to evaluate.

tip sheet — Reading and Writing Rhetorically

- **It is important to consider rhetorical context as you read and write.** Think about how the following four elements have shaped or might shape a text:
  - who the *author* is, and what background and experience he or she brings to the text
  - who the intended *audience* is
  - what issue or *topic* the author is addressing
  - what the author's *purpose* is for writing

- **Genres are approaches to writing situations that share some common features, or conventional expectations.** As you read and write texts, consider the form of writing you're asked to read or produce: Is it a recognizable genre? What kinds of conventional expectations are associated with the genre? How should you shape your text in response to those expectations?

- **Reading rhetorically means reading with an eye toward how the four elements of author, audience, topic, and purpose work together** to influence the way an author shapes a text, verbal or visual or otherwise.

- **Writing rhetorically means crafting your own text based on an understanding of the four elements of your rhetorical context.** Specifically, you consider how your understanding of the rhetorical context should affect the choices you make as a writer, or how your understanding should ultimately shape your text.

- **A rhetorical analysis is a formal piece of writing that examines the different elements of the rhetorical context of a text.** It also often considers how these elements work together to explain the shape of a text targeted for analysis.

Developing Arguments

Many writing situations, both academic and non-academic, require us
as writers to persuade audiences on a particular topic — that is, to
develop an argument. When we refer to arguments, we don't mean heated,
emotional sparring matches. Rather, we use **argument** to refer to the
process of making a logical case for a particular position, interpretation,
or conclusion. Of course we all experience and participate in these kinds
of arguments around us every day as we decide where to eat dinner with
friends, what classes to take, or which movie to download or concert to see.
We are immersed in these kinds of popular arguments constantly through
advertisements, marketing campaigns, social media posts, and texting with
friends, and so we are adept at critically thinking about arguments and persuasion in those contexts.

In academic settings, arguments are frequently more
developed and nuanced because the authors are arguing
for a particular interpretation or conclusion or action
based on the results of research. To make such an argument effectively, academics must develop clear, persuasive
texts through which to present their research. These arguments are built on **claims** — arguable assertions — that
are supported with evidence from research. The unifying
element of any academic argument is its primary or central claim, and although most sustained arguments make
a series of claims, there is usually one central claim that
makes an argument a coherent whole. Our goal in this
chapter is to introduce you to some of the basic principles of argumentation and to help you write clear central
claims and develop successful arguments, especially in
your academic writing.

ANDREA TSURUMI

Understanding Proofs and Appeals

Aristotle, a rhetorician in ancient Greece, developed a method of analyzing arguments that can be useful to us in our own reading and writing today. He explained that arguments are based on a set of proofs that are used as evidence to support a claim. He identified two kinds of proofs: inartistic and artistic. **Inartistic proofs** are based on factual evidence, such as statistics, raw data, or contracts. **Artistic proofs**, by contrast, are created by the writer or speaker to support an argument. Many arguments contain a combination of inartistic and artistic proofs, depending on what facts are available for support. Aristotle divided the complex category of artistic proofs into three kinds of **rhetorical appeals** that speakers and writers can rely on to develop artistic proofs in support of an argument:

- Appeals to **ethos** are based on credibility or character. An example might be a brand of motor oil that is endorsed by a celebrity NASCAR driver. Another example could be a proposal for grant money to conduct a research study that discusses the grant writer's experience in successfully completing similar research studies in the past. In both examples, the speaker's or writer's experiences (as a NASCAR driver or as an established researcher) are persuasive elements in the argument.

- Appeals to **logos** are based on elements of logic and reason. An example might be an argument for change in an attendance policy that reveals a correlation between attendance and grades. The argument relies on logic and reason because it presents a relationship between attendance and grades and draws a connection to the policy, emphasizing how a change in the policy might affect grades.

- Appeals to **pathos** are based on emotions. Emotion can be a powerful motivator to convince an audience to hear an argument. An example might include telling the story of a program that helps homeless teenagers complete high school by finding shelter, food, and social support that enables them to improve their living conditions. Perhaps the program is in need of financial assistance in order to continue helping homeless teens. A story that features one or two specific teens who have come through the program and successfully completed high school would be an example of an appeal to emotion.

These types of appeals are present in arguments in both academic and non-academic settings. Many arguments, and often the most effective ones, include elements of more than one kind of appeal, using several strategies to persuade an audience. Based on the example above about a program that helps homeless teens, imagine that there is a campaign to solicit financial donations from the public to support the program. Now consider how much more persuasive that campaign would be if other appeals were used in addition to an emotional appeal. The campaign might develop an argument that includes raw data and statistics (an inartistic proof), the advice of civic leaders or sociological experts (ethos), the demonstration of a positive cause-and-effect relationship of the program's benefits in teens' lives (logos), along with a story of one teen, describing how she became homeless and how the program helped to get her back on her feet (pathos). Understanding the structure of arguments, and knowing the potential ways you can develop your own arguments to persuade an audience, will help you to write more effectively and persuasively.

INSIDE WORK **Writing about Arguments**

Choose a text to read that makes a claim. Consider something that interests you—perhaps an advertisement, or even your college's or university's website. Write about the kinds of rhetorical appeals you notice. Do you see evidence of ethos? Logos? Pathos? Is the argument drawing on statistics or raw data, an inartistic proof? Why do you think the author(s) or designer(s) structured the argument in this way? To answer this question, you'll also need to consider the rhetorical context. Who is the author, and who is the intended audience? What is the topic, and what is the purpose of the argument? In other words, what is the ultimate goal of the argument? ❱

Making Claims

As we mentioned earlier, the unifying element of any academic argument is its primary or central claim. In American academic settings, the central claim is often (but not always) presented near the beginning of a piece so that it can tie the elements of the argument together. A form of the central claim that you're likely familiar with is the **thesis statement**. Thesis statements, whether revealed in an argument's introduction or delayed and presented later in an argument (perhaps even in the conclusion), are central claims of arguments that are typical of writing that is primarily focused on civic concerns, as well as writing in some academic fields such as those in the humanities (see Chapter 7).

Imagine for a moment that you've been asked to write an argument taking a position on a current topic like cell phone usage, and you must decide whether or not to support legislation to limit cell phone use while driving. In this instance, the statement of your position is your claim. It might read something like this: "We should support legislation to limit the use of cell phones while driving," or "We should not support legislation to limit the use of cell phones while driving." Although there are many types of claims, the statement "We should pass legislation to limit the use of cell phones" is a claim of proposal or policy, indicating that the writer will propose some action or solution to a problem. We could also explore claims of definition

("Cheerleading is a sport") or claims of value ("Supporting a charity is a good thing to do"), just to name a few.

Literary analysis, a genre commonly taught in high school English classes, usually presents a thesis statement as part of the introduction. You may be familiar with a thesis statement that reads something like this: "Suzanne Collins's *Hunger Games* is a dystopian novel that critiques totalitarian regimes and empowers young women who are far too often marginalized and oppressed." This thesis statement makes a claim in support of a specific interpretation of the story. Regardless of the specific type of claim offered, the argument that follows it provides evidence to demonstrate why an audience should find the claim persuasive.

THESIS VERSUS HYPOTHESIS

In an academic setting, thesis statements like those typical of arguments in the humanities are not the only kind of unifying claim you might encounter. In fact, arguments in the natural and social sciences are often organized around a statement of hypothesis, which is different from a thesis statement. Unlike a thesis statement, which serves to convey a final position or conclusion on a topic or issue that a researcher has arrived at based on study, a **hypothesis** is a proposed explanation or conclusion that is usually either confirmed or denied on the basis of rigorous examination or experimentation later in a paper. This means that hypothesis statements are, in a sense, still under consideration by a writer or researcher. A hypothesis is a proposed answer to a research question. Thesis statements, in contrast, represent a writer or researcher's conclusion(s) after much consideration of the issue or topic.

Consider the following examples of a hypothesis and a thesis about the same topic:

Hypothesis	Thesis
Decreased levels of sleep will lead to decreased levels of academic performance for college freshmen.	College freshmen should get at least seven hours of sleep per night because insufficient sleep has been linked to emotional instability and poor academic performance.

The hypothesis example above includes several elements that distinguish it from the thesis statement. First, the hypothesis is written as a prediction, which indicates that the researcher will conduct a study to test the claim. Additionally, it is written in the future tense, indicating that an experiment or study will take place to prove or disprove the hypothesis. The thesis statement, however, makes a claim that indicates it is already supported by evidence gathered by the researcher. A reader would expect to find persuasive evidence from sources later in that essay.

We highlight this distinction in types of claims to underscore that there is no single formula for constructing a good argument in all academic contexts. Instead, expectations for strong arguments are bound up with the expectations of particular writing communities. If you write a lab report with the kind of thesis statement that usually appears in a literary analysis, your work would likely convey the sense that you're a novice to the community of writers and researchers who expect a hypothesis statement instead of a thesis statement. One of the goals of this text is to help you develop awareness of how the expectations for good argumentation change from one academic context to the next.

Developing Reasons

When writing an academic argument that requires a thesis statement, you can choose how detailed to make that thesis statement. When we introduced thesis statements as a type of claim, we asked you to consider two possible statements on the topic of cell phone use while driving: "We should/should not support legislation to limit the use of cell phones while driving." You can also refer to these two possible forms as **simple thesis statements** because they reveal a writer's central position on a topic but do not include any reasoning as support for that position. When reasons are included as logical support, then you can think about the thesis statement as a **complex thesis statement**:

Simple Thesis: We should support legislation to limit the use of cell phones while driving.

Reasons: They are an unnecessary distraction.

They increase the incidence of accidents and deaths.

When you combine the simple statement of position or belief with the reasons that support it, then you have a more complex, and fuller, thesis statement:

Complex Thesis: We should support legislation to limit the use of cell phones because they are an unnecessary distraction for drivers and because they increase needless accidents and deaths on our roadways.

Although constructing complex thesis statements allows you to combine your statement of position, or your central claim, with the reasons you'll use to defend that position, you may frequently encounter arguments that do not provide the reasons as part of the thesis. That is, some writers, depending on their rhetorical context, prefer to present a simple thesis and then reveal the reasons for their position throughout their argument. Others choose to write a thesis that both establishes their position and provides the reasoning for it early on. An advantage of providing a complex thesis statement is that it offers a road map to the reader for the argument that you will develop.

INSIDE WORK   **Constructing Thesis Statements**

Generate a list of six to eight current social issues that require you to take a position. Consider especially issues that are important to your local community. Choose one or two to focus on for the other parts of this activity.

Next, explore multiple positions. Consider competing positions you can take for each of the issues you identified. Write out a simple thesis statement for those positions. Be careful not to limit your positions to pros and cons, especially if you can think of alternative positions that might be reasonable for someone to argue. Often, there are multiple sides to an issue, and we miss the complexity of the issue if we only acknowledge two sides. Then, list as many reasons as you can think of to support each of those positions. It might be helpful to connect your simple statement of thesis to your reasons using the word *because*. This activity can help you to strengthen your argument by anticipating rebuttals or counterarguments. We'll take these issues up later in the chapter.

For example:

Claim: The U.S. Congress should enact legislation to prohibit animal testing for cosmetics manufactured or sold in the United States.

Reasons:

because _____.

because _____.

because _____.

Alternate Claim: The U.S. Congress should not enact legislation to prohibit animal testing for cosmetics manufactured or sold in the United States.

Reasons:

because _____.

because _____.

because _____.

Alternate Claim: The decision to prohibit animal testing for cosmetics manufactured or sold in the United States should be made at the state level and not by the federal government.

Reasons:

because _____.

because _____.

because _____.

Finally, combine your simple thesis with your reasoning to construct a complex thesis for each potential position. Write out your thesis statements. ❯

Supporting Reasons with Evidence

Reasons that support a claim are not particularly powerful unless there is evidence to back them up. Evidence that supports an argument can take the form of any of the rhetorical appeals. Let's look again at the complex thesis from the previous section: "We should support legislation to limit the use of cell phones because they are an unnecessary distraction for drivers and because they increase needless accidents and deaths on our roadways." In order to generate the reasons, the writer relied on what he already knew about the dangers of cell phone use. Perhaps the writer had recently read a newspaper article that cited statistics concerning the number of people injured or killed in accidents as a direct result of drivers using their phones instead of paying attention to the roadways. Or perhaps the writer had read an academic study that examined attention rates and variables affecting them in people using cell phones. Maybe the writer even had some personal knowledge or experience to draw upon as evidence for her or his position. Strong, persuasive arguments typically spend a great deal of time unpacking the logic that enables a writer to generate reasons in support of a particular claim, and that evidence can take many forms.

Personal Experience   You may have direct experience with a particular issue or topic that allows you to speak in support of a position on that topic. Your personal experience can be a rich resource for evidence. Additionally, you may know others who can provide evidence based on their experiences with an issue. Stories of personal experience often appeal to either ethos (drawing on the credibility of the writer's personal experience) or pathos (drawing on readers' emotions for impact). Sometimes these stories appeal to both ethos and pathos at the same time. Imagine the power of telling the story of someone you know who has been needlessly injured in an accident because another driver was distracted by talking on the phone.

Expert Testimony   Establishing an individual as an expert on a topic and using that person's words or ideas in support of your own position can be an effective way of bolstering your own ethos while supporting your central claim. However, the use of expert testimony can be tricky, as you need to carefully establish what makes the person you're relying on for evidence an actual expert on the topic or issue at hand. You must also consider your audience—whom would your audience consider to be an expert? How would you determine the expert's reputation within that community? The use of expert testimony is quite common in academic argumentation. Researchers often summarize, paraphrase, or cite experts in their own discipline, as well as from others, to support their reasoning. If you've ever taken a class in which your instructor asked you to use reputable

Learn more about entering academic conversations.

Hear criminologist Michelle Richter comment on types of research in her field.

sources to support your argument, then you've probably relied on expert testimony to support a claim or reason already. As evidence for our complex thesis, imagine the effectiveness of citing experts who work for the National Transportation and Safety Board about their experiences investigating accidents that resulted from inattentive driving due to cell phone use.

Statistical Data and Research Findings Statistics frequently serve as support in both popular and academic argumentation. Readers tend to like numbers, partly because they seem so absolute and scientific. However, it is important, as with all evidence, to evaluate statistical data for bias. Consider where statistics come from and how they are produced, if you plan to use them in support of an argument. Additionally, and perhaps most important, consider how those statistics were interpreted in the context of the original research reported. What were the study's conclusions? Imagine the effectiveness of citing recently produced statistics (rates of accidents) on the highways in your state from materials provided by your state's Department of Transportation.

Writers also often present the findings, or conclusions, of a research study as support for their reasons and claims. These findings may sometimes appear as qualitative, rather than just statistical, results or outcomes.

When selecting the types and amounts of evidence to use in support of your reasons, be sure to study your rhetorical context and pay particular attention to the expectations of your intended audience. Some audiences, especially academic ones, are less likely to be convinced if you only provide evidence that draws on their emotions. Other audiences may be completely turned off by an argument that relies only on statistical data for support.

So far, we've discussed several types of evidence that are typically used in the construction of arguments—personal experience, expert testimony, statistical data and research findings. Collecting the data you need to make a strong argument can seem like a daunting task at times. It's important to keep in mind, though, that the amount of evidence you provide and the types of data your argument requires will depend entirely on the kind of argument you are constructing, as well as on the potential audience you want to persuade. Therefore, it's essential that you analyze and understand your audience's expectations when selecting support for your argument. Above all, select support that your audience will find credible, reliable, and relevant to your argument.

Choose any one of the complex thesis statements you constructed in the "Inside Work" activity on pages 64–65. Then identify two potential target audiences for your arguments. Freewrite for five to ten minutes in response to the following questions about these audiences' likely expectations for evidence.

- What does each audience already know about your topic? That is, what aspects of it can you assume they already have knowledge about?

- What does each audience need to know? What information do you need to make sure to include?

- What does each audience value in relation to your topic? What kinds of information will motivate them, interest them, or persuade them? How do you know?

- What sources of information about your topic might your audiences find reliable, and what sources would they question? Why? ❭

Understanding Assumptions

Any time you stake a claim and provide a reason, or provide evidence to support a reason, you are assuming something about your audience's beliefs and values, and it is important to examine your own assumptions very carefully as you construct arguments. Though assumptions are often unstated, they function to link together the ideas of two claims.

Let's consider a version of the claim and reason we've been looking at throughout this section to examine the role of assumptions: "We should support legislation to limit the use of cell phones while driving because they increase needless accidents and deaths on our roadways." In this instance, the claim and the reason appear logically connected, but let's identify the implied assumptions that the reader must accept in order to be persuaded by the argument:

Claim:	We should support legislation to limit the use of cell phones while driving.
Reason:	They increase needless accidents and deaths on our highways.
Implied Assumptions:	We should do whatever we can to limit accidents and deaths.
	Legislation can reduce accidents and deaths.

Many audiences would agree with these implied assumptions. As a result, it would likely be unnecessary to make the assumptions explicit or provide support for them. However, you can probably imagine an instance when a given audience would argue that legislating people's behavior does not affect how people actually behave. To such an audience, passing laws to regulate the use of cell phones while driving might seem ineffective. As a result, the audience might actually challenge the assumption(s) upon which your argument rests, and you may need to provide evidence to support the implied assumption that "legislation can reduce accidents and deaths."

A writer who is concerned that an audience may attack his argument by pointing to problematic assumptions might choose to explicitly state the assumption and provide support for it. In this instance, he might consider whether precedents exist (e.g., the effect of implementing seat belt laws, or statistical data from other states that have passed cell phone use laws) that could support his assumption that "legislation can reduce accidents and deaths."

INSIDE WORK **Considering Assumptions and Audience**

In the previous activity, you considered the most appropriate kinds of evidence for supporting thesis statements for differing audiences. This time, we ask you to identify the assumptions in your arguments and to consider whether or not those assumptions would require backing or additional support for varying audiences.

Begin by identifying the assumption(s) for each of your thesis statements. Then consider whether or not those assumptions need backing as the intended audience for your argument changes to the following:

- a friend or relative

- a state legislator

- an opinion column editor

- a professional academic in a field related to your topic ❱

Anticipating Counterarguments

Initially, it may strike you as odd to think of counterarguments as a strategy to consider when constructing an argument. However, anticipating **counterarguments**—the objections of those who might disagree with you—may actually strengthen your argument by forcing you to consider competing chains of reasoning and evidence. In fact, many writers actually choose to present counterarguments, or rebuttals of their own arguments, as part of the design of their arguments.

Why would anyone do this? Consider for a moment that your argument is like a debate. If you are able to adopt your opponent's position and then explain why that position is wrong, or why her reasoning is flawed, or in what ways her evidence is insufficient to support her own claim, then you support your own position. This is what it means to offer a **rebuttal** to potential counterarguments. Of course, when you provide rebuttals, you must have appropriate evidence to justify dismissing part or all of the counterargument. By anticipating and responding to counterarguments, you also strengthen your own ethos as a writer on the topic. Engaging counterarguments demonstrates that you have considered multiple positions and are knowledgeable about your subject.

You can also address possible counterarguments by actually conceding to an opposing position on a particular point or in a limited instance. Now, you're probably wondering: Why would anyone do this? Doesn't this mean losing your argument? Not necessarily. Often, such a concession reveals that you're developing a more complex argument and moving past the pro/con positions that can limit productive debate.

Imagine that you're debating an opponent on a highly controversial issue like free college tuition. You're arguing that tuition should be free, and your opponent makes the point that free tuition could have the effect of lowering the quality of education an institution is able to offer. You might choose to concede this possibility, but counter it by explaining how varying tuition costs among different kinds of universities contribute to socioeconomic stratification. Though you acknowledge the validity of your opponent's concerns, you are able to make a case that the social damage caused by the current system makes that risk acceptable. That is, you could **qualify** your position by acknowledging your opponent's concerns and explaining why you feel that your argument is still valid. In this case, your opponents' points are used to adjust or to qualify your own position, but this doesn't negate your argument. Your position may appear even stronger precisely because you've acknowledged the opponent's points and refined the scope of your argument as a result.

Insider's View
Figuring out the "right" side
MIKE BROTHERTON, ASTRONOMY

"In science, we're really worried about which side is right, and you discuss both sides only to the extent of figuring out which one's right. It's not one opinion versus another. It's one set of ideas supported by a certain set of observations against another set of ideas supported, or not supported, by the same set of observations, and trying to figure out which one is a better explanation for how things work."

🔲 **LaunchPad**

Hear more about writing to solve problems.

INSIDE WORK   **Dealing with Counterarguments**

Throughout this section, you've been working with a series of claims that you constructed. You've linked those claims to reasons as support, and you've considered the kinds of evidence most appropriate for your theses in light of particular audiences. You've also considered the likely acceptability of your assumptions, according to various potential audiences. This time, consider possible counterarguments for your thesis statements.

- Who might argue against you?
- What might their arguments be?

- What will their arguments be based on?
- How might you use a counterargument to actually support your own claim?

Brainstorm a list of instances in which you might want to concede a point or two as a means of strengthening your own position. ❱

Analyzing Arguments

One way to understand the process of developing a persuasive argument is to study how others structure theirs. If you'll recall, in Chapter 3 we discussed how visual texts, like verbal ones, construct rhetorical situations. In the same way, visual texts may also seek to persuade an audience, and they may use many of the techniques explored throughout this chapter.

The following papers present arguments about visual texts. In the first, Jack Solomon, a professional writer, explores how advertisements reflect what he sees as contradictory impulses in the American character. In the second, Timothy Holtzhauser, a student writer, examines the argument strategies employed in a 1943 ad for American war bonds. As you engage with their arguments, keep in mind that each writer is both making an argument and analyzing an argument simultaneously, so you'll want to consider their texts from both perspectives. Also keep in mind that their arguments are supported by evidence found in their own research. We'll explore how to conduct research in more detail in Chapter 5.

Insider Example
Professional Analysis of an Advertisement

In the following passage from "Masters of Desire: The Culture of American Advertising," Jack Solomon uses *semiotics*—a method for studying and interpreting cultural signs and symbols—to analyze the arguments made in two advertisements. As you read Solomon's argument, try to identify which elements of argument discussed in this chapter he uses in his analysis.

Excerpt from **"Masters of Desire: The Culture of American Advertising"**

JACK SOLOMON

JACK SOLOMON

The American dream . . . has two faces: the one communally egalitarian and the other competitively elitist. This contradiction is no accident; it is fundamental to the structure of American society. Even as America's great myth of equality celebrates the virtues of mom, apple pie, and the girl or boy next door, it also lures us to achieve social distinction, to rise above the crowd and bask alone in the glory. This land is your land and this land is my land, Woody Guthrie's populist anthem tells us, but we keep trying to increase the "my" at the expense of the "your." Rather than fostering contentment, the American dream breeds desire, a longing for a greater share of the pie. It is as if our society were a vast high-school football game, with the bulk of the participants noisily rooting in the stands while, deep down, each of them is wishing he or she could be the star quarterback or head cheerleader.

For the semiotician, the contradictory nature of the American myth of equality is nowhere written so clearly as in the signs that American advertisers use to manipulate us into buying their wares. "Manipulate" is the word here, not "persuade"; for advertising campaigns are not sources of product information, they are exercises in behavior modification. Appealing to our subconscious emotions rather than to our conscious intellects, advertisements are designed to exploit the discontentments fostered by the American dream, the constant desire for social success and the material rewards that accompany it. America's consumer economy runs on desire, and advertising stokes the engines by transforming common objects—from peanut butter to political candidates—into signs of all the things that Americans covet most.

But by semiotically reading the signs that advertising agencies manufacture to stimulate consumption, we can plot the precise state of desire in the audiences to which they are addressed. In this chapter, we'll look at a representative sample of ads and what they say about the emotional climate of the country and the fast-changing trends of American life. Because ours is a highly diverse, pluralistic society, various advertisements may say different things depending on their intended audiences, but in every case they say something about America, about the status of our hopes, fears, desires, and beliefs.

Let's begin with two ad campaigns conducted by the same company that bear out Alexis de Tocqueville's observations about the contradictory nature of American society: General Motors' campaigns for its Cadillac and Chevrolet lines. First, consider an early magazine ad for the Cadillac Allanté. Appearing as a full-color, four-page insert in *Time*, the ad seems to say "I'm special—and so is this car" even before we've begun to read it. Rather than being printed on the ordinary, flimsy pages of the magazine, the Allanté spread appears on glossy coated stock. The unwritten message

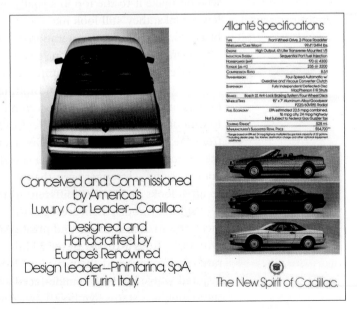

here is that an extraordinary car deserves an extraordinary advertisement, and that both car and ad are aimed at an extraordinary consumer, or at least one who wishes to appear extraordinary compared to his more ordinary fellow citizens.

Ads of this kind work by creating symbolic associations between their product and what is most coveted by the consumers to whom they are addressed. It is significant, then, that this ad insists that the Allanté is virtually an Italian rather than an American car—an automobile, as its copy runs, "Conceived and Commissioned by America's Luxury Car Leader—Cadillac" but "Designed and Handcrafted by Europe's Renowned Design Leader—Pininfarina, SpA, of Turin, Italy." This is not simply a piece of product information; it's a sign of the prestige that European luxury cars enjoy in today's automotive marketplace. Once the luxury car of choice for America's status drivers, Cadillac has fallen far behind its European competitors in the race for the prestige market. So the Allanté essentially represents Cadillac's decision, after years of resisting the trend toward European cars, to introduce its own European import—whose high cost is clearly printed on the last page of the ad. Although $54,700 is a lot of money to pay for a Cadillac, it's about what you'd expect to pay for a top-of-the-line Mercedes-Benz. That's precisely the point the ad is trying to make: the Allanté is no mere car. It's a potent status symbol you can associate with the other major status symbols of the 1980s.

American companies manufacture status symbols because American consumers want them. As Alexis de Tocqueville recognized a century and a half ago, the competitive nature of democratic societies breeds a desire for social distinction, a yearning to rise above the crowd. But given the fact that those who do make it to the top in socially mobile societies have often risen from the lower ranks, they still look like everyone else. In the socially immobile societies of aristocratic Europe, generations of fixed social conditions produced subtle class signals. The accent of one's voice, the shape of one's nose, or even the set of one's chin immediately communicated social status. Aside from the nasal bray and uptilted head of the Boston Brahmin, Americans do not have any native sets of personal status signals. If it weren't for his Mercedes-Benz and Manhattan townhouse, the parvenu Wall Street millionaire often couldn't be distinguished from the man who tailors his suits. Hence, the demand for status symbols, for the objects that mark one off as a social success, is particularly strong in democratic nations—stronger even than in aristocratic societies, where the aristocrat so often looks and sounds different from everyone else.

Status symbols, then, are signs that identify their possessors' place in a social hierarchy, markers of rank and prestige. We can all think of any number of status symbols—Rolls-Royces, Beverly Hills mansions, even Shar Pei puppies (whose rareness has rocketed them beyond Russian wolfhounds as status pets and has inspired whole lines of wrinkle-faced stuffed toys)—but how do we know that something is a status symbol? The explanation is quite simple: when an object (or puppy!) either costs a lot of money or requires influential connections to possess, anyone who possesses it must also possess the necessary means and influence to acquire it. The object itself really doesn't matter, since it ultimately disappears behind the presumed social potency of its owner. Semiotically, what matters is the signal it sends, its value as a sign of power. One traditional sign of social distinction is owning a country estate and enjoying the peace and privacy that attend it. Advertisements for Mercedes-Benz, Jaguar, and Audi automobiles thus frequently feature drivers motoring quietly along a country road, presumably on their way to or from their country houses.

Advertisers have been quick to exploit the status signals that belong to body language as well. As Hegel observed in the early nineteenth century, it is an ancient aristocratic prerogative to be seen by the lower orders without having to look at them in return. Tilting his chin high in the air and gazing down at the world under hooded eyelids, the aristocrat invites observation while refusing to look back. We can find such a pose exploited in an advertisement for Cadillac Seville in which an elegantly dressed woman goes out for a drive with her husband in their new Cadillac. If we look closely at the woman's body language, we see her glance inwardly with a satisfied smile on her face but not outward toward the camera that represents our gaze. She is glad to be seen by us in her Seville, but she isn't interested in looking at us!

Ads that are aimed at a broader market take the opposite approach. If the American dream encourages the desire to arrive, to vault above the mass, it also fosters a desire to be popular, to "belong." Populist commercials accordingly transform products into signs of belonging, utilizing such common icons as country music, small-town life, family picnics, and farmyards. All of these icons are incorporated in GM's "Heartbeat of America" campaign for its Chevrolet line. Unlike the Seville commercial, the faces in the Chevy ads look straight at us and smile. Dress is casual, the mood upbeat. Quick camera cuts take us from rustic to suburban to urban scenes, creating an American montage filmed from sea to shining sea. We all "belong" in a Chevy.

Discussion Questions

1. Jack Solomon sets up an interesting contrast between "manipulate" and "persuade" at the beginning of this excerpt. How does his description of these ads mirror our understanding of arguments? In your own words, how would you describe the differences he establishes between manipulating and persuading?

2. In Solomon's analysis of the Cadillac and Chevrolet ads, where does he address the claims and reasons given by the advertisers to buy their products? Do the ads address assumptions?

3. How does Solomon characterize the appeals made by both advertisements? Where does he describe appeals to ethos? Logos? Pathos?

Insider Example
Student Analysis of an Advertisement

Timothy Holtzhauser, a student in a first-year writing class, wrote the following analysis of an advertisement as a course assignment. He used elements of rhetorical analysis and argument analysis to understand the persuasive effects of the advertisement he chose. Notice, also, that he followed Modern Language Association (MLA) style conventions, especially when citing sources within his paper and documenting them at the end of the paper. (See Chapter 5 and the Appendix for additional information on documentation styles.)

Timothy Holtzhauser

ENG 101-79

February 13, 2018

Rhetoric of a 1943 War Bonds Ad

From the front covers of magazines at the store, to the ads by Google on sidebars of websites, to the incessant commercials on television, advertisements are visible everywhere. Whether the advertisement announces or insinuates its purpose, all advertisements attempt to change the audience's manner of thinking or acting. In "Masters of Desire: The Culture of American Advertising," Jack Solomon describes the motive behind advertising as pure and simple manipulation: "'Manipulate' is the word here, not 'persuade'; for advertising campaigns are not sources of product information, they are exercises in behavior modification" (60). Even the most innocent advertisement performs this maneuver, and the "Death Warrant . . . US War Bonds" advertisement drawn by S. J. Woolf is no different. This 1943 ad, printed in the *New York Daily News* for Bloomingdale's department store, not only encourages the purchase of U.S. war bonds by exaggerating Hitler's negative aspects, but also depicts the growing influence and activism of the United States during this era.

> The main claim, or thesis

When this advertisement appeared, the United States was rapidly becoming more involved in the hostilities of World War II. While not yet engaged in the war in Europe, the United States was providing supplies and manpower for the war in the Pacific, and the government was in serious need of funds to keep the war machine rolling. The main method that the government used to obtain these funds was selling war bonds and advertising, to push the sale of these bonds. War bonds were used as a tool to raise money for the government by selling certificates that promised a return on the investment after a period of time in exchange for the investment. In New York City, publishing city of the *New York Daily*

> The next two paragraphs provide the reader with historical context for the ad and its publication. This information clarifies the rhetorical situation for readers and sets the stage for the analyses of the ad's elements that follow.

News and home of Bloomingdale's main store, there was tremendous outrage at the atrocities being committed as a result of the war. Due to this, the general public showed interest in ending the war, especially the war in the Pacific. For the most part, the city trended toward the progressive democratic mind-set and agreed with the mostly Democrat-controlled government of the era (Duranti 666). While factors such as these propelled the citizens to purchase bonds as the advertisement suggests, there were other factors resisting this push as well. Particularly important was the ever-present aftermath of the Great Depression. The combination of these factors created a mixed feeling about the purchase of war bonds, but the fear of Hitler's reign continuing tended to bias the populace toward purchasing the bonds.

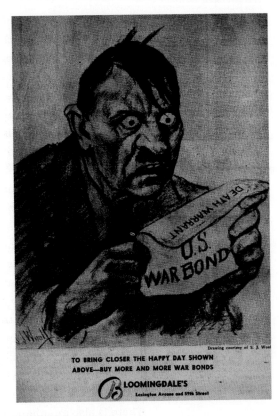

TO BRING CLOSER THE HAPPY DAY SHOWN
ABOVE—BUY MORE AND MORE WAR BONDS

BLOOMINGDALE'S
Lexington Avenue and 59th Street

At the time of the release of this ad, the *New York Daily News* was a fairly new newspaper in New York City, as it had been initially released about twenty years beforehand. Even as a new publication, it had an extremely wide readership due to its tabloid format, which focused on images, unlike other New York papers. At the time of the printing of this ad, the *Daily News* was known to be slightly biased toward the democratic mind-set common among the citizens of the city ("New York Daily News"). The publishing of this advertisement at this time could be viewed as an appeal to ethos in order to push the patriotic sense of the paper. The advertisement can also be seen as an appeal to ethos by Bloomingdale's, as the company was seeking to portray itself as a patriotic firm. With that context in mind, several components of the advertisement make more sense and can be more effectively analyzed.

The most prominent feature in the advertisement is Hitler's face, and in particular, his facial expression. Woolf's image here uses two primary components to make the facial expression stand out: the humorously exaggerated bug-eyed stare and the dropped jaw. The effect created by these two factors is compounded by the addition of the buck teeth and

The analysis now focuses on specific elements of the ad. In this paragraph, the student analyzes features of Hitler's face: the bug eyes, the dropped jaw, the tufts of hair. These, he suggests, express Hitler's fear of American strength, which stems at least partially from the selling and purchasing of war bonds.

the protruding ears. The bug eyes commonly serve in American imagery to express shock, and they perform that role excellently here in this advertisement. The dropped jaw is used very frequently as well, especially in cartoons, and here it strengthens the shocked expression. The buck teeth and protruding ears are two images that are used in American culture to convey the idea of a buffoon. In addition to these features, Woolf comically adds in two tufts of hair in imitation of devil horns to further enhance Hitler's evil image. When these two are added to the previous facets, it creates an image of a completely dumbfounded and baffled Hitler. The image was designed in this manner to enhance the feeling that purchasing U.S. war bonds would benefit society by eliminating the severe hindrance known as Hitler.

The next feature that stands out is the death warrant and war bond itself and Hitler's hands clutching it. Woolf draws Hitler's hands in a manner that makes them appear to be tightly gripping the paper as in anger. The paper itself shows only the words "death warrant" and "U.S. War Bonds," but one can infer from the context that the warrant is for Hitler. The fact that the warrant is printed on a war bond suggests that the U.S. government completely backs the killing of Hitler and will take action to see it through. The document appeals to the viewer's logos through the suggestion that war bonds will end the war sooner and save countless lives in the process. There is also an inherent appeal to ethos in the suggestion of the character of Bloomingdale's as a firm that strongly opposes the horrors committed by Hitler and his followers. In addition, there is an appeal to pathos, with the ad attempting to home in on the audience's moral code. This apparent encouragement of killing Hitler, coupled with the text at the bottom of the advertisement, creates a mood of vengeance directed toward Hitler.

The writer shifts focus to analyze the ad's caption.

The next major feature of the advertisement is the caption at the bottom of the image, which reads, "To bring closer the happy day shown above — buy more and more war bonds." The image shown above the text in most scenarios would not be considered a happy day for most people. The thought of death is normally enough to ruin anyone's day, but this image banks on the public having a burning vengeance that justifies the end of Hitler. The idea of vengeance is generally viewed as having serious negative repercussions, but this ad portrays the idea in a positive manner by making an appeal to the audience's logos. The appeal here could best be described as sacrificing one to save millions. The caption also makes an appeal to pathos in the manner that it tries to connect with the viewer's sense of morals that Hitler has almost definitely broken in numerous ways.

The next aspect of the advertisement that stands out is the use of shading. Woolf's decision here may have been influenced by requirements of the *Daily News* at the time, but even viewed in that light it has a rhetorical effect on the advertisement. The usage of shading here creates the appearance of an unfinished image, further enhancing the idea that Hitler has just been served his death warrant hot off the press by the United States and its war bonds. It also creates a worried cast to Hitler's face through the heavy shading in the creases along his jawline. The overall image of Hitler created through the use of shading comes off as dark and sinister, representative of the common American's view on Hitler's character. In contrast, the war bond is virtually untouched by shading, leaving it nearly white. This creates the image of a beacon of hope shining through the darkness that provides a means to eliminate this terror. Additionally, the presence of a heavily shaded advertisement among the more crisp images, popular among tabloids, accents this advertisement and its message.

The final aspect of the advertisement that draws major attention is the overall construction of the image. The layout emphasizes the two key components of the advertisement: Hitler's face and the war bond. Not only does this accentuate the relationship between buying war bonds and bringing the hammer down on Hitler, but it also provides further depth to the image's rhetorical context. Hitler is posed hunched over as if to imply a deformity in his body and represent a deformity of his mind. The statement here runs on the classic American stereotype that a malformed person is either inferior or evil, a stereotype popularly used in comical representations such as this one. In addition, the hunched posture can be interpreted as the weight of the American war machine, fueled by the war bond purchases, dragging Hitler down to end his reign of terror.

With each of these analyzed aspects in mind, the advertisement can serve as an effective description of the period similar to what Jack Solomon suggests is possible in "Masters of Desire." He uses the following statement to show how advertisements are indicative of the culture of their audiences: "But by semiotically reading the signs that advertising agencies manufacture to stimulate consumption, we can plot the precise state of desire in the audiences to which they are addressed" (61). Based upon the patriotic push shown through this advertisement's attack on Hitler and visualization of

Notice how the ending addresses elements of the paper's thesis statement, or how the ad "depicts the growing influence and activism of the United States during this era."

handing him a death warrant, the advertisement shows the general patriotic mood of America at the time. Given the war footing of the country during this era, this patriotic pride fits well into the time frame. It also shows the growing influence of the United States across the world. Up until this point in time, America was not taken very seriously, and U.S. foreign policy was mostly designed to ignore the rest of the world and preserve America. With the serving of the death warrant to Hitler shown in this advertisement, the change in ideology is starkly apparent. Instead of the wait-and-see mentality common in America before World War II, the highly proactive and aggressive nature of America today begins to show. For a small snippet in a tabloid newspaper, this advertisement packs quite a rhetorical punch.

Taking into account all the elements of this advertisement, rhetorical and otherwise, the advertisement creates an astounding patriotic push for the purchase of war bonds through exaggeration and establishes the United States as a globally significant force through the implications of the death warrant for a foreign citizen. All aspects used in this advertisement work well to cleverly goad readers of the paper to purchase war bonds from Bloomingdale's, holding true to Jack Solomon's statement about advertisements not seeking to provide information, but to manipulate the audience. In the end, however, this advertisement does not convey the negative connotation often associated with manipulative advertising; rather, it uses manipulative elements to try to create a better future for the readers.

Works Cited

Bloomingdale's. Advertisement. *New York Daily News.* 1943.

Duranti, Marco. "Utopia, Nostalgia, and World War at the 1939–40 New York World's Fair." *Journal of Contemporary History,* vol. 41, no. 4, 2006, pp. 663–83.

"New York Daily News." *Encyclopaedia Britannica Online,* 2016. www.britannica.com/topic/New-York-Daily-News.

Solomon, Jack. "Masters of Desire: The Culture of American Advertising." *The Signs of Our Time: Semiotics: The Hidden Messages of Environments, Objects, and Cultural Images.* Jeremy P. Tarcher, 1988, pp. 59–76.

Discussion Questions

1. Where does Timothy Holtzhauser state his thesis? Why do you think he phrases his thesis in the way that he does?

2. How does Timothy use logos in his own argument? Why do you think he relies on logos to support his claim?

3. Who is the intended audience for this argument?

4. What scholarly or popular conversation(s) is Timothy joining in?

5. Which claim(s) do you find most convincing and least convincing for Timothy's rhetorical situation? Why?

Composing a Rhetorical Analysis of an Advertisement

For this project, we ask you to consider the ways in which rhetorical context and appeals work together in an advertisement to create an argument.

- To begin, choose a print or online advertisement that you can analyze based on its rhetorical context and the appeals it uses to persuade the intended audience.

- Then, drawing on the principles of rhetorical analysis from Chapter 3 and the discussion of developing arguments in this chapter, compose an analysis examining the ad's use of appeals in light of the rhetorical situation the ad constructs.

RHETORICAL CONTEXT (SEE CHAPTER 3)
Central Question: How do the elements of the rhetorical context affect the way the advertisement is structured?

Author _____

Audience _____

Topic _____

Purpose _____

RHETORICAL APPEALS
Central Question: What appeals does the advertisement use, and why?

Ethos _____

Logos _____

Pathos _____

Keep in mind that a rhetorical analysis makes an argument, so your analysis should have a central claim that you develop based on what you observed, through the frameworks of rhetorical context and rhetorical appeals, in the advertisement. Make your claim clear, and then support it with reasons and evidence from the advertisement.

- **Presenting an argument is different from merely stating an opinion.** Presenting and supporting an argument mean establishing a claim that is backed by reasons and evidence.

- **The unifying element of any academic argument is its primary or central claim.** A unifying claim may take the form of a thesis, a hypothesis, or a more general statement of purpose. There are numerous kinds of claims, including claims of value, definition, and policy.

- **Reasons are generated from and supported by evidence.** Evidence may take the form of inartistic proofs (including statistics and raw data) or artistic proofs, including the rhetorical appeals of ethos (appeal to credibility), logos (appeal to reason and logic), and pathos (appeal to emotion).

- **Claims presented as part of a chain of reasoning are linked by (often) unstated assumptions.** Assumptions should be analyzed carefully for their appropriateness (acceptability, believability) in a particular rhetorical context.

- **Considering and/or incorporating counterarguments is an excellent way to strengthen your own arguments.** You may rebut counterarguments, or you may concede (or partially concede) to them and qualify your own arguments in response.

- **Analyzing others' arguments is a good way to develop your skills at arguing,** particularly in an academic context.

Academic Research

Conducting Research

Research projects have all kinds of starting points. Sometimes we start them because a course instructor or an employer asks us to. At other times, we embark on research projects because we want to learn about something on our own. In all these cases, though, the research we undertake typically responds to a question or to a set of questions that we need to answer. These are called **research questions**. Constructing research questions and narrowing them to focus specifically on the relevant information needed to answer them is usually the first step in any research project, especially in an academic context.

DEVELOPING A RESEARCH QUESTION

For many students, choosing a subject to research can be incredibly difficult. Whenever you have free rein to choose the topic of a research project, one way to start is by thinking about issues that really matter to you. Writers tend to do their best work when writing about issues in which they have a personal investment. Even if you're conducting research in a course with a topic that has been assigned, you should always consider how you might approach the topic from an angle that matters to you or that brings in your unique point of view. Your personal investment and level of interest in the topic of your research can greatly impact the kinds of questions you ask of that topic, but they may also influence your level of commitment to, and the quality of, your research.

Another challenge many students face is narrowing down a solid research question once they've selected an issue of interest. If a research question is too broad, then it may not be feasible to respond to it adequately in the scope of your research assignment. If it's too narrow, though, it

ANDREA TSURUMI

might not be researchable; in other words, you might not be able to find enough sources to support a solid position on the issue. A good research question has an appropriately narrow scope and can be answered with available resources in the space and time allowed to do so.

A focused question sometimes comes from reading previously published materials on a topic or issue. If you are able to review what others have already written on a topic before conducting a study or making an argument of your own on that topic, then you will know what still needs to be understood, explained, or debated. In this way, you may identify a gap in what is already known or understood about a topic in order to build a research question that, when answered, could help fill that gap. This is how researchers continue to contribute to ongoing conversations.

As you work on drafting a research question, keep these five criteria in mind:

- **Personal Investment** Is this an issue you care about? If the issue is too broad, is there a way you can narrow down the topic to an aspect of the issue that is of the most importance to you?
- **Debatable Subject** Could two reasonable people looking at evidence about this issue come to different conclusions?
- **Researchable Issue** Can you locate or collect adequate evidence to support a position on this issue?
- **Feasibility** Is the scope of the research question manageable, given the amount of time you have to research the issue and the amount of space in which you will make your argument?
- **Contribution** Will your response to your question contribute to the ongoing conversation about the issue?

INSIDE WORK **Writing a Research Question**

As you begin your research project, you should identify a research question that will guide your research and keep you on track. Start by brainstorming a list of possible research questions for ten minutes, and then use the five criteria above to narrow down your list to a research question that might work for you. If your answer to any of the questions is a definitive "No," then the research question might not be a good choice, or you might need to revise it to make it work for your research project. ▶

 LaunchPad

A political scientist emphasizes the importance of supporting evidence.

CHOOSING PRIMARY AND SECONDARY SOURCES

You can gather several different types of sources to respond to a research question. When considering sources to gather, you should look for those that provide specific evidence to address aspects of your research question.

Remember to keep your target audience in mind as you select evidence, taking into account the kinds of evidence that would likely be most convincing to your audience.

To respond to any research question, you must collect evidence to prove or disprove a hypothesis or to support or refute a claim. Once you have identified a solid research question, then you must decide whether you need to collect primary and/or secondary sources to support your research aims.

Primary sources include the results of data that researchers might collect on their own. If you're making a claim about how to interpret a work of art and you've studied the piece carefully for images and symbols that you discuss in your argument, for instance, then the work of art is your primary source. Or perhaps you've designed and conducted a survey of people's experiences with a particular social phenomenon, like culture shock. In this case, the results you've gathered from your survey are a primary source from which you can provide evidence to answer a research question or support an argument about the experience of culture shock. Other forms of primary sources include original historical documents and responses from interviews you may have conducted.

Insider's View
Primary research in writing studies
MORIAH McCRACKEN, WRITING STUDIES

"I like to try to introduce my students to qualitative research in their first year, when our students have to interview a professor. Sometimes I'll help them develop survey questions and questionnaires so they can have that kind of experience, and I'll teach them about double-entry notebooks so they can do some observations in the classroom. I like to bring in qualitative methods so that students realize there are different kinds of questions to ask, and depending on my question, I'm going to have to try something a little bit different and learn how to do this kind of research in my discipline."

LaunchPad
Find additional advice on doing primary research.

INSIDE WORK   **Collecting Primary Evidence**

Freewrite for five to ten minutes about a time in the past when you had to collect data on your own to answer a research question.

- Why were you collecting the data? What question were you trying to answer?
- What data did you collect, and how did you collect it? Did you observe something? Conduct a survey? Interview someone?
- If you were to try to answer that research question now, what data would you collect? Would you do anything differently? Why or why not? ▶

Based on the scope of your argument and the expectations of your audience, you may also need to engage **secondary sources**, or research collected by and/or commented on by others. Let's say that your literature professor wants you to offer an interpretation of a poem. You study the poem carefully as your primary source and arrive at a conclusion or claim about the work. But imagine that the assignment also requires you to use scholarly opinions to support your own position or interpretation. As a result, you spend time in the library or searching online databases to locate articles or books by scholars who provide their own interpretations or perspectives on the poem. The articles or books you rely on to support your interpretation are secondary sources because the interpretations were developed by others, commenting on the poem. Likewise, if you cite as part of your own argument the results of a survey published in an academic article, then that article serves as a secondary source of information to you. Other secondary sources include newspapers and magazines, textbooks, and encyclopedias. Many of the researched arguments you'll produce in college will require you to use both primary and secondary sources as support.

INSIDE WORK Using Primary and Secondary Sources

Read Timothy Holtzhauser's ad analysis on pages 74–78 of Chapter 4. After reviewing his analysis, look at the list of works cited at the end of his essay. Then answer the following questions.

- What primary source(s) does Timothy use to support his argument? Why do you think he chooses the primary source(s) he does?

- What would the impact be if Timothy didn't use primary sources in his argument? Would his argument be more or less persuasive to his audience?

- What secondary sources does Timothy use to support his argument?

- Why do you think he chooses these particular secondary sources? What impact do they have on the development of his argument?

- If Timothy had only used primary sources and no secondary sources, what would the impact have been on the persuasiveness of his argument? ❭

SEARCHING FOR SOURCES

In Part Two, we discuss collecting primary sources to support claims in specific disciplinary areas or genres in more detail. In the rest of this chapter, though, we provide support for collecting secondary sources, which build a foundation for research and writing in academic contexts. Even if the main evidence used to support an academic research project comes from primary sources, secondary sources can provide an overview of what other scholars have already argued with regard to a particular issue or topic. Keep in mind that academic writing and research essentially comprise a series of extended conversations about different issues, and secondary sources help you understand what part of the conversation has already happened before you start researching a topic on your own, or before you consider entering an established conversation on a topic or issue.

Identifying Search Terms

The school, college, or university you attend likely offers many avenues to help navigate the processes for conducting library research at your institution. Most of these processes include searching for source materials online. When you search for secondary sources online to support the development of a research study or to support a claim in an argument, it's important to consider your **search terms**, the key words and phrases you'll use while you're searching. Let's say that you're interested in understanding the effects of using cell phones while driving, a topic we explored in Chapter 4. In such a case, you might begin your research with a question that reads something like this:

What are the effects of using cell phones while driving?

The first step in your research process would likely be to find out what others have already written about this issue. To start, then, you might temporarily rephrase your research question to ask:

What have others written or argued about the effects of using cell phones while driving?

To respond, you'll need to identify the key terms of your question that will focus your search for secondary sources about the subject. You might highlight some of the key terms in the question:

What have others written or argued about the effects of using **cell phones** while **driving**?

If you started your search by typing "cell phones and driving" into Google, your search would return millions of results:

These results include links to images of people on cell phones in their cars, to news articles, and to statistics from insurance companies, to name a few. In the figure above, the first three items in the list and the ones in the sidebar are all sponsored advertisements. You might want to seek out non-sponsored links in the list. After careful evaluation, you may decide that some of these sources of data would be useful for your research, but you can also see that the results produce far too many hits to manage. There's simply no way you can comb through the millions of hits to find information that is appropriate for your purposes. As a result, you may choose to narrow your search to something that emerges as a specific issue, like "reaction time." If you narrowed your search to "cell phones and reaction time," you would see results like this:

Focusing your research terms in this way narrows the scope of your search somewhat further, but you still have far too many results to review. One concern to keep in mind, then, is that basic Google searches are not very useful in helping to locate the kinds of sources you might rely on for your research, especially in an academic context. If you want to understand, more specifically, what scholars have written about your topic, then you need to find scholarly or academic sources as support. A basic Google search doesn't filter different kinds of sources, so it's not generally very helpful.

Instead, you might choose to search Google Scholar to understand the ongoing conversation among scholars about your topic. Conducting a search for "cell phones and driving accidents and reaction time" in Google Scholar returns tens of thousands of results:

If you take a close look at the left-hand side of the screen, however, you'll notice that you can limit your search in several additional ways. By limiting the search to sources published since 2014, you can reduce your results significantly:

You can continue refining your search until you end up with a more manageable number of hits to comb through. Although the number is still large, thousands of results are more manageable than millions. Of course, you would likely need to continue narrowing your results. As you conduct this narrowing process, you are simultaneously focusing in on the conversation you originally wanted to understand: what scholars have written about your topic. Consider the criteria that would be most meaningful for your project as you refine your search by revising your search terms.

INSIDE WORK   **Generating Search Terms**

Think of a controversial social issue that interests you. We chose driving while using a cell phone, but you should choose something you would potentially be interested in learning more about. Then follow these instructions, preferably working with classmates.

- Brainstorm the search terms you would use for that topic. What terms would you enter into a web search engine?

- List your search terms in the box for Round 1 below, and then try doing a search using your preferred web search engine.

- How many hits did you get? Write the number in the box for Round 1.

- Switch seats with a classmate so that you can look at someone else's search terms. Should the search be narrowed? If so, revise your classmate's search terms to narrow them slightly. Write those in the box for Round 2. Try the search, and record the number of hits.

- Follow the instructions again for Rounds 3 and 4.

	Search Terms	Number of Hits
Round 1		
Round 2		
Round 3		
Round 4		

After you have finished the exercise, reflect on the following questions.

- How did your classmates narrow your search terms? What changes worked well, and what changes didn't work as well?

- If you were going to write advice for students using web search engines for research, what advice would you give about search terms? ▶

Keep in mind that general search engines such as Google are not always the best places to conduct academic research, although they can often be useful starting points. Experienced researchers generally rely on more specialized databases to find the kinds of sources that will support their research most effectively.

Using Journal Databases

If you are conducting academic research, then one of the first types of sources you should look for is peer-reviewed journal articles. You may wonder why we don't recommend beginning your search by scouring your library's catalog for books. The answer is that academic books, which are often an excellent source of information, generally take much longer to make their way through the publishing process before they appear in libraries. Publishing the results of research in academic journal articles, however, is a faster method for academics to share their work with their scholarly communities. Academic journals, therefore, are a valuable resource precisely because they offer insight into the most current research being conducted in a field.

Additionally, like other scholarly work, most academic journals publish research only after it has undergone rigorous scrutiny through a peer-review process by other scholars in the relevant academic field. Work that has gone through the academic peer-review process has been sent out, with the authors' identifying information removed, and reviewed by other scholars who determine whether it makes a sufficiently significant contribution to the field to be published. Work published in a peer-reviewed academic journal has been approved not only by the journal's editor but also by other scholars in the field.

If you've ever browsed through your school's library, you've probably noticed that there are thousands of academic journals, and many are available online and easy to locate via the Internet. If you're associated with a college or university, you likely have access to a wide array of online academic journals that can be explored through databases via the library's website. You can search general library databases by refining search terms, as we discussed in the examples of using Google, but you can also find relevant resources by searching in specific disciplinary databases.

Searching for Journal Articles by Discipline

One way of searching for journal articles through your school's library is to explore the academic databases by subject or discipline. These databases usually break down the major fields of study into the many subfields that make up smaller disciplinary communities. Individual schools, colleges, and universities choose which databases they subscribe to. In the following image from the North Carolina State University's library website, you can see that agriculture is divided into various subfields: agricultural economics, animal science, crop science, and so on.

Let's say you need to find information on post-traumatic stress disorder (PTSD) among veterans of the Iraq War that began in March 2003. You spend some time considering the subfields of the social sciences where you're most likely to find research on PTSD: history, sociology, political science, and psychology, for instance. If you choose to focus on the psychological aspects of PTSD, then you would likely select "Social Sciences" and then "Psychology." When you select "Psychology" from the list of available disciplines, typically you'll see a screen that identifies major research databases in psychology, along with some related databases. Choosing the database at the top of the page, "PsycINFO," gains you access to one of the most comprehensive databases in that field of study.

Psychology

Databases

PsycINFO

PsycINFO, from the American Psychological Association (APA), contains more than 2 million citations and summaries of scholarly journal articles, book chapters, books, and dissertations, all in psychology and related disciplines, dating as far back as the 1800s. The database also includes information about the psychological aspects of related fields such as medicine, psychiatry, nursing, sociology, education, pharmacology, physiology, linguistics, anthropology, business, law and others. Journal coverage, which spans 1887 to present, includes international material selected from nearly 2,000 periodicals in more than 25 languages.

Selecting "PsycINFO" grants access to the PsycINFO database via a search engine — in this case, EbscoHOST. You can now input search terms such as "PTSD and Iraq War veterans" to see your results.

Limit To ⌄

☐ Linked Full Text
☐ References Available
☐ Peer Reviewed

2006 | Publication Date | 2014

Show More

Source Types ⌄

☑ All Results
☐ Academic Journals (12)
☐ Books (1)

Notice that the search engine allows you to refine your search in a number of ways, very similar to the criteria that you can use in Google Scholar: you can limit the years of publication for research articles, you can limit the search to sources that are available full-text online, you can limit the search to peer-reviewed journal articles, and more. If you limit your search for "PTSD and Iraq War veterans" to peer-reviewed journal articles available in full-text form online, then the results look something like this:

Searching: PsycINFO | Choose Databases
☐ Suggest Subject Terms

PTSD and Iraq war veterans | SU Subjects ▾ | Search Clear ?

AND ▾ | Select a Field (option... ▾

AND ▾ | Select a Field (option... ▾ ⊕ ⊖

Basic Search Advanced Search Search History ▸

Refine Results

Current Search

Find all my search terms:
SU PTSD and Iraq war veterans

Limiters
Linked Full Text ☒
Peer Reviewed ☒

Limit To
☑ Linked Full Text
☐ References Available
☑ Peer Reviewed

Search Results: 1 - 8 of 8   Relevance ▾ Page Options ▾ ⏍ Share ▾

1. The effects of alcohol problems, **PTSD**, and combat exposure on nonphysical and physical aggression among **Iraq** and Afghanistan **war veterans**.
Stappenbeck, Cynthia A.; Hellmuth, Julianne C.; Simpson, Tracy; Jakupcak, Matthew; Psychological Trauma: Theory, Research, Practice, and Policy, Vol 6(1), Jan, 2014. pp.65-72. Publisher: Educational Publishing Foundation [Journal Article]
Subjects: Aggressive Behavior; Alcohol Abuse; Combat Experience; Posttraumatic Stress Disorder; War; Adulthood (18 yrs & older); Male; Female
Cited References: (66)
🗎 HTML Full Text 📄 PDF Full Text FindText @ NCSU

2. Perceived barriers to care among **veterans** health administration patients with posttraumatic stress disorder.
Ouimette, Paige; Vogt, Dawne; Wade, Michael; Tirone, Vanessa; Greenbaum, Mark A.; Kimerling, Rachel; Laffaye, Charlene; Fitt, Julie E.; Rosen, Craig S.; Psychological Services, Vol 8(3), Aug, 2011. pp.212-223. Publisher: Educational Publishing Foundation [Journal Article]
Subjects: Military Veterans; Posttraumatic Stress Disorder; Stigma; War; Treatment Barriers; Adulthood (18 yrs & older); Young Adulthood (18-29 yrs); Thirties (30-39 yrs); Middle Age (40-64 yrs); Aged (65 yrs & older); Male; Female
Cited References: (40) Times Cited in this Database: (10)

You can now access the texts of journal articles that you find interesting or that might be most relevant to your research purposes. Depending on the number and content of the results, you may choose to revise your search terms and run the search again.

INSIDE WORK   **Generating Sources from an Academic Database**

For this activity, use the same controversial social issue you relied on to complete the previous Inside Work activity, for which you generated and refined possible search terms to assess the number of hits, as possible sources, you could locate. This time, however, you should conduct your search using a more specialized academic database that is appropriate to your topic, such as PsycINFO or Sociological Abstracts. If you do not have access to such a database, then you may choose to use Google Scholar as an alternative.

Input each of the four sets of search terms generated in your previous Inside Work activity into the database and record the number of hits yielded. As you conduct your search, using each of the search terms, take a few minutes to peruse the kinds of results that are generated by each search.

	Search Terms	Number of Hits
Round 1		
Round 2		
Round 3		
Round 4		

After you have finished the exercise, reflect on the following questions:

- In what ways are the results of your academic database search similar to those you found from a web search engine? In what ways are the results different?

- Which of your search terms yielded the highest and lowest number of hits? How do these results compare to your previous results? What factors, besides using different terms, could account for any difference in the results?

- If you were going to write advice for students using academic databases to locate sources for a research project, what advice would you give them? ▶

Insider's View
On distinguishing scholarly sources
JONATHAN MORRIS, POLITICAL SCIENCE

"We have to teach our students what's scholarly literature and what isn't. Peer-review journal articles, books — that's scholarly literature. When you pull things off of Wikipedia, when you go even to newspaper articles from the *New York Times* — that's not scholarly research. They need to know that differentiation."

LaunchPad

Get expert advice on finding scholarly sources.

EVALUATING SOURCES

Distinguishing between Scholarly and Popular Sources

Using search engines to find relevant sources is fairly easy. The difficult part is deciding which sources are worth your time. If you are working on an academic paper, it is particularly useful to be able to distinguish between popular and scholarly sources.

Depending on your research and writing context, you might be able to use both scholarly and popular sources to support your research. However, in some writing situations it is most appropriate to rely primarily on scholarly sources. For this reason, you should understand the difference between scholarly and popular sources, which comes down to a matter of audience and the publication process. **Scholarly sources** are produced for an audience of other scholars, and **popular sources** are produced for a general audience. Scholarly sources have undergone a peer-review process prior to publication, while popular sources typically have been vetted only by an editor. Generally speaking, popular sources are not very useful for supporting academic research. Let's examine a number of publication types in terms of the kind of information, scholarly or popular, they most often provide:

Examples of Scholarly Sources

- **Academic Journals**   Most journal articles are produced for an audience of other scholars, and the vast majority are peer-reviewed before they are published in academic journals.

- **Books Published by Academic Presses**   Academic presses publish books that also go through the peer-review process. You can sometimes identify academic presses by their names (e.g., a university press), but sometimes you need to dig deeper to find out whether a press generally publishes scholarly or popular sources. Looking at the press's website can often help answer that question.

Examples of Popular Sources

- **Newspapers**   Most newspaper articles are reviewed by editors for accuracy and reliability. However, they typically provide only information that would be of interest to a general audience. They are not specifically intended for an academic audience. A newspaper might report the results of a study published in an academic journal, but it will generally not publish original academic research.

- **Magazines**   Like newspaper articles, magazine articles are typically reviewed by editors and are intended for a general reading audience, not an academic one.

Although it may seem easy to classify sources into one of these two categories, in fact it is often difficult to determine if a source is scholarly or not. Understanding the nature of scholarly and popular sources and recognizing their differences as you conduct your research will help you develop more effective arguments.

Scholarly works, for instance, are typically built on other sources, so they generally include references to other works that are documented in the text and listed in a complete bibliography at the end. Imagine for a moment, though, that you locate a study published on the Internet that you think would be a really good source for your research. It looks just like an article that might appear in a journal, and it has a bibliography that includes other academic sources. However, as part of your analysis of the source, you discover that the article, published only on a website, has never been published by a journal. Is this a scholarly work? It might be. Could this still be a useful scholarly work for your purposes? Perhaps. Still, as a writer and researcher, you would need to know that the article you're using as part of your own research has never been peer-reviewed or published by a journal or an academic press. This means that the validity of the work has never been assessed by other experts in the field. If you use the source in your own work, you would probably want to indicate that it has never been peer-reviewed or published in an academic journal as part of your discussion of that source.

Answering the following questions about your sources can help you evaluate their credibility and reliability:

1. Who are the authors?
2. Who is the intended audience?

3. Where is the work published?

4. Does the work rely on other reputable sources for information?

5. Does the work seem biased?

As a writer, you must ultimately make the decisions about what is or is not an appropriate source, based on your goals and an analysis of your audience. Answering the questions above can help you assess the appropriateness of sources.

INSIDE WORK **Evaluating Sources**

For this exercise, either look at the sample essay from Timothy Holtzhauser on pages 74–78 of Chapter 4 or look at an essay that you wrote for a class in the past. Choose one of the references listed in the essay's bibliography, and write answers to the following questions.

- Who are the authors? Do they possess any particular credentials that make them experts on the topic? With what institutions or organizations are the authors associated?

- Who is the intended audience — the general public or a group of scholars? How do you know?

- Where is the work published? Do works published there undergo a peer-review process?

- Does the work rely on other reputable sources for information? What are those sources, and how do you know they are reputable?

- Does the work seem biased? How do you know this? Is the work funded or supported by individuals or parties who might have a vested interest in the results? If so, is there a potential conflict of interest? ▶

SUMMARIZING, PARAPHRASING, AND QUOTING FROM SOURCES

Once you've located and studied the sources you want to use in a research paper, then you're ready to begin considering ways to integrate that material into your own work. There are a number of ways to integrate the words and ideas of others into your research, and you've likely already had experience summarizing, paraphrasing, and quoting from sources as part of an academic writing assignment. For many students, though, the specifics of how to summarize, paraphrase, and quote accurately are often unclear, so we'll walk through these processes in some detail.

Summarizing

Summarizing a text is a way of condensing the work to its main ideas. A summary therefore requires you to choose the most important elements of a text and to answer these questions: *What* is this work really trying to say, and *how* does it say it? Composing a summary of a source can be valuable for a number of reasons. Writing a summary can help you carefully analyze the content of a text and understand it better, but a summary can also help you identify and keep track of the sources you want to use in the various parts of your research. You may sometimes be able to summarize a source in only a sentence or two. We suggest a simple method for analyzing a source and composing a summary:

1. Read the source carefully, noting the **rhetorical context**. Who composed the source? For whom is the source intended? Where was it published? Identify the source and provide answers to these questions at the beginning of your summary, as appropriate.

2. Identify the **main points**. Pay close attention to topic sentences at the beginnings of paragraphs, as they often highlight central ideas in the overall structure of an argument. Organize your summary around the main ideas you identify.

3. Identify **examples**. You will want to be able to summarize the ways the writer illustrates, exemplifies, or argues the main points. Though you will likely not discuss all of the examples or forms of evidence you identify in detail as part of your summary, you will want to comment on one or two, or offer some indication of how the writer supports his or her main points.

The following excerpt is taken from the text of Jack Solomon's "Masters of Desire: The Culture of American Advertising," which appears on pages 70–73 in Chapter 4:

> Status symbols, then, are signs that identify their possessors' place in a social hierarchy, markers of rank and prestige. We can all think of any number of status symbols — Rolls-Royces, Beverly Hills mansions, even Shar Pei puppies (whose rareness and expense has rocketed them beyond Russian wolfhounds as status pets and has even inspired whole lines of wrinkle-faced stuffed toys) — but how do we know that something is a status symbol? The explanation is quite simple: when an object (or puppy!) either costs a lot of money or requires influential connections to possess, anyone who possesses it must also possess the necessary means and influence to acquire it. The object itself really doesn't matter, since it ultimately disappears behind the presumed social potency of its owner. Semiotically, what matters is the signal it sends, its value as a sign of power. One traditional sign of social distinction is owning a country estate and enjoying the peace and privacy that attend it. Advertisements for Mercedes-Benz, Jaguar, and Audi automobiles thus frequently feature drivers motoring quietly along a country road, presumably on their way to or from their country houses.

A summary of this part of Solomon's text might read something like this:

> In "Masters of Desire: The Culture of American Advertising," Jack Solomon acknowledges that certain material possessions may be understood as representations of an individual's rank or status. He illustrates this point by identifying a number of luxury automobiles that, when observed, cause us to consider the elevated economic status of the vehicles' owners (63).

You'll notice that this summary eliminates discussion of the specific examples Solomon provides. Further, it removes any discussion of the concept of semiotics. Though Solomon's ideas are clearly condensed and the writer of this summary has carefully selected the ideas to be summarized in order to further his or her own aims, the core of Solomon's idea is accurately represented.

Paraphrasing

Sometimes a writer doesn't want to summarize a source because condensing its ideas risks losing part of its importance. In such a case, the writer has to choose whether to paraphrase or quote directly from the source. **Paraphrasing** means translating the author's words and sentence structure into your own for the purpose of making the ideas clear for your audience. A paraphrase may be the same length or even longer than the part of a text being paraphrased, so the purpose of paraphrase is not really to condense a passage, as is the case for summary.

Often, writers prefer to paraphrase sources rather than to quote from them, especially if the exact language from the source isn't important, but the ideas are. Depending on your audience, you might want to rephrase highly technical language from a scientific source, for example, and put it in your own words. Or you might want to emphasize a point the author makes in a way that isn't as clear in the original language. Many social scientists and most scientists routinely paraphrase sources as part of the presentation of their own research because the results they're reporting from secondary sources are more important than the exact language used to explain the results. Quotations should be reserved for instances when the exact language of the original source is important to the point being made. Remember that paraphrasing requires you to restate the passage in your own words and in your own sentence structure. Even if you are putting the source's ideas in your own words, you must acknowledge where the information came from by providing an appropriate citation.

The following paragraph was taken from William Thierfelder's article "Twain's *Huckleberry Finn*," published in *The Explicator*, a journal of literary criticism.

> An often-noted biblical allusion in *Huckleberry Finn* is that comparing Huck to the prophet Moses. Like Moses, whom Huck learns about from the Widow Douglas, Huck sets out, an orphan on his raft, down the river. In the biblical story, it is Moses's mother who puts him in his little "raft," hoping he will be found. In the novel, Huck/Moses takes charge of his own travels. . . .

Inappropriate Paraphrase

William Thierfelder suggests that Huckleberry is often compared to the prophet Moses. Huck, an orphan like Moses, travels down a river on a raft (194).

Although some of the language has been changed and the paraphrase includes documentation, this paraphrase of the first two sentences of Thierfelder's passage is inappropriate because it relies on the language of the original text and employs the author's sentence structure. An appropriate paraphrase that uses new language and sentence structure might look like this:

> William Thierfelder notes that numerous readers have linked the character of Huckleberry Finn and the biblical figure of Moses. They are both orphans who take a water journey, Thierfelder argues. However, Moses's journey begins because of the actions of his mother, while Huck's journey is undertaken by himself (194).

Quoting

Depending on your rhetorical context, you may find that **quoting** the exact words of a source as part of your argument is the most effective strategy. The use of quotations is much more common in some academic fields than in others. Writers in the humanities, for example, often quote texts directly because the precise language of the original is important to the argument. You'll find, for instance, that literary scholars often quote a short story or poem (a primary source) for evidence. You may also find that a secondary source contains powerful or interesting language that would lose its impact if you paraphrased it. In such circumstances, it is entirely appropriate to quote the text. Keep in mind that your reader should always be able to understand why the quotation is important to your argument. We recommend three methods for integrating quotations into your writing. (The examples below follow American Psychological Association style conventions; see "Understanding Documentation Systems" on pages 99–101 and the Appendix for more information about documentation styles.)

1. **Attributive Tags**   Introduce the quotation with a tag (with words like *notes, argues, suggests, posits, maintains,* etc.) that attributes the language and ideas to its author. Notice that different tags suggest different relationships between the author and the idea being cited. For example:

   > De Niet, Tiemens, Lendemeijer, Lendemei, and Hutschemaekers (2009) argued, "Music-assisted relaxation is an effective aid for improving sleep quality in patients with various conditions" (p. 1362).

2. **Further Grammatical Integration**   You may also fully integrate a quotation into the grammar of your own sentences. For example:

   > Their review of the research revealed "scientific support for the effectiveness of the systematic use of music-assisted

relaxation to promote sleep quality" in patients (De Niet et al., 2009, p. 1362).

3. **Introduce with Full Sentence + Punctuation**   You can also introduce a quotation with a full sentence and create a transitional link to the quotation with punctuation, like the colon. For example:

The study reached a final conclusion about music-assisted relaxation: "It is a safe and cheap intervention which may be used to treat sleep problems in various populations" (De Niet et al., 2009, p. 1362).

INSIDE WORK **Summarizing, Paraphrasing, and Quoting from Sources**

Choose a source you have found on a topic of interest to you, and find a short passage (only one or two sentences) from the source that provides information that might be useful in your own research. Then complete the following steps and write down your responses.

1. Summarize the passage. It might help to look at the larger context in which the passage appears.

2. Paraphrase the passage, using your own words and sentence structure.

3. Quote the passage, using the following three ways to integrate the passage into your own text:
   – attributive tags
   – grammatical integration
   – full sentence + punctuation

For your own research, which approach (summarizing, paraphrasing, quoting) do you think would be most useful? Consider your writing context and how you would use the source. ❱

AVOIDING PLAGIARISM

Any language and ideas used in your own writing that belong to others must be fully acknowledged and carefully documented, with both in-text citations and full bibliographic documentation. Failure to include either of these when source materials are employed could lead to a charge of **plagiarism**, perhaps the most serious of academic integrity offenses. The procedures for documenting cited sources vary from one rhetorical and disciplinary context to another, so you'll always want to clarify the expectations for documentation with your instructor when responding to an assigned writing task. Regardless, you should always acknowledge your sources when you summarize, paraphrase, or quote, and be sure to include the full information for your sources in the bibliography of your project.

Understanding Plagiarism

Most schools, colleges, and universities have established definitions of plagiarism and penalties or sanctions that may be imposed on students found guilty of plagiarism. You should become familiar with the definitions of plagiarism used by your institution as well as by your individual instructors.

- Locate a resource on campus (e.g., a student handbook or the website of your institution's Office of Student Conduct) that provides a definition of plagiarism from the perspective of your institution. You may discover that in addition to defining plagiarism, your institution provides avenues of support to foster academic integrity and/or presents explanations of the consequences or penalties for violating rules of academic integrity.

- Locate a resource from one of your classes (e.g., a course website, a course syllabus) that provides a definition of plagiarism from the perspective of one of your instructors.

- Consider what is similar about the two definitions. Consider the differences between them. What do these similarities and differences reveal about your instructor's expectations and those of the larger academic community in which you participate? ❿

Insider's View
On accidental plagiarism
KAREN KEATON JACKSON, WRITING STUDIES

"Many students come in who are already familiar with using direct quotations. But when it comes to paraphrasing and summarizing, that's when I see a lot of accidental plagiarism. So it's really important for students to understand that if you don't do the research yourself, or if you weren't there in the field or doing the survey, then it's not your own idea and you have to give credit."

 LaunchPad
Hear more on avoiding plagiarism.

UNDERSTANDING DOCUMENTATION SYSTEMS

Documentation systems are often discipline-specific, and their conventions reflect the needs and values of researchers and readers in those particular disciplines. For these reasons, you should carefully analyze any writing situation to determine which documentation style to follow. You'll find examples of specific documentation systems in the disciplinary chapters in Part Two. Here are some of the most common ones:

Modern Language Association (MLA)

MLA documentation procedures are generally followed by researchers in the humanities. One of the most important elements of the in-text citation requirements for the MLA documentation system is the inclusion of page numbers in a parenthetical reference. Though page numbers are used in other documentation systems for some in-text citations (as in the APA system when quoting a passage directly), page numbers in MLA are especially important because they serve as a means for readers to assess your use of sources, both primary and secondary, and are used whether you are quoting, paraphrasing, or summarizing a passage. Page numbers enable readers to quickly identify cited passages and evaluate the evidence: readers may verify that you've accurately represented a source's intent when citing the author's words, or that you've fully examined all the elements at play in your analysis of a photograph or poem. Of course, this kind of examination is important in all disciplines, but it is especially the case in the humanities, where evidence typically takes the form of words and images. Unlike some other documentation systems, the MLA system does not require dates for in-text citations, because scholars in this field often find that past discoveries or arguments are just as useful today as when they were first observed or published. Interpretations don't really expire; their usefulness remains valid across exceptionally long periods of time. Learn more about the style guides published by the Modern Language Association, including the *MLA Handbook*, along with more information about the MLA itself, at www.mla.org.

American Psychological Association (APA)

APA documentation procedures are followed by researchers in many areas of the social sciences and related fields. Although you will encounter page numbers in the in-text citations for direct quotations in APA documents, you're much less likely to find direct quotations overall. Generally, researchers in the social sciences are less interested in the specific language or words used to report research findings than they are in the results or conclusions. Therefore, social science researchers are more likely to paraphrase information than to quote information. Additionally, in-text documentation in the APA system requires the date of publication for research (see the examples on p. 209, and consult the Appendix for more information). This is a striking distinction from the MLA system. Social science research that was conducted fifty years ago may not be as useful as research conducted two years ago, so it's important to cite the date of the source in the text of the argument. Imagine how different the results would be for a study of the effects of violence in video games on youth twenty years ago versus a study conducted last year. Findings from twenty years ago probably have very little bearing on the contemporary social context and would not reflect the same video game content as today's games. As a result, the APA system requires the date of research publication as part of the in-text citation. The date enables readers to quickly evaluate the currency, and therefore the appropriateness, of the research being referenced. Learn more about the *Publication Manual of the American Psychological Association* and the APA itself at its website: www.apa.org.

The Council of Science Editors (CSE)

As the name suggests, the CSE documentation system is most prevalent among disciplines of the natural sciences, although many of the applied fields in the sciences, like engineering and medicine, rely on their own documentation systems. As in the other systems described here, CSE requires writers to document all materials derived from sources. Unlike MLA or APA, however, CSE allows multiple methods for in-text citations, corresponding to alternative forms of the reference page that appears at the end of research reports. For more detailed information on CSE documentation, consult the latest edition of *Scientific Style and Format: The CSE Manual for Authors, Editors, and Publishers.* You can learn more about the Council of Science Editors at its website: www.councilscienceeditors.org.

Writing an Annotated Bibliography

WRITING PROJECT

The annotated bibliography is a common genre in several academic disciplines because it provides a way to compile and take notes on — that is, annotate — resources that are potentially useful in a research project. **Annotated bibliographies** are essentially lists of citations, formatted in a consistent documentation style, that include concise summaries of source material. Some annotated bibliographies include additional commentary about the sources — perhaps evaluations of their usefulness for the research project or comments about how the sources complement one another within the bibliography (possibly by providing multiple perspectives). Annotated bibliographies are usually organized alphabetically, but longer bibliographies can be organized topically or in sections with subheadings. Each source entry gives the citation first and then a paragraph or two of summary, as in this example using MLA style:

Carter, Michael. "Ways of Knowing, Doing, and Writing in the Disciplines." *College Composition and Communication,* vol. 58, no. 3, 2007, pp. 385–418.

In this article, Carter outlines a process for helping faculty across different academic disciplines to understand the conventions of writing in their disciplines by encouraging them to think of disciplines as "ways of doing." He provides examples from his own interactions with faculty members in several disciplines, and he draws on data collected from these interactions to describe four "metagenres" that reflect ways of doing that are shared across multiple disciplines: problem-solving, empirical inquiry, research from sources, and performance. Finally, he concludes that the metagenres revealed by examining shared ways of doing can help to identify "metadisciplines."

For this assignment, you should write an annotated bibliography that seeks to find sources that will help you respond to a specific research question. Your purpose in writing the annotated bibliography is threefold: (1) to organize and keep track of the sources you've found on your own topic, (2) to better understand the relationships among different sources that address your topic, and (3) to demonstrate knowledge of the existing research about it.

To meet this purpose, choose sources that will help answer your research question, and think about a specific audience who might be interested in the research you're presenting. Your annotated bibliography should include the following elements.

- An introduction that clearly states your research question and describes the scope of your annotated bibliography.

- As many as eight to twelve sources (depending on the scope of the sources and the number of perspectives you want to represent), organized alphabetically. If you choose a different organization (e.g., topical), explain how you have organized your annotated bibliography in the introduction.

- An annotation for each source that includes:
  - A summary of the source that gives a concise description of the main findings, focused on what is most important for responding to your research question
  - Relevant information about the authors or sponsors of the source to indicate credibility, bias, perspective, and the like
  - An indication of what this source brings to your annotated bibliography that is unique and/or how it connects to the other sources
  - A citation (see the Appendix) in a consistent documentation style

---

WRITING PROJECT

Developing a Supported Argument on a Controversial Issue

For this writing assignment, you will apply your knowledge from Chapter 4 about developing an argument and from this chapter on finding and documenting appropriate sources. The sources you find will be evidence for the argument you develop. We ask you to make a claim about a controversial issue that is of importance to you and support that claim with evidence to persuade a particular audience of your position. As you write, you might follow the steps below to develop your argument.

- Begin by identifying an issue that you care about and likely have some experience with. We all write best about things that matter to us. For many students, choosing an issue that is specific to their experience or local context makes a narrower, more manageable topic to write about. For example, examining recycling options for students on your college campus would be more manageable than tackling the issue of global waste and recycling.

- Once you have identified an issue, start reading about it to discover what people are saying and what positions they are taking. Use the suggestions in this chapter to find scholarly sources about your issue so that you can "listen in on" the conversations already taking place about your issue. You might find that you want to narrow your topic further based on what you find.

- As you read, begin tracking the sources you find. These sources can serve as evidence later for multiple perspectives on the issue; they will be useful both in supporting your claim and in understanding counterarguments.

- Identify a clear claim you would like to support, an audience you would like to persuade, and a purpose for writing to that audience. Whom should you talk to about your issue, and what can they do about it?

As you work to develop your argument, consider the various elements of an argument you read about in Chapter 4.

- Identify a clear central claim, and determine if it should have a simple or complex thesis statement.

- Develop clear reasons for that claim, drawn from your knowledge of the issue and the sources you have found.

- Choose evidence from your sources to support each reason that will be persuasive to your audience, and consider the potential appeals of ethos, logos, and pathos.

- Identify any assumptions that need to be explained to or supported for your audience.

- Develop responses to any counterarguments you should include in your argument.

Insider Example
Student Argument on a Controversial Issue

The following sample student argument, produced in a first-year writing class, illustrates many of the principles discussed in Chapters 4 and 5. As you read, identify the thesis, reasons, and sources used as support for the argument. Notice also that the student writer, Jack Gomperts, followed CSE style conventions throughout his paper, in response to his instructor's direction to choose a documentation style appropriate to the subject of his argument.

Evaluating Hydration Levels in High School Athletes

Jack Gomperts

Professor Melton
English 101
Project 4

Evaluating Hydration Levels in High School Athletes

Every day, high school athletes across the country put themselves at risk of heat-related injury, and even death, by failing to hydrate properly. Many athletes arrive at practice dehydrated, and abandon proper hydration throughout activity. This habit not only puts athletes at an increased risk of injury, but also decreases their performance (Gibson-Moore 2014). Numerous researchers have explored exactly when and how much fluid an athlete needs to maintain proper hydration. Some experimenters focus on which fluids, such as water, sports drinks, milk, juice, or various other drink options, produce the best hydration. The most important factor in making sure athletes maintain hydration, however, is not telling them how to obtain hydration, but rather testing their hydration status. Often, athletes forget or ignore hydration when coaches simply tell them to stay well hydrated. If athletes know that they will undergo testing for hydration every day, they will be more likely to take action to achieve the proper hydration status. Scientists possess dozens of methods for testing hydration in athletes, and urine specific gravity and body mass measurements are the most practical for everyday use. Urine specific gravity requires only one drop of urine from an athlete, and body mass measurements require athletes to step on a scale. In addition, athletes must sign a contract with their school before participating in any athletic event associated with the school. Schools use these contracts to ensure that they are not liable for any injury experienced by an athlete. However, most schools do not include any information about hydration in their contracts, thus exposing athletes to severe risk. Altogether, schools should alter their athletic contracts to include hydration testing for athletes with urine specific gravity and body mass measurements.

Argument begins by establishing a problem that exists

Establishes the need for further exploration and action with regard to hydration in athletes

Does this author identify or imply a particular audience for this argument? If so, who do you believe that audience might be?

Establishes a two-part central claim or position of the argument: schools should alter contracts to include hydration testing and they should use urine specific gravity and body mass measurements as the means to test hydration.

Every year, 10,000 high school athletes in the United States suffer from dehydration (Center for Disease Control and Prevention 2010). This staggering number only includes injuries that health professionals have diagnosed and does not account for the numerous athletes who suffer from dehydration without realizing it. Personally, I have never witnessed an athlete who was diagnosed with a heat-related illness, but I have seen several athletes suffer injuries that trace back to dehydration. I played on several sports teams throughout my high school career and witnessed a common theme; coaches often tell athletes to stay hydrated, but fail to explain the importance of hydration. At many football games, several of my teammates suffered from cramps caused by dehydration. During my senior year of high school, an athlete collapsed at three of my cross-country meets because of over-heating.

The athletes who neglected proper hydration at my school did not do so without consequences. Many of them experienced concussions; at least ten to twelve athletes from various sports at my school received concussions every year. According to Dr. Meehan, "Every time you get [a concussion], there's some effect on the brain that doesn't go away, concussions have a cumulative effect" (Costa 2015). Concussions negatively impact student-athletes for their entire lives, whereas most sports-related injuries do not have detrimental long-term effects. Scientists believe a strong correlation exists between hydration statuses and concussion risks. They have begun to study cerebrospinal fluid, which surrounds the brain and reduces the impact of heavy blows. With less fluid, athletes have a smaller cushion for their brain; scientists believe even a two percent decrease in hydration severely decreases the amount of cerebrospinal fluid (DripDrop 2016).

Consider the kinds of evidence the writer relies on this paragraph, including evidence from personal experience. Are they effective? What function does this paragraph serve in the overall structure of the student's argument?

How does this paragraph support part of the writer's central position about testing athletes' levels of hydration? What reason is supported here?

In addition to concussions, dehydration can also lead to a variety of heat-related illnesses, such as heat cramps, heat exhaustion, heat stroke, or even death. Heat cramps cause involuntary muscle contractions and can be treated by stretching and rehydration. Heat exhaustion causes redness of skin, profuse sweating, nausea, and vomiting, and is treated as a medical emergency by immediate rehydration and applying ice to the core. Heat stroke is the complete inability to thermo-regulate and causes clammy skin, cease of sweating, dizziness, nausea, and possible unconsciousness. In order to treat a person experiencing these symptoms, medical professionals immediately cool them in an ice bath or transport them to a trauma center (Gallucci 2014). Despite the consequences, many athletes and coaches overlook the problem of dehydration. According to the National Center for Catastrophic Sports Injury Research (2009), 40 high school football players have died from heat stroke since 1995. In addition, they report that dozens of athletes are hospitalized every year for heat-related illnesses, which directly correlates to hydration status. When as many as two thirds of young athletes arrive at practice dehydrated (Southwest Athletic Trainers' Association 2013), it is evident that high school athletic policies must be improved.

Once schools recognize the problem of dehydration, there are many possible solutions. Of the various methods, a combination of urine specific gravity and body mass measurements would be the most convenient and effective for daily use. Since urine specific gravity is easy to use and accurate, schools should utilize its capabilities. This system analyzes a drop of urine on the stage of a refractometer to evaluate the level of hydration in the athlete. If the device shows a value between 1.001 and 1.012, the athlete is likely over-hydrated. A value between 1.013 and 1.029 shows

This paragraph functions to support the writer's reasoning for his central position. What is the reason he presents to support his central claim or thesis?

How effectively does the writer incorporate evidence from statistics?

Provides reasoning to support this particular method of hydration testing proper hydration, and values above 1.030 show dehydration (Armstrong 2005). The device needed to take these measurements can cost anywhere from $60 to $400 (Lopez 2006)—a small price for teams to pay to ensure the safety of their athletes. According to Armstrong (2005), urine specific gravity is the best method to test hydration in an everyday setting because of its reliability, accuracy, and ease of use. Scientists possess several additional methods for testing hydration. These methods, however, are not practical for athletes on a daily basis, although they produce a higher level of accuracy than urine specific gravity. For instance, urine specific gravity loses accuracy as athletes' muscle mass increases. Hamouti et al. (2010) found that urine specific gravity devices falsely classify athletes with high muscle mass as dehydrated far more often than athletes with low muscle mass.

Due to the slightly inaccurate measurements produced by urine specific gravity, coaches should use body mass measurements in addition to urine specific gravity to test hydration. Body mass measurements are even more efficient and less expensive to record than urine specific gravity measurements. In order for coaches to use body mass measurements to determine hydration, they must simply weigh their athletes before and after every practice. If the athletes' mass decreases by more than two percent, they are dehydrated (Armstrong 2005). In addition, if their body mass decreases by more than two percent from the beginning of practice one day to the beginning of practice the next day, they are likely dehydrated. Body mass measurements provide a good estimate of hydration status. Recognizing that the body mass of high school athletes constantly changes due to growth, eating habits, and several other factors, coaches should use body mass measurements in addition to urine specific gravity. They should use urine specific gravity once

Writer provides further reasoning to support the methods of testing hydration levels in athletes

Writer ties together issues related to measuring hydration levels in order to support his contention that certain steps are necessary on the athletes at the beginning of the season, and two to three times randomly throughout the season. This system will provide the coaches with more accurate results than body mass measurements, while not requiring athletes to place a drop of urine on a device every day. This process will ensure the safety of athletes on a daily basis and drastically decrease their risk for illness or death.

Despite the many benefits of hydration testing, some people might disagree with this proposal. Some might argue that regulating hydration status invades the privacy of an athlete and assumes unnecessary control of an athlete's life. I propose that students should decide how much fluid they need, how often they need it, and which drinks best produce hydration. Lopez (2006), Maughan (2010), and Johannsen (2015) all argue for different amounts and types of fluid for proper hydration. These decisions should be left to the athlete since each athlete differs in how much fluid they need for hydration. The schools should only take responsibility for making sure that their athletes are well hydrated. Schools and athletic organizations have put dozens of rules in place to ensure the safety of athletes, like the types of hits allowed in football. If schools have the authority to make rules that protect football players, schools have the power to implement rules and regulations that concern hydration. If implementing hydration regulations can save just one life, schools should do so as quickly as possible. A life is worth more than the few hundred dollars spent on urine specific gravity devices and portable scales. A life is worth more than the slight hassle of taking a few minutes before and after practice to measure athletes' body mass. These rules, however, could have potentially saved the 40 lives that have been lost since 1995 because of heat-related illnesses (National Center for Catastrophic Sports Injury Research 2009). Hydration

> The writer acknowledges a potential counterargument. How does he use sources and evidence to refute the counterargument?

testing might have prevented several thousand athletes from experiencing heat-related illness every year, or saved dozens of athletes from hospitalization. The slight intrusion on athletes' privacy is well worth saving dozens of lives.

In addition to the intrusion on athletes, some people might argue that coaches already carry immense responsibility, and adding these tests would place a heavier burden on the coaches. However, the coaches' job is to teach the athletes how to improve their play and to keep them safe from injury. The hydration requirements I propose align directly with a coach's responsibility. Although it could be considered a burden to require coaches to measure athletes' hydration status, this burden takes no more than 20 minutes a day to complete. Additionally, these regulations exist in accordance with the coach's job, which is to protect his or her athletes, and enhance the athletes' performance however possible. These tests will help coaches do their job more fully and provide better care for their athletes.

Altogether, hydration should be tested in athletes with a combination of urine specific gravity and body mass measurements because these tests will ensure that athletes are practicing and performing under safe conditions. Dehydration poses a problem in high schools all across America because many teens do not understand the importance of proper hydration. Therefore, they arrive at practice dehydrated, which leads to thousands of injuries a year. I propose that to solve this problem, schools should include a policy in their athletic contract regarding hydration. This policy should require athletes to be subject to three to four urine specific gravity tests throughout the season and two daily body mass measurements. Even though people might argue that these tests intrude on athletes' privacy and place a burden on coaches, the tests are capable of saving

The author identifies another possible counterargument. What evidence is provided to refute the counterargument? Is that evidence convincing to you? Why or why not?

Can you identify other potential counterarguments that might undermine the writer's position here?

Do any of the writer's statements, presented in the conclusion to the argument, surprise you as a reader? Why or why not?

dozens of lives. I believe that this insignificant burden is well worth the sacrifice. I further propose that each athlete should be held responsible for determining how he or she can best achieve hydration. While researchers continue to find the best ways for athletes to maintain hydration, schools must take responsibility by implementing regulations to reduce the dangers associated with dehydration in athletics.

Are you convinced by this argument? Do you agree with the writer's position? Why or why not?

References

Armstrong LE. 2005. Hydration assessment techniques [Internet]. Nutr Res. [accessed 2016 Dec 9]; 63(6):S40-S54. Available from: https://www.ncbi.nlm.nih.gov/pubmed /16028571

Center for Disease Control and Prevention. 2010. Heat illness among high school athletes—United States, 2005-2009 [Internet]. Morb Mortal Wkly Rep. [accessed 2016 Dec 9]; 59(32):1009-1053. Available from: https://www.cdc.gov /mmwr/preview/mmwrhtml/mm5932a1.htm

Coe S, Williams R. 2011. Hydration and health [Internet]. Nutr Bull. [accessed 2016 Dec 9]; 36(2):259-266. Available from: http://onlinelibrary.wiley.com/doi/10.1111/j.1467-3010 .2011.01899.x/abstract

Costa S. 2015. Just how dangerous are sports concussions, anyway?: Concussions cause the brain to dangerously move back and forth inside the skull [Internet]. Huffington Post. [accessed 2016 Dec 9]. Available from: http://www.huffingtonpost.com/entry /the-truth-about-concussions_us_564a0043e4b045bf3deff7fc

DripDrop Hydration. 2016. Does dehydration increase an athlete's risk for concussion? [Internet]. [accessed 2016 Dec 9]. Available from: http://dripdrop.com /dehydration-increase-athletes-risk-concussion/

Gallucci J. 2014. Soccer injury prevention and treatment: A guide to optimal performance for players, parents and coaches. New York (NY): Demos Medical Publishing. p. 157-159.

Gibson-Moore H. 2014. Hydration and health [Internet]. Nutr Bull. [accessed 2016 Dec 9]; 39(1):4-8. Available from: http://onlinelibrary.wiley.com/doi/10.1111/nbu .12039/full

Notice the mix of sources the writer relies upon, both popular and academic, as well as any primary and secondary forms of research.

Notice the kinds of sources the author uses as support. If he were to conduct additional research for support, what kind of additional sources would you recommend he look to in order to strengthen his argument?

Hamouti N, Del Coso J, Avila A, Mora-Rodriquez R. 2010. Effects of athletes' muscle mass on urinary markers of hydration status [Internet]. Euro J Appl Physiol. [accessed 2016 Dec 9]; 109(2):213-219. Available from: https://www.ncbi.nlm.nih.gov/pubmed/20058021

Johannsen NM, Earnest CP. 2015. Fluid balance and hydration for human performance. In: Greenwood M, Cooke MB, Ziegenfuss T, Kalman DS, Antonio J, editors. Nutritional supplements in sports and exercise. Cham, Switzerland: Springer International Publishing. p. 105-119.

Lopez RM, Casa DJ. 2006. Hydration for athletes: What coaches can do to keep their athletes healthy and performing their best [Internet]. Coaches' Quarterly. [accessed 2016 Dec 9]. Available from: https://www.wiaawi.org/Portals/0/PDF/Sports/Wrestling/hydration4athletes.pdf

Maughan RJ, Shirreffs SM. 2010. Dehydration and rehydration in competitive sport [Internet]. Scand J Med Sci. [accessed 2016 Dec 9]; 20(3):40-47. Available from: http://onlinelibrary.wiley.com/doi/10.1111/j.1600-0838.2010.01207.x/abstract

National Center for Catastrophic Sports Injury Research (US) [NCCSIR]. 2009. Annual survey of football injury research: 1931-2008 [Internet]. [accessed 2016 Dec 9]. p. 2-29. Available from: http://nccsir.unc.edu/files/2014/05/FootballAnnual.pdf

Southwest Athletic Trainers' Association. 2013. Statistics on youth sports safety [Internet]. [accessed 2016 Dec 9]. Available from: http://www.swata.org/statistics/

Discussion Questions

1. Whom do you think Jack Gomperts is targeting as his audience in this assignment? Why do you think that is his audience?

2. What is Jack's thesis, and what does he provide as the reasons and evidence for his claim?

3. What assumptions connect his thesis to his reasons? Additionally, what assumptions would his audience have to accept in order to find his evidence persuasive? Really dig into this question, because this area is often where arguments fall apart.

4. What counterarguments does Jack address in his argument? Why do you think he addresses these particular counterarguments? Can you think of others that he might have addressed?

5. What kinds of sources does Jack rely on in his argument? How does he integrate them into his argument, and why do you think he has made those choices?

6. What would make this argument more persuasive and effective?

---

tip sheet **Academic Research**

- **Research typically begins with a research question, which establishes the purpose and scope of a project.** As you develop research questions, keep in mind the following evaluative criteria: personal investment, debatable subject, researchable issue, feasibility, and contribution.

- **A researcher who has established a clear focus for her research, or who has generated a claim, must decide on the kinds of sources needed to support the research focus:** primary, secondary, or both.

- **While both scholarly and popular sources may be appropriate sources of evidence in differing contexts, be sure to understand what distinguishes these types of sources** so that you can choose evidence types purposefully.

- **Primary sources are the results of data that researchers might collect on their own.** These results could include data from surveys, interviews, or questionnaires. **Secondary sources include research collected by and/or commented on by others.** These might include information taken from newspaper articles, magazines, scholarly journal articles, and scholarly books, to name a few.

- **Keep in mind that as you conduct research, you will likely have to refine your search terms.** This process involves carefully selecting or narrowing the terms you use to locate information via search engines or databases.

- **Be aware of the challenges of conducting basic searches for sources via Internet search engines** like Google. While Google Scholar may be a better means of searching for sources in the academic context, researchers often rely on more specialized research databases.

- **Peer-reviewed academic journals are an excellent source of information for academic arguments.** The publication process for journal articles is typically much faster than for books, so using journal articles allows you access to the most current research.

- **Be aware of the strategies you can use to integrate the ideas of others into your own writing:** summarizing, paraphrasing, and/or quoting.

- **When you integrate the words or ideas of others, take care to ensure that you are documenting their words and ideas carefully to avoid instances of plagiarism,** and make sure you understand what constitutes plagiarism at your institution and/or in your individual classes. Follow appropriate rules for documenting your sources and constructing a bibliography. In academic contexts, this often means using MLA, APA, or CSE documentation systems.

PART TWO

Inside Academic Writing

ANDREA TSURUMI

PART TWO

Inside Academic Writing

6

Reading and Writing in Academic Disciplines 119

7

Reading and Writing in the Humanities 139

8

Reading and Writing in the Social Sciences 183

9

Reading and Writing in the Natural Sciences 240

10

Reading and Writing in the Applied Fields 292

CHAPTER 6

Reading and Writing in Academic Disciplines

The four chapters that follow this one introduce four broad disciplinary areas in higher education: humanities, social sciences, natural sciences, and applied fields. While some differences distinguish each of these areas, certain similarities show shared values that provide ways to analyze and understand the conventions of writing and research in those areas.

To help you navigate these chapters, we have organized Chapters 7 through 9 around the same key concerns:

- **Research in the Discipline**   Every academic discipline has established conventions of research. One thing that unites them is the importance of **observation**. Whether you're a humanities scholar observing texts, or a social scientist observing human behavior, or a scientist observing the natural world, careful methods of observation are central to developing research questions and writing projects in each disciplinary area. Similarly, all disciplines rely on the concepts of **primary research** and **secondary research**. (If you gather data of your own, you're doing primary research. If you gather data by studying the research of others, you're doing secondary research. See pages 60–62 for more on different types of research.) Academic writers in a variety of disciplines engage in both primary and secondary research and find that they inform each other. For example, a social scientist studying human behavior might conduct secondary research first to learn what others have done and to develop her research questions. Then she might conduct primary research to test a hypothesis and report results. Similarly, a humanities scholar

ANDREA TSURUMI

"I think students should consider that writing has to be and should be different in various situations. Students need to go through a kind of meta-process of thinking about their own writing, one that allows them to see that the skills they learn in first-year writing can transfer. When students go into their history class or psychology class, for instance, the expectations may be different, but they'll see how they can transfer what they've learned in first-year writing to that situation."

LaunchPad

Learn more about rhetorical situations.

studying historical documents might conduct secondary research to develop a review of literature that will lead to a guiding research question. That research question could then lead him to conduct primary research that includes analyzing a historical document to develop a thesis about his interpretation of that document.

- **Conventions of Writing in the Discipline** Each academic discipline has expectations about academic writing in its field. The chapters that follow this one all include sections that describe and help you analyze the **conventions** of writing in the disciplines, using the principles of rhetoric (the strategies of communication and persuasion) introduced in Part One and in this chapter.

- **Genres in the Discipline** Each chapter also provides examples of **genres**, or common types of writing, that often cross disciplines. These *Insider Examples* of writing, not only by professionals in the disciplines but also by students entering the discipline and composing in particular genres, are annotated to reveal key features that prompt your own analysis of them.

Chapter 10 then explores the kinds of genres produced in a number of applied fields, including health fields, education, business, and law.

Additionally, the chapters share other common features to help you broaden your understanding of each disciplinary area: *Insider's View* excerpts of scholars discussing disciplinary writing; *Inside Work* activities that prompt you to reflect on what you've learned; *Writing Projects* that help you develop your own academic compositions; and *Tip Sheets* that summarize key information.

Throughout these chapters, we ask you to analyze and practice writing in various academic disciplines. Keep in mind, though, that we *do not* expect you to master the writing of these communities by taking just one class or by reading one book. Instead, we introduce you to the concepts associated with **disciplinary discourse**, or the writing and speaking that is specific to different disciplines. Using these concepts, you can analyze future writing situations and make choices appropriate to the rhetorical contexts. It's worth noting that such rhetorical awareness may help you enter other **discourse communities**, or groups that share common values and similar communication practices, outside of your college classes as well, both socially and professionally.

Disciplinary conventions and styles are not just patterns to follow; rather, they represent shared values. In other words, there's a reason why academic texts are communicated in the way that they are: scholars in the same discipline might have similar ways of thinking about an issue, and they follow common ways of researching and investigating that represent their shared values and perspectives. The information we offer you on different academic disciplinary conventions in this book is not necessarily something to memorize, but rather something to analyze through the frame of *rhetorical context*. Ultimately, we want you to be able to look at an academic genre and determine:

1. What is the rhetorical context?
2. What conventions are present in the genre?

As you write for different courses throughout your college career, this ability will help you determine and follow the expectations of writing for the different academic contexts you encounter. It will also help you read the assignments in your other classes because you'll understand some of the reasons that texts are written in the way that they are.

Analyzing Genres and Identifying Conventions of Academic Writing

As you know, different writing situations call for different types of writing. Different types of writing—from short items such as tweets, bumper stickers, and recipes to longer and more complex compositions such as Ph.D. dissertations, annual reports, and novels—are called genres. We mentioned genres in Part One, but we want to dive a little deeper here to talk about the kinds of genres you'll encounter in academic contexts and how to analyze them. Scholars write in many different genres depending on their disciplinary areas, the kinds of work they do, and the situation in which they're writing. You have probably written in several different academic genres in your education already. You might have written a literary analysis in an English class, a lab report in a science class, a bibliography for a research paper, and maybe a personal narrative. Each of these genres has a distinct purpose and set of expectations that you must be familiar with in order to communicate effectively with your intended audience. In this text, you'll find information about writing in many of these genres—such as literary/artistic interpretations, rhetorical analyses, annotated bibliographies, reviews of literature, lab reports, and memos—with the ultimate goal of learning to analyze the rhetorical context so that you can determine the expected conventions of a genre in any writing situation.

Genres are not always bound by discipline, however. Some genres recur across disciplines because writers' purposes can be quite similar even in different fields. You'll find that the conventions of some genres are similar from one

"I think the three skills that students need to write in college settings are all tied into the rhetorical situation. If they can think about audience, purpose, and form, I think that will at least get them ready to start asking the kinds of questions they need of their professors to determine, how am I going to shape this for this particular audience, this particular discipline, this particular professor?"

LaunchPad

Learn more about analyzing genres.

disciplinary area to another. As you read Chapters 7 through 10 on humanities, the social sciences, the natural sciences, and applied fields, pay attention to which genres are repeated and how the conventions of those genres shift or remain constant from one disciplinary context to another.

You'll notice that similar writing situations within, and even sometimes across, disciplines call for a similar genre. In other words, academics might approach a piece of writing in the same (or a similar) way even though they come from different academic disciplines.

For example, you'll notice that scholars in all disciplines write reviews of literature for their research. Likewise, when reporting on the results of a research study, many academics follow the **IMRaD (Introduction, Methods, Results, and Discussion) format**, or a variation of it, to record and publish the results of their research, regardless of their discipline. There might be some subtle differences from one discipline or one situation to another, but common elements are evident. Literature reviews and IMRaD reports are two examples of common genres of academic writing.

As we begin to talk about specific disciplinary contexts, keep in mind these strategies to analyze the conventions of academic writing. When you read and write academic texts, you'll want to:

- understand the overall rhetorical context of the piece of writing: the author, the audience, the topic, and the purpose for writing
- identify and understand the disciplinary area—humanities, social sciences, natural sciences, applied fields—and make connections to what you know about that discipline
- identify the conventions of writing for that genre, including which elements of structure, language, and reference (explained below) govern the writing situation
- analyze the persuasive strategies used, if the author is developing an argument. (What claims are presented? How are they supported by reasons and evidence? What assumptions are in play?)

These analytical strategies will help you to approach any academic writing situation confidently and effectively.

"Aspiring scientists often don't appreciate the importance of communication skills. Science doesn't count until it's communicated to the rest of the scientific community, and eventually the public. Moreover, scientists must write all sorts of things to have a successful career, from journal articles to grant applications to press releases.

"Probably the most important thing to do well when writing as a scientist is simply to get everything right. Science is a methodology for developing reliable information about the world we live in, and getting things wrong is the surest way for scientists to lose their reputation; and for a scientist, reputation is the coin of the realm. While nearly everyone scientifically inclined finds getting things right to be an obvious and principal goal, it is also critically important to identify the audience of any particular piece of writing and address that audience in an effective way. The writing examples included in this text are all targeted for a different readership, and that represents a primary difference between them.

"Scientists write and are asked to write for all sorts of audiences. This isn't an easy task, but success in that adaptation can be the difference between a great career and failure, so it's important to treat it seriously. There isn't magic to this, and while brilliance can be challenging to achieve, competence can certainly be learned. It just takes some practice and thought."

Adapting to Different Rhetorical Contexts: An Academic Writer at Work

Even though some genres are more common in specific disciplines than others, many scholars write in more than one genre on a regular basis. Scholars write for different rhetorical contexts all the time, and they adapt their writing to the audience, topic, and purpose of the occasion. We'd like to take an in-depth look at one scholar's writing to show you an example of how he shifts the conventions of his writing for different contexts—often academic, but sometimes more general. We've chosen to look at a scholar in a scientific field that is rarely discussed in English classes: astronomy. Mike Brotherton is an astronomer at the University of Wyoming, and we'll look at two types of writing that he does on a regular basis. Brotherton writes scholarly articles in his field to report on his research to an audience of other academics—his peers. He also sometimes writes press releases about his research, and these are intended to help journalists report news to the general public. Each piece of writing represents a different genre that follows unique conventions for that rhetorical context, but together they show us the varying ways that Brotherton shares his work in the field of astronomy. Both of these rhetorical contexts call for an awareness of different genre conventions.

Reflecting on a Discipline

In his Insider's View, "Scientists must write all sorts of things," Mike Brotherton makes several generalizations about science, scientists, and scientific writing. Which of these comments, if any, surprised you, and which ones didn't? Explain why. ❯

Using Rhetorical Context to Analyze Academic Writing

In Chapter 3, we introduced the concept of rhetorical context for analyzing different kinds of writing. Now we want to turn your attention toward the range of academic texts you might encounter in college and beyond to understand their unique rhetorical contexts. First we'll take a look at a piece of writing that Mike Brotherton composed for an audience of journalists who might be interested in research he conducted. Brotherton wrote a press release to communicate the results of his research in a genre familiar to journalists. As you read the press release, which we've annotated, keep in mind the elements of rhetorical context that are useful in analyzing all kinds of writing:

- *author* (who is the writer, and what does he or she bring to the text?)
- *audience* (for whom is the text intended?)
- *topic* (what issue is the text addressing?)
- *purpose* (why did the author write the text?)

Specifically, consider the following questions:

- How might Brotherton's position as the *author* of the press release influence the way he wrote it? What might have been different if someone else had written the press release after talking to him about his research?
- Who is the *audience* for this piece? What choices do you think Brotherton made that were specific to his audience for the press release?
- How does the *topic* of the press release affect the choices Brotherton made? Would you have made different choices to approach the topic for a general audience? What would they be?
- What is the *purpose* for writing the press release? How might that influence Brotherton's choices as a writer? Do you think he has met that purpose? Why or why not?

Excerpt from **Hubble Space Telescope Spies Galaxy/ Black Hole Evolution in Action**

MIKE BROTHERTON

JUNE 2ND, 2008 — A set of 29 Hubble Space Telescope (HST) images of an exotic type of active galaxy known as a "post-starburst quasar" show that interactions and mergers drive both galaxy evolution and the growth of super-massive black holes at their centers. Mike Brotherton, Associate Professor at the University of Wyoming, is presenting his team's findings today at the American Astronomical Society meeting in St. Louis, Missouri. Other team members include Sabrina Cales, Rajib Ganguly, and Zhaohui Shang of the University of Wyoming, Gabriella Canalizo of the University of California at Riverside, Aleks Diamond-Stanic of the University of Arizona, and Dan Vanden Berk of the Penn State University. The result is of special interest because the images provide support for a leading theory of the evolution of massive galaxies, but also show that the situation is more complicated than previously thought.

> Identifies the **topic** of the research study and its relevant findings

> Identifies members of the research team, who are all **authors** of the study upon which the press release is based

> Fulfills the **purpose** of a press release by stating the importance of the research project. Appears in the first paragraph to make it prominent for the audience

Over the last decade, astronomers have discovered that essentially every galaxy harbors a super-massive black hole at its center, ranging from 10,000 times the mass of the sun to upwards of 1,000,000,000 times solar, and that there exists a close relationship between the mass of the black hole and properties of its host. When the black holes are fueled and grow, the galaxy becomes active, with the most luminous manifestation being a quasar, which can outshine the galaxy and make it difficult to observe.

> Provides relevant background information about the topic for the audience

In order to explain the relationships between galaxies and their central black holes, theorists have proposed detailed models in which both grow together as the result of galaxy mergers. This hierarchical picture suggests that large galaxies are built up over time through the assembly of smaller galaxies with corresponding bursts of star formation, and that this process also fuels the growth of the black holes, which eventually ignite to shine as quasars. Supernova explosions and their dusty debris shroud the infant starburst until the activated quasar blows out the obscuration.

Brotherton and his team turned the sharp-eyed Hubble Space Telescope and its Advanced Camera for Surveys to observe a subset of these post-starburst quasars that had the strongest and most luminous stellar content. Looking at these systems 3.5 billion light-years away, Hubble, operating without the distortions of an atmosphere, can resolve sub-kiloparsec scales necessary to see nuclear structure and host galaxy morphology.

> Provides a brief overview of the study's methods

"The images started coming in, and we were blown away," said Brotherton. "We see not only merger remnants as in the prototype of the class, but also post-starburst quasars with interacting companion galaxies, double nuclei, star-bursting rings, and all sorts of messy structures."

Astronomers have determined that our own Milky Way galaxy and the great spiral galaxy of Andromeda will collide three billion years from now. This event will create massive bursts of star formation and most likely fuel nuclear activity a few hundred million years later. Hubble has imaged post-starburst quasars three and a half billion light-years away, corresponding to three and a half billion years ago, and three and a half billion years from now our own galaxy is probably going to be one of these systems.

This work is supported by grants from NASA, through the Space Telescope Science Institute and the Long-Term Space Astrophysics program, and the National Science Foundation.

Acknowledges funding support for the research project, giving credit to funding agencies that might also be audiences for the journalists' news articles

Insider's View
The audience for a press release is very general
MIKE BROTHERTON, ASTRONOMY

"It isn't always the case that scientists write their own press releases. Often, there are writers on staff at various institutions who specialize in writing press releases and who work with scientists. I've written press releases solo (e.g., the contribution included here) and in collaboration with staff journalists at the University of Texas, Lawrence Livermore National Laboratory, and the University of Wyoming. Press releases should be able to be run as news stories themselves and contain enough content to be adapted or cut to length. The audience for a press release is very general, and you can't assume that they have any background in your field. You have to tell them why your result is important, clearly and briefly, and little else.

"While I don't think my effort here is bad, it is far from perfect and suffers one flaw. Reporters picking up press releases want to know what single result they should focus upon. They want to keep things simple. I tried to include several points in the release, rather than focusing on a single result. Some reporters became distracted about the notion that the Milky Way and Andromeda would someday merge and might become a post-starburst galaxy, which was not a result of my research project. Even though it gave the work some relevance, in hindsight I should have omitted it to keep the focus on the results of my research."

INSIDE WORK   **Reflecting on Rhetorical Context**

In his Insider's View, "The audience for a press release is very general," Mike Brotherton explains some of the specifics of writing a press release and what he sees as the strengths and weaknesses of his own press release. Review the press release with Brotherton's comments in mind, and explain whether you agree with his assessment of it. What advice might you give him for revising the press release? ❱

Using Structure, Language, and Reference to Analyze Genre Conventions

Earlier, we introduced two questions that are central to analyzing an academic text:

1. What is the rhetorical context?
2. What conventions are present in the text?

Understanding the rhetorical context is the first step toward understanding how a particular genre works. Knowing the audience and purpose for writing helps us to identify the situations in which different genres occur. In order to understand fully how a genre works, you must also understand the conventions that are present in the text and whether they follow the expectations for conventions in that genre.

To understand the conventions that are present in the text, though, we need an additional framework for analysis. The categories of **structure**, **language**, and **reference (SLR)*** offer more specific help in analyzing the conventions of genres at a deeper level. Although discourse conventions vary from discipline to discipline, once you understand how to analyze writing through these categories, you can determine what conventions and choices are appropriate for nearly any writing situation.

- **Structure, or Format and Organization** Written texts are often organized according to specific disciplinary conventions. For example, scholars in the social sciences and natural sciences usually organize experimental study reports with an introduction first, followed by a description of their research methods, then their data/results, then the analysis of that data, and finally a discussion and conclusion (IMRaD format, discussed in more detail in Chapters 8 and 9 on the social sciences and natural sciences). By contrast, scholars in the humanities tend to write and value essays that are driven by a clear thesis (or main claim: what you are trying to prove) near the beginning of the essay that indicates the direction the argument will take. Scholars in the humanities also don't tend, as much, to use headings to divide a text.

- **Language, or Style and Word Choice** The language used in academic writing follows disciplinary conventions. Consider the use of qualifiers (words such as *might*, *could*, *likely*), which are often used in the natural and social sciences to indicate the interpretive power of the data collected and to help persuade an audience to accept the results because they are not

---

*The SLR concept originated in the following essay: Patricia Linton, Robert Madigan, and Susan Johnson. "Introducing Students to Disciplinary Genres: The Role of the General Composition Course." *Language and Learning Across the Disciplines*, vol. 1, no. 2, 1994, pp. 63-78.

Get astronomer Mike
Brotherton's take
on qualifying and
hedging.

generalizing inappropriately (*The positive correlation between the variables* *likely indicates a strong relationship between the motivation of a student and his or her achievement of learning objectives*). When qualifiers are used in the humanities, however, they often demonstrate uncertainty and weaken an argument (*Hamlet's soliloquies in acts 2 and 4 might provide an interesting comparison because they frame the turning point of the play in act 3*).

- **Reference, or Citation and Documentation** The conventions of how scholars refer to one another's work can also shift by discipline. You might already know, for example, that many scholars in the humanities use the documentation style of the Modern Language Association (MLA), while those in the social sciences generally use the style guide published by the American Psychological Association (APA). More citation styles are listed and discussed in the Appendix. Conventions for how often scholars quote, paraphrase, and summarize one another's work can also vary.

In the next example of Mike Brotherton's work, we'll look at the abstract and introduction to a scholarly journal article that he wrote with several co-authors. If we start with an understanding of the rhetorical context—that Brotherton and his co-authors are writing with the *purpose* of sharing research results and the *audience* of fellow astronomers—then we can move to understanding the conventions that are present in this type of writing. Considering the *structure*, *language*, and *reference conventions* used in the piece provides insight into the way such writing is structured within the sciences—and specifically in the field of astronomy.

As you read the excerpt from Brotherton's co-authored article, notice the structure, language, and reference conventions. The article contains a lot of specific scientific language, and for the purpose of your analysis right now it's not important to understand the concepts as much as it is to recognize some of the elements that make this writing unique from other writing you may have encountered in English classes in the past. Consider the following questions:

- Even though the entire article is not included, what conclusions can you draw about its **structure**? What comes first in the article, and how is it organized in the beginning?

- How would you describe the **language** that Brotherton and his co-authors choose to use in the article? What does it tell you about the audience for the article?

- What **reference conventions** does the article follow? Does the documentation style used for the parenthetical references look familiar? How often are other scholars cited, and what is the context for citing their work? What purpose do those references serve in the article?

Excerpt from **A Spectacular Poststarburst Quasar**

M. S. BROTHERTON, WIL VAN BREUGEL, S. A. STANFORD, R. J. SMITH, B. J. BOYLE, LANCE MILLER, T. SHANKS, S. M. CROOM, AND ALEXEI V. FILIPPENKO

ABSTRACT

We report the discovery of a spectacular "poststarburst quasar" UN J10252–0040 ($B = 19$; $z = 0.634$). The optical spectrum is a chimera, displaying the broad Mg II $\lambda2800$ emission line and strong blue continuum characteristic of quasars, but is dominated in the red by a large Balmer jump and prominent high-order Balmer absorption lines indicative of a substantial young stellar population at similar redshift. Stellar synthesis population models show that the stellar component is consistent with a 400 Myr old instantaneous starburst with a mass of $\leq 10^{11} M_{\odot}$. A deep, K_s-band image taken in ~0″.5 seeing shows a point source surrounded by asymmetric extended fuzz. Approximately 70% of the light is unresolved, the majority of which is expected to be emitted by the starburst. While starbursts and galaxy interactions have been previously associated with quasars, no quasar ever before has been seen with such an extremely luminous young stellar population.

The language is highly specific and technical.

1. INTRODUCTION

Headings indicate a particular kind of structure.

Is there a connection between starbursts and quasar activity? There is circumstantial evidence to suggest so. The quasar 3C 48 is surrounded by nebulosity that shows the high-order Balmer absorption lines characteristic of A-type stars (Boroson & Oke 1984; Stockton & Ridgeway 1991). PG 1700+518 shows a nearby starburst ring (Hines et al. 1999) with the spectrum of a 10^8 yr old starburst (Stockton, Canalizo, & Close 1998). Near-IR and CO mapping reveals a massive (~$10^{10} M_{\odot}$) circumnuclear starburst ring in I Zw 1 (Schinnerer, Eckart, & Tacconi 1998). The binary quasar member FIRST J164311.3+315618B shows a starburst host galaxy spectrum (Brotherton et al. 1999).

In addition to these individual objects, *samples* of active galactic nuclei (AGNs) show evidence of starbursts. Images of quasars taken with the *Hubble Space Telescope* show "chains of emission nebulae" and "near-nuclear emission knots" (e.g., Bahcall et al. 1997). Seyfert 2 and radio galaxies have significant populations of ~100 Myr old stars (e.g., Schmitt, Storchi-Bergmann, & Cid Fernandes 1999). Half of the ultraluminous infrared galaxies (ULIRGs) contain simultaneously an AGN and recent (10–100 Myr) starburst activity in a 1–2 kpc circumnuclear ring (Genzel et al. 1998).

The advent of *IRAS* provided evidence for an evolutionary link between starbursts and AGNs. The ULIRGs ($L_{IR} > 10^{12} L_{\odot}$) are strongly interacting merger systems with copious molecular gas [$(0.5–2) \times 10^{10} M_\odot$] and dust heated by both starburst and AGN power sources. The ULIRG space density is sufficient to form the quasar parent population. These facts led Sanders et al. (1988) to hypothesize that ULIRGs represent the initial dust-enshrouded stage of a quasar. Supporting this hypothesis is the similarity in the evolution of the quasar luminosity density and the star formation rate (e.g., Boyle & Terlevich 1998; Percival & Miller 1999). Another clue is that supermassive black holes appear ubiquitously in local massive galaxies, which may be out-of-fuel quasars (e.g., Magorrian et al. 1998). AGN activity may therefore reflect a fundamental stage of galaxy evolution.

> Introduction references multiple prior studies by other scholars.

We report here the discovery of a poststarburst quasar. The extreme properties of this system may help shed light on the elusive AGN-starburst connection. We adopt $H_0 = 75$ km s^{-1} Mpc^{-1} and $q_0 = 0$.

INSIDE WORK   **Reflecting on an Academic Article**

In his Insider's View "Accuracy trumps strong writing," Mike Brotherton provides some guidelines for analyzing the conventions of his scientific article through the lenses of structure, language, and reference. Write down a few points he makes about each lens that will be helpful when you approach reading a scientific article on your own.

Insider's View
Accuracy trumps strong writing
MIKE BROTHERTON, ASTRONOMY

"The audience for a scientific journal should be experts in your field but also beginning graduate students. Articles should be specific, succinct, and correct. For better or worse, in scientific articles it is necessary to use a lot of qualifications, adverbs, and modifying phrases, to say exactly what you mean even though the result is not as strong or effective.

Accuracy trumps strong writing here, although there is plenty of room for good writing. Every piece of writing, fiction or non-fiction, should tell an interesting story. The format for a scientific article is rather standard.

"There is also an abstract that gives a summary of all the parts of the paper. In many instances, the entire paper is not read but skimmed, so being able to find things quickly and easily makes the paper more useful. Audiences for scientific papers are often measured only in the dozens, if that. While popular papers can be read and used by thousands, most papers have a small audience and contribute to advancement in some niche or other, which may or may not turn out to be important.

"Some people cite heavily, and some people don't cite as heavily. And, again, you need to keep in mind your audience and what's appropriate. In writing a telescope proposal, for instance, which is not quite the same as a scientific article but has the same conventions, some reviewers want you to cite a lot of things just to prove that you know the field. This is especially true for beginning students writing proposals."

- Reread the excerpt from "A Spectacular Poststarburst Quasar" (see pp. 129–30) and reflect on any new things you notice.

- Read the excerpt again, this time with an eye to rhetorical context (author, audience, topic, and purpose for writing). Try to generalize about the usefulness of the two approaches to your reading.

- Annotate a paper you've written for another class, noting the rhetorical context and the genre conventions as we have in our annotations on the press release and the scholarly article. What practices about your own writing do these approaches suggest? ❭

Writing a Genre Analysis of an Academic Article

WRITING PROJECT

For this project, you will analyze a full-length article in a discipline of your choice, published in an academic journal. Your instructor may assign an article or may ask you to seek his or her approval for the article you choose to use for this project.

Using the following guiding questions, describe the basic genre features of the article you've chosen to study:

1. What is the rhetorical context? Consider the author, audience, topic, and purpose of the article.

2. What conventions are present the text? Consider the structure, language, and reference conventions of the article.

Once you have described the genre features of the article, consider the choices the writer or writers made when they wrote the article. Why did they write the article in the way that they did? How do these genre features work together?

The introduction to your paper should name the article you will analyze, describe the primary methods you will use to analyze it, and explain the goal of your analysis—to analyze an academic article. The body of your paper might be organized around the two guiding questions, or you might focus on one or two of the genre features that are of specific interest in your article. Of course, you can subdivide the features you are analyzing to address specific elements of the larger categories. For example, if you were analyzing conventions of language, you could address the use of qualifiers, the use of first person, and so on, providing examples from the article and commenting on their usefulness for the writer. In your conclusion, reflect on what you've found. Are there other issues still to be addressed? What other rhetorical strategies could be explored to analyze the work further? How effective are the strategies the author used, given the intended audience?

Writing a Comparative Genre Analysis

WRITING PROJECT

The goal of this writing project is to allow you to consider further the shifts in rhetorical situation and genre expectations for writing across two disciplinary areas.

To begin, you'll need to locate two articles on the same topic in academic journals representing different disciplines. For example, you might find two articles discussing the issue of increasing taxes on the wealthy to deal with the U.S. national debt. You might find one article written by an economist that addresses the impact of the national debt and projects the feasibility of different solutions, and another article written by a humanist discussing how the media has portrayed the issue.

Once you have identified your two articles, use the following guiding questions to describe the basic genre features of the articles you've chosen to study:

1. What are the rhetorical contexts? Consider the authors, audiences, topic, and purposes of the articles.

2. What conventions are present in the texts? Consider the structure, language, and reference conventions of the articles.

Once you have described the genre features of the articles, consider the choices the writer or writers made when they wrote the article. Why did they write the article in the way that they did? How do these genre features work together?

You might also consider other elements of the articles: what kinds of questions the authors ask and what kinds of evidence they draw upon, for example. Formulate a thesis that assesses the degree to which the genre features in each category compare or contrast. Organize your analysis in a way that helps your reader follow the main points you want to make about your comparison. Throughout your paper, develop your comparisons and contrasts by illustrating your findings with examples from the texts. For example, if you find that one article (perhaps from the humanities) uses the active voice almost exclusively, then provide some examples. If the other article relies heavily on the passive voice, then provide examples of this use. End each section with a consideration of the implications of your findings: What does it say about the sciences that claims are often hedged by qualifiers? Do not avoid discussing findings that might contradict your assumptions about writing in these two academic domains. Instead, study them closely and try to rationalize the authors' rhetorical decision-making.

WRITING PROJECT

Comparing Scholarly and Popular Articles

Choose a scholarly article and an article written for a more general audience on a common topic. You might reread the discussion of the differences between scholarly and popular articles in Chapter 5 as you're looking for articles to choose. Then use these guiding questions to analyze the two texts as distinct, but perhaps related, genres:

1. What are the rhetorical contexts? Consider the authors, audiences, topic, and purposes of the articles.

2. What conventions are present in the texts? Consider the structure, language, and reference conventions of the articles.

In your comparison of the rhetorical contexts and the decisions the authors have made about conventions, consider the questions below:

1. How do the rhetorical contexts for writing compare?

2. Which genre conventions are similar, and which ones are different?

3. Why do you think the authors made the choices that they did in writing?

Translating Scholarly Writing for Different Rhetorical Contexts

At times, writing for an academic context, like Mike Brotherton's work, must be repurposed for presentation in another, more general context. Sometimes the writer does the translating, and sometimes other writers may help communicate the importance of a piece of scholarly writing to another audience.

Insider Example
Student Translation of a Scholarly Article

Jonathan Nastasi, a first-year writing student, translated a scholarly article about the possible habitability of another planet from the journal *Astronomy & Astrophysics* into a press release for a less specialized audience. He condensed the information into a two-page press release for a potential audience interested in publishing these research results in news venues. Also, he followed his writing instructor's advice to apply MLA style even though the article he summarized is scientific.

Release Date: 18 September 2014

Contact: W. von Bloh

bloh@pik-potsdam.de

Potsdam Institute for Climate Impact Research

Life May Be Possible on Other Planets

New data shows that a new planet found outside of our solar system may be habitable for life.

RALEIGH (SEPTEMBER 18, 2014) — A study from the Potsdam Institute for Climate Impact Research shows that a planet in another solar system is in the perfect position to harbor life. Additionally, the quantity of possibly habitable planets in our galaxy is much greater than expected.

Gliese 581g is one of up to six planets found to be orbiting the low-mass star Gliese 581, hence its name. Gliese 581g and its other planetary siblings are so-called "Super Earths," rocky

An artist's rendition of Gliese 581g orbiting its star.

planets from one to ten times the size of our Earth. This entire system is about twenty light-years away from our Sun. W. Von Bloh, M. Cuntz, S. Franck, and C. Bounama from the Potsdam Institute for Climate Impact Research chose to research Gliese 581g because of its size and distance from its star, which make it a perfect candidate to support life.

A planet must be a precise distance away from a star in order to sustain life. This distance is referred to as the habitable zone. According to Von Bloh et al., the habitable zones "are defined as regions around the central star where the physical conditions are favourable for liquid water to exist at the planet's surface for a period of time sufficient for biological evolution to occur." This "Goldilocks" zone can be affected by a number of variables, including the temperature of the star and the composition of the planet.

The actual distance of Gliese 581g from its star is known; the goal of this study was to find out if the planet is capable of supporting life at that distance. The researchers began by finding the habitable zone of the star Gliese 581—specifically, the zone that allowed for photosynthesis. Photosynthesis is the production of oxygen from organic life forms and is indicative of life. In order for the planet to harbor this kind of life, a habitable zone that allows for a specific concentration of CO_2 in the atmosphere as well as liquid water would have to be found.

The scientists used mathematical models based on Earth's known attributes and adjusted different variables to find out which scenarios yielded the best results. Some of these variables include surface temperature, mass of the planet, and geological activity. The scientists also considered settings where the surface of the planet was all-land, all-water, or a mix of both.

Considering all of these scenarios, Von Bloh et al. determined that the habitable zone for Gliese 581g is between 0.125 and 0.155 astronomical units, where an astronomical unit is the distance between the Earth and the Sun. Other studies conclude that the *actual* orbital distance of Gliese 581g is 0.146 astronomical units. Because Gliese 581g is right in the middle of its determined habitable zone, the error and uncertainty in the variables that remain to be determined are negligible.

However, the ratio of land to ocean on the planet's surface is key in determining the "life span" of the habitable zone. The habitable zone can shift over time due to geological phenomena caused by a planet having more land than ocean. According to Von Bloh et al., a planet with a land-to-ocean ratio similar to ours would remain in the habitable zone for about seven billion years, shorter than Gliese 581g's estimated age. In other words, if Gliese 581g has an Earth-like composition, it cannot sustain life. But if the ratio is low (more ocean than land), the planet will remain in its habitable zone for a greater period of time, thus allowing for a greater chance of life to develop.

The researchers conclude that Gliese 581g is a strong candidate for life so long as it is a "water world." According to the authors, water worlds are defined as "planets of non-vanishing continental area mostly covered by oceans."

The discovery of Gliese 581g being a strong candidate for sustaining life is especially important considering the vast quantity of planets just like it. According to NASA's *Kepler Discoveries* Web page, the Kepler telescope alone has found over 4,234 planet candidates in just five years. With the collaboration of other research, 120 planets have been deemed "habitable," according to *The Habitable Exoplanets Catalog*.

"Our results are another step toward identifying the possibility of life beyond the Solar System, especially concerning Super-Earth planets, which appear to be more abundant than previously surmised," say the authors. More and more scientists are agreeing with the idea that extraterrestrial life is probable, given the abundance of Earth-like planets found in our galaxy already. If this is true, humanity will be one step closer to finding its place in the universe.

"[W]e have to await future missions to identify the pertinent geodynamical features of Gl[iese] 581g . . . to gain insight into whether or not Gl[iese] 581g harbors life," write the researchers. The science community agrees: continued focus in researching the cosmos is necessary to confirm if we have neighbors.

The full journal article can be found at http://www.aanda.org.prox.lib.ncsu.edu/articles/aa/full_html/2011/04/aa16534-11/aa16534-11.html.

Astronomy & Astrophysics, published by EDP Sciences since 1963, covers important developments in the research of theoretical, observational, and instrumental astronomy and astrophysics. For more information, visit http://www.aanda.org/.

Works Cited

"About Astronomy & Astrophysics." *Astronomy & Astrophysics*, www
.aanda.org/about-aa.

Annual Review of Astronomy and Astrophysics. Annual Reviews, 2014, www
.annualreviews.org/journal/astro.

Cook, Lynette. "Planets of the Gliese 581 System." *NASA Features*, NASA,
29 Sept. 2010, www.nasa.gov/topics/universe/features/Gliese_581.html.

The Habitable Exoplanets Catalog. Planetary Habitability Laboratory, 2 Sept.
2014, phl.upr.edu/projects/habitable-exoplanets-catalog.

Kepler Discoveries. NASA, 24 July 2014, kepler.nasa.gov/Mission/discoveries/.

Kepler Launch. NASA, 2 Apr. 2014, www.nasa.gov/mission_pages/kepler/
launch/.

Von Bloh, W., et al. "Habitability of the Goldilocks Planet Gliese 581g:
Results from Geodynamic Models." *Astronomy & Astrophysics*, vol. 528,
no. A133, 2011. *Summon*, doi:10.1051/0004-6361/201116534.

Discussion Questions

1. Who was Jonathan Nastasi's audience as he wrote his press release? What cues in the writing tell you whom Jonathan views as his audience?

2. How well did he tailor his description of the research to that audience?

3. What is the purpose behind Jonathan's communication of the research findings?

4. What other genre might work for translating this research to a public audience? What would Jonathan need to do differently in that rhetorical situation?

WRITING PROJECT

Translating a Scholarly Article for a Public Audience

The goal of this project is to translate a scholarly article for a public audience. To do so, you will first analyze the scholarly article rhetorically and then shift the genre through which the information in your article is reported. You will produce two documents in response to this assignment:

- the translation of your scholarly article
- a written analysis of the choices you made as you wrote your translation

IDENTIFY YOUR NEW AUDIENCE, PURPOSE, AND GENRE

To get started, you'll need to identify a new audience and purpose for the information in your selected article. The goal here is to shift the audience from an academic one to a public one and to consider whether the purpose for reporting the information also shifts. You may, for instance, choose to report the findings of the article in a magazine targeted toward a general audience of people who are interested in science, or you may choose to write a newspaper article that announces the research findings. You might also choose to write a script for a news show that reports research findings to a general television audience. Notice that once the rhetorical situation shifts, a new genre with unique conventions is often called for. The genre you produce will be contingent on the audience you're targeting and the purpose for writing: magazine article, newspaper article, news show script.

ANALYZE THE EXPECTATIONS OF YOUR GENRE

Closely analyze an example or two of the kind of genre you're attempting to create, and consider how those genre examples fulfill a particular purpose and the expectations of the target audience. Your project will be assessed according to its ability to reproduce those genre expectations, so you will need to explain, in detail, the choices you had to make in the construction of your piece. Be sure that you're able to explain those choices. In addition to thinking about the audience and purpose, consider the structure, language, and reference conventions of the genre.

CONSTRUCT THE GENRE

At this point, you're ready to begin constructing or translating the article into the new genre. The genre you're producing could take any number of forms. As such, the form, structure, and development of your ideas are contingent on the genre of public reporting you're attempting to construct. If you're constructing a magazine article, for example, then the article you produce should really look like one that would appear in a magazine. Try to mirror how the genre would appear in a real situation.

WRITE THE ANALYSIS

Once your translation is complete, compose a reflective analysis. As part of your analysis, consider the choices you made as you constructed your translation. Offer a rationale for each of your decisions that connects your translation to your larger rhetorical context and the conventions of the genre. For example, if you had to translate the title of the scholarly article for a public audience, explain why your new title is the most appropriate one for your public audience.

tip sheet

Reading and Writing in Academic Disciplines

- **You should not expect to master the writing of every academic discipline by reading one book,** even this one.

- **It's important to become familiar with key concepts of disciplinary writing in academic discourse communities:** *research* expectations; *conventions* (expectations) of writing; *genres* (types) of writing.

- **Genres are not always bound by discipline, although their conventions may vary somewhat from discipline to discipline.** For example, you can expect to write literature reviews in many different courses across the curriculum.

- **Analyzing academic writing is a multistep process.**
  1. Understand the rhetorical context (author, audience, topic, purpose for writing).
  2. Identify the disciplinary area and what you know about it.
  3. Identify the conventions of writing for that genre, including *structure*, *language*, and *reference* expectations.
  4. Analyze the persuasive strategies if the writer is developing an argument.

- **Remember SLR.** The acronym for *structure*, *language*, and *reference* offers categories that can help you determine genre conventions and choices appropriate for most writing situations. These categories are particularly useful in academic writing situations.
  - *Structure* concerns how texts are organized. *Example:* IMRaD—signifying Introduction, Methods, Results, and Discussion—is a common format in both the social and natural sciences.
  - *Language* encompasses conventions of style or word choice. *Example:* Active voice is typically favored in the humanities, and passive voice is more characteristic of writing in the social and natural sciences.
  - *Reference* concerns the ways writers engage source material, including their use of conventions of citation and documentation. *Example:* Many humanities scholars use MLA style; many social science scholars use APA style.

- **Academic research is important beyond the academy.** Therefore, academic writing that conveys such research often must be repurposed—translated—for different venues and audiences.

Reading and Writing in the Humanities

Introduction to the Humanities

An interest in exploring the meaning, or interpretation, of something and how it reflects on the human experience is one of the defining characteristics of the **humanities** that sets it apart from the social sciences, the natural sciences, and applied fields. Look at the tree at the bottom of this page, and see if you recognize any fields within the humanities with which you're already familiar.

Scholars in the humanities are interested in, and closely observe, human thought, creativity, and experience. The American Council of Learned Societies explains that humanistic scholars "help us appreciate and understand what distinguishes us as human beings as well as what unites us." Scholars in the humanities ask questions such as these:

- What can we learn about human experience from examining the ways we think and express ourselves?
- How do we make sense of the world through various forms of expression?
- How do we interpret what we experience, or make meaning for ourselves and for others?

Professor John McCurdy teaches history at Eastern Michigan University. McCurdy's research focuses on the history of early America, and he teaches courses on the colonial era and the American Revolution. In his Insider's View comments, he offers thoughts on what humanists do and value, as well as the kind of research questions they ask. These comments come from an interview with him about his writing and about research in the humanities in general.

ANDREA TSURUMI

139

TEXTS AND MEANING

To understand the human condition and respond to these questions, humanists often turn to artifacts of human culture that they observe and interpret. These might be films, historical documents, comic strips, paintings, poems, religious artifacts, video games, essays, photographs, and songs. They might even include graffiti on the side of a building, a social media status update, or a YouTube video.

In addition to tangible artifacts, humanist writers might turn their attention to events, experiences, rituals, or other elements of human culture to develop meaning. When Ernest Hemingway wrote *Death in the Afternoon* about the traditions of bullfighting in Spain, he carefully observed and interpreted the meaning of a cultural ritual. And when historians interpret Hemingway's text through the lens of historical context, or when literary scholars compare the book to Hemingway's fiction of a later period, they are extending that understanding of human culture. Through such examination and interpretation of specific objects of study, scholars in the humanities can create artistic texts and develop theories that explain human expression and experience.

In this chapter, we'll often refer to artifacts and events that humanistic scholars study as **texts**. The ability to construct meaning from a text is an essential skill within the scholarship of the humanities. In high school English classes, students are often asked to interpret novels, poetry, or plays. You've likely written such analyses in the past, so you've developed a set of observational and interpretive skills that we'd like to build upon in this chapter. The same skills, such as the observational skills that lead you to find evidence in a literary text to develop and support an interpretation, can also help you analyze other kinds of texts.

INSIDE WORK Thinking about Texts

Write your responses to the following questions.

- What experiences do you already have with interpretation of texts in the humanities? Have you had to write a formal interpretation of a text before? If so, what questions did you ask?
- Imagine a text with which you are familiar. It might be a novel, a song, a painting, a sculpture, a play, a building, or a historical document. Brainstorm a list of *why* questions that you could ask about that text. ▶

OBSERVATION AND INTERPRETATION

You probably engage every day in observation of the kinds of things studied in the humanities, but you might not be doing it in the systematic way that humanistic scholars do. When you listen to music, how do you make meaning? Perhaps you listen to the words, the chord progressions, or repeated phrases. Or maybe you look to specific matters of context such as who wrote the song, what other music the artist has performed, and when it was recorded. You might consider how it is similar to or different from other songs. In order to understand the song's meaning, you might even think about social and cultural events surrounding the period when the song was recorded. These kinds of observational and interpretive acts are the very things humanists do when they research and write; they just use careful methods of observing, documenting, and interpreting that are generally more systematic than what most of us do when listening to music for enjoyment. Humanists also develop theories of interpretation or build on the theories of others in order to help still other scholars determine how to observe and interpret texts and find meaningful connections among them. In this chapter, you will learn about some of those methods of observation and interpretation, and you will also have the opportunity to practice some of the kinds of writing and research typically seen in the humanities.

INSIDE WORK Observing and Asking Questions

For this activity, pick a place to sit and observe, and bring something to write with. You might choose to do the activity in your dorm room or apartment, your workplace, a classroom, outside, in a restaurant or coffee shop, or at a gym, to name a few possibilities. For ten minutes, freewrite about all the things you see around you that could be "texts" that a humanist might interpret. Then think about the kinds of questions that a humanist might ask about those texts. Try to avoid writing about the actual activities people are engaging in; human behavior is more within the realm of the social sciences, not the humanities. Instead, think creatively about the kinds of artifacts that a humanist might analyze to understand and interpret human experience.

For example, if you observe and write in a coffee shop, you might consider the following artifacts, or texts.

- **The Sign or Logo Used for the Store**   Is there a logo? What does it include? How is it designed, and why? Is there a slogan? Whom might it relate to? What does it say about the store?

- **The Clothing of the People Working behind the Counter**   Do they have a dress code? Are they wearing uniforms? If so, what do the colors, materials, and/or style of the uniforms represent? What do they potentially tell you about the values of the business?

- **The Furniture**   Is it comfortable? New? Old? How is it arranged? What might the coffee shop be communicating to customers through that arrangement?

- **The Music Playing in the Background**   Is there music? What is playing? How loud is the music? What mood does it convey? Does it match the arrangement of the rest of the space? What emotions might the music evoke from customers?

- **The Materials Used to Serve Coffee**   Are the cups and napkins recycled? Does the store use glass or ceramic cups that can be washed and reused? Are there slogans or logos on the materials? If so, what do they say? What does the store communicate to customers through the materials used?

- **The Menu**   What kinds of items does the coffee shop serve? What language is used to describe menu items? How are the items written on the menu? Where is it displayed? Is food served? If so, what types of food are available, and what does that communicate to customers?

See how many different texts you can identify and how many questions you can generate. You might do this activity separately in the same place with a partner and then compare notes. What texts did you and your partner find in common? Which ones did you each identify that were unique? Why do you think you noticed the things you did? What was the most interesting text you identified? ❱

 LaunchPad

Hear more about the different kinds of texts scholars draw on in their research.

Research in the Humanities

The collection of information, or data, is an integral part of the research process for scholars in all academic disciplines. The data that researchers collect form the foundation of evidence they use to answer a question. In the humanities, data are generally gathered from texts. Whether you're reading a novel, analyzing a sculpture, or speculating on the significance of a cultural ritual, your object of analysis is a text and the primary source of data you collect to use as evidence typically originates from that text.

Academic fields within the humanities have at their heart the creation and interpretation of texts. A history scholar may pore through photographs of Civil War soldiers for evidence to support a claim. An actor in a theater class might scour a script in order to develop an interpretation of a character he will perform onstage. And those who are primarily the creators of texts—visual artists, novelists, poets, playwrights, screenwriters, musicians—read widely in the field in order to master elements of style and contribute to their art in original and innovative ways. In the humanities, it's all about the text. Humanists are either creators or interpreters of texts, and often they are both.

To understand the research and writing in a specific disciplinary area, it is important to know not only what the objects of study are but also what methods scholars in that area use to analyze and study the objects of their attention. In the humanities, just as in other disciplines, scholars begin with observation. They closely observe the texts that interest them, looking for patterns, meaning, and connections that will help generate and support an interpretation. Humanists use their observations to pose questions about the human condition, to gather evidence to help answer those questions, and to generate theories about the human experience that can extend beyond one text or set of texts.

INSIDE WORK **Observing and Interpreting Images**

Consider each of the following images—graffiti (A), a painting (B), and a movie poster (C)—as texts that have something to say about human experience. Write your ideas in response to the following questions.

- What does the image mean?
- How do you make meaning from the image? What do you analyze to make meaning?
- What does the image make you think about?
- What emotion does the artist want you to feel? What aspect of the text do you base this on?
- Why do you think someone created this image? ❯

SKIP BOLEN/EPA/REX/SHUTTERSTOCK

A. Graffiti as Text

LUNCHEON OF THE BOATING PARTY, 1880–81 (OIL ON CANVAS)/RENOIR, PIERRE AUGUSTE (1841–1919)/ PHILLIPS COLLECTION/THE PHILLIPS COLLECTION, WASHINGTON, D.C., USA/BRIDGEMAN IMAGES

B. Painting as Text

© MOVIESTORE COLLECTION LTD/ALAMY

C. Movie Poster as Text

THE ROLE OF THEORY IN THE HUMANITIES

When scholars in the humanities analyze and interpret a text, they often draw on a specific theory of interpretation to help them make meaning. Theories in the humanities offer a particular perspective through which to understand human experience. Sometimes those perspectives are based on ideas about *how* we make meaning from a text; such theories include Formalism (sometimes called New Criticism, though it is far from new), Reader Response, and Deconstruction. Other theories, such as Feminist Theory and Queer Theory, are based more on ideas about how identity informs meaning-making. Still other theories, such as New Historicism, Postcolonialism, and Marxism, are centrally concerned with how historical, social, cultural, and other contexts inform meaning.

These are only a few of the many prominent theories of humanistic interpretation, barely scratching the surface of the theory-building work that has taken place in the humanities. Our goal is not for you to learn specific names of theories at this point, though. Rather, we want you to understand that when scholars in the humanities draw on a theory in the interpretation of a text, the theory gives them a *lens* through which to view the text and a set of questions they might ask about it. For example, they might ask:

- When was the text written, and what major social forces might have influenced the text at the time? (New Historicism)

- What characters exhibit the most power in their relationships to their partners? (Feminism)

- What kinds of tensions does the artifact create for the viewer through its use of shading and lighting? (New Criticism)

Different theories lead to different sets of questions and varying interpretations of the same text.

CLOSE READING IN THE HUMANITIES

To develop clear claims about the texts they're interpreting, scholars in the humanities must closely observe their texts and learn about them. Close observation might involve the kinds of reading strategies we discussed in Chapter 3, especially if the text is alphabetic (i.e., letter based), such as a book, a story, or a poem. One method that humanities scholars use is **close reading**, or careful observation of a text. It's possible to do a close reading of a story, of course, but you can also do a close reading of non-alphabetic texts such as films, buildings, paintings, events, or songs.

Most college students are highly skilled at reading for content knowledge, or for information, because that's what they're most often asked to do as students. This is what a professor generally expects when assigning a reading from a textbook. As you read such texts, you're primarily trying to figure out what the text is saying rather than thinking about how it functions, why the author makes certain stylistic choices, or how others might interpret the text. As we mentioned in Chapter 3, you might also read to be entertained, to learn, or to communicate.

Close observation or *reading* in the humanities, however, requires our focus to shift from reading for information to reading to understand how a text functions and how we can make meaning of it. Because texts are the primary sources of data used in humanistic research, it's important for those who work in the humanities to examine how a text conveys meaning to its audience. This kind of work—observing a text critically to analyze what it means and how it conveys meaning—is what we call close reading.

Insider Example
Professional Close Reading

In the following example of a close reading of a text, Dale Jacobs discusses how he constructs meaning from comics. He argues that comics are more complicated to interpret than texts composed only of words (e.g., a novel or short story) because graphic novel readers must also interpret visual, gestural, and spatial language at work in the panels. In doing so, Jacobs offers his own observation. Furthermore, he concludes his interpretation by calling on instructors to challenge students to think critically about how they construct meaning from texts. As you read his article, you might reflect on this question: When reading a text, how do you make meaning?

More Than Words: Comics as a Means of Teaching Multiple Literacies

DALE JACOBS

Over the last several years, comics have been an ever more visible and well-regarded part of mainstream culture. Comics are now reviewed in major newspapers and featured on the shelves of independent and chain bookstores. Major publishing houses such as Pantheon publish work in the comics medium, including books such as Marjane Satrapi's *Persepolis* and David B.'s *Epileptic*. Educational publishers such as Scholastic are also getting in on the act; in January 2005, Scholastic launched its own graphic novels imprint, Graphix, with the publication of Jeff Smith's highly acclaimed Bone series. At the NCTE [National Council of Teachers of English] Annual Convention, graphic novels and comics are displayed in ever greater numbers. School and public libraries are building graphic novels collections to try to get adolescents into the library. Comics have, indeed, emerged from the margins into the mainstream.

With all this activity and discussion surrounding comics, it is timely to consider how we as literacy teachers might think about the practice of using comics in our classrooms and how this practice fits into ongoing debates about comics and literacy. In examining these links between theory and practice, I wish to move beyond seeing the reading of comics as a debased or simplified word-based literacy. Instead, I want to advance two ideas: (1) reading comics involves a complex, multimodal literacy; and (2) by using comics in our classrooms, we can help students develop as critical and engaged readers of multimodal texts.

THE HISTORY OF ATTITUDES TOWARD COMICS AND LITERACY

Prior to their current renaissance, comics were often viewed, at best, as popular entertainment and, at worst, as a dangerous influence on youth. Such attitudes were certainly prevalent in the early 1950s when comics were at their most popular, with critics such as Fredric Wertham voicing the most strenuous arguments against comics in his 1954 book *Seduction of the Innocent* (for an extended discussion of this debate, see Dorrell, Curtis, and Rampal). Wertham baldly asserts that "[c]omic books are death on reading" (121). He goes on, "Reading troubles in children are on the increase. An important cause of this increase is the comic book. A very large proportion of children who cannot read well habitually read comic books. They are not really readers, but gaze mostly at the pictures, picking up a word here and there. Among the worst readers is a very high percentage of comic-book addicts who spend very much time 'reading' comic books. They are book-worms without books" (122). According to this thinking, children who read comic books are not really reading; they are simply looking at the pictures as a way to avoid engaging in the complex processes of learning to read. The problem, according to Wertham, is that in reading comics children focus far too much on the image to make meaning and avoid engaging with the written word, a semiotic system that Wertham clearly sees as both more complex and more important. Though he sees the visuality of comics as dangerous, Wertham shares the notion with current proponents of comics that the visual is more easily ingested and interpreted than the written. Whether the visual acts as a hindrance or a help to the acquisition of word-based literacy, the key idea remains that the visual is subservient to the written.

When I was growing up in the 1970s, I never saw comics in school or in the public library unless they were being read surreptitiously behind the cover of a novel or other officially sanctioned book. Over the last decade, however, there has been a movement to claim a value for comics in the literacy education of children. Comics have made their way into schools mainly as a scaffold for later learning that is perceived to be more difficult, in terms of both the literate practices and content involved. For example, *Comics in Education*, the online version of Gene Yang's final project for his master's degree at California State

University, Hayward, embodies thinking that is typical of many educators who advocate the use of comics in the classroom. Yang, a teacher and cartoonist, claims that the educational strength of comics is that they are motivating, visual, permanent, intermediary, and popular. In emphasizing the motivational, visual permanency (in the way it slows down the flow of information), intermediacy, and the popular, such approaches inadvertently and ironically align themselves with Wertham's ideas about the relationship between word and image, even while bringing comics into the mainstream of education. Comics in this formulation are seen simply as a stepping stone to the acquisition of other, higher skills. As a teaching tool, then, comics are seen primarily as a way to motivate through their popularity and to help slow-learning students, especially in the acquisition of reading skills (see Haugaard; Koenke). While I agree with these attempts to argue for the value of comics in education, such an approach has limited value.

Libraries have also been important in the reconsideration of the place of comics as appropriate texts for children in their literacy learning and acquisition. Recently, many librarians have been arguing for the introduction of comics into library collections, usually in the form of graphic novels, as a way to get children into the library and interested in reading. The main thrust of this argument is that the presence of graphic novels will make the library seem cool and interesting, especially among the so-called reluctant readers, mainly adolescent boys, who seem to show little interest in reading or in libraries (see Crawford; Simmons). Graphic novels can compete with video games, television, and movies, giving the library the advantage it needs to get this specifically targeted demographic through the door. Many public libraries and librarians have seen the power of comics and graphic novels as a tool for drawing young people into the library, getting them first to read those comics and then building on that scaffold to turn them into lifelong readers. Again, while I agree with the inclusion of comics and graphic novels in library collections, such an approach places severe limitations on the possibilities of our uses of the medium as literacy educators.

To think through these ideas, let's assume that this strategy has some of its desired effects in drawing reluctant readers into the library and coaxing them to read. What can we then say about the effects of this approach and its conception of comics and their relation to developing literate practices? On the one hand, the use of graphic novels is seen as one strategy in teaching and encouraging literacy and literate practices; on the other hand, graphic novels are still regarded as a way station on the road to "higher" forms of literacy and to more challenging and, by implication, worthwhile texts. I'm not trying to suggest that reading comics or graphic novels exists apart from the world of word-based texts as a whole or the complex matrix of literacy acquisition. Rather, I'm simply pointing out that in the development of children's and adolescents' literacies, reading comics has almost always been seen as a debased form of word-based literacy, albeit an important intermediate step to more advanced forms of textual literacy, rather than as a complex form of multimodal literacy.

COMICS AS MULTIMODAL LITERACY: THE THEORY

If we think about comics as multimodal texts that involve multiple kinds of meaning making, we do not give up the benefits of word-based literacy instruction but strengthen it through the inclusion of visual and other literacies. This complex view of literacy is touched on but never fully fleshed out in two excellent recent articles on comics and education: Rocco Versaci's "How Comic Books Can Change the Way Our Students See Literature: One Teacher's Perspective" and Bonny Norton's "The Motivating Power of Comic Books: Insights from Archie Comic Readers." By situating our thinking about comics, literacy, and education within a framework that views literacy as occurring in multiple modes, we can use comics to greater effectiveness in our teaching at all levels by helping us to arm students with the critical-literacy skills they need to negotiate diverse systems of meaning making.

I'm going to offer an example of how comics engage multiple literacies by looking at Ted Naifeh's *Polly and the Pirates*, but first let me give a brief outline of these multiple systems of meaning making. As texts, comics provide a complex environment for the negotiation of meaning, beginning with the layout of the page itself. The comics page is separated into multiple panels, divided from each other by gutters, physical or conceptual spaces through which connections are made and meanings are negotiated; readers must fill in the blanks within these gutters and make connections between panels. Images of people, objects, animals, and settings, word balloons, lettering, sound effects, and gutters all come together to form page layouts that work to create meaning in distinctive ways and in multiple realms of meaning making. In these multiple realms of meaning making, comics engage in what the New London Group of literacy scholars calls *multimodality*, a way of thinking that seeks to push literacy educators, broadly defined and at all levels of teaching, to think about literacy in ways that move beyond a focus on strictly word-based literacy. In the introduction to the New London Group's collection, *Multiliteracies: Literacy Learning and the Design of Social Futures*, Bill Cope and Mary Kalantzis write that their approach "relates to the increasing multiplicity and integration of significant modes of meaning-making, where the textual is also related to the visual, the audio, the spatial, the behavioural, and so on.... Meaning is made in ways that are increasingly multimodal—in which written-linguistic modes of meaning are part and parcel of visual, audio, and spatial patterns of meaning" (5). By embracing the idea of multimodal literacy in relation to comics, then, we can help students engage critically with ways of making meaning that exist all around them, since multimodal texts include much of the content on the Internet, interactive multimedia, newspapers, television, film, instructional textbooks, and many other texts in our contemporary society.

Such a multimodal approach to reading and writing asserts that in engaging with texts, we interact with up to six design elements, including linguistic, audio, visual, gestural, and spatial modes, as well as multimodal design, "of a different order to the others as it represents the patterns of interconnections among the other modes" (New London Group 25). In the first two pages from *Polly and the Pirates*, all of these design elements are present, including a textual and visual representation of the audio element. Despite the existence of these multiple modes of meaning making, however, the focus in thinking about the relationship between comics and education is almost always on the linguistic element, represented here by the words in the words balloons (or, in the conventions of comics, the dialogue from each of the characters) and the narrative text boxes in the first three panels (which we later find out are also spoken dialogue by a narrator present in the story).

As discussed earlier, comics are seen as a simplified version of word-based texts, with the words supplemented and made easier to understand by the pictures. If we take a multimodal approach to texts such as comics, however, the picture of meaning making becomes much more complex. In word-based texts, our interaction with words forms an environment for meaning making that is extremely complex. In comics and other multimodal texts, there are five other elements added to the mix. Thought about in this way, comics are not just simpler versions of word-based texts but can be viewed as the complex textual environments that they are.

COMICS AS MULTIMODAL LITERACY: *POLLY AND THE PIRATES* IN THE CLASSROOM

In comics, there are elements present besides words, but these elements are just as important in making meaning from the text. In fact, it is impossible to make full sense of the words on the page in isolation from the audio, visual, gestural, and spatial. For example, the first page of *Polly and the Pirates* (the first issue of a six-issue miniseries) opens with three panels of words from what the reader takes to be the story's narrative voice. Why? Partially it is because of *what* the words say—how they introduce a character and begin to set up the story—but also it is because of the text boxes that enclose the words. That is, most people understand from their experiences of reading comics at some point in their history that words in text boxes almost always contain the story's narrative voice and denote a different kind of voice than do words in dialogue balloons. What's more, these text boxes deviate in shape and design from the even rectangles usually seen in comics; instead, they are depicted more like scrolls, a visual element that calls to mind both the time period and genre associated with pirates. Not only does this visual element help to place the reader temporally and generically, but it, along with lettering and punctuation, also aids in indicating tone, voice inflection, cadence, and emotional tenor by giving visual representation to the text's audio element. We are better able to "hear" the narrator's voice because we can see what words are emphasized by the bold lettering, and we associate particular kinds of voices with the narrative voice of a pirate's tale, especially emphasized here by the shape of the text boxes. Both the visual and the audio thus influence the way we read the words in a comic, as can be seen in these three opening panels.

It seems to me, however, that the key lies in going beyond the way we make meaning from the words alone and considering the other visual elements, as well as the gestural and spatial. If I were teaching this text, I would engage students in a discussion about how they understand what is going on in the story and how they make meaning from it. Depending on the level of the class, I would stress different elements at varying levels of complexity. Here I will offer an example of how I make meaning from these pages and of some of the elements I might discuss with students.

In talking about the visual, I would consider such things as the use of line and white space, shading, perspective, distance, depth of field, and composition. The gestural refers to facial expression and body posture, while the spatial refers to the meanings of environmental and architectural space, which, in the case of comics, can be conceived as the layout of panels on the page and the relation between these panels through use of gutter space. The opening panel depicts a ship, mainly in silhouette, sailing on the ocean; we are not given details, but instead see the looming presence of a ship that we are led to believe is a pirate ship by the words in the text boxes. The ship is in the center of an unbordered panel and is the only element in focus, though its details are obscured. The unbordered panel indicates openness, literally and metaphorically, and this opening shot thus acts much in the same way as an establishing shot in a film, orienting us both in terms of place and in terms of genre. The second panel pulls in closer to reveal a silhouetted figure standing on the deck of the ship. She is framed between the sails, and the panel's composition draws our eyes toward her as the central figure in the frame. She is clearly at home, one arm thrust forward while the other points back with sword in hand, her legs anchoring herself securely as she gazes across the ocean. The third panel pulls in even farther to a close-up of her face, the top half in shadow and the bottom half showing a slight smile. She is framed by her sword on the left and the riggings of the ship on the right, perfectly in her element, yet obscured from our view. Here and in the previous panel, gestural and visual design indicate who is the center of the story and the way in which she confidently belongs in this setting. At the same time, the spatial layout of the page and the progression of the panels from establishing shot to close-up and from unbordered panels to bordered and internally framed panels help us to establish the relationship of the woman to the ship and to the story; as we move from one panel to the next, we must make connections between the panels that are implied by the gutter. Linguistic, visual, audio, gestural, and spatial elements combine in these first three panels to set up expectations in the reader for the type of story and its narrative approach. Taken together, these elements form a multimodal system of meaning making.

What happens in the fourth panel serves to undercut these expectations as we find out that the narrative voice actually belongs to one of the

characters in the story, as evidenced by the shift from text box to dialogue balloon even though the voice is clearly the same as in the first three panels of the page. Spatially, we are presented with a larger panel that is visually dominated by the presence of a book called *A History of the Pirate Queen*. This book presumably details the story to which we had been introduced in the first three panels. The character holding the book is presenting it to someone and, because of the panel's composition, is also effectively presenting it to us, the readers. The gesture becomes one of offering this story up to us, a story that simultaneously becomes a romance as well as a pirate story as evidenced by the words the character says and the way she says them (with the bold emphasis on *dream* and *marry*). At this point, we do not know who this character is or to whom she is speaking, and the answers to these questions will be deferred until we turn to the second page.

On the first panel of page 2, we see three girls, each taking up about a third of the panel, with them and the background in focused detail. Both the words and facial expression of the first girl indicate her stance toward the story, while the words and facial expression of the second girl indicate her indignation at the attitude of the first girl (whom we learn is named Sarah). The third girl is looking to the right, away from the other two, and has a blank expression on her face. The next panel depicts the second and third girls, pulling in to a tighter close-up that balances one girl on either side of the panel and obscures the background so that we will focus on their faces and dialogue. The unbordered panel again indicates openness and momentary detachment from their surroundings. Polly is at a loss for words and is not paying attention to the other girl, as indicated by the ellipses and truncated dialogue balloons, as well as her eyes that are pointing to the right, away from the other girl. Spatially, the transition to panel 3 once more encloses them in the world that we now see is a classroom in an overhead shot that places the students in relation to the teacher. The teacher's words restore order to the class and, on a narrative level, name the third of the three girls and the narrative voice of the opening page. The story of the pirates that began on page 1 is now contained within the world of school, and we are left to wonder how the tensions between these two stories/worlds will play out in the remaining pages. As you can see, much more than words alone is used to make meaning in these first two pages of *Polly and the Pirates*.

CONCLUSION

My process of making meaning from these pages of *Polly and the Pirates* is one of many meanings within the matrix of possibilities inherent in the text. As a reader, I am actively engaging with the "grammars," including discourse and genre conventions, within this multimodal text as I seek to create/negotiate meaning; such a theory of meaning making with multimodal texts acknowledges the social and semiotic structures that surround us and within which we exist, while at the same time it recognizes individual agency and experience in the creation of meaning. Knowledge of linguistic, audio, visual, gestural, and spatial conventions within comics affects the ways in which we read and the meanings we assign to texts, just as knowledge of conventions within word-based literacy affects the ways in which those texts are read. For example, the conventions discussed above in terms of the grammar of comics would have been available to Naifeh as he created *Polly and the Pirates*, just as they are also available to me and to all other readers of his text. These conventions form the underlying structure of the process of making meaning, while familiarity with these conventions, practice in reading comics, interest, prior experience, and attention given to that reading all come into play in the exercise of agency on the part of the reader (and writer). Structure and agency interact so that we are influenced by design conventions and grammars as we read but are not determined by them; though we are subject to the same set of grammars, my reading of the text is not necessarily the same as that of someone else.

Reading and writing multimodal texts, then, is an active process, both for creators and for readers who by necessity engage in the active production of meaning and who use all resources available to them based on their familiarity with the comics medium and its inherent grammars, their histories, life experiences, and interests. In turn, every act of creating meaning from a multimodal text, happening as it does at the intersection of structure and agency, contributes to the ongoing process of becoming a multimodally literate person. By teaching students to become conscious and critical of the ways in which they make meaning from multimodal texts such as comics, we can also teach students to become more literate with a wide range of multimodal texts. By complicating our view of comics so that we do not see them as simply an intermediary step to more complex word-based literacy, we can more effectively help students become active creators, rather than passive consumers, of meaning in their interactions with a wide variety of multimodal texts. In doing so, we harness the real power of comics in the classroom and prepare students for better negotiating their worlds of meaning.

WORKS CITED

B., David. *Epileptic*. New York: Pantheon, 2005.

Cope, Bill, and Mary Kalantzis. "Introduction: Multiliteracies: The Beginnings of an Idea." *Multiliteracies: Literacy Learning and the Design of Social Futures*. Ed. Bill Cope and Mary Kalantzis. New York: Routledge, 2000. 3–8.

Crawford, Philip. "A Novel Approach: Using Graphic Novels to Attract Reluctant Readers." *Library Media Connection* 22.5 (Feb. 2004): 26–28.

Dorrell, Larry D., Dan B. Curtis, and Kuldip R. Rampal. "Book-Worms without Books? Students Reading Comic Books in the School House." *Journal of Popular Culture* 29 (Fall 1995): 223–34.

Haugaard, Kay. "Comic Books: Conduits to Culture?" *The Reading Teacher* 27.1 (Oct. 1973): 54–55.

Koenke, Karl. "The Careful Use of Comic Books." *The Reading Teacher* 34.5 (Feb. 1981): 592–95.

McCloud, Scott. *Understanding Comics: The Invisible Art*. New York: Harper, 1993.

Naifeh, Ted. *Polly and the Pirates* 1 (Sept. 2005): 1–2.

New London Group, The. "A Pedagogy of Multiliteracies: Designing Social Futures." *Multiliteracies: Literacy Learning and the Design of Social Futures*. Ed. Bill Cope and Mary Kalantzis. New York: Routledge, 2000. 9–37.

Norton, Bonny. "The Motivating Power of Comic Books: Insights from Archie Comic Readers." *The Reading Teacher* 57.2 (Oct. 2003): 140–47.

Satrapi, Marjane. *Persepolis*. New York: Pantheon, 2003.

Simmons, Tabitha. "Comic Books in My Library?" *PNLA Quarterly* 67.3 (Spring 2003): 12, 20.

Versaci, Rocco. "How Comic Books Can Change the Way Our Students See Literature: One Teacher's Perspective." *English Journal* 91.2 (Mar. 2001): 61–67.

Wertham, Fredric. *Seduction of the Innocent*. New York: Rinehart, 1954.

Yang, Gene. *Comics in Education*. 2003. 29 Aug. 2006 <http://www.humblecomics.com/comicsedu/index.html>.

Discussion Questions

1. In your own words, describe how Jacobs constructs meaning from the comics panels analyzed in this article.

2. What do you think he means by the phrase *multimodal text*?

3. Study one of the comics panels for a minute, and consider how you make meaning from it. Freewrite for five minutes about your own process for making sense of what the comic means.

4. Freewrite for five minutes discussing something you were asked to interpret in the past: perhaps a painting, a novel, a poem, or something else. How did you make meaning of what you were observing and interpreting?

STRATEGIES FOR CLOSE READING AND OBSERVATION

For most of us, when we observe a printed text closely, we highlight, underline, and take notes in the margins. If we're analyzing a visual or aural text, we might take notes on our thoughts, observations, and questions. We might keep a separate notebook or computer file in which we expand on our notes or clarify meaning. As with any skill, the more you practice these steps, the better you'll become at interpretation. We encourage you to take detailed notes, underline passages if applicable, and actively engage with a text when conducting your observation.

We recommend two specific data-collection steps for humanistic inquiry. First, we suggest that you take notes in the margins for a printed text or on a separate sheet of paper as you read, view, or listen to a text to be interpreted. These notes will draw your attention to passages that may serve as direct evidence to support points you'll make later. Additionally, you can elaborate in more detail when something meaningful in the text draws your attention. Jotting down page numbers, audio/video file time markers, and paragraph numbers is often a helpful step for cataloging your notes. The key is to commit fully to engaging with a text by systematically recording your observations.

Second, we recommend developing a **content/form-response grid** to organize the essential stages of your interpretation. The "content" is what happens in the text, and the "form" is how the text's creator structures the piece. In the case of a painting, you might comment on the materials used, the artist's technique, the color palette and imagery choice, or the historical context of the piece. In the case of a religious or political text, you might examine style, language, and literary devices used. The "response" is your interpretation of what the elements you've identified might mean.

Now read the opening paragraphs from "The Story of an Hour," a very brief short story by Kate Chopin published in 1894 that is now recognized as a classic work of American literature. The excerpt includes a student's notes in the margins followed by a content/form-response grid. Notice the frequency of notes the student takes in the margins and the kinds of questions she asks at this early stage. She offers a fairly equal balance of questions and claims. Pay attention to how she follows the two steps of humanistic inquiry mentioned above:

1. Examine the text and take careful notes. Try keeping marginal notes (if appropriate) and/or a separate notebook or sheets of paper to expand on your notes.

2. Complete a content/form-response grid based on the notes you collect.

Excerpt from **The Story of an Hour**

KATE CHOPIN

Knowing that Mrs. Mallard was afflicted with a heart trouble, great care was taken to break to her as gently as possible the news of her husband's death. It was her sister Josephine who told her, in broken sentences; veiled hints that revealed in half concealing. Her husband's friend Richards was there, too, near her. It was he who had been in the newspaper office when intelligence of the railroad disaster was received, with Brently Mallard's name leading the list of "killed." He had only taken the time to assure himself of its truth by a second telegram, and had hastened to forestall any less careful, less tender friend in bearing the sad message.

Heart trouble? I wonder what kind of trouble.

The news of her husband's death is delivered by her sister.

She did not hear the story as many women have heard the same, with a paralyzed inability to accept its significance. She wept at once, with sudden, wild abandonment, in her sister's arms. When the storm of grief had spent itself she went away to her room alone. She would have no one follow her.

Why would she act differently from other women hearing the same kind of news?

Interesting comparison. The storm-like quality of her grief.

There stood, facing the open window, a comfortable, roomy armchair. Into this she sank, pressed down by a physical exhaustion that haunted her body and seemed to reach into her soul.

Why is she "exhausted"? Interesting word choice.

She could see in the open square before her house the tops of trees that were all aquiver with the new spring life. The delicious breath of rain was in the air. In the street below a peddler was crying his wares. The notes of a distant song which some one was singing reached her faintly, and countless sparrows were twittering in the eaves.

There are lots of images of life here. This really contrasts with the dark news of the story's opening.

This student's annotations can be placed into a content/form-response grid that helps her keep track of the ideas she had as she read and observed closely, both for information (*what*) and for ways the text shaped her experience of it (*how*). Notice that the student uses the Content/Form section to summarize the comments from her annotations, and then she reflects on her annotations in the Response section:

Content/Form Notes (*what* and *how*)	Response (What effect does it have on me?)
Heart trouble? I wonder what kind of trouble.	*There's a mystery here. What's wrong with Mrs. Mallard's heart?*
The news of her husband's death is delivered by her sister.	*Interesting that a female relative is chosen to deliver the news. A man would be too rough?*
Why would she act differently from other women hearing the same kind of news?	*I wonder what is special about Mrs. Mallard that causes her reaction to be different. Is she putting on a show? Story says her reaction was "sudden" and "wild."*
Why is she "exhausted"? Interesting word choice.	*Maybe this has to do with her heart condition or with how physically draining her mourning is.*
There are lots of images of life here. This really contrasts with the dark news of the story's opening.	*This is a sudden change in feeling. Everything is so calm and pleasant now. What happened?*

The purpose of this activity is to construct meaning from the text based on the student's close observation of it. This is an interpretation. We can already see that major complexities in the story are beginning to emerge in the student's response notes—such as the importance of the story's setting and the change that occurs in Mrs. Mallard.

Because content/form-response grids like the one above allow you to visualize both your ideas and how you arrived at those ideas, we recommend using this activity any time you have to observe a text closely in order to interpret its meaning. For a non-alphabetic text, start with the content/form-response grid and use it to log your initial notes as you observe; then reflect later. In the end, such an activity provides a log of details that can help explain how you arrived at a particular conclusion or argument about the text.

INSIDE WORK **Annotating a Text**

Use this activity as an opportunity to practice close reading. Read the whole text of Kate Chopin's "The Story of an Hour" on pages 157–59, and then annotate the text as you read, paying particular attention to the following elements.

- **Content:** what is being said (the facts, the events, and who the characters are)
- **Form:** how it is being said (the style, language, literary techniques, and narrative perspective)

A follow-up activity at the conclusion of the story asks you to draw a content/ form-response grid like the example above. It's important to take extensive marginal notes (perhaps one or two comments per paragraph) and highlight and underline passages as you read the story. These notes will help shape your content/form-response grid and will strengthen your interpretation. We encourage you to expand on your notes on a separate sheet of paper while you read the story. ◗

The Story of an Hour

KATE CHOPIN

Knowing that Mrs. Mallard was afflicted with a heart trouble, great care was taken to break to her as gently as possible the news of her husband's death.

It was her sister Josephine who told her, in broken sentences; veiled hints that revealed in half concealing. Her husband's friend Richards was there, too, near her. It was he who had been in the newspaper office when intelligence of the railroad disaster was received, with Brently Mallard's name leading the list of "killed." He had only taken the time to assure himself of its truth by a second telegram, and had hastened to forestall any less careful, less tender friend in bearing the sad message.

She did not hear the story as many women have heard the same, with a paralyzed inability to accept its significance. She wept at once, with sudden, wild abandonment, in her sister's arms. When the storm of grief had spent itself she went away to her room alone. She would have no one follow her.

There stood, facing the open window, a comfortable, roomy armchair. Into this she sank, pressed down by a physical exhaustion that haunted her body and seemed to reach into her soul.

She could see in the open square before her house the tops of trees that were all aquiver with the new spring life. The delicious breath of rain was in the air. In the street below a peddler was crying his wares. The notes of a distant song which some one was singing reached her faintly, and countless sparrows were twittering in the eaves.

There were patches of blue sky showing here and there through the clouds that had met and piled one above the other in the west facing her window.

She sat with her head thrown back upon the cushion of the chair, quite motionless, except when a sob came up into her throat and shook her, as a child who has cried itself to sleep continues to sob in its dreams.

She was young, with a fair, calm face, whose lines bespoke repression and even a certain strength. But now there was a dull stare in her eyes, whose gaze was fixed away off yonder on one of those patches of blue sky. It was not a glance of reflection, but rather indicated a suspension of intelligent thought.

There was something coming to her and she was waiting for it, fearfully. What was it? She did not know; it was too subtle and elusive to name. But she felt it, creeping out of the sky, reaching toward her through the sounds, the scents, the color that filled the air.

Now her bosom rose and fell tumultuously. She was beginning to recognize this thing that was approaching to possess her, and she was striving to beat it back with her will—as powerless as her two white slender hands would have been.

When she abandoned herself a little whispered word escaped her slightly parted lips. She said it over and over under her breath: "free, free, free!" The vacant stare and the look of terror that had followed it went from her eyes. They stayed keen and bright. Her pulses beat fast, and the coursing blood warmed and relaxed every inch of her body.

She did not stop to ask if it were or were not a monstrous joy that held her. A clear and exalted perception enabled her to dismiss the suggestion as trivial.

She knew that she would weep again when she saw the kind, tender hands folded in death; the face that had never looked save with love upon her, fixed and gray and dead. But she saw beyond that bitter moment a long procession of years to come that would belong to her absolutely. And she opened and spread her arms out to them in welcome.

There would be no one to live for during those coming years; she would live for herself. There would be no powerful will bending hers in that blind persistence with which men and women believe they have a right to impose a private will upon a fellow-creature. A kind intention or a cruel intention made the act seem no less a crime as she looked upon it in that brief moment of illumination.

And yet she had loved him—sometimes. Often she had not. What did it matter! What could love, the unsolved mystery, count for in face of this possession of self-assertion which she suddenly recognized as the strongest impulse of her being!

"Free! Body and soul free!" she kept whispering.

Josephine was kneeling before the closed door with her lips to the keyhole, imploring for admission. "Louise, open the door! I beg, open the door—you will make yourself ill. What are you doing, Louise? For heaven's sake open the door."

"Go away. I am not making myself ill." No; she was drinking in a very elixir of life through that open window.

Her fancy was running riot along those days ahead of her. Spring days, and summer days, and all sorts of days that would be her own. She breathed a quick prayer that life might be long. It was only yesterday she had thought with a shudder that life might be long.

She arose at length and opened the door to her sister's importunities. There was a feverish triumph in her eyes, and she carried herself unwittingly like a goddess of Victory. She clasped her sister's waist, and together they descended the stairs. Richards stood waiting for them at the bottom.

Some one was opening the front door with a latchkey. It was Brently Mallard who entered, a little travel-stained, composedly carrying his grip-sack and umbrella. He had been far from the scene of accident, and did not even know there had been one. He stood amazed at Josephine's piercing cry; at Richards' quick motion to screen him from the view of his wife.

But Richards was too late.

When the doctors came they said she had died of heart disease—of joy that kills.

INSIDE WORK · **Preparing a Content/Form-Response Grid**

Based on your annotations and notes, construct a content/form-response grid modeled after the example on page 156. Be sure to include your responses to the items you identify in the Content/Form column. Remember that in this case "content" relates to what happens in the story, and "form," in the context of a literary text, relates to how the writer makes the story function through style, narrative perspective, and literary techniques.

Once you've completed your close reading, you might pair up with a classmate or two and share your content/form-response grids. When doing so, consider the following questions as part of your discussion.

- What facts or events did you note about the story?
- What did you notice about the ways Chopin shapes your experience of the story? What style or literary techniques did you note?
- What patterns do you see in the notes you've taken in the Form column? What repeated comments did you make, or what elements strike you in a similar way? How would you explain the meaning of those patterns? ▶

RESPONDING TO THE INTERPRETATIONS OF OTHERS

Before, during, and after observing a text, humanistic scholars also draw on the work of other scholars to build and support their interpretations. If you were interpreting Chopin's story, for example, you might review the notes you made in your content/form-response grid, search for interesting patterns, and then see if other scholars have noticed the same things. You might look for an element of the story that doesn't make sense to you and see if another scholar has

LaunchPad

Learn more about incorporating sources into your writing.

already offered an interpretation. If you agree with the interpretation, you might cite it as support for your own argument. If you disagree, you might look for evidence in the story to show why you disagree and then offer your own interpretation.

As in other disciplines, scholars in the humanities draw on the work of others to make sure they're contributing something new to the ongoing conversation about the artifact, event, or phenomenon they're studying. They also read the work of others to determine if they agree or disagree with an interpretation. Because of the importance of specific language and detail in the humanities, scholars in the humanities often quote one another's exact words, and they also quote directly from their primary sources. We'll discuss some of the reasons for these conventions, and others, in the next section.

Conventions of Writing in the Humanities

Some writing conventions are shared across different fields in the humanities. Because the kinds of texts humanistic scholars examine can vary so much, though, there are also sometimes distinctions in writing conventions among its various fields. One of the challenges of learning the conventions of a disciplinary discourse community is figuring out the specific expectations for communicating with a specific academic audience. In this section, we turn our attention from *research in the humanities* to examine and interpret artifacts themselves, to *strategies of rhetorical analysis* that help us examine how scholars in the humanities write about those artifacts.

Many scholars learn about disciplinary writing conventions through imitation and examination of articles in their fields. Recall that in Chapter 6 we introduced a three-part method for analyzing texts by examining the conventions of structure, language, and reference. Applying this analytical framework to professional writing in the various humanities fields can help you further understand conventions appropriate for any given subfield. An awareness of the conventions for writing in any academic context may facilitate your success in writing in those contexts.

Shelley Garrigan teaches Spanish language and literature at North Carolina State University. As Garrigan describes in her Insider's View, scholars learn conventions of writing in their field through a variety of means, including learning from peers.

STRUCTURAL CONVENTIONS

From your experience in high school, you might already be familiar with common structural features of writing in the humanities. Arguments in the humanities are generally "thesis-driven"; that is, they make an interpretive claim about a text and then support that claim with specific evidence from the text and sometimes with material from other sources that support their interpretation. By contrast, arguments in the social sciences and the natural sciences are usually driven by a hypothesis that must be tested in order to come to a conclusion, which encourages a different structure (see Chapters 8 and 9). First we'll talk about how humanistic scholars develop research questions and thesis statements. Then we'll turn our attention to a common structure that many students learn in secondary school to support their thesis statements with evidence, which is loosely based on the structure of the thesis-driven argument, and we'll compare it with published scholarship in the humanities.

DEVELOPING RESEARCH QUESTIONS AND THESIS STATEMENTS

An important part of the interpretation process is using observations to pose questions about a text. From these close observations, humanists develop *research questions* that they answer through their research. A research question in the humanities is the primary question a scholar asks about a text or set of texts. It is the first step in interpretation because questions grow out of our observations and the patterns or threads that we notice. A *thesis statement* is an answer to a research question and is most persuasive when supported by logical evidence. Thesis statements are discussed in more detail in

Insider's View
The research is going to support your own ideas
KAREN KEATON JACKSON, WRITING STUDIES

"When we talk about what the paper should look like, I let them know that the research part of your paper is not the longest part. I always say the longest part of your paper is this brainchild, your program that you're coming up with. And I say that purposely because I don't want the research running your paper. This is your paper, your voice. The research is going to support your own ideas.

"I think this sends the message that there's more to it than this; you can be more creative and not just rely on the research."

LaunchPad

Get expert advice on incorporating research.

Chapter 4 as the central claim of an argument. It's important to note that developing a research question works best when it is generated prior to writing a thesis statement. Novice writers can sometimes overlook this crucial step in the writing process and attempt to make a thesis statement without formulating a well-realized research question first.

As John McCurdy mentions earlier in this chapter, some of the most important questions for humanists begin by asking, "Why?" Why does George befriend Lenny in *Of Mice and Men*? Why did Pablo Picasso begin experimenting with cubism in his paintings in the early 1900s? Why did President Lincoln frequently use religious imagery and language in public discourse? To answer such questions, humanistic scholars must collect evidence to support their claims, and in the humanities, evidence often originates from texts.

Many students confess to struggling with the process of writing a good thesis statement. A key to overcoming this hurdle is to realize that a good thesis statement comes first from asking thoughtful questions about a text and searching for answers to those questions through observation.

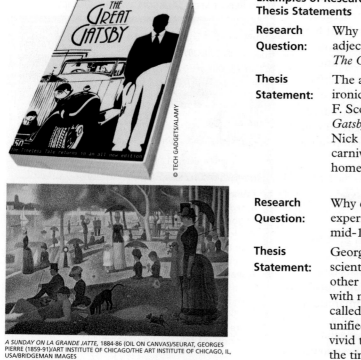

© TECH GADGETS/ALAMY

A SUNDAY ON LA GRANDE JATTE, 1884-86 (OIL ON CANVAS)/SEURAT, GEORGES PIERRE (1859-91)/ART INSTITUTE OF CHICAGO/THE ART INSTITUTE OF CHICAGO, IL, USA/BRIDGEMAN IMAGES

Examples of Research Questions and Corresponding Thesis Statements

Research Question: Why does F. Scott Fitzgerald use the adjective *great* to describe Gatsby in *The Great Gatsby*?

Thesis Statement: The adjective *great* is used both ironically and derisively throughout F. Scott Fitzgerald's novel *The Great Gatsby*, as evidenced by the use of Nick Carraway as the narrator and the carnival-like depictions of Gatsby's home and parties.

Research Question: Why did Georges-Pierre Seurat experiment with pointillism in the mid-1800s?

Thesis Statement: Georges-Pierre Seurat drew upon the scientific research of Ogden Rood and other color theorists to create paintings with minute brushstrokes in a style now called pointillism, which Seurat believed unified optically to make colors more vivid than in traditional painting styles of the time.

Once you have carefully observed a text, gathered thorough notes, and developed a content/form-response grid as discussed earlier in the chapter, you're in a great position to begin brainstorming and drafting research questions. We encourage open-ended questions (*who, what, when, where, why,* and *how*) as opposed to closed questions (questions that can be answered with a *yes* or *no*) as a pivotal step before drafting a thesis statement. Scholars in the humanities often start by asking questions that begin with *why,* but you might also consider questions of *what* and *how.*

INSIDE WORK Developing *Why, What,* and *How* Questions

The process of asking questions after conducting a close reading of a text is part of interpretation, and it can help you generate effective research questions to guide the development of a thesis. In this activity, we walk you through developing research questions from your notes on "The Story of an Hour." You could easily follow these steps after observing another kind of text as well.

1. Review your notes on "The Story of an Hour," and develop three questions about the story's content and form using *Why* as a starter word.

2. Next, develop three questions using *What* as your starter word. Try to focus your questions on different aspects of the story's characters, language, style, literary techniques, or narrative perspective.

3. Then use *How* as a starter word to develop three more questions. Again, write your questions with a different aspect of the story as the central focus for each. That is, don't just repeat the same questions from your *What* or *Why* list, inserting *How* instead. Think of different questions that can help address the story's meaning.

Try sharing your questions with a fellow student, and discuss which ones might lead to promising thesis statements to ground an extended interpretation. Effective research questions have the following characteristics:

- They can be answered with specific evidence from the text and from your notes: an effective research question can be answered with evidence and not just feelings or opinions.

- They can be answered in more than one way (i.e., they might require you to make a claim as opposed to being questions of fact): an effective research question is debatable. ▶

DEVELOPING EFFECTIVE THESIS STATEMENTS

The thesis statement, or the central claim, asserts *what* the author intends to prove, and it may also provide insight into *how* it will be proven. Providing both of these elements in a thesis allows writers to establish a blueprint for the structure of their entire argument—what we describe as a complex thesis statement in Chapter 4. Based on the thesis alone, a reader can determine the central claim and see how the writer intends to go about supporting it.

In the following example, Sarah Ray provides a thesis for her interpretation of Chopin's "The Story of an Hour." Notice that she includes clues as to how she will prove her claim in the thesis statement itself:

Blueprint for how Sarah will prove her claim

Sarah's interpretation of the story, provided as a clear claim

Through Mrs. Mallard's emotional development and the concomitant juxta-position of the vitality of nature to the repressive indoors, Chopin exposes the role of marriage in the oppression of one's true self and desires.

Although it's not uncommon for thesis statements in humanistic scholarship to remain implied, as opposed to being stated explicitly, most interpretations explicitly assert a claim close to the beginning of the argument, often in the introductory paragraph (or, in a longer piece, paragraphs). Thesis statements may appear as single-sentence statements or may span multiple sentences.

Notice, for example, how Zenia Kish, a professor of American studies, states her claim at the end of the introductory section to her article "'My FEMA People': Hip-Hop as Disaster Recovery in the Katrina Diaspora." In the full text of the article, Kish builds up to this statement through several paragraphs of explanation, which all contribute to her thesis statement, shown here:

Blueprint for how Kish will prove her claim

Reasons provided for Kish's claim

Clear statement of Kish's claim

I will examine how both national and local New Orleans artists identify with and rebel against the forces of marginalization that produced different senses of being a refugee, and also how they exploit marginality and the hustle as strategies to return home, however different or new that home may be. Providing listeners with an affective mapping of the social, economic, and discursive contradictions that produced the Katrina diaspora as refugees, post-Katrina hip-hop is a critical site for interrogating the ongoing tragedy of African American bodies that don't matter. (p. 673)

INSIDE WORK **Drafting Thesis Statements**

Review the questions and responses you drafted in the "Developing *Why, What,* and *How* Questions" Inside Work activity. Some scholars use "I" in thesis statements, like the example from Zenia Kish, while others avoid using "I." Make sure you pay attention to requirements for the particular type of writing you're doing in your discipline. (Don't hesitate to ask your professor if "I" statements are acceptable.) You can always edit the thesis statement later to take out "I" if needed, but sometimes it helps when figuring out what you want to say to include yourself in the statement. So, for now, consider structuring your responses to any three of your questions as separate thesis statements, using an "I" statement in the following form.

By examining _____ (a, b, c, etc.—the evidence you have found), I argue that _____ (your claim).

Example Thesis Statement: **By examining Mrs. Mallard's emotional development and the juxtaposition of the vitality of nature to the repressive indoors in the story, I argue that Chopin exposes the role of marriage in the story to show the oppression of a person's true self and desires.**

Now test the appropriateness of your claim by asking the following questions about it.

- **Is the thesis debatable?**   Claims in the humanities are propositions, not statements of fact. For example, the assertion that "The Story of an Hour" deals with a wife's response to the news of her husband's death is a fact. It is not, therefore, debatable and will not be a very useful thesis. If, however, we assert that the wife's response to her husband's death demonstrates some characteristic of her relationship with her husband and with the institution of marriage, then we're proposing a debatable claim. This is a proposition we can try to prove, instead of a fact that is already obviously true.

- **Is the thesis significant?**   Claims about texts should offer substantial insight into the meaning of the artifacts. They should account for as much of the artifacts as possible and avoid reducing their complexity. Have you paid attention to all of the evidence you collected, and have you looked at it in context? Are you considering all of the possible elements of the text that might contribute to your interpretation?

- **Does the thesis contribute to an ongoing scholarly conversation?**   Effective thesis statements contribute to an ongoing conversation without repeating what others have already said about the text. How does the claim extend, contradict, or affirm other interpretations of the text?

Once you've analyzed Chopin's story and constructed two separate thesis statements, consider sharing them with a classmate, identifying strengths and weaknesses in both. How is your claim both argumentative and significant? How many direct quotes from the story would help support your points? Which of the two thesis statements offers a more significant insight into the story's meaning? ❯

FIVE-PARAGRAPH ESSAYS AND OTHER THESIS-DRIVEN TEMPLATES

Many students learn to write academic arguments following a template taught in primary and secondary school as the **five-paragraph essay**. This template places a thesis, or claim, at the front of the argument (often at the end of an introductory paragraph), devotes the body of the essay to supporting the thesis, and then offers a final paragraph of conclusion that connects all the parts of the argument by summarizing the main points and reminding readers of the argument's overall significance.

 LaunchPad

See more on the transition into college writing.

While the premise behind this structure is based on some conventions of the humanities, following the template too closely could get you into trouble. Not every thesis has three points to prove, for example, giving you three body paragraphs in which to present evidence. And sometimes an introduction needs to be longer than one paragraph—as in the case of Zenia Kish's article "'My FEMA People': Hip-Hop as Disaster Recovery in the Katrina Diaspora," discussed below. The elements of the template that tend to be consistent in scholarship in the humanities, though, are these:

- Thesis statements generally appear toward the beginning of the argument in an introduction that explains the scope and importance of the topic.

- The body of the argument presents evidence gathered from the text to support the thesis.

- The conclusion connects the parts of the argument together to reinforce the thesis, summarizing the argument's important elements and reminding readers of its overall significance.

A template such as this one can provide a useful place to start as you organize your argument, but be careful not to allow a template to restrict your argument by oversimplifying your understanding of how humanistic scholars structure their writing.

OTHER STRUCTURAL CONVENTIONS IN THE HUMANITIES

There are other conventional structural features of writing in the humanities that you should consider when you begin a project in the discipline.

Title

Scholars in the humanities value the artistic and creative use of language, and titles of their work often reflect that value. In contrast to articles in the social sciences and the natural sciences, which often have descriptive titles that directly state the topic of study, articles in the humanities tend to have titles that play with language in creative ways, sometimes using quotations from the text in interesting ways. Humanistic scholars are also notorious for their love of subtitles. Here are a few examples:

- *Burlesque West: Showgirls, Sex, and Sin in Postwar Vancouver*
- "'The Fault of Being Purely French': The Practice and Theory of Landscape Painting in Post-Revolutionary France"
- "Reforming Bodies: Self-Governance, Anxiety, and Cape Colonial Architecture in South Africa, 1665–1860"
- "Resident Franchise: Theorizing the Science Fiction Genre, Conglomerations, and the Future of Synergy"

Paragraphs and Transitions

In arguments in the humanities, paragraphs tend to link back to the thesis by developing a reason and providing evidence. The paragraphs are often connected through **transitional words or phrases** (e.g., *similarly, in addition, in contrast, for example*) that guide readers by signaling shifts between and among the parts of an argument. These words and phrases help the reader understand the order in which the reasons are presented and how one paragraph connects to the preceding one.

LANGUAGE CONVENTIONS IN THE HUMANITIES

Writing in the humanities generally follows several conventions of language use that might sound familiar because they're often taught in English classes. Keep in mind, though, that even though these conventions are common in the humanities, they aren't necessarily conventional in other disciplinary areas.

Descriptive and Rhetorical Language

Writers in the humanities often use language that is creative or playful, not only when producing artistic texts but sometimes also when writing interpretations of texts. For example, you might notice that writing in the humanities uses figurative language and rhetorical devices (similes, metaphors, and alliteration, for example) more often than in other disciplines. Because writers in the humanities are studying texts so closely, they often pay similarly close attention to the text they're creating, and they take great care to choose precise, and sometimes artistic, language. In many cases, the language not only conveys information; it also engages in rhetorical activity of its own.

Active Voice

Writing in the humanities tends to privilege the use of the active voice rather than the passive voice. Sentences written in the **active voice** clearly state the subject of the sentence, the agent, as the person or thing doing the action. By contrast, the **passive voice** inverts the structure of the sentence, obscuring or eliminating mention of the agent. Let's look at three simple examples.

> **Active Voice:** The girl chased the dog.
>
> **Passive Voice (agent obscured):** The dog was chased by the girl.
>
> **Passive Voice (agent not mentioned):** The dog was chased.

In the first example, the girl is the subject of the sentence and the person (the agent) doing the action—chasing. In the second sentence, the girl is still there, but her presence is less prominent because the dog takes the subject's position at the beginning of the sentence. In the final sentence, the girl is not mentioned at all.

Now let's look at an example from a student paper in the humanities to understand why active voice is usually preferred. In her interpretation of "The Story of an Hour" (printed in full on pp. 174–80), Sarah Ray writes this sentence in the introduction, using active voice:

> **Active Voice:**   Kate Chopin presents a completely different view of marriage in "The Story of an Hour," published in 1894.

If Sarah were to write the sentence in the passive voice, eliminating the agent, it would look like this:

> **Passive Voice:**   A completely different view of marriage is presented in "The Story of an Hour," published in 1894.

In this case, the active voice is preferred because it gives credit to the author, Kate Chopin, who created the story and the character. Scholars in the humanities value giving credit to the person doing the action, conducting the study, or creating a text. Active voice also provides the clearest, most transparent meaning—another aspect of writing that is valued in the humanities.

Hedging

In the humanities, writers sometimes hedge the claims that they make when interpreting a text, even though they are generally quite fervent about defending their arguments once established. In fact, the sentence that you just read contains not one but three **hedges**, or qualifiers. Take a look:

> In the humanities, writers tend to hedge the claims that they make when interpreting a text.

Each highlighted phrase limits the scope of the claim in a way that is important to improve accuracy and to allow for other possibilities. In contrast, consider the next claim:

> Writers hedge the claims that they make.

If we had stated our claim that way, not only would it not be true, but you would immediately begin to think of exceptions. Even if we had limited the claim to writers in the humanities, you still might find exceptions to it. As the original sentence is written, we've allowed for other possibilities while still identifying a predominant trend in humanities writing.

Humanistic scholars hedge their claims for several reasons. The disciplines of the humanities don't tend to claim objectivity or neutrality in their research (for more detail, see Chapters 8 and 9), so they allow for other interpretations of and perspectives on texts. As an example, take a look at the first sentence of Dale Jacobs's Conclusion from his article printed earlier in the chapter:

> My process of making meaning from these pages of *Polly and the Pirates* is one of many meanings within the matrix of possibilities inherent in the text. (par. 16)

In this example, Jacobs not only hedges the interpretation he has offered, but he explicitly states that there are many possible meanings in the text he has just analyzed.

REFERENCE CONVENTIONS IN THE HUMANITIES

Scholars in the humanities frequently cite the work of others in their scholarship, especially when supporting an interpretation of a text. They often quote the language from their primary sources exactly instead of summarizing or paraphrasing, because the exact words or details included in the primary source might be important to the argument.

Engagement with Other Scholars

When humanistic scholars cite the work of other scholars, they show how their research contributes to ongoing conversations about a subject—whether they're agreeing with a previous interpretation, extending someone else's interpretation, or offering an alternative one. These citations can strengthen their own argument and provide direct support by showing that another scholar had a similar idea or by demonstrating how another scholar's ideas are incorrect, imprecise, or not fully developed.

As we mentioned in Chapter 5, you can integrate the work of others into your writing by paraphrasing, summarizing, or quoting directly. Scholars in the humanities use all these options, but they quote directly more often than scholars in other disciplines because the exact language or details from their primary sources are often important to their argument.

Take a look at this example from Zenia Kish's article "'My FEMA People': Hip-Hop as Disaster Recovery in the Katrina Diaspora," which originally appeared in the academic journal *American Quarterly*. She situates her argument about the message of hip-hop music after Hurricane Katrina within the work of another scholar, Hazel Carby, who had written about the cultural meaning of the blues. Although Carby was writing about a genre that preceded hip-hop, Kish makes a connection between Carby's interpretation of the blues and her own interpretation of the message of hip-hop at a particular point in history:

> Where the early blues served to "sp[ea]k the desires which were released in the dramatic shift in social relations that occurred in a historical moment of crisis and dislocation," as Hazel Carby observes (36), I would argue that the post-Katrina moment is the first time that mainstream American hip-hop has taken up the thematic of contemporary black migration as a mass phenomenon in any significant way. (p. 674)

Establishing Focus/Stance

Most scholars in the humanities include references to the work of others early in their writing to establish what the focus and stance of their own research will be. Because abstracts appear in humanities scholarship less frequently than in social sciences and natural sciences research, the introduction to an article in the humanities provides a snapshot of how the researcher is positioning himself or herself in the ongoing conversation about an object of study.

As you read scholarship in the humanities, notice how frequently the text references or cites secondary sources in the opening paragraphs. Look at this example from the second page of Dale Jacobs's article on teaching literacy through the use of comics, on page 145 of this chapter. Jacobs situates his work historically among work published about comics in the 1950s, and he also references the research of other scholars who had already written about that history in more detail:

> Prior to their current renaissance, comics were often viewed, at best, as popular entertainment and, at worst, as a dangerous influence on youth. Such attitudes were certainly prevalent in the early 1950s when comics were at their most popular, with critics such as Fredric Wertham voicing the most strenuous arguments against comics in his 1954 book *Seduction of the Innocent* (for an extended discussion of this debate, see Dorrell, Curtis, and Rampal). (par. 3)

In these two sentences, Jacobs positions his work within that of other scholars, showing how it's connected to and distinct from it. Also, by citing the work of Dorrell, Curtis, and Rampal, Jacobs doesn't have to write a lengthy history about a period that's tangentially related to his argument but not central to it.

DOCUMENTATION

A few documentation styles are prevalent in the humanities, and those styles tend to highlight elements of a source that are important in humanistic study. Many scholars in the humanities, especially in literature and languages, follow the documentation style of the Modern Language Association (MLA). Scholars in history and some other disciplines of the humanities follow the *Chicago Manual of Style* (CMS). When using CMS, scholars can choose between two systems of citations: the notes and bibliography system or the author-date system. In the humanities, researchers generally use the notes and bibliography system.

The values of the humanities are most prevalent in the in-text citations of both MLA and CMS. In MLA, in-text citations appear in parenthetical references that include the author's last name and a page number, with no comma in between (Miller-Cochran et al. 139). The page number is included regardless of whether the cited passage was paraphrased, summarized, or quoted—unlike in other common styles like APA, where page numbers are usually given only for direct quotations. One reason for including the page number in the MLA in-text citation is that humanistic scholars highly value the original phrasing of an argument or passage and might want to look at the original source. The page number makes searching easy for the reader, facilitating the possibility of examining the original context of a quotation or the original language of something that was paraphrased or summarized.

CMS style also supports looking for the information in the original source by giving the citation information in a footnote on the same page as the referenced material. Additionally, CMS allows authors to include descriptive details in a footnote that provides more information about where a citation came from in a source.

INSIDE WORK **Analyzing Scholarly Writing in the Humanities**

Answer the following questions about a scholarly article in the humanities. You might choose to focus on an article from Part 3 of this book or find another article on a topic that interests you more.

A. Structural Elements

- **Title**   Does the title of the interpretation seek to entertain, to challenge, or to impress the reader somehow? Does the title reveal anything about the writer and his or her relationship to the intended audience?

- **Thesis**   Can you identify a clear statement of thesis? Where is it located? Does the thesis preview the stages of the claim that will be discussed throughout the paper? In other words, does the thesis explicitly or implicitly provide a "blueprint" for guiding the reader through the rest of the paper? If so, what is it?

- **Paragraphs and Transitions**   Look closely at four successive body paragraphs in the paper. Explain how each paragraph relates to the paper's guiding thesis. How does the writer transition between each of the paragraphs such that his or her ideas in each one stay linked together?

B. Language Elements

- **Descriptive and Rhetorical Language**   Is the language of the text meant only to convey information, or does it engage in rhetorical activity? In other words, do similes, metaphors, or other rhetorical devices demonstrate attempts to be creative with language? If so, what are they?

- **Voice**   Is the voice of the text primarily active or passive?

- **Conviction and Hedging**   Is the writer convinced that his or her interpretation is correct? If so, in what way(s) does specific language convey that conviction? Alternatively, if the writer doesn't seem convinced of the certainty of his or her argument, is there evidence of hedging? That is, does the writer qualify statements with words and phrases such as *tend, suggest, may, it is probable that,* or *it is reasonable to conclude that*? What is the significance of hedging?

C. Reference Elements

- **Engagement with Other Scholars**   Choose two or three examples from the article showing the author's use of another scholar's words or ideas, if appropriate. Explain how the writer uses the words and ideas of another to support his or her own argument. Keep in mind that a writer may use another's words or ideas as direct support by showing that another scholar has the same or similar ideas, or by demonstrating how another scholar's ideas are incorrect, imprecise, or not fully developed. Also, does the writer use block quotations? Does he or she fully integrate others' words and ideas in his or her own sentences? Further, notice the writer's attitude toward other scholars: Does he or she treat other scholars' ideas fully and respectfully? Is there praise for others' ideas? Or are their ideas quickly dismissed? Is there any evidence of hostility in the writer's treatment of other voices?

- **Establishing Focus/Stance** How frequently does the text reference or cite secondary source materials in the opening paragraphs? What function do such citations or references serve in the article's overall organization?

- **Documentation** Look closely at examples of internal documentation as well as the writer's Works Cited or References page. What form of documentation applies? Why might the chosen documentation system be appropriate for writing about texts in the humanities? ❱

Insider's View
Academics often write for other academics

SHELLEY GARRIGAN, SPANISH LANGUAGE AND LITERATURE

COURTESY OF SHELLEY GARRIGAN

"I write academic articles and am currently editing a book-length manuscript. The articles that I have are peer-reviewed and published in academic journals, in which the readership is largely limited to other specialists in my field or in fields that touch upon what I study. Although the book has the possibility of inviting a wider range of readers, it is contracted with an academic press, and so the reading public that it may attract will most likely also be associated with or limited to academia."

Genres of Writing in the Humanities

The disciplines included under the umbrella of the humanities vary widely, but several genres occur frequently across disciplines. In her Insider's View response to interview questions, Shelley Garrigan, an associate professor of Spanish at North Carolina State University, describes the kind of academic writing that she does most frequently.

Similar to scholars in the social sciences and the natural sciences, scholars in the humanities often present their research at conferences and publish their work in journal articles and books. In some fields of the humanities, books are highly valued, and scholars here tend to work individually more frequently than scholars in the social sciences and the natural sciences. Also, many scholars in the humanities engage in creative work and might present it at an art installation, reading, or exhibit.

TEXTUAL INTERPRETATION

One of the primary genres that humanities researchers write is an interpretation of a text or set of texts. The research methods and activities outlined in this chapter provide support for interpretations of texts in a variety of fields in the humanities. A **textual interpretation** makes a clear claim about the object of study and then supports that claim with evidence from the text, and often with evidence drawn from the interpretations of other scholars.

Interpreting a Text

WRITING PROJECT

In this Writing Project, you'll complete a close reading and offer an interpretation of a text for an audience of your peers. Begin by selecting a text that you find particularly interesting. You may choose from a host of categories, including the ones listed here.

paintings	advertisements
photographs	short stories
sculptures	poems
buildings	music videos or recordings

As a model for reading closely, follow the procedures outlined earlier in this chapter for creating a content/form-response grid. As you read, view, listen to, and/or study the text and make notes, consider the ways you are interacting with the text by creating a content/form-response grid: *What* are you learning, and *how* is the text itself shaping your experience of it?

Once your close reading is complete, formulate a thesis (or a claim) about the text. You'll need to provide evidence to support your thesis from the text itself. You might also include evidence from secondary sources as support. (See Chapter 4 for more information on developing a clear thesis and Chapter 5 for gathering secondary sources.) Remember that depending on the scope of your thesis, your interpretation may or may not require you to do additional research beyond your close reading of the text. As you compose your interpretation, also keep in mind the conventions of structure, language, and reference that typically appear in scholarship in the humanities. Integrate them into your interpretation as appropriate.

Insider Example
Student Interpretation of a Text

In the following essay, "Till Death Do Us Part: An Analysis of Kate Chopin's 'The Story of an Hour,'" Sarah Ray offers an interpretation of Chopin's story that relies on close observation of the text for support. Read her essay below, and pay particular attention to her thesis statement and to her use of evidence. Note how her thesis responds to the question, "How does Mrs. Mallard's marriage function in the story?" Sarah didn't use outside scholars to support her interpretation, so you could also consider how secondary sources might have provided additional support for her claim.

Sarah Ray

ENG 101

10 April 201-

FORM: Ray uses a common line from marriage vows to indirectly indicate that she focuses on the role of marriage in her interpretation.

Till Death Do Us Part: An Analysis of Kate Chopin's

"The Story of an Hour"

The nineteenth century saw the publication of some of the most renowned romances in literary history, including the novels of Jane Austen and the Brontë sisters, Charlotte, Emily, and Anne. While their stories certainly have lasting appeal, they also inspired an unrealistic and sometimes unattainable ideal of joyful love and marriage. In this romanticized vision, a couple is merely two halves of a whole; one without the other compromises the happiness of both. The couple's lives, and even destinies, are so intertwined that neither individual worries about what personal desires and goals are being forsaken by commitment to the other. By the end of the century, in her "The Story of an Hour" (1894), Kate Chopin presents a completely different view of marriage. Through the perspective of a female protagonist, Louise Mallard, who believes her husband has just died, the author explores the more challenging aspects of marriage in a time when divorce was rare and disapproved of. Through Mrs. Mallard's emotional development and the concomitant juxtaposition of the vitality of nature to the repressive indoors, Chopin explores marriage as the oppression of one's true self and desires.

"The Story of an Hour" begins its critique of marriage by ending one, when the news of Brently Mallard's death is gently conveyed to his wife, Louise. Chopin then follows Mrs. Mallard's different emotional stages in response to her husband's death. When the news is initially broken to Louise, "[s]he did not hear the story as many women have heard the same, with a paralyzed inability to accept its

CONTENT: Ray clearly states her thesis and provides a preview about how she will develop and support her claim.

CONTENT: In this paragraph, Ray develops the first part of her thesis, the stages of Mrs. Mallard's emotional development.

significance" (Chopin par. 3). She instead weeps suddenly and briefly, a "storm of grief" that passes as quickly as it had come (par. 3). This wild, emotional outburst and quick acceptance says a great deal about Louise's feelings toward her marriage. "[S]he had loved [her husband]—sometimes" (par. 15), but a reader may infer that Louise's quick acceptance implies that she has considered an early death for her spouse before. That she even envisions such a dark prospect reveals her unhappiness with the marriage. She begins to see, and even desire, a future without her husband. This desire is expressed when Louise is easily able to see past her husband's death to "a long procession of years to come that would belong to her absolutely" (par. 13). Furthermore, it is unclear whether her "storm of grief" is genuine or faked for the benefit of the family members surrounding her. The "sudden, wild abandonment" (par. 3) with which she weeps almost seems like Louise is trying to mask that she does not react to the news as a loving wife would. Moreover, the display of grief passes quickly; Chopin devotes only a single sentence to the action. Her tears are quickly succeeded by consideration of the prospects of a future on her own.

Chopin uses the setting to create a symbolic context for Louise's emotional outburst in response to the news of her husband's death. Louise is informed of Brently's death in the downstairs level of her home: "It was her sister Josephine who told her, in broken sentences; veiled hints that revealed in half concealing" (par. 2). No mention is made of windows, and the only portal that connects to the outside world is the door that admits the bearers of bad news. By excluding a link to nature, Chopin creates an almost claustrophobic environment to symbolize the oppression Louise feels from her marriage. It is no mistake that this setting plays host to Mrs. Mallard's initial

FORM: Ray primarily uses active voice to clarify who is doing the action in her sentences.

emotional breakdown. Her desires have been suppressed throughout her relationship, and symbolically, she is being suffocated by the confines of her house. Therefore, in this toxic atmosphere, Louise is only able to feel and show the emotions that are expected of her, not those that she truly experiences. Her earlier expression of "grief" underscores this disconnect, overcompensating for emotions that should come naturally to a wife who has just lost her husband, but that must be forced in Mrs. Mallard's case.

FORM: Ray uses transitions between paragraphs that indicate her organization and connect different ideas.

Chopin continues Mrs. Mallard's emotional journey only after she is alone and able to process her genuine feelings. After her brief display of grief has run its course, she migrates to her upstairs bedroom and sits in front of a window looking upon the beauty of nature. It is then and only then that Louise gives in not only to her emotions about the day's exploits, but also to those feelings she could only experience after the oppression of her husband died with him—dark desires barely explored outside the boundaries of her own mind, if at all. They were at first foreign to her, but as soon as Louise began to "recognize this thing that was approaching to possess her . . . she [strove] to beat it back with her will" (par. 10). Even then, after the source of her repression is gone, she fights to stifle her desires and physical reactions. The habit is so engrained that Louise is unable to release her emotions for fear of the unknown, of that which has been repressed for so long. However, "her bosom rose and fell tumultuously . . . When she abandoned herself a little whispered word escaped her slightly parted lips. She said it over and over under her breath: 'free, free, free!' . . . Her pulses beat fast, and the coursing blood warmed and relaxed every inch of her body" (pars. 10, 11). When she's allowed to experience them, Louise's feelings and desires provide a glimpse into a possible joyous future without her husband, a future where "[t]here would be no powerful will bending hers in that blind persistence with which men and women believe they have a right to impose" (par. 14). Her marriage is over, and Louise appears finally to be able to liberate her true identity and look upon the future with not dread but anticipation.

The author's setting for this scene is crucial in the development of not only the plot but also her critique of marriage. Chopin sought to encapsulate the freedom Louise began to feel in her room with this scene's depiction of nature. For example, Chopin describes the view from Louise's bedroom window with language that expresses its vitality: "She could see in the open square before her house the tops of trees that were all aquiver with the new spring life" (par. 5). She goes on to say, "The delicious breath of rain was in the air. In the street below a peddler was crying his wares . . . and countless sparrows were twittering in the eaves" (par. 5). The very adjectives and phrases used to describe the outdoors seem to speak of bustling activity and life. This is in stark contrast to the complete lack of vivacity in the description of downstairs.

The language used in the portrayal of these contrasting settings is not the only way Chopin strives to emphasize the difference between the two. She also uses the effect these scenes have on Mrs. Mallard to convey their meaning and depth. On the one hand, the wild, perhaps faked, emotional outburst that takes place in the stifling lower level of the house leaves Louise in a state of "physical exhaustion that haunted her body and seemed to reach into her soul" (par. 4). On the other hand, Louise "[drank] in a very elixir of life through that open window" (par. 18) of her bedroom through which nature bloomed. Because the author strove to symbolize Mrs. Mallard's marriage with the oppressive downstairs

FORM: When making assumptions about the author's intentions, Ray sometimes uses hedging words—in this case, "seem to."

and her impending life without her husband with the open, healing depiction of nature, Chopin suggests that spouses are sometimes better off without each other because marriage can take a physical toll on a person's well-being while the freedom of living for no one but one's self breathes life into even the most burdened wife. After all, "[w]hat could love, the unsolved mystery, count for in face of this possession of self-assertion" (par. 15) felt by Mrs. Mallard in the wake of her emancipation from oppression?

Chopin goes on to emphasize the healing capabilities and joy of living only for one's self by showing the consequences of brutally taking it all away, in one quick turn of a latchkey. With thoughts of her freedom of days to come, "she carried herself unwittingly like a goddess of Victory. She clasped her sister's waist, and together they descended the stairs" (par. 20). Already Chopin is preparing the reader for Mrs. Mallard's looming fate. Not only is she no longer alone in her room with the proverbial elixir of life pouring in from the window, but also she is once again sinking into the oppression of the downstairs, an area that embodies all marital duties as well as the suffocation of Louise's true self and desires. When Brently Mallard enters the house slightly confused but unharmed, the loss of her newly found freedom is too much for Louise's weak heart to bear. Chopin ends the story with a hint of irony: "When the doctors came they said she had died of heart disease—of joy that kills" (par. 23). It may be easier for society to accept that Mrs. Mallard died of joy at seeing her husband alive, but in all actuality, it was the violent death of her future prospects and the hope she had allowed to blossom that sent Louise to the grave. Here lies Chopin's ultimate critique of marriage: when there was no other viable escape, only death could provide freedom from an oppressive marriage. By killing

Louise, Chopin solidifies this ultimatum and also suggests that even death is kinder when the only other option is the slow and continuous addition of the crushing weight of marital oppression.

In "The Story of an Hour," Kate Chopin challenges the typical, romanticized view of love and marriage in the era in which she lived. She chooses to reveal some of the sacrifices one must make in order to bind oneself to another in matrimony. Chopin develops these critiques of marriage through Louise Mallard's emotional responses to her husband's supposed death, whether it is a quick, if not faked, outburst of grief, her body's highly sexualized awakening to the freedoms to come, or the utter despair at finding that he still survives. These are not typical emotions for a "grieving" wife, and Chopin uses this stark contrast as well as the concomitant juxtaposition of nature to the indoors to further emphasize her critique. Louise Mallard may have died in the quest to gain independence from the oppression of her true self and desires, but now she is at least "[f]ree! Body and soul free!" (par. 16).

CONTENT: Ray provides a broad summary of her argument in the concluding paragraph.

CONTENT: In her last sentence, Ray reveals a portion of the significance of the story to an understanding of marital oppression.

FORM: Ray cites her source using MLA format.

Work Cited

Chopin, Kate. "The Story of an Hour." 1894. Ann Woodlief's
Web Study Texts, www.vcu.edu/engweb/webtexts/hour.

Discussion Questions

1. Describe how Sarah Ray's thesis is both debatable and significant.

2. How does the author use evidence from the text to support her interpretation?

3. How has she organized her interpretation?

4. How could it help Sarah's interpretation if she looked at the work of other scholars who have studied Chopin's story?

ARTISTIC TEXTS

Many scholars in the humanities are creators of artistic texts. It has been said about artistic texts that when you create them, they're the arts, and when you study them, they're the humanities. This formulation oversimplifies somewhat, but it's helpful as shorthand for thinking about the relationship between arts and humanities. Artistic texts can occur in many different forms and media. Some of the more common artistic texts that students create include the following:

paintings	songs	stories
sculptures	pottery	video games
poems	models	short films

The process that you follow to create an artistic text will vary according to the type of text you create. In a writing class, an instructor might ask you to create an artistic text and then reflect on the process of creating it. Additionally, he or she might ask you to interpret your own text or that of another student.

Creating an Artistic Text

In this three-part project, you'll create a text, reflect on the process of creating it, and then develop a preliminary interpretation of the text. Your assessment will be based primarily on your reflection on and close reading of your text. We encourage you to try something new; indeed, you might discover a talent you didn't realize you had, or you might understand something new about the creative process by trying an art form you haven't experimented with before.

PART 1

Choose an art form that you'd like to experiment with for this activity. You might try something that you've done before, or you might want to experiment with something new. Some possibilities are listed below.

- sketching or painting a figure or a landscape
- composing a poem or a song
- using a pottery wheel or sculpting with clay
- writing a short story
- creating an advertisement or Public Service Announcement for an issue important to you
- designing a video game
- directing a (very) short film

PART 2

After completing the creative portion of this project, respond to the following prompts for reflection about the process of creating the text. First reflect on the process of creating your text and what you learned from it.

- What was the most challenging part of the project for you?
- What was the most enjoyable part of the project?
- What did you discover about yourself as you participated in this activity?
- Did you find yourself trying to imitate other examples you've seen, heard, or experienced, or were you trying to develop something very different?
- What inspired you as you were working?

PART 3

Once you've reflected on the process of creating your text, examine the text closely and take notes regarding the elements of it that you see as important to its meaning. Once you've developed notes, do the following.

1. Complete a content/form-response grid to highlight the notes you see as most important for constructing meaning from the text. Be sure to articulate responses about why you see each note as important and relevant toward interpreting meaning.

2. Brainstorm a list of *how*, *what*, and *why* questions regarding various aspects of the text related to its meaning(s).

3. Select one or two questions that seem most promising to try and answer. You should be able to draw direct evidence from the text (and your notes) that supports your answer.

4. Select and rewrite the best question that has evidence, and then write a thesis statement.

You should construct the remainder of your interpretation of the text based on the thesis statement. Try to develop an interpretation that's organized with clear reasons and evidence (see Chapter 4). Use examples actually taken from your text as evidence.

---

tip sheet — **Reading and Writing in the Humanities**

- **In the humanities, scholars seek to understand and interpret human experience.** To do so, they often create, analyze, and interpret texts.

- **Scholars in the humanities often conduct close readings of texts** to interpret and make meaning from them, and they might draw on a particular theoretical perspective to ask questions about those texts.

- **Keeping a content/form-response grid can help you track important elements of a text** and your response to them as you do a close reading.

- **Writing in the humanities often draws on the interpretations of others,** either as support or to position an interpretation within prior scholarship.

- **Arguments in the humanities generally begin with a thesis statement** that asserts what the author intends to prove, and it may also provide insight into how the author will prove it. Each section of the argument should provide support for the thesis.

Reading and Writing in the Social Sciences

Introduction to the Social Sciences

Social scientists study human behavior and interaction along with the systems and social structures we create to organize our world. Professionals in the fields of the **social sciences** help us understand why we do what we do as well as how processes (political, economic, personal, etc.) contribute to our lives. As the image at the bottom of this page shows, the social sciences encompass a broad area of academic inquiry that comprises numerous fields of study. These include sociology, psychology, anthropology, communication studies, and political science, among others.

Maybe you've observed a friend or family member spiral into addictive or self-destructive behavior and struggled to understand how it happened. Maybe you've spent time wondering how cliques were formed and maintained among students in your high school, or how friends are typically chosen. Perhaps larger social issues like war, poverty, or famine concern you the most. If you've ever stopped to consider any of these kinds of issues, then you've already begun to explore the world of the social sciences.

Social scientist Kevin Rathunde, who teaches at the University of Utah, shares his perspective on the work and writing of social scientists in Insider's View features in this chapter. Excerpts from Rathunde's paper entitled "Middle School Students' Motivation and Quality of Experience: A Comparison of Montessori and Traditional School Environments,"

ANDREA TSURUMI

Social scientists care about the conditions that allow people to connect

KEVIN RATHUNDE, SOCIAL SCIENCES

COURTESY OF KEVIN RATHUNDE

"There are many branches of social science. In general, as the name 'social science' implies, the main focus of scientific action and dialogue is on people and social processes. My training was in an interdisciplinary program on human development at the University of Chicago. As a result, my perspective on social science tends to reach across disciplinary boundaries. I also work in an interdisciplinary department at the University of Utah. The professional conversations I have with colleagues—both within and outside of my department—are wide-ranging. If there is a common denominator to them, it might be the well-being of individuals, families, and society. Social scientists care about the conditions that allow people to connect with others, participate in the lives of their communities, and reach their full potential."

which he wrote and published with his colleague Mihaly Csikszentmihalyi in the *American Journal of Education*, also appear throughout this chapter. Rathunde and Csikszentmihalyi's study investigated the types of educational settings that contribute to the best outcomes for students. Specifically, they compared traditional public school environments with those of Montessori schools to assess how students learn, interact, and perceive the quality of their experiences in these differing environments.

As a social scientist, you might study issues like therapy options for autism, the effects of substance abuse on families, peer pressure, the dynamics of dating, social networking websites, stress, or the communication practices of men and women. You might study family counseling techniques or the effects of divorce on teens. Or perhaps you might wonder (as Rathunde and Csikszentmihalyi do) about the effects of differing educational environments on student satisfaction and success.

Whatever the case may be, if you're interested in studying human behavior and understanding why we do what we do, you'll want to consider further how social scientists conduct research and how they present their results in writing. As in all the academic domains, progress in the social sciences rests upon researchers' primary skills at making observations of the world around them.

INSIDE WORK **Observing Behavior**

For this activity, pick a place to sit and observe people. You can choose a place that you enjoy going to regularly, but make sure you can observe and take notes without being interrupted or distracted. For example, you might observe people in your school's library or another space on campus. Try to avoid places where you could feel compelled to engage in conversation with people you know.

For ten minutes, freewrite about the people around you and what they're doing. Look for the kinds of interactions and engagements that characterize their behavior. Then draft some questions that you think a social scientist observing the same people might ask about them. For example, if you wrote about behaviors you observed in a college classroom or lecture hall, you might consider questions like the ones listed here.

- How are students arranged around the room? What does the seating arrangement look like? What effect does the room's arrangement have on classroom interaction, if any?

- What are students doing? Are they taking notes? Writing? Sleeping? Typing? Texting? Listening? Doing something else?

- Are students doing different things in different parts of the room, or are the activities similar throughout the room? Why?

- What is the instructor doing in the classroom? Where is he or she positioned? How are students responding?

- Are students using technology? If so, what kinds of technology? What are they using the technology to do?

- If people are interacting with one another in the classroom, what are they talking about? How are they interacting? How are they positioned when they interact? Are numerous people contributing to the conversation? Is someone leading the conversation? If so, how?

See how many different behaviors, people, and interactions you can observe and how many questions you can generate. You might do this activity in the same place with a partner and then compare notes. What did you or your partner find in common? What did you each observe that was unique? Why do you think you noticed the things you did? What was the most interesting thing you observed? ❱

Research in the Social Sciences

As we've indicated, the social sciences comprise a diverse group of academic fields that aim to understand human behavior and systems. But it may be difficult to see the commonalities among these disciplines that make it possible to refer to them as social sciences. One of the ways we can link these disciplines and the values they share, beyond their basic concern for why and how people do things, is by considering how social scientists conduct and report their research.

THE ROLE OF THEORY

Unlike in the natural sciences, where research often takes place in a laboratory setting under controlled conditions, research in the social sciences is necessarily "messier." The reason is fairly simple: human beings and the systems they organize cannot generally be studied in laboratory conditions, where variables are controlled. For this reason, social scientists do not generally establish fixed laws or argue for absolute truths, as natural scientists sometimes do. For instance, while natural scientists are able to argue, with certainty, that a water molecule contains two atoms of hydrogen and one of oxygen, social scientists cannot claim to know the absolute fixed nature of a person's psychology (why a person does what she does in any particular instance, for example) or that of a social system or problem (why homelessness persists, for instance).

Much social science research is therefore based on **theories of human behavior and human systems**, which are propositions that scholars use to explain specific phenomena. Theories can be evaluated on the basis of their ability to explain why or how or when a phenomenon occurs, and they generally result from research that has been replicated time and again to confirm their accuracy, appropriateness, and usefulness. Still, it's important to understand that theories are not laws; they are not absolute, fixed, or perfect explanations. Instead, social science theories are always being refined as research on particular social phenomena develops. The Rathunde and Csikszentmihalyi study we highlight in the Insider's View boxes, for instance, makes use of goal theory and optimal experience theory as part of the research design to evaluate the type of middle school environment that best contributes to students' education.

Insider Example
Exploring Social Science Theory

Read the following excerpt from Kalervo Oberg's "Cultural Shock: Adjustment to New Cultural Environments," and then reflect on his theory by answering the questions that follow the selection. Oberg (1901–1973) was a pioneer in economic anthropology and applied anthropology, and his foundational work in this study has been cited hundreds of times by sociologists and anthropologists who are interested in the phenomenon. Oberg himself coined the term *culture shock*.

Excerpt from **Cultural Shock: Adjustment to New Cultural Environments**

KALERVO OBERG

Culture shock is precipitated by the anxiety that results from losing all our familiar signs and symbols of social intercourse. These signs or cues include the thousand and one ways in which we orient ourselves to the situations of daily life: when to shake hands and what to say when we meet people, when and how to give tips, how to give orders to servants, how to make purchases, when to accept and when to refuse invitations, when to take statements seriously and when not. Now these cues—which may be words, gestures, facial expressions, customs, or norms—are acquired by all of us in the course of growing up and are as much a part of our culture as the language we speak or the beliefs we accept. All of us depend for our peace of mind and our efficiency on hundreds of these cues, most of which we do not carry on the level of conscious awareness.

Now when an individual enters a strange culture, all or most of these familiar cues are removed. He or she is like a fish out of water. No matter how broad-minded or full of good will you may be, a series of props have been knocked from under you, followed by a feeling of frustration and anxiety. People react to the frustration in much the same way. First they *reject* the environment which causes the discomfort: "the ways of the host country are bad because they make us feel bad." When Americans or other foreigners in a strange land get together to grouse about the host country and its people—you can be sure they are suffering from culture shock. Another phase of culture shock is *regression*. The home environment suddenly assumes a tremendous importance. To an American everything American becomes irrationally glorified. All the difficulties and problems are forgotten and only the good things back home are remembered. It usually takes a trip home to bring one back to reality.

SYMPTOMS OF CULTURE SHOCK

Some of the symptoms of culture shock are: excessive washing of the hands; excessive concern over drinking water, food, dishes, and bedding; fear of physical contact with attendants or servants; the absent-minded, far-away stare (sometimes called "the tropical stare"); a feeling of helplessness and a desire for dependence on long-term residents of one's own nationality; fits of anger over delays and other minor frustrations; delay and outright refusal to learn the language of the host country; excessive fear of being cheated, robbed, or injured; great concern over minor pains and irruptions of the skin; and finally, that terrible longing to be back home, to be able to have a good cup of coffee and a piece of apple pie, to walk into that corner drugstore, to visit one's relatives, and, in general, to talk to people who really make sense.

Individuals differ greatly in the degree in which culture shock affects them. Although not common, there are individuals who cannot live in foreign countries. Those who have seen people go through culture shock and on to a satisfactory adjustment can discern steps in the process. During the first few weeks most individuals are fascinated by the new. They stay in hotels and associate with nationals who speak their language and are polite and gracious to foreigners.

This honeymoon stage may last from a few days or weeks to six months depending on circumstances. If one is a very important person he or she will be shown the show places, will be pampered and petted, and in a press interview will speak glowingly about progress, good will, and international amity, and if he returns home he may well write a book about his pleasant if superficial experience abroad.

But this Cook's tour type of mentality does not normally last if the foreign visitor remains abroad and has seriously to cope with real conditions of life. It is then that the second stage begins, characterized by a hostile and aggressive attitude towards the host country. This hostility evidently grows out of the genuine difficulty which the visitor experiences in the process of adjustment. There is maid trouble, school trouble, language trouble, house trouble, transportation trouble, shopping trouble, and the fact that people in the host country are largely indifferent to all these troubles. They help but they just don't understand your great concern over these difficulties. Therefore, they must be insensible and unsympathetic to you and your worries. The result, "I just don't like them." You become aggressive, you band together with your fellow countrymen and criticize the host country, its ways, and its people. But this criticism is not an objective appraisal but a derogatory one. Instead of trying to account for conditions as they are through an honest analysis of the actual conditions and the historical circumstances which have created them, you talk as if the difficulties you experienced are more or less created by the people of the host country for your special discomfort. You take refuge in the colony of your countrymen and its cocktail circuit, which often becomes the fountain-head of emotionally charged labels known as stereotypes. This is a peculiar kind of invidious shorthand which caricatures the host country and its people in a negative manner. The "dollar-grasping American" and the "indolent Latin American" are samples of mild forms of stereotypes. The use of stereotypes may salve the ego of someone with a severe case of culture shock but it certainly does not lead to any genuine understanding of the host country and its people. This second stage of culture shock is in a sense a crisis in the disease. If you overcome it, you stay; if not, you leave before you reach the stage of a nervous breakdown.

If the visitor succeeds in getting some knowledge of the language and begins to get around by himself, he is beginning to open the way into the new cultural environment. The visitor still has difficulties but he takes a "this is my cross and I have to bear it" attitude. Usually in this stage the visitor takes a superior attitude to people of the host country. His sense of humor begins to exert itself. Instead of criticizing he jokes about the people and even cracks jokes about his or her own difficulties. He or she is now on the way to recovery. And there is also the poor devil who is worse off than yourself whom you can help, which in turn gives you confidence in your ability to speak and get around.

In the fourth stage your adjustment is about as complete as it can be. The visitor now accepts the customs of the country as just another way of living. You operate within the new milieu without a feeling of anxiety although there are moments of strain. Only with a complete grasp of all the cues of social intercourse will this strain disappear. For a long time the individual will understand what the national is saying but he is not always sure what the national means. With a complete adjustment you not only accept the foods, drinks, habits, and customs, but actually begin to enjoy them. When you go on home leave you may even take things back with you and if you leave for good you generally miss the country and the people to whom you have become accustomed.

Discussion Questions

1. In your own words, define what you think Kalervo Oberg means by *culture shock*.

2. What are the four stages of culture shock, according to Oberg?

3. Oberg's essay was written more than half a century ago. In what ways does it seem dated? In what ways does it strike you as still valid or relevant?

INSIDE WORK   **Tracing a Theory's Development**

As we indicated, theories in the social sciences exist to be developed and refined over time, based on our developing understandings of a social phenomenon as a result of continued research. Conduct a search (using the web or your academic database access) to determine if you can make a rough estimate as to how often Oberg's theory of culture shock has been cited in published research. You might even make a timeline, or another visual representation, of what you find. As you look at the research, identify any evidence or indicators that the theory has been updated or altered since its first appearance. In what ways has the theory been refined? ❱

RESEARCH QUESTIONS AND HYPOTHESES

As we've noted throughout this book, research questions are typically formulated on the basis of observations. In the social sciences, such observations focus on human behavior, human systems, and/or the interactions between the two. Observations of a social phenomenon can give rise to questions about how a phenomenon operates or what effects it has on people or, as Rathunde suggests, how it could be changed to improve individuals' well-being. For example, in their social science study, "'Under the Radar': Educators and Cyberbullying in Schools," W. Cassidy, K. Brown, and M.

Jackson (2012) offer the following as guiding research questions for their investigation:

> Our study of educators focused on three research questions: Do they [educators] consider cyberbullying a problem at their school and how familiar are they with the extent and impact among their students? What policies and practices are in place to prevent or counter cyberbullying? What solutions do they have for encouraging a kinder online world? (p. 522)

Research that is designed to inform a theory of human behavior or to provide data that contributes to a fuller understanding of some social or political structure (i.e., to answer a social science research question) also often begins with the presentation of a *hypothesis*. As we saw in Chapter 4, a hypothesis is a testable proposition that provides an answer or predicts an outcome in response to the research question(s) at hand. It's important to note that not all social science reports include a statement of hypothesis. Some social science research establishes its focus by presenting the questions that guide researchers' inquiry into a particular phenomenon instead of establishing a hypothesis. C. Kerns and K. Ko (2009) present the following hypothesis, or predicted outcome, for their social science study, "Exploring Happiness and Performance at Work." The researchers make a prediction concerning what they believed their research would show before presenting their findings later in their research report:

> The intent of this analysis was to review how happiness and performance related to each other in this workplace. It is the authors' belief that for performance to be sustained in an organization, individuals and groups within that organization need to experience a threshold level of happiness. It is difficult for unhappy individuals and work groups to continue performing at high levels without appropriate leadership intervention. (p. 5)

Hypotheses differ from *thesis statements*, which are more commonly associated with arguments in the humanities. While thesis statements offer researchers' final conclusions on a topic or issue, hypothesis statements offer a predicted outcome. The proposition expressed in a hypothesis may be either accepted or rejected based on the results of the research. For example, an educational researcher might hypothesize that teachers' use of open-ended questioning increases students' level of participation in class. However, the researcher wouldn't be able to confirm or reject such a hypothesis until the end of his or her research report.

INSIDE WORK   **Developing Hypotheses**

1. For five minutes, brainstorm *social science* topics or issues that have affected your life. One approach is to consider issues that are causing you stress in your life right now. Examples might include peer pressure, academic performance, substance abuse, dating, or a relative's cancer treatment.

2. Once you have a list of topics, focus on two or three that you believe have had the greatest impact on you personally. Next, generate a list of possible

research questions concerning the topics that, if answered, would offer you a greater understanding of them. Examples: *What triggers most people to try their first drink of alcohol? What types of therapies are most effective for working with children on the autism spectrum? What kinds of technology actually aid in student learning?*

3. When you've reached the stage of proposing a possible answer to one or more of your questions, then you're ready to state a hypothesis. Try proposing a *hypothesis*, or testable proposition, as an answer to one of the research questions you've posed. For example, if your research question is "What triggers most people to try their first drink of alcohol?" then your hypothesis might be "Peer pressure generally causes most people to try their first drink of alcohol, especially for those who try their first drink before reaching the legal drinking age." ▶

METHODS

Research in the diverse fields of the social sciences is, as you probably suspect, quite varied, and social scientists collect data to answer their research questions or test their hypotheses in several different ways. Their choice of methods is directly influenced by the kinds of questions they ask in any particular instance, as well as by their own disciplinary backgrounds. In his Insider's View on page 192, Kevin Rathunde highlights the connection between the kinds of research questions a social scientist asks and the particular methods the researcher uses to answer those questions.

We can group most of the research you're likely to encounter in the fields of the social sciences into three possible types: quantitative, qualitative, and mixed methods. Researchers make choices about which types of methods they'll employ in any given situation based on the nature of their line of inquiry. A particular research question may very well dictate the methods used to answer that question. If you wanted to determine the number of homeless veterans in a specific city, for instance, then collecting numerical, or quantitative, data would likely suffice to answer that question. However, if you wanted to know what factors affect the rates of homelessness among veterans in your community, then you would need to do more than tally the number of homeless veterans. You'd need to collect a different type of data to help construct an answer—perhaps responses to surveys or interview questions.

Quantitative Methods

Quantitative studies include those that rely on collecting numerical data and performing statistical analyses to reveal findings in research. Basic statistical data, like those provided by *means* (averages), *modes* (most often occurring value), and *medians* (middle values), are fundamental to quantitative social science research. More sophisticated statistical procedures commonly used in professional quantitative studies include correlations, chi-square tests, analysis of variance (ANOVA), and multivariate analysis of variance (MANOVA), as well as regression model testing, just to name a few. Not all statistical procedures are appropriate in all situations, however, so researchers must carefully select procedures based on the nature of their data and the kinds of findings they seek. Researchers who engage in advanced statistical procedures as part of their methods are typically highly skilled in such procedures. At the very least, these researchers consult or work in cooperation with statisticians to design their studies and/or to analyze their data.

You may find, in fact, that a team of researchers collaborating on a social science project often includes individuals who are also experienced statisticians. Obviously, we don't expect you to be familiar with the details of statistical procedures, but it's important that you be able to notice when researchers rely on statistical methods to test their hypotheses and to inform their results.

Also, you should take note of how researchers incorporate discussion of such methods into their writing. In the following example, we've highlighted a few elements in the reporting that you'll want to notice when reading social science studies that make use of statistical procedures:

- **Procedures**   What statistical procedures are used?

- **Variables**   What variables are examined in the procedures?

- **Results**   What do the statistical procedures reveal?

- **Participants**   From whom are the data collected, and how are those individuals chosen?

In their study, Rathunde and Csikszentmihalyi report on the statistical procedures they used to examine different types of schools:

> The first analysis compared the main motivation and quality-of-experience variables across school type (Montessori vs. traditional) and grade level (sixth vs. eighth) using a two-way MANCOVA with parental education, gender, and ethnic background as covariates. Significant differences were found for school context (Wilks's lambda = .84, $F(5, 275) = 10.84$, $p < .001$), indicating that students in the two school contexts reported differences in motivation and quality of experience. After adjusting for the covariates, the multivariate eta squared indicated that 17 percent of the variance of the dependent variables was associated with the school context factor. The omnibus test for grade level was not significant (Wilks's lambda = .99, $F(5, 275) = .68$, $p = .64$) indicating that students in sixth and eighth grade reported similar motivation and quality of experience. Finally, the omnibus test for the interaction of school context x grade level was not significant (Wilks's lambda = .97, $F(5, 275) = 2.02$, $p = .08$). None of the multivariate tests for the covariates—parental education, gender, and ethnic background—reached the .05 level. (p. 357)

Variables examined, participants or populations involved in the study, and statistical procedure employed—MANCOVA, or a multivariate analysis of covariance—are identified.

Results of the statistical procedure are identified.

Qualitative Methods

Qualitative studies generally rely on language, observation, and reporting of individual human experiences to reveal findings in research. Research reports often communicate these methods through the form of a study's results, which rely on in-depth narrative reporting. Methods for collecting data in qualitative studies include interviews, document analysis, surveys, and observations.

We can see examples of these methods put into practice in Barbara Allen's "Environmental Justice, Local Knowledge, and After-Disaster Planning in New Orleans" (2007), published in the academic social science journal *Technology and Society*. In this example, we've highlighted a few elements in the reporting that you'll want to notice when reading qualitative research methods:

- **Method**   What method of data collection is used?
- **Data**   What data is gathered from that method?
- **Results**   What are the results? What explanation do the researchers provide for the data, or what meaning do they find in the data?
- **Participants**   From whom is the data collected, and how are these individuals chosen?

> Six months after the hurricane I contacted public health officials and researchers, many of whom were reluctant to talk. One who did talk asked that I did not use her name, but she made some interesting observations. According to my informant, health officials were in a difficult position. Half a year after the devastation, only 25% of the city's residents had returned; a year after the

Participants

Data-collection method: interview

storm, that number rose to about 40%. Negative publicity regarding public health issues would deter such repatriation, particularly families with children who had not returned in any large numbers to the city. The informant also told me to pursue the state public health websites where the most prominent worries were still smoking and obesity, not Hurricane Katrina. While the

information on various public health websites did eventually reflect concerns about mold, mildew, and other contamination, it was never presented as the health threat that independent environmental scientists, such as Wilma Subra, thought it was. (pp. 154–55)

. . .

About five months after Hurricane Katrina, I received an e-mail from a high school student living in a rural parish west of New Orleans along the Mississippi River (an area EJ advocates have renamed Cancer Alley). After Hurricane Katrina, an old landfill near her house was opened to receive waste and began emitting noxious odors. She took samples of the "black ooze" from the site and contacted the Louisiana Department of Environmental Quality, only to be told that the landfill was accepting only construction waste, and the smell she described was probably decaying gypsum board. I suspect her story

will be repeated many times across south Louisiana as these marginal waste sites receive the debris from homes and businesses ruined by the hurricane. The full environmental impact of Hurricane Katrina's waste and its hastily designated removal sites will not be known for many years. (p. 155)

Mixed Methods

Studies that make use of both qualitative and quantitative data-collection techniques are generally referred to as **mixed-methodology studies**. Rathunde and Csikszentmihalyi's study used mixed methods: the authors report findings from both qualitative and quantitative data. In this excerpt, they share results from qualitative data they collected as they sought to distinguish among the types of educational settings selected for participation in their study:

> After verifying that the demographic profile of the two sets of schools was similar, the next step was to determine if the schools differed with respect to the five selection criteria outlined above. We used a variety of qualitative sources to verify contextual differences, including observations by the research staff; teacher and parent interviews; school newsletters, information packets, mission statements, and parent teacher handbooks; summaries from board of education and school council meetings; and a review of class schedules and textbook choices discussed in strategic plans. These sources also provided information about the level of middle grade reform that may or may not have been implemented by the schools and whether the label "traditional" was appropriate. (p. 64)

However, Rathunde and Csikszentmihalyi's central hypothesis, "that students in Montessori middle schools would report more positive perceptions of their school environment and their teachers, more often perceive their classmates as friends, and spend more time in collaborative and/or individual work rather than didactic educational formats such as listening to a lecture" (p. 68), was tested by using quantitative methods:

> The main analyses used two-way multivariate analysis of covariance (MANCOVA) with school type (Montessori vs. traditional) and grade level (sixth vs. eighth) as the two factors. Gender, ethnicity, and parental education were covariates in all of the analyses. Overall multivariate F tests (Wilks's lambda) were performed first on related sets of dependent variables. If an overall F test was significant, we performed univariate ANOVAs as follow-up tests to the MANCOVAs. If necessary, post hoc analyses were done using Bonferroni corrections to control for Type I errors. Only students with at least 15 ESM signals were included in the multivariate analyses, and follow-up ANOVAs used students who had valid scores on all of the dependent variables. (p. 68)

Addressing Bias

Because social scientists study people and organizations, their research is considered more valuable when conducted within a framework that minimizes the influence of personal or researcher bias on the study's outcome(s). When possible, social scientists strive for **objectivity** (in quantitative research) or **neutrality** (in qualitative research) in their research. This means that researchers undertake all possible measures to reduce the influence of biases on their research. Bias is sometimes inevitable, however, so social science research places a high value on honesty and transparency in the reporting of data. Each of the methods outlined above requires social scientists to engage in rigorous procedures and checks (e.g., ensuring appropriate sample sizes and/or using multiple forms of qualitative data) to ensure that the influence of any biases is as limited as possible.

📷 **LaunchPad**

A political scientist weighs in on avoiding bias.

INSIDE WORK   **Considering Research Methods**

In the previous activity, we asked you to consider possible hypotheses, or testable propositions, to the research questions you posed. Now choose one of your hypothesis statements, and consider the types of methods that might be appropriate for testing the hypothesis. Think about the kinds of data you'll generate from the different methods.

- Would quantitative, qualitative, or mixed research methods be the most appropriate for testing your hypothesis? Why?

- What specific methods would you use—statistical procedures, surveys, observations, interviews? Why?

- Who would you want to have participate in your research? From whom would you need to collect your data in order to answer your research question? ❯

THE IRB PROCESS AND USE OF HUMAN SUBJECTS

All research, whether student or faculty initiated and directed, must treat its subjects, or participants, with the greatest of care and consider the ethical implications of all its procedures. Although institutions establish their own systems and procedures for verifying the ethical treatment of subjects, most of these include an **institutional review board (IRB)**, or a committee of individuals whose job is to review research proposals in light of ethical concerns for subjects and applicable laws. Such proposals typically include specific forms of documentation that identify a study's purpose; rigorously detail the research procedures to be followed; evaluate potential risks and rewards of a study, especially for study participants; and ensure (whenever possible) that participants are fully informed about a study and the implications of their participation in it.

We encourage you to learn more about the IRB process at your own institution and, when appropriate, to consider your own research in light of the IRB policies and procedures established for your institution. Many schools maintain informational, educational, and interactive websites. You'll notice similarities in the mission statements of institutional review boards from a number of colleges and universities:

> **Duke University:** To ensure the protection of human research subjects by conducting scientific and ethical review of research studies while providing leadership and education for the research community.

> **The George Washington University:** To support [the] research community in the conduct of innovative and ethical research by providing guidance, education, and oversight for the protection of human subjects.

> **Maricopa County Community College District:** [T]o review all proposed research involving human subjects to ensure that subjects are treated ethically and that their rights and welfare are adequately protected.

Conventions of Writing in the Social Sciences

In light of the variety of research methods used by social scientists, it's not surprising that there are also a number of ways social scientists report their research findings. In this section, we highlight general conventional expectations of *structure*, *language*, and *reference* that social scientists follow to communicate their research to one another. Understanding these conventions, we believe, can help foster your understanding of this academic domain more broadly.

Aya Matsuda is a linguist and social science researcher at Arizona State University, where she studies the use of English as an international language, the integration of a "World Englishes" perspective into U.S. education, and the ways bilingual writers negotiate identity. In her Insider's View, Matsuda explains that she learned the conventions of writing as a social scientist, and more particularly as a linguist, "mostly through writing, getting feedback, and revising."

As Matsuda also suggests, reading can be an important part of understanding the writing of a discipline. Furthermore, reading academic writing with a particular focus on the rhetorical elements used is a powerful way to acquire insight into the academic discipline itself, as well as a way to learn the literacy practices that professional writers commonly follow in whatever academic domain you happen to be studying.

STRUCTURAL CONVENTIONS AND IMRaD FORMAT

Structural conventions within the fields of the social sciences can vary quite dramatically, but the structure of a social science report should follow logically from the type of study conducted or the methodological framework (quantitative, qualitative, or mixed-methods) it employs. The more quantitative a study is, the more likely its reporting will reflect the conventions for scientific research, using IMRaD format. Qualitative studies, though, sometimes appear in other organizational forms that reflect the particular qualitative methods used in the study. But just as numerous fields within the social sciences rely on quantitative research methods, so too do many social scientists report their results according to the conventional form for scientific inquiry: *IMRaD (Introduction, Methods, Results, and Discussion) format.*

Introduction

The introduction of a social science report establishes the context for a study, providing appropriate background on the issue or topic under scrutiny. The introduction is also where you're likely to find evidence of researchers' review of previous scholarship on a topic. As part of these reviews, researchers typically report what's already known about a phenomenon or what's relevant in the current scholarship for their own research. They may also situate their research goals within some gap in the scholarship—that is, they explain how their research contributes to the growing body of scholarship on the phenomenon under investigation. If a theoretical perspective drives a study, as often occurs in more qualitative studies, then the introduction may also contain an explanation of the central tenets or the parameters of the researchers' theoretical lens. Regardless, an introduction in the social sciences generally builds to a statement of specific purpose for the study. This may take the form of a hypothesis or thesis, or it may appear explicitly as a general statement of the researchers' purpose, perhaps including a presentation of research questions. The introduction to Rathunde and Csikszentmihalyi's study provides an example:

Provides an introduction to the topic at hand: the problem of motivation for adolescents in middle school. The problem is situated in the scholarship of others.

> The difficulties that many young adolescents encounter in middle school have been well documented (Carnegie Council on Adolescent Development 1989, 1995; Eccles et al. 1993; U.S. Department of Education 1991). During this precarious transition from the elementary school years, young adolescents may begin to doubt the value of their academic work and their abilities to succeed (Simmons and Blyth 1987; Wigfield et al. 1991). A central concern of many studies is motivation (Anderman and Maehr 1994); a disturbingly consistent finding associated with middle school is a drop in students' intrinsic motivation to learn (Anderman et al. 1999; Gottfried 1985; Harter et al. 1992).

Reviews relevant scholarship: the researchers review previous studies that have bearing on their own aims—addressing the decline in motivation among students.

> Such downward trends in motivation are not inevitable. Over the past decade, several researchers have concluded that the typical learning environment in middle school is often mismatched with adolescents' developmental needs (Eccles et al. 1993). Several large-scale research programs have focused on the qualities of classrooms and school cultures that may enhance student achievement and motivation (Ames 1992; Lipsitz et al. 1997; Maehr and Midgley 1991). School environments that provide a more appropriate developmental fit (e.g., more relevant tasks, student-directed learning, less of an emphasis on grades and competition, more collaboration, etc.) have been shown to enhance students' intrinsic, task motivation (Anderman et al. 1999).

Identifies researchers' particular areas of interest

> The present study explores the issues of developmental fit and young adolescents' quality of experience and motivation by comparing five Montessori middle schools to six "traditional" public middle schools. Although the Montessori educational philosophy is primarily associated with early childhood education, a number of schools have extended its core principles to early adolescent education. These principles are in general agreement with the reform proposals associated with various motivation theories (Anderman et al. 1999; Maehr and Midgley 1991), developmental fit theories (Eccles et al. 1993), as well as insights from various recommendations for middle school reform (e.g., the Carnegie Foundation's "Turning Points" recommendations; see Lipsitz et al. 1997). In addition, the Montessori philosophy is consistent with the theoretical and practical implications of optimal experience (flow) theory (Csikszentmihalyi and Rathunde 1998). The present study places a special emphasis on students' quality of experience in middle school. More specifically, it uses the Experience Sampling Method (ESM) (Csikszentmihalyi and Larson 1987) to compare the school experiences of Montessori middle school students with a comparable sample of public school students in traditional classrooms. (pp. 341–42)

Although the introductory elements of Rathunde and Csikszentmihalyi's study actually continue for a number of pages, these opening paragraphs reveal common rhetorical moves in social science research reporting: establishing a topic of interest, reviewing the scholarship on that topic, and connecting the current study to the ongoing scholarly conversation on the topic.

Methods

Social science researchers are very particular about the precise reporting of their methods of research. No matter what the type of study (quantitative, qualitative, or mixed-methods), researchers are very careful not only to identify the methods used in their research but also to explain why they chose certain ones, in light of the goals of their study. Because researchers want to reduce the influence of researcher bias and to provide enough context so others might replicate or confirm their findings, social scientists make sure that their reports thoroughly explain the kinds of data they have collected and the precise procedures they used to collect that data (interviews, document analysis, surveys, etc.). Also, there is often much discussion of the ways the data were interpreted or analyzed (using case studies, narrative analysis, statistical procedures, etc.).

An excerpt from W. Cassidy, K. Brown, and M. Jackson's study on educators and cyberbullying provides an example of the level of detail at which scholars typically report their methods:

> Each participant chose a pseudonym and was asked a series of 16 in-depth, semi-structured, open-ended questions (Lancy, 2001) and three closed-category questions in a private setting, allowing their views to be voiced in confidence (Cook-Sather, 2002). Each 45- to 60-minute audiotaped interview was conducted by one of the authors, while maintaining a neutral, nonjudgmental stance in regards to the responses (Merriam, 1988).

Provides highly specific details about data-collection methods, and emphasizes researchers' neutral stance

> Once the interviews were transcribed, each participant was given the opportunity to review the transcript and make changes. The transcripts were then reviewed and re-reviewed in a backward and forward motion (Glaser & Strauss, 1967; McMillan & Schumacher, 1997) separately by two of the three researchers to determine commonalities and differences among responses as well as any salient themes that surfaced due to the frequency or the strength of the response (Miles & Huberman, 1994). Each researcher's analysis was then compared with the other's to jointly determine emergent themes and perceptions.

Provides detailed explanation of procedures used to support the reliability of the study's findings

> The dominant themes were then reviewed in relation to the existing literature on educators' perceptions and responses to cyberbullying. The approach taken was "bottom-up," to inductively uncover themes and contribute to theory, rather than apply existing theory as a predetermined frame for analysis (Miles & Huberman, 1994). (p. 523)

Connects the research to the development of theory

You'll notice that the researchers do not simply indicate that the data were collected via interviews. Rather, they go to some lengths to describe the kinds of interviews they conducted and how they were conducted, as well as how those interviews were analyzed. This level of detail supports the writers' ethos, and it further highlights their commitment to reducing bias in their research. Similar studies might also report the interview questions at the end of the report in an appendix. Seeing the actual questions helps readers interpret the results on their own and also provides enough detail for readers to replicate the study or test the hypothesis with a different population, should they desire to do so. Readers of the study need to understand as precisely as possible the methods for data collection and analysis.

Results

There can be much variety in the ways social science reports present the results, or findings, of a study. You may encounter a section identified by the title "Results," especially if the study follows IMRaD format, but you may not find that heading at all. Instead, researchers often present their results by using headings and subheadings that reflect their actual findings. As examples, we provide here excerpts from two studies: (1) Rathunde and Csikszentmihalyi's 2005 study on middle school student motivation, and (2) Cassidy, Brown, and Jackson's 2012 study on educators and cyberbullying.

In the Results section of their report, Rathunde and Csikszentmihalyi provide findings from their study under the subheading "Motivation and Quality-of-Experience Differences: Nonacademic Activities at School." Those results read in part:

> Follow-up ANCOVAs were done on each of the five ESM variables. Table 3 summarizes the means, standard errors, and significance levels for each of the variables.

Table 3

Univariate F-Tests for Quality of Experience in Nonacademic Activities at School by School Context

ESM Measure	School Context		F-test	p
	Montessori (N = 131)	Traditional (N = 150)		
Flow (%)	11.0 (1.7)	17.3 (1.6)	7.19	.008
Affect	.32 (.05)	.14 (.05)	6.87	.009
Potency	.22 (.05)	.16 (.05)	1.90	NS
Motivation	−.03 (.05)	−.12 (.05)	1.70	NS
Salience	−.38 (.04)	−.19 (.04)	11.14	.001

Means are z-scores (i.e., zero is average experience for the entire week) and are adjusted for the covariates gender, parental education, and ethnicity. Standard errors appear in parentheses. Flow percent indicates the amount of time students indicated above-average challenge and skill while doing nonacademic activities.

Consistent with the relaxed nature of the activities, students in both school contexts reported higher levels of affect, potency, and intrinsic motivation in nonacademic activities, as well as lower levels of salience and flow (see table 2). In contrast to the findings for academic work, students in both groups reported similar levels of intrinsic motivation and potency. In addition, students in the traditional group reported significantly more flow in nonacademic activities, although the overall percentage of flow was low. Similar to the findings for academic activities, the Montessori students reported better overall affect, and despite the fact that levels of salience were below average for both student groups, the traditional students reported that their activities were more important. (pp. 360–61)

> Result
>
> Result
>
> Result
>
> Result

You'll notice that in this section, the researchers remain focused on reporting their findings. They do not, at this point, go into great detail about what those findings mean or what the implications are.

Cassidy, Brown, and Jackson also report their findings in a Results section, and they subdivide their findings into a number of areas of inquiry (identified in the subheadings) examined as part of their larger study. Only the results are presented at this point in the article; they are not yet interpreted:

RESULTS

Familiarity with technology

Despite the district's emphasis on technology, the educators (except for two younger teachers and one vice-principal) indicated that they were not very familiar with chat rooms and blogs, were moderately familiar with YouTube and Facebook and were most familiar with the older forms of communication — email and cellular phones.

> Results

Cyberbullying policies

We asked respondents about specific cyberbullying policies in place at their school and their perceived effectiveness. Despite the district's priorities around technology, neither the school district nor either school had a specific cyberbullying policy; instead educators were supposed to follow the district's bullying policy. When VP17-A was asked if the district's bullying handbook effectively addressed the problem of cyberbullying, he replied: "It effectively addresses the people that are identified as bullying others [but] it doesn't address the educational side of it . . . about what is proper use of the Internet as a tool."

> Result

P14-B wanted to see a new policy put in place that was flexible enough to deal with the different situations as they arose. VP19-B thought that a cyberbullying policy should be separate from a face-to-face bullying policy since the impact on students is different. He also felt that there should be a concerted district policy regarding "risk assessment in which you have a team that's trained at determining the level of threat and it should be taken very seriously whether it's a phone threat, a verbal threat, or a cyber threat." Participants indicated that they had not considered the idea of a separate cyberbullying policy before the interview, with several commenting that they now saw it as important. (pp. 524, 526–27)

> Result

Visual Representations of Data   The Results section of a report may also provide data sets in the form of tables and/or figures. Figures may appear as photos, images, charts, or graphs. When you find visual representations of data in texts, it's important that you pause to consider these elements carefully. Researchers typically use *tables* when they want to make data sets, or raw data, available for comparisons. These tables, such as the one Rathunde and Csikszentmihalyi include in their study of middle school students' motivation, present variables in columns and rows, as seen above.

Table 1

Comparison of Montessori and Traditional Middle School Samples on Various Background Variables

Background Variable	School Context	
	Montessori	Traditional
Ethnicity (%):		
European American	72.6	74.9
Asian American	10.2	7.8
Latino	1.9	3.4
African American	12.7	12.6
Other	2.6	1.2
Parental education	5.5	5.4
Home resources	29.6	29.5
School-related:		
Parental discussion	2.41	2.49
Parental involvement	2.11	2.10
Parental monitoring	1.69	1.66
Number of siblings	1.8	2.0
Mother employment (%)	71.6	74.1
Father employment (%)	83.7	88.1
Intact (two-parent) family (%)	81.0	84.0
Grade point average	1.97	1.93

Note. None of the differences reported in the table were statistically significant.

In this instance, the "background variable[s]" used to describe the student populations are listed in the column, and the rows compare values from two "school context[s]," Montessori and traditional schools. The table's title reveals its overall purpose: to compare "Montessori and Traditional Middle School Samples on Various Background Variables." Rathunde and Csikszentmihalyi describe the contents of their table this way:

> Table 1 summarizes this comparison. The ethnic diversity of the samples was almost identical. Both shared similar advantages in terms of high parental

education (baccalaureate degree or higher), high rates of two-parent families, high family resources, and other indicators of strong parental involvement in their children's education. Although only one-third of the Montessori students received grades, *t*-tests indicated that both samples were comprised of good students (i.e., they received about half As and half Bs). (p. 356)

Researchers use *figures* when they want to highlight the results of research or the derived relationships between data sets or variables. *Graphs*, a type of figure, contain two axes—the horizontal x-axis and the vertical y-axis. The relationship between variables on these axes is indicated by the cells of overlap between the two axes in the body of the figure. Conventionally, the *x-axis* identifies an independent variable, or a variable that can be controlled; by contrast, the *y-axis* identifies the dependent variable, which is dependent on the variable identified in the x-axis. Here's a figure from Rathunde and Csikszentmihalyi's study:

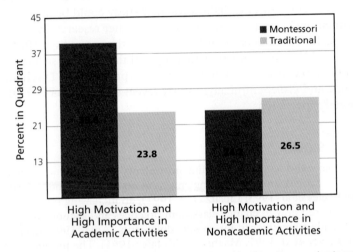

Figure 2. Percentage of undivided interest in academic and nonacademic activities

As with tables, the titles of figures reveal their overall purpose. In this case, the researchers demonstrate the "[p]ercentage of undivided interest in academic and nonacademic activities." Reading the figure, in this instance, comes down to identifying the percentage of "undivided interest" that students in Montessori and traditional middle schools (revealed in different colors, as the legend indicates) expressed in the quadrants "High Motivation and High Importance in Academic Activities" and "High Motivation and High Importance in Nonacademic Activities." Colored cells in the body of the graph reveal the percentages. Rathunde and Csikszentmihalyi note about this figure: "[O]n the key variable undivided interest, students in the traditional group reported a slightly higher percent of high-motivation and high-importance activities; this noteworthy change from academic activities is illustrated in figure 2" (p. 361).

Whenever you see charts or figures in social science reports, you should take time to do the following:

- study the titles carefully
- look for legends, which provide keys to understanding elements in the chart or figure
- identify the factors or variables represented, and understand how those factors or variables are related, as well as how they are measured
- look closely for possible patterns

Discussion

The Discussion of a social science report explains the significance of the findings in light of the study's aims. This is also where researchers reflect on the study more generally, highlight ways their study could be improved (often called "limitations"), and/or identify areas of further research that the study has brought to light. Researchers sometimes lay out the groundwork for continued research, based on their contribution, as part of the ongoing scholarly conversation on the topic or issue at hand. A few excerpts from the Discussion section of Rathunde and Csikszentmihalyi's study reveal their adherence to these conventional expectations:

DISCUSSION

Reveals why their study is important to the ongoing conversation on this topic

Given the well-documented decline in students' motivation and engagement in middle school, and the ongoing emphasis on middle school reform (Cross 1990; Eccles et al. 1993; Lipsitz et al. 1997), an increasing number of studies have explored how to change classroom practices and school cultures in ways that provide a healthier fit for young adolescents (Ames 1992; Eccles et al. 1993; Felner et al. 1997; Maehr and Midgley 1991). The present study adds to this area of research by comparing the motivation and quality of experience of students from five Montessori middle schools and six traditional middle schools. (p. 362)

. . .

Discusses important findings

Results from the study showed that while engaged in academic work at school, Montessori students reported higher affect, potency (i.e., feeling alert and energetic), intrinsic motivation (i.e., enjoyment, interest), and flow experience than students from traditional middle schools. (p. 363)

. . .

Identifies limitations in the study and an area for possible future research

The present study did not look at whether such experiential differences translated into positive achievement and behavioral outcomes for the students. This is an important topic for future research. (p. 363)

Following are some additional structural conventions to consider when you are reading or writing in the fields of the social sciences.

OTHER STRUCTURAL CONVENTIONS

Conclusion

On occasion, researchers separate out coverage of the implications of their findings (as part of a Discussion section) from other elements in the Discussion. When this occurs, these researchers typically construct a separate Conclusion section in which they address conventional content coverage of their study's limitations, as well as their findings' implications for future research.

Titles

Research reports in the social sciences, as in the natural sciences, tend to have rather straightforward titles that are concise and that contain key words highlighting important components of the study. Titles in the social sciences tend not to be creative or rhetorical, although there is a greater tendency toward creativity in titles in qualitative studies, which are more typically language driven than numerically driven. The title of Barbara Allen's study reported in the academic journal *Technology in Society*, for instance, identifies the central issues her study examined as well as the study location: "Environmental Justice, Local Knowledge, and After-Disaster Planning in New Orleans." Similarly, the title of Rathunde and Csikszentmihalyi's article is concise in its identification of the study's purpose: "Middle School Students' Motivation and Quality of Experience: A Comparison of Montessori and Traditional School Environments."

Abstracts

Another structural feature of reports in the social sciences is the abstract. **Abstracts** typically follow the title of the report and the identification of the researchers. They provide a brief overview of the study, explaining the topic or issue under study, the specific purpose of the study and its methods, and offering a concise statement of the results. These elements are usually summarized in a few sentences. Abstracts can be useful to other researchers who want to determine if a study might prove helpful for their own work or if the methods might inform their own research purposes. Abstracts thus serve to promote collaboration among researchers. Though abstracts appear at the beginning of research reports, they're typically written after both the study and the research report are otherwise completed. Abstracts reduce the most important parts of a study into a compact space.

The following example from Rathunde and Csikszentmihalyi illustrates a number of the conventions of abstracts:

> This study compared the motivation and quality of experience of demographically matched students from Montessori and traditional middle school programs. Approximately 290 students responded to the Experience Sampling Method (ESM) and filled out questionnaires. Multivariate analyses showed

The study's purpose is identified.

Methods are briefly outlined.

Results are provided.

Implications of the research findings are noted.

that the Montessori students reported greater affect, potency (i.e., feeling energetic), intrinsic motivation, flow experience, and undivided interest (i.e., the combination of high intrinsic motivation and high salience or importance) while engaged in academic activities at school. The traditional middle school students reported higher salience while doing academic work; however, such responses were often accompanied by low intrinsic motivation. When engaged in informal, nonacademic activities, the students in both school contexts reported similar experiences. These results are discussed in terms of current thought on motivation in education and middle school reform.

Acknowledgments

Acknowledgment sections sometimes appear at the end of social science reports. Usually very brief, they offer a quick word of thanks to organizations and/or individuals who have helped to fund a study, collect data, review the study, or provide another form of assistance during the production of the study. This section can be particularly telling if you're interested in the source of a researcher's funding. Barbara Allen's "Environmental Justice, Local Knowledge, and After-Disaster Planning in New Orleans" contains the following Acknowledgments section:

> ACKNOWLEDGMENTS
>
> I would like to thank Carl Mitcham, Robert Frodeman, and all the participants of the Cities and Rivers II conference in New Orleans, March 21–25, 2006. The ideas and discussions at this event enabled me to think in a more interdisciplinary manner about the disaster....
>
> In addition, I would like to thank the American Academy in Rome for giving me the time to think and write about this important topic. Conversations with my colleagues at the academy were invaluable in helping me to think in new ways about historic preservation and rebuilding. (p. 159)

References

The documentation system most often used in the social sciences is the style regulated by the American Psychological Association, which is referred to as **APA format**. (For more details about APA style conventions, see p. 100 of Chapter 5 and the Appendix.) Studies in the social sciences end with a References page that follows APA guidelines—or the formatting style used in the study, if not APA.

Appendices

Social science research reports sometimes end with one or more appendices. Items here are often referenced within the body of the report itself, as appropriate. These items may include additional data sets, calculations, interview questions, diagrams, and images. The materials typically offer context or support for discussions that occur in the body of a research report.

INSIDE WORK **Observing Structural Features**

Although we've discussed a number of structural expectations for reports in the social sciences, we need to stress again that these expectations are conventional. As such, you'll likely encounter numerous studies in the social sciences that rely on only a few of these structural features or that alter the conventional expectations in light of the researchers' particular aims. For this activity, we'd like you to do the following.

- Select a social science topic.
- Locate two articles published in peer-reviewed academic journals that address some aspect of your selected topic.
- Compare and contrast the two articles in terms of their structural features. Note both (1) instances when the articles follow the conventional expectations for social science reporting as explained in this chapter, and (2) instances when the articles alter or diverge from these expectations. Speculate as to the authors' reasoning for following the conventional expectations or diverging from them. ▶

LANGUAGE CONVENTIONS

As with structural conventions, the way social scientists use language can vary widely with respect to differing audiences and/or genres. Nevertheless, we can explore several language-level conventional expectations for writing in the social sciences. In the following sections, we consider the use of both active and passive voice, as well as the use of hedging (or hedge words) to limit the scope and applicability of assertions.

Active and Passive Voice

Many students have had the experience of receiving a graded paper back from an English teacher in high school and discovering that a sentence or two was marked for awkward or inappropriate use of the passive voice. This problem occurs fairly often as students acclimate their writing to differing disciplinary communities. As we discussed in Chapter 7, the passive voice usually appears with less frequency in the fields of the humanities, but writers in the social sciences and natural sciences use it more frequently, and with good purpose. (For a fuller discussion and examples of the differences between active and passive voice constructions, see pp. 167–68 in Chapter 7.)

You may wonder why anyone would want to add words unnecessarily or remove altogether the actor/agent from a sentence. The passive voice is often preferable in writing in the social sciences and natural sciences because, although it may seem wordy or unclear to some readers in some instances, skillful use of the passive voice can actually foster a sense that researchers are acting objectively or with neutrality. This does not mean that natural or social scientists are averse to the active voice. However, in particular instances, the passive voice can go a long way toward supporting an ethos of objectivity, and its use appears most commonly in the Methods sections of social science reports. Consider these two sentences that might appear in the Methods section of a hypothetical social science report:

Active Voice: We asked participants to identify the factors that most influenced their decision.

Passive Voice: Participants were asked to identify the factors that most influenced their decision.

With the agent, *we*, removed, the sentence in passive voice deemphasizes the researchers conducting the study. In this way, the researchers maintain more of a sense of objectivity or neutrality in their report.

Hedging

Another language feature common to writing in the social sciences is hedging. Hedging typically occurs when researchers want to make a claim or propose an explanation but also want to be extremely careful not to overstep the scope of their findings based on their actual data set. Consider the following sentences:

Participants seemed to be anxious about sharing their feelings on the topic.

Participants were anxious about sharing their feelings on the topic.

When you compare the two, you'll notice that the first sentence "hedges" against making a broad or sweeping claim about the participants. The use of *seemed to be* is a hedge against overstepping, or saying something that may or may not be absolutely true in every case. Other words or phrases that are often used to hedge include the following, just to name a handful:

probably	perhaps
some	possibly
sometimes	might
likely	it appears that
apparently	partially

Considering that social scientists make claims about human behavior, and that participants in a study may or may not agree with the conclusions, it's perhaps not surprising that writers in these fields often make use of hedging.

INSIDE WORK **Observing Language Features**

Use the two articles you located for the previous Inside Work exercise, in which you compared and contrasted their structural conventions.

- This time, study the language of the articles for instances of the two language conventions we've discussed in this section. Try to determine in what sections of the reports passive voice and hedging occur most frequently.

- Offer a rationale for your findings. If you find more instances of the use of passive voice in the Methods sections than in the Results sections, for instance, attempt to explain why that would be the case. Or, if you find more instances of verbal hedging in the Results sections than in the Methods sections, what do you think explains those findings? ❱

REFERENCE CONVENTIONS

The style guide for writing followed in most (but not all) social science fields is the *Publication Manual of the American Psychological Association* (APA). Many referencing conventions of the social sciences are governed by the APA, and some are worth examining in more detail.

In-Text Documentation

One of the distinguishing features of the APA method for documenting sources that are paraphrased, summarized, or cited as part of a report is the inclusion of a source's year of publication as part of the parenthetical notation in or at the end of a sentence in which a source is used. We can compare this to the MLA documentation system described in Chapter 6 through the following examples:

MLA: The study reports that "in some participants, writing block appears to be tied to exhaustion" (Jacobs 23).

APA: The study reports that "in some participants, writing block appears to be tied to exhaustion" (Jacobs, 2009, p. 23).

Although these examples by no means illustrate all the differences between MLA and APA styles of documentation, they do highlight the elevated importance that social science fields place on the year of a source's publication. Why? Imagine that you're reading a sociological study conducted in 2010 that examines the use of tobacco products among teenagers. The study references the finding of a similar study from 1990. By seeing the date of the referenced study in the in-text citation, readers can quickly consider the usefulness of the 1990 study for the one being reported on. Social scientists value recency, or the most current data possible, and their documentation requirements reflect this preference.

Summary and Paraphrase

Another reference distinction among the academic domains concerns how writers reference others' ideas. You've probably had experience writing papers for teachers who required you to cite sources as support for your ideas. You may have done this by copying the language directly from a source. If so, then you noted that these words belonged to another person by putting quotation marks around them and by adding a parenthetical comment identifying the source of the cited language. These practices hold true for writers in the social sciences as well.

However, as you become more familiar with the reference practices of researchers in these fields, you'll discover that social scientists quote researchers in other fields far less frequently than scholars in the humanities do. Why is this so? For humanist scholars, language is of the utmost importance, and how someone conveys an idea can seem almost inseparable from the idea being conveyed. Additionally, for humanists, language is often the "unit of measure"—that is, *how* someone says something (like a novelist or a poet) is actually *what* is being studied. Typically, this is not the case for social science researchers (with the exception of fields such as linguistics and communication, although they primarily address how study participants say something and not how prior research reported its findings). Instead, social scientists tend to be much more interested in other researchers' methodology and findings than they are in the language through which those methods or finding are conveyed. As a result, social scientists are more likely to summarize or paraphrase source materials than to quote them directly.

INSIDE WORK **Observing Reference Features**

In this section, we've suggested that two areas of conventional reference features in social science writing are (1) the elevated position of year of publication in the internal documentation of source material, and (2) the preference among social scientists for summarizing and paraphrasing sources.

- Use the same two studies that you examined for the last two Inside Work activities.

- Based on the principle that social scientists are concerned with the recency of research in their areas, examine the References page (the ending bibliography) for each study. How does the form of entries on the References page reflect the social science concern with the recency of sources?

- Look more closely at the introductions of the two articles, and note the number of times in each article another source is referenced. Count the number of times these sources are paraphrased, summarized, or quoted directly. Based on your findings, what can you conclude about the ways social scientists reference source material? ❱

Genres of Writing in the Social Sciences

Scholars in the social sciences share the results of their research in various ways. As Aya Matsuda reveals in her Insider's View, social scientists write in a variety of forms for differing venues. They might, for instance, present their work at a conference or publish their research results in a journal or a book.

In this section, we offer descriptions of, and steps for producing, two of the most common types of writing, or genres, required of students in introductory-level courses in the social sciences. These are the literature review and the theory-response paper. As genres, literature reviews and responses to social science theories sometimes appear as parts of other, longer works. Sometimes, though, they stand alone as complete works.

THE LITERATURE REVIEW

The literature review (also referred to as a review of scholarship) is one of the most common genres you will encounter in academic writing. Though this chapter is dedicated to writing in the social sciences, and the literature review genre occurs quite frequently in the social sciences, you can find evidence of reviews of scholarship in virtually every academic field—including the humanities, the natural sciences, and applied fields. The skills required for this genre are thus important to the kinds of inquiry that occur across all the academic disciplines.

At its core, the **literature review** is an analysis of published resources related to a specific topic. The purposes of a literature review may vary: students and researchers may conduct a review of scholarship simply to establish what research has already been conducted on a topic, or the review may make a case for how new research can fill in gaps or advance knowledge about a topic. In the former situation, the resulting literature review may appear as a freestanding piece of writing; in the latter, a briefer review of scholarship may be embedded at the start (usually in the introduction) of a research study.

In fact, most published scholarly articles include a review of literature in the first few pages. Besides serving as a means to identify a gap in the scholarship or a place for new scholarship, a literature review helps to establish

Insider's View
There are many kinds of writing that applied linguists do
AYA MATSUDA, LINGUISTICS

COURTESY OF AYA MATSUDA

"My writing is mostly in the form of research papers that are published as articles in scholarly journals or chapters in scholarly books. I also review other applied linguists' manuscripts and write evaluation reports on them, usually to help journal editors decide whether or not to publish manuscripts in their journals. I also write book reviews that are published in scholarly journals. But because of the 'real-life' nature of the kinds of questions my field addresses, there are many other kinds of writing that applied linguists do. Textbooks, articles in newspapers and general magazines, policies, consultation reports, and public education materials (e.g., brochures) are some examples of other types of writing that my colleagues do. Grant writing is also an important kind of writing that researchers in my field do."

researchers' credibility by demonstrating their awareness of what has been discovered about a particular topic or issue. It further respectfully acknowledges the hard work of others within the community of scholarship. Equally important, the literature review illustrates how previous studies interrelate. A good literature review may examine how prior research is similar and different, or it may suggest how a group of researchers' work developed over several years and how scholars have advanced the work of others.

Insider Example
An Embedded Literature Review

Read the first two paragraphs of "Happiness in Everyday Life: The Uses of Experience Sampling," a social science study reported by Mihaly Csikszentmihalyi and Jeremy Hunter, as an example of a review of scholarship that is embedded within a larger study report. As you read, consider the purposes of a literature review to which it responds, including:

- reviewing what is known on a topic or issue
- identifying a gap in scholarship
- establishing the researchers' ethos

Excerpt from **Happiness in Everyday Life: The Uses of Experience Sampling**

MIHALY CSIKSZENTMIHALYI AND JEREMY HUNTER

MIHALY CSIKSZENTMIHALYI

PHOTO BY WILLIAM VASTA

INTRODUCTION

Current understanding of human happiness points at five major effects on this emotion. These are, moving from those most impervious to change to those that are most under personal control: genetic determinants, macro-social conditions, chance events, proximal environment, and personality. It is not unlikely that, as behavioral geneticists insist, a "set level" coded in our chromosomes accounts for perhaps as much as half of the variance in self-reported happiness (Lykken & Tellegen, 1996; Tellegen et al., 1988). These effects are probably mediated by temperamental traits like extraversion, which are partly genetically determined and which are in turn linked to happiness (Myers, 1993). Cross-national comparisons suggest that macro-social conditions such as extreme poverty, war, and social injustice are all obstacles to happiness (Inglehart &

This section of the study's introduction establishes what is known about the topic at hand. It reviews the scholarship of others.

Klingemann, 2000; Veenhoven, 1995). Chance events like personal tragedies, illness, or sudden strokes of good fortune may drastically affect the level of happiness, but apparently these effects do not last long (Brickman et al., 1978; Diener, 2000). One might include under the heading of the proximal environment the social class, community, family, and economic situation—in other words, those factors in the immediate surroundings that may have an impact on a person's well-being. And finally, habits and coping behaviors developed by the individual will have an important effect. Hope, optimism, and the ability to experience flow can be learned and thus moderate one's level of happiness (Csikszentmihalyi, 1997; Seligman, 2002).

In this paper, we present a method that allows investigators to study the impact of momentary changes in the environment on people's happiness levels, as well as its more lasting, trait-like correlates. Research on happiness generally considers this emotion to be a personal trait. The overall happiness level of individuals is measured by a survey or questionnaire, and then "happy" people—those who score higher on a one-time response scale—are contrasted with less happy ones. Whatever distinguishes the two groups is then assumed to be a condition affecting happiness. This perspective is a logical outcome of the methods used, namely, one-time measures. If a person's happiness level is measured only once, it is by definition impossible to detect intra-individual variations. Yet, we know quite well that emotional states, including happiness, are quite volatile and responsive to environmental conditions.

How does this review of previous scholarship affect your view of the writers? What does it say about them?

Reveals the researchers' purpose in the context of the review of scholarship. Identifies a space, or gap, in the scholarship for investigation.

WRITING A LITERATURE REVIEW

The scope of a freestanding literature review can vary greatly, depending on the knowledge and level of interest of the investigator conducting the review. For instance, you may have very little knowledge about autism, so your review of the scholarship might be aimed at learning about various aspects of the condition and issues related to it. If this is the case, your research would cast a pretty wide net. However, let's say you're quite familiar with certain critical aspects of issues related to autism and are interested in one aspect in particular—for example, the best therapies for addressing autism in young children. If this is the case, then you could conduct a review of scholarship with a more focused purpose, narrowing your net to only the studies that address your specific interest. Regardless of the scope of your research interest, though, literature reviews should begin with a clear sense of your topic. One way to narrow the focus of your topic is by proposing one or more research questions about it. (See Chapter 5 for more support for crafting such research questions.)

Once you've clearly established your topic, the next step is to conduct your research. The research you discover and choose to read, which may be quite substantial for a literature review, is chosen according to the scope of your research interest. (For help in narrowing a search based on key terms in your research question, see Chapter 5.) Here are some tips to conducting research:

- As you search for and review possible sources, pay particular attention to the *abstracts* of studies, as they may help you quickly decide if a study is right for your purposes.

- Unless your review of scholarship targets the tracing of a particular thread of research across a range of years, you should probably focus on the most current research available.

- After you've examined and gathered a range of source materials, determine the best way to keep track of the ideas you discover. Many students find this is a good time to produce an annotated bibliography as a first step in creating a literature review. (See Chapter 5, pp. 101–2 for more help on constructing annotated bibliographies.)

Another useful strategy for organizing your sources is a **source synthesis chart**. We recommend this as a way to visualize the areas of overlap in your research, whether for a broad focus (*What are researchers studying with regard to autism?*) or a more narrow one (*What are the best therapies for addressing autism in young children?*). Here's an abbreviated example of a source synthesis chart for a broad review of scholarship on autism:

| Authors of Study | Topics We Expect to Emerge in Scholarship | | | |
	Issues of Diagnosis	*Treatments*	*Debate over Causes*	*Wider Familial Effects*
Solomon et al. (2012)	pp. 252–55 Notes: emphasizes problems families face with diagnosis	pp. 257–60 Notes: examines and proposes strategies for family therapists	p. 253 Notes: acknowledges a series of possible contributing factors	
Vanderborght et al. (2012)		pp. 359–67 (results) Notes: examines use of robot for storytelling		
Grindle et al. (2012)		pp. 208–313 (results) Notes: school-based behavioral intervention program (ABA)		p. 229 Notes: home-based therapy programs
Lilley (2011)	pp. 135–37 Notes: explores the roles of mothers in diagnosis processes	pp. 143–51 Notes: explores rationales and lived experiences of ABA and non-ABA supporters		

In this case, the studies that we read are named in the column under "Authors of Study." The topics or issues that we anticipated would emerge from our review of the sources are shown in the top row. Based on our reading of a limited number of studies, four at this point, we can already discern a couple of areas of overlap in the scholarship: the diagnosis of autism in children, and intervention programs for children with autism. We can tell which researchers talked about what issues at any given time because we've noted the areas (by page number, along with some detail) where they addressed these issues. The empty cells in the synthesis chart reveal that our review of the sources, thus far at least, suggests there is less concern for those topics. We should note, however, that our review of sources is far from exhaustive. If you're able to create a visual representation of your research such as this one, then you're well on your way to creating a successful literature review. Keep in mind that the more detailed you can make your synthesis chart, the easier your process may be moving forward.

The last step before writing is perhaps the most challenging. You must synthesize the sources. **Synthesizing sources** is the process of identifying and describing the relationships between and among researchers' ideas or approaches: What trends emerge? Does the Grindle et al. study say something similar to the Lilley study about behavioral interventions? Something different? Do they share methods? Do they approach the issue of behavioral interventions similarly or differently? Defining the relationships between the studies and making these relationships explicit is critically important to your success. As you read the sources, you'll likely engage in an internal process of comparing and contrasting the researchers' ideas. You might even recognize similarities and differences in the researchers' approaches to the topic. Many of these ideas will probably be reflected in your synthesis chart, and you might consider color-coding (or highlighting in different colors) various cells to indicate types of relationships among the researchers you note.

A quick review of the abstract to "The Experience of Infertility: A Review of Recent Literature," a freestanding literature review published in the academic journal *Sociology of Health and Illness*, demonstrates the areas of synthesis that emerged from the professionals' examination of recent research on infertility:

> About 10 years ago Greil published a review and critique of the literature on the socio-psychological impact of infertility. He found at the time that most scholars treated infertility as a medical condition with psychological consequences rather than as a socially constructed reality. This article examines research published since the last review. More studies now place infertility within larger social contexts and social scientific frameworks, although clinical emphases persist. Methodological problems remain, but important improvements are also evident. We identify two vigorous research traditions in the social scientific study of infertility. One tradition uses primarily quantitative techniques to study clinic patients in order to improve service delivery and to

Four synthesis points: (1) more recent studies approach the topic of infertility differently; (2) there remains a focus on examining infertility from a clinical viewpoint; (3) there are still questions about research methods, but there have also been "important improvements" in methods; (4) two trends emerged from these scholars' review of the current research.

assess the need for psychological counseling. The other tradition uses primarily qualitative research to capture the experiences of infertile people in a sociocultural context. We conclude that more attention is now being paid to the ways in which the experience of infertility is shaped by social context. We call for continued progress in the development of a distinctly sociological approach to infertility and for the continued integration of the two research traditions identified here.

Another example, this one a brief excerpt from the introduction to Csikszentmihalyi and Hunter's "Happiness in Everyday Life: The Uses of Experience Sampling," demonstrates the kind of synthesis that typically appears in reviews of scholarship when they're embedded as part of a larger study:

Cross-national comparisons suggest that macro-social conditions such as extreme poverty, war, and social injustice are all obstacles to happiness (Inglehart & Klingemann, 2000; Veenhoven, 1995). Chance events like personal tragedies, illness, or sudden strokes of good fortune may drastically affect the level of happiness, but apparently these effects do not last long (Brickman et al., 1978; Diener, 2000).

Writing a Literature Review

Your goal in this writing project, a freestanding literature review, is to provide an overview of the research that has been conducted on a topic of interest to you.

THE INTRODUCTION

The opening of your literature review should introduce the topic you're exploring and assess the state of the available scholarship on it: What are the current areas of interest? What are the issues or elements related to a particular topic being discussed? Is there general agreement? Are there other clear trends in the scholarship? Are there areas of convergence and divergence?

THE BODY

Paragraphs within the body of your literature review should be organized according to the issues or synthesized areas you're exploring. For example, based on the synthesis chart shown earlier, we might suggest that one of the body sections of a broadly focused review of scholarship on autism concern issues of diagnosis. We might further reveal, in our topic sentence to that section of the literature review, that we've synthesized the available research in this area and that it seems uniformly to suggest that although many factors have been studied, no credible studies establish a direct link between any contributing factor and the occurrence of autism in children. The rest of that section of our paper would explore the factors that have been examined in the research to support the claim in our topic sentence.

Keep in mind that the body paragraphs should be organized according to a claim about the topic or ideas being explored. They should not be organized merely as successive summaries of the sources. Such an organization does not promote effective synthesis.

THE CONCLUSION

Your conclusion should reiterate your overall assessment of the scholarship. Notify your readers of any gaps you've determined in the scholarship, and consider suggesting areas where future scholarship can make more contributions.

TECHNICAL CONSIDERATIONS

Keep in mind the conventions of writing in the social sciences that you've learned about throughout this chapter. Use APA documentation procedures for in-text documentation of summarized, paraphrased, and cited materials, as well as for the References page at the end of your literature review.

Insider Example
Student Literature Review

William O'Brien, a first-year writing student who had a particular interest in understanding the effects of sleep deprivation, composed the following literature review. As you read, notice how William's text indicates evidence of synthesis both between and among the sources he used to build his project. Notice also that he follows APA style conventions in his review.

Effects of Sleep Deprivation: A Literature Review

William O'Brien

North Carolina State University

Effects of Sleep Deprivation: A Literature Review

Introduction

Everybody knows the feeling of having to struggle through a long day after a night of poor sleep, or sometimes even none at all. You may feel groggy, cloudy, clumsy, or unable to think of simple things. Sometimes you may even feel completely fine but then get angry or frustrated at things that normally would not affect you. No matter how you deal with it on that particular day, the reality is that even slight sleep deprivation can have extremely negative effects on mental ability. These effects are amplified when poor sleep continues for a long period of time. In a society with an ever-increasing number of distractions, it is becoming harder for many people to get the recommended amount of sleep. Sleep issues plague the majority of the U.S. population in one way or another. The Centers for Disease Control recognizes insufficient sleep as a public health epidemic.

A lot of research is being conducted relating to sleep and sleep deprivation, and for good reason. Most researchers seem to agree that short-term sleep deprivation has purely negative effects on mental functioning in general. However, the particular types of effects caused by poor sleep are still being debated, as are the long-term implications of sleep deprivation. The questions for researchers, then, are under what circumstances do these negative effects begin to show, to what extent do they show, and most significant, what exactly are these negative effects?

Short-Term Effects of Sleep Deprivation

In order to examine the direct and immediate effects of sleep deprivation, numerous researchers rely on experimentation, to control for other variables, for results. Research by Minkel et al. (2012) identified a gap in the

The writer establishes the general topic, sleep deprivation, in the opening paragraph.

SYNTHESIS POINT: scholars agree on the negative effects of short-term sleep deprivation.

SYNTHESIS POINT: questions remain about the effects of long-term sleep deprivation.

Focuses on scholarship that uses experimental studies to examine the effects of short-term sleep deprivation.

research relating to how sleep deprivation affects the stress response (p. 1015). In order to test how inadequate sleep affects the stress response, the researchers divided healthy adults into two groups. Participants in the first group acted as the control and were allowed a 9-hour sleeping opportunity during the night. The second group was not allowed to sleep at all during that night. The next day, the participants completed stressful mental tasks (primarily math) and were asked to report their stress levels and mood via visual scales (Minkel et al., 2012, pp. 1016-1017). The researchers hypothesized that insufficient sleep would increase the stress response to each stressor as compared to the rested group, and that sleep loss would increase the stress response in proportion to the severity of the stressor (p. 1016). Their findings, however, showed that while the negative response to stressors was more profound for the sleep-deprived group, the differences in stress response between groups were not significant for the high-stressor condition. Still, the research clearly showed that sleep-deprived people have "significantly greater subjective stress, anger, and anxiety" in response to low-level stressors (p. 1019).

Research by Jugovac and Cavallero (2012) also focused on the immediate effects of sleep deprivation on attention. This study's purpose was to research the effects of sleep deprivation on attention through three attentional networks: phasic alerting, covert orienting, and executive control (Jugovac & Cavallero, 2012, p. 115). The study tested 30 young adults using the Attention Network Test (ANT), the Stanford Sleepiness Scale (SSS), and the Global Vigor-Affect Scale (GVA) before and after a 24-hour sleep deprivation period (p. 116). (All participants were subjected to sleep deprivation, because the tests before the sleep deprivation

Links the two studies reviewed according to their similar focus on short-term effects of sleep deprivation

served as the control.) The findings built upon the idea that sleep deprivation decreases vigilance and that it impairs the "executive control" attentional network, while appearing to leave the other components (alerting and orienting) relatively unchanged (pp. 121-122). These findings help explain how one night of missed sleep negatively affects a person's attention, by distinguishing the effects on each of the three particular attentional networks.

Research by Giesbrecht, Smeets, Leppink, Jelicic, and Merckelbach (2013) focused on the effects that short-term sleep deprivation has on dissociation. This research is interesting and different from the other research in that it connects sleep deprivation to mental illness rather than just temporarily reduced mental functioning. The researchers used 25 healthy undergraduate students and kept all participants awake throughout one night. Four different scales were used to record their feelings and dissociative reactions while being subjected to two different cognitive tasks (Giesbrecht et al., 2013, pp. 150-152). The cognitive tasks completed before the night of sleep deprivation were used to compare the results of the cognitive tasks completed after the night of sleep deprivation. Although the study was small and the implications are still somewhat unclear, the study showed a clear link between sleep deprivation and dissociative symptoms (pp. 156-158).

It is clear that sleep deprivation negatively affects people in many different ways. These researchers each considered a different type of specific effect, and together they form a wide knowledge base supporting the idea that even a very short-term (24-hour) loss of sleep for a healthy adult may have multiple negative impacts on mental and emotional well-being. These effects include increased anxiety, anger,

> The writer links this study to the continuing discussion of short-term effects of sleep deprivation but also notes a difference.

> This paragraph provides a summative synthesis, or an overview of the findings among the sources reviewed.

and stress in response to small stressors (Minkel et al., 2012), inhibited attention—the executive control attentional network more specifically (Jugovac & Cavallero, 2012)—and increased dissociative symptoms (Giesbrecht et al., 2013).

Long-Term Effects of Sleep Deprivation

Although the research on short-term effects of sleep deprivation reveals numerous negative consequences, there may be other, less obvious, implications that studies on short-term effect cannot illuminate. In order to better understand these other implications, we must examine research relating to the possible long-term effects of limited sleep. Unfortunately, long-term sleep deprivation experiments do not seem to have been done and are probably not possible (due to ethical reasons and safety reasons, among other factors). A study by Duggan, Reynolds, Kern, and Friedman (2014) pointed out the general lack of previous research into the long-term effects of sleep deprivation, but it examined whether there was a link between average sleep duration during childhood and life-long mortality risk (p. 1195). The researchers analyzed data from 1,145 participants in the Terman Life Cycle Study from the early 1900s, which measured bedtime and wake time along with year of death. The amount of sleep was adjusted by age in order to find the deviations from average sleep time for each age group. The data were also separated by sex (Duggan et al., 2014, pp. 1196-1197). The results showed that, for males, sleeping either more or less than the regular amount of time for each age group correlated with an increased life-long mortality risk (p. 1199). Strangely, this connection was not present for females. For males, however, this is a very important finding. Since we can surmise that the childhood sleep patterns are independent of and unrelated to any underlying health issues that ultimately cause the deaths later

The writer shifts to an examination of the long-term effects of sleep deprivation and acknowledges a shift in the methods for these studies.

on in life, it is more reasonable to assume causation rather than simply correlation. Thus, the pattern that emerged may demonstrate that too little, or too much, sleep during childhood can cause physiological issues, leading to death earlier in life, which also reaffirms the idea that sleep is extremely important for maintaining good health.

While this study examined the relationship between sleep duration and death, a study by Kelly and El-Sheikh (2014) examined the relationship between sleep and a slightly less serious, but still very important, subject: the adjustment and development of children in school over a period of time. The study followed 176 third grade children (this number dropped to 113 by the end of the study) as they progressed through school for five years, recording sleep patterns and characteristics of adjustment (Kelly & El-Sheikh, 2014, pp. 1137-1139). Sleep was recorded both subjectively through self-reporting and objectively though "actigraphy" in order to assess a large variety of sleep parameters (p. 1137). The study results indicated that reduced sleep time and poorer-quality sleep are risk factors for problems adjusting over time to new situations. The results also indicate that the opposite effect is true, but to a lesser extent (p. 1146).

From this research, we gain the understanding that sleep deprivation and poor sleep quality are related to problems adjusting over time. This effect is likely due to the generally accepted idea that sleep deprivation negatively affects cognitive performance and emotional regulation, as described in the Kelly and El-Sheikh article (2014, pp. 1144-1145). If cognitive performance and emotional regulation are negatively affected by a lack of sleep, then it makes sense that the sleep-deprived child would struggle to adjust over time as compared to a well-rested child. This hypothesis has

> Establishes one of the study's central findings related to long-term effects of sleep deprivation

important implications. It once again affirms the idea that receiving the appropriate amount of quality sleep is very important for developing children. This basic idea does not go against the research by Duggan et al. (2014) in any way; rather, it complements it. The main difference between each study is that the research by Duggan et al. shows that too much sleep can also be related to a greater risk of death earlier in life. Together, both articles provide evidence that deviation from the appropriate amount of sleep causes very negative long-term effects, including, but certainly not limited to, worse adjustment over time (Kelly & El-Sheikh, 2014) and increased mortality rates (Duggan et al., 2014).

Provides a summative synthesis that examines relationships between the sources and considers implications of findings

Conclusion

This research provides great insight into the short-term and long-term effects of sleep deprivation. Duggan et al. (2014) showed increased mortality rates among people who slept too much as well as too little. This result could use some additional research. Through the analysis of each article, we see just how damaging sleep deprivation can be, even after a short period of time, and thus it is important to seriously consider preventative measures. While sleep issues can manifest themselves in many different ways, especially in legitimate sleep disorders such as insomnia, just the simple act of not allowing oneself to get enough sleep every night can have significant negative effects. Building on this, there seems to be a general lack of discussion on *why* people (who do not have sleep disorders) do not get enough time to sleep. One possible reason is the ever-increasing number of distractions, especially in the form of electronics, that may lead to overstimulation. Another answer may be that high demands placed on students and adults through school and work, respectively, do not give them time to sleep enough.

Conclusion acknowledges what appears as a gap in the scholarship reviewed

The most probable, yet most generalized, answer, however, is that people simply do not appropriately manage their time in order to get enough sleep. People seem to prioritize everything else ahead of sleeping, thus causing the damaging effects of sleep deprivation to emerge. Regardless, this research is valuable for anyone who wants to live a healthy lifestyle and function at full mental capacity. Sleep deprivation seems to have solely negative consequences; thus, it is in every person's best interests to get a full night of quality sleep as often as possible.

References

Duggan, K., Reynolds, C., Kern, M., & Friedman, H. (2014).
    Childhood sleep duration and lifelong mortality risk.
    Health Psychology, *33*(10), 1195-1203. doi:10.1037
    /hea0000078

Giesbrecht, T., Smeets, T., Leppink, J., Jelicic, M., &
    Merckelbach, H. (2013). Acute dissociation after one
    night of sleep loss. *Psychology of Consciousness:
    Theory, Research, and Practice*, *1*(S), 150-159.
    doi:10.1037/2326-5523.1.S.150

Jugovac, D., & Cavallero, C. (2012). Twenty-four hours of
    total sleep deprivation selectively impairs attentional
    networks. *Experimental Psychology*, *59*(3), 115-123.
    doi:10.1027/1618-3169/a000133

Kelly, R., & El-Sheikh, M. (2014). Reciprocal relations between
    children's sleep and their adjustment over time.
    Developmental Psychology, *50*(4), 1137-1147. doi:10.1037
    /a0034501

Minkel, J., Banks, S., Htaik, O., Moreta, M., Jones, C.,
    McGlinchey, E., Simpson, N., & Dinges, D. (2012). Sleep
    deprivation and stressors: Evidence for elevated negative
    affect in response to mild stressors when sleep deprived.
    Emotion, *12*(5), 1015-1020. doi:10.1037/a0026871

THEORY RESPONSE ESSAY

Faculty in the fields of the social sciences often ask students to apply a social science theory to their own experiences. Psychology, sociology, and communication professors may ask students to use a psychological, sociological, or communication theory as a lens through which to explain their own or others' behaviors. Assignments like these involve writing a **theory response essay**. These assignments are popular for a number of reasons: (1) they allow students to engage with the fundamental elements of social sciences (theories); (2) they allow students to attend to the basic processes of data collection that are common in the social sciences; and (3) they are often quite engaging for faculty to read and are among the most interesting for students to write.

Whether you're using elements of Freud's dream theories to help understand your own dreams or you're using an interpersonal communication theory to understand why people so easily engage with you, the theory you're working with provides the frame for your analysis of some event or action. The theory is the core of any theory response.

Precisely because the theory is the core of such a writing project, it's crucial that in the beginning stage of such a project, you work with a theory that is actually applicable to the event, action, or phenomenon you want to understand better. You also want to choose a theory that genuinely interests you. Luckily, theories of human behavior and human system interactions abound. If you aren't assigned a theory for the project, then consider the places where you might go about locating a workable theory. Textbooks in the social sciences frequently make reference to theories, and numerous academic websites maintain lists and explanations of social science theories. Here are a few categories of theories that students often find interesting:

birth order theories   friendship theories

parenting style theories   stage theories of grieving

addiction theories

If you're unable to locate a workable theory that's "ready-made" for application to some experience(s), then consider building a theory based on your reading of a social science study. Though this certainly makes completing the assignment challenging, it is not without rewards.

Personal Experience

Regardless of whether you're working with a particular theory or constructing a theory of behavior based on one or more studies, consider making a list of the "moments" or events in your life that the theory might help you understand further. Your next step might be to write out detailed descriptions of those events as you see or remember them. Capture as much detail as you can, especially if you're writing from memory. Then apply the theory (all of its component parts) to your event or moment to see what it can illuminate for you: Where does it really help you understand something? Where does it fail to help? How might the theory need to change to account for your experiences?

Others' Experiences

Some instructors might ask you to collect and analyze the experiences of others. If you're assigned to do this, then you'll need to consider a data-collection method very carefully and ask your instructor if there are specific procedures at your institution that you should follow when collecting data from other people. We recommend, for now, that you think about the methods most commonly associated with qualitative research: observations, interviews, and open-ended surveys. These rich data-producing methods are most likely to provide the level of detail about others' experiences needed to evaluate the elements of your theory. Trying to understand others' experiences in light of the theory you're working with means considering the same analytical questions that you applied to your own experiences: Where does the theory really help you understand something? Where does it fail to help? How might the theory need to change to account for the experiences of those in your study?

WRITING PROJECT

Writing a Theory Response

The goal of this writing project is to apply a theoretical framework from an area of the social sciences to your own experiences, to the experiences of others, or to both. The first step is to choose a theoretical framework that has some relevance to you, providing ample opportunity to reflect on and write about your own experiences in relation to the theory.

THE INTRODUCTION

The introduction to your study should introduce readers to the theory and explain all of its essential elements. You should also be clear about whether you're applying the theory to your own experiences, to the experiences of others, or to both. In light of the work you did applying the theory, formulate a thesis that assesses the value of the theory for helping to understand the "moments," events, or phenomena you studied.

THE BODY

The body can be organized in a number of ways. If your theory has clear stages or elements, then you can explain each one and apply it to relevant parts of your experiences or those of others. If the theory operates in such a way that it's difficult to break into parts or stages or elements, then consider whether or not it's better to have subheadings that identify either (1) the themes that emerged from your application, or (2) your research subjects (by pseudonym). In this case, your body sections would be more like case studies. Ultimately, the organization strategy you choose will depend on the nature of the theory you're applying and the kinds of events you apply it to. The body of your project should establish connections among the theory's component elements.

THE CONCLUSION

The conclusion of your study should assert your overall assessment of the theory's usefulness. Reiterate how the theory was useful and how it wasn't. Make recommendations for how it might need to be changed in order to account for the experiences you examined in light of the theory.

TECHNICAL CONSIDERATIONS

Keep in mind the conventions of writing in the social sciences that you've learned about throughout this chapter. Use APA documentation procedures for in-text documentation of summarized, paraphrased, and cited materials, as well as for the References page at the end of your study.

Insider Example
Student Theory Response Paper

Matt Kapadia, a first-year writing student, was interested in understanding the ways people rationalize their own successes and failures. In the following paper, he analyzes and evaluates a theory about the social science phenomenon of attribution (as described at changingminds.org) through the lenses of both his own and others' experiences. As you read Matt's paper, pay close attention to the moments when he offers evaluation of the theory. Ask yourself if his evaluation in each instance makes sense to you, based on the evidence he provides. Notice also that he follows APA style conventions in his paper.

Evaluation of the Attribution Theory

Matt Kapadia

North Carolina State University

Evaluation of the Attribution Theory

In an attempt to get a better sense of control, human beings are constantly attributing cause to the events that happen around them (Straker, 2008). Of all the things people attribute causes to, behavior is among the most common. The attribution theory aims to explain how people attribute the causes of their own behaviors compared to the behaviors of those around them. Behaviors can be attributed to both internal and external causes. Internal causes are things that people can control or are part of their personality, whereas external causes are purely circumstantial and people have no control over the resulting events (Straker, 2008). The attribution theory uses these internal and external causes to explain its two major components: the self-serving bias and the fundamental attribution error. The self-serving bias evaluates how we attribute our own behaviors, whereas the fundamental attribution error evaluates how we attribute the behaviors of those around us (Straker, 2008). This paper evaluates how applicable the attribution theory and its components are, using examples from personal experience as well as data collected from others. Based on the findings of this evaluation, I believe the attribution theory holds true on nearly all accounts; however, the category of the self-serving bias might need revision in the specific area dealing with professionals in any field of study or in the case of professional athletes.

Attribution Theory: An Explanation

The foundation of the attribution theory is based in the nature of the causes people attribute behaviors to, whether it be internal or external. A person has no control over an external cause (Straker, 2008). An example would be a student failing a math test because the instructor used the

> The writer establishes a thesis that includes an evaluation of the theory's usefulness in various contexts.

> In this paragraph and the next two, the writer reviews and exemplifies the component parts of the theory. That is, the writer offers an explanation of the theory, with examples to illustrate points, as appropriate.

wrong answer key. In this case, the student had no control over the grade he received, and it did not matter how much he had studied. A bad grade was inevitable. A person can also attribute behavioral causes to internal causes. Internal causes are in complete control of the person distributing the behavior and are typically attributed to part of the individual's personality (Straker, 2008). An example would be a student getting a poor grade on his math test because he is generally lazy and does not study. In this case, the student had complete control of his grade and chose not to study, which resulted in the poor grade. These two causes build up to the two major categories within the attribution theory.

The first major category of the attribution theory is that of self-serving bias. This category explores how people attribute causes to their own behaviors. It essentially states that people are more likely to give themselves the benefit of the doubt. People tend to attribute their poor behaviors to external causes and their good behaviors to internal causes (Straker, 2008). An example would be a student saying he received a poor grade on a test because his instructor does not like him. In this case, the student is attributing his poor behavior, making a poor grade on the test, to the external cause of his instructor not liking him. However, following the logic of the theory, if the student had made a good grade on the test, then he would attribute that behavior to an internal cause such as his own good study habits.

The second category of the attribution theory, the fundamental attribution error, states the opposite of the self-serving bias. The fundamental attribution error talks about how people attribute cause to the behaviors of those around them. It states that people are more likely to attribute others' poor behaviors to internal causes and their good behaviors to external causes (Straker, 2008). An example would be a student saying his friend got a better grade on the math test than him because the instructor likes his friend more. The student jumps to the conclusion that his friend's good grade was due to the external cause of the instructor liking the friend more. Moreover, if his friend had done poorly on the test, the student would most likely attribute the poor grade to an internal factor, such as his friend not studying for tests.

Personal Experiences

A situation from my personal experiences that exemplifies the ideas of the attribution theory is my high school golfing career. For my first two years of high school, I performed relatively poorly on the golf course. My team consistently placed last in tournaments, and I ranked nowhere near the top golfers from neighboring high schools. I blamed my performance on factors such as the wind and flat-out bad luck. At the same time, I attributed my teammates' poor performances to factors such as not practicing hard enough to compete in tournament play. In doing this, I became no better a golfer because I was denying that the true cause of my poor scores was the fact that I was making bad swings and not putting in the hours of work needed to perform at a higher level. I finally recognized this during my junior year of high school. I started to realize that blaming everything but myself was getting me nowhere and that the only way to improve was to take responsibility for my own play. I started practicing in areas where my game needed improvement and putting in hours at the driving range to improve my swing memory. In doing this, I became a much better player; by the time my senior season came around, I was ranked one of the top golfers in my conference and one of the best amateur players in the state of North Carolina. However, my team still did not perform

The writer details a particular personal experience that he'll later analyze through the lens of the theory.

well due to my teammates' performance, which I continued to attribute to their poor practice habits.

In this section, the writer analyzes his experiences through the lens of the theory.

This experience reflects the attribution theory in several ways. I displayed self-serving bias in my early years of high school golf. I attributed all of my poor performances to external causes, such as the wind, that I could not control. At the same time, I was displaying the fundamental attribution error in attributing my teammates' poor performances to internal causes such as not practicing hard enough. Throughout my high school golf career, I displayed the ideas of the attribution theory's category of the fundamental attribution error. However, during my junior and senior seasons my attributions moved away from the attribution theory's category of the self-serving bias. I began to attribute my poor performance to internal causes instead of the external causes I had previously blamed for my mishaps.

I believe that this is generally true for any athlete or professional seeking improvement in his or her prospective field. If a person continues to follow the ideas discussed in the category of the self-serving bias, he is not likely to improve at what he is trying to do. If Tiger Woods had constantly attributed his bad play to external causes and not taken responsibility for his actions as internal causes, he would have never become the best golfer in the world. Without attributing his poor behaviors to internal causes, he would have never gained the motivation to put in the hours of work necessary to make him the best. This observation can be applied to any other professional field, not only athletics. Personal improvement is only likely to take place when a person begins to attribute his or her poor behaviors to internal causes. I believe athletes and professionals represent problem areas for the theory of self-serving bias. However, the ideas of the fundamental attribution error generally hold true.

Experiences of Others

To evaluate the attribution theory, I conducted an experiment to test both the fundamental attribution error and the self-serving bias. The test subjects were three friends in the same class at North Carolina State University: MEA101, Introduction to Geology. The students were asked to write down if their grades were good or bad on the first test of the semester ("good" meant they received an 80 or higher on the test, and "bad" meant they received below an 80). After the three students had done this for themselves, they were asked to attribute the grades of the others to a cause. This activity provided a clear sample of data that could test the validity of the self-serving bias and the fundamental attribution error. The reason I chose a group of friends versus a group of random strangers was that when people know each other they are more likely to attribute behavioral causes truthfully, without worrying about hurting anyone's feelings.

For the purposes of this experiment, the test subjects will be addressed as Students X, Y, and Z to keep their names confidential. The results of the experiment were as follows. The first student, Student X, received a "bad" grade on the test and attributed this to the instructor not adequately explaining the information in class and not telling the students everything the test would ultimately cover. However, Students Y and Z seemed to conclude that the reason Student X got a "bad" grade was because he did not study enough and is generally lazy when it comes to college test taking. Student Y received a "good" grade on the test and attributed this to studying hard the night before and to the fact that the test was relatively easy if one studied the notes. Students X and Z seemed to conclude that Student Y is a naturally smart student who usually receives good grades on tests regardless of how

The writer provides some insight into his methods for collecting data on the experiences of others.

In this section, the writer provides the results of his data collection.

much he or she studies. Finally, Student Z received a "bad" grade on the test and attributed this to the instructor not covering the material on the test well enough for students to do well, a similar response to Student X. However, Students X and Y attributed Student Z's poor grade to bad study habits and not taking the class seriously.

In this section, the writer discusses the implications of his findings for his overall evaluation of the theory.

These results tend to prove the ideas of both of the attribution theory's categories. Student X attributed his poor grade to the external cause of the instructor not covering the material well enough, demonstrating the self-serving bias. Students Y and Z attributed Student X's poor grade to the internal cause of Student X not studying hard enough and being a generally lazy college student, exemplifying the ideas of the fundamental attribution error. Student Y attributed her good grade to the internal cause of good study habits, also exemplifying the self-serving bias. However, Students X and Z felt that the reason for Student Y's success was the external cause of being a naturally good student who does well with or without studying, reflecting the ideas of the fundamental attribution error. Student Z's results also hold true to the theory. Student Z attributed his poor grade to the external cause of the instructor not covering the material adequately, a belief shared by Student X. Also holding true to the fundamental attribution error, both Students X and Y attributed Student Z's failure to the internal cause of poor study habits. Based on the findings of this experiment, I can say that both the fundamental attribution error and the self-serving bias hold true on all accounts.

Conclusion

The writer concludes his response paper by reviewing his overall evaluation of the theory in light of his own and others' experiences he analyzed.

Overall, I believe the attribution theory's categories of the self-serving bias and the fundamental attribution error are very applicable to everyday life. Based on the data gathered through personal experiences and the experiences of others through the experiment described in this analysis, I believe the theory holds true in the vast majority of situations where people attribute causes to behaviors and/or actions. The only area needing revisions is the self-serving bias when applied to the specific situations of professionals in a field of study or in the case of professional athletes. In both situations, improvement must occur in order to become a professional, and the only way this is likely to happen is by accepting internal fault for poor behaviors. By accepting internal fault, a person gains the motivation to put in the hours of work necessary to learn and improve at what he or she is trying to do. Without this improvement and learning, the ability to reach the professional level is slim to none. This displays the exact opposite of the attribution ideas that are described in the self-serving bias. With the exception of this small niche of situations that falsify the self-serving bias, the validity of the attribution theory is confirmed on all accounts.

Reference

Straker, D. (2008). *Attribution theory*. Retrieved from
changingminds.org: http://changingminds.org
/explanations/theories/attribution_theory.htm

- **Observation plays a critical role in the social sciences.** The academic fields of the social sciences, including sociology, psychology, anthropology, communication studies, and political science, among others, make observations about human behavior and interactions, as well as the systems and social structures we create to organize the world around us.

- **Social science research rests on theories of human behavior and human systems,** propositions that are used to explain specific phenomena. Social science research contributes to the continual process of refining these theories.

- **Researchers in the social sciences typically establish a hypothesis,** or a testable proposition that provides an answer or predicts an outcome in response to the research question(s) at hand, at the beginning of a research project.

- **Social science researchers must make choices about the types of methods they use** in any research situation, based on the nature of their line of inquiry and the kind of research question(s) they seek to answer. They may use a quantitative, qualitative, or mixed-methods research design to collect data for analysis.

- **Social scientists must guard against bias in their research.** They rely on rigorous procedures and checks (e.g., ensuring appropriate sample sizes and/or using multiple forms of qualitative data) to ensure that the influence of any biases is as limited as possible.

- **IMRaD format—Introduction, Methods, Results, and Discussion—is a common structure used for the organization of research reports in the social sciences.** Although research reports in the social sciences may appear in any number of forms, much of the scholarship published in these fields appears in the IMRaD format.

- **The passive voice and hedging are uses of *language* that characterize, for good reason,** social scientific writing.

- **APA style is the most common documentation style used for *reference* in** the fields of the social sciences.

- **The genres of the literature review and the theory response paper are often produced in the fields of the social sciences.**

Reading and Writing in the Natural Sciences

Introduction to the Natural Sciences

Each of us has likely observed something peculiar in the natural world and asked, "Why does it do that?" or "Why does that happen?" Perhaps you've observed twinkling stars in the night sky and wanted to know why such distant light seems to move and pulse. Or perhaps you've wondered why, as you drive, trees closer to your car appear to rush by much faster than trees in the distance. Maybe you can recall the first time you looked at a living cell under a microscope in a biology course and wondered about the world revealed on the slide.

For most scientists, observation of natural phenomena is the first step in the process of conducting research. Something in the natural world captures their attention and compels them to pose questions. Some moments of scientific observation are iconic—such as Newton's observation of an apple falling from a tree as inspiration for his theory of gravity.

We interviewed Sian Proctor, a geologist at South Mountain Community College in Phoenix, Arizona, where she teaches classes in physical, environmental, and historical geology. Proctor has participated in several unique research team experiences, including the Hawaii Space Exploration Analog and Simulation (HI-SEAS) Mars habitat, the NASA Spaceflight and Life Sciences Training Program (she was a finalist for the 2009 NASA Astronaut Program), and the PolarTREC (Teachers and Researchers Exploring and Collaborating) program in Barrow, Alaska. Her work has taken her out

ANDREA TSURUMI

of the college/university setting many times. In her Insider's View, she describes the varied places in which scientists conduct observations and collect data as part of their work to understand the natural world.

Proctor's description of her field explains that those who work in the **natural sciences** study observable phenomena in the natural world and search for answers to the questions that spark their interests about these phenomena. The disciplines of the natural sciences include a wide array of fields of academic research, including those in agricultural and life sciences, as well as physical sciences. As Proctor's own life experiences suggest, the search for understanding of natural phenomena can take scientists to many different places, and there is much variety in the ways they engage in research. One aspect that holds this diverse group of disciplines together, though, is a set of common values and procedures used in conducting research. You're probably already familiar with or at least have heard about the **scientific method**, a protocol for conducting research in the sciences that includes the following elements, or steps:

1. Observe.
2. Ask a research question.
3. Formulate a hypothesis.
4. Test the hypothesis.
5. Explain the results.

In this chapter, we describe a process of writing activities involved in scientific research. We present a four-step **scientific writing process** that maps onto the elements of the scientific method. The process begins with careful observation of natural phenomena and leads to the development of research questions. This step is followed by an investigation that culminates in the reporting or publication of the research:

1. Observe and describe.
2. Speculate.
3. Experiment.
4. Report.

The following table illustrates how the elements of the scientific method map onto a scientific writing process:

Before we delve too deeply into the research and writing practices of students and scholars of the sciences and how they connect, though, let's consider some of the areas of inquiry that make up the natural sciences.

Astronomy, biology, chemistry, earth science, physics, and mathematics are some of the core disciplinary areas within the natural sciences. Each area of inquiry includes numerous areas of specialty, or fields. For example, quantum physics, acoustics, and thermodynamics are three fields of physics. Conservation biology and marine science are fields of biology. Ecology (the study of organisms and their relationships to their environments) also operates under the umbrella of biology.

Interdisciplinary research is quite common in the natural sciences. An **interdisciplinary field** is an area of study in which different disciplinary perspectives or methods are combined into one. In such instances, methods for data collection often associated with one field may be used within another field of study. Consider biochemistry and biophysics, two interdisciplinary fields. In biochemistry, methods often associated with chemistry research are useful in answering questions about living organisms and biological systems. A biochemist may study aspects of a living organism such as blood alkalinity and its impact on liver function. Likewise, researchers in biophysics may use methods typical of physicists to answer research questions about biological systems. Biophysicists, for instance, might use the methodology of physics to unlock the mysteries of human DNA.

Research in the Natural Sciences

No matter the specific fields in which scientists work, they all collect, analyze, and explain data. Scientists tend to embrace a shared set of values, and as a result they typically share similar desires about how best to conduct research. The importance of any scientific study and its power to explain a natural phenomenon, then, are largely based on how well a researcher or research team designs and carries out a study in light of the shared values and desires of the community's members.

Completing the steps of a research project in a logical order and reporting the results accurately are keys to mastering research and writing in the natural sciences. You must observe and describe an object of study before you can speculate as to what it is or why it does what it does. Once you've described and speculated about a particular phenomenon, and posed a research question and a hypothesis about it, then you're positioned well to construct an experiment (if appropriate) and collect data to test whether your hypothesis holds true. When you report the results of your research, you must describe these steps and the data collected accurately and clearly. These research and writing steps build on one another, and we explore each step in more detail moving forward.

We interviewed biomedical scientist Paige Geiger, who teaches in the Department of Molecular and Integrative Physiology at the University of Kansas Medical Center, where she conducts experimental research in a laboratory on the effects of exercise and age on muscle metabolism and insulin resistance in Type II diabetes. In her Insider's View, she describes the kind of work that natural scientists do in her field and the importance of conducting careful, thorough data collection in the sciences.

Natural scientists collect evidence through systematic observation and experimentation, and they value methods that are quantifiable and replicable. In some instances, the natural sciences are described as "hard" sciences and the social sciences as "soft." This distinction stems from the tendency for natural scientists to value quantitative methods over qualitative methods, whereas social scientists often engage in both forms of data collection and sometimes combine quantitative and qualitative methods in a single study. (See Chapter 8,

Insider's View
We value innovation, ideas, accurate interpretation of data, and scientific integrity
PAIGE GEIGER, MOLECULAR AND INTEGRATIVE PHYSIOLOGY

COURTESY OF PAIGE GEIGER

"A biomedical scientist performs basic research on questions that have relevance to human health and disease, biological processes and systems. We design scientific studies to answer a particular research question and then report our results in the form of a manuscript for publication. Good science is only as good as the research study design itself. We value innovation, ideas, accurate interpretation of data, and scientific integrity. There is an honor system to science that the results are accurate and true as reported. Manuscripts are peer-reviewed, and there is inherent trust and belief in this system."

pp. 191–95, for more discussion of quantitative and qualitative methods.) Natural scientists value experiments and data collection processes that can be repeated to achieve the same or similar results, often for the purposes of generalizing their findings. Social scientists acknowledge the fluidity and variability of social systems and therefore also highly value qualitative data, which helps them to understand more contextual experiences.

INSIDE WORK **Considering a Natural Science Topic**

Generate a list of natural science topics or issues that interest you. Include any you may have read about or heard about recently, perhaps in a magazine or blog or from a television news report. Then select one for further consideration. Try to focus on a topic in which you're genuinely interested or for which you have some concern. If you're currently taking a natural science course or studying in one of the fields of the natural sciences, you might consider a topic that has emerged from your classroom or laboratory experiences. Answer the following questions.

- What is the topic?

- What do you think scientists are currently interested in discovering about this topic? What would you like to know about the topic?

- Could the topic be addressed by researchers in more than one field of the sciences? Is the topic multidisciplinary in nature? What fields of the natural sciences are currently exploring or could potentially explore the topic?

- How do or could scientists observe and collect data on some aspect of the topic?

- In a broader sense, how does the topic connect with you personally? ▶

OBSERVATION AND DESCRIPTION IN THE NATURAL SCIENCES

Observing in the natural world is an important first step in scientific inquiry. Indeed, the first step of the scientific method is observation, as we show in the table on page 242. Beyond simple observation, though, researchers in the natural sciences conduct **systematic observations** of their objects of study. A systematic approach to observation requires a researcher to follow a regular, logical schedule of observation and to conduct focused and *neutral* observations of the object of study. In other words, the researcher tries to minimize or eliminate any bias about the subject matter and simply records everything he or she experiences, using the five senses. These observations, when written up to share with others as part of a research report, form the basis of description of the object of study. In order to move from observation to description, researchers must keep careful notes about their systematic observations. We discuss one method of tracking those observations, an observation logbook, on pages 258–70.

Read student Kedric Lemon's account of his observations (on pp. 260–70) of various batteries, which he completed between October 11 and October 19, 2017, as part of his observation logbook. Then answer the following questions.

- What do you know about who the author is, based on the language used in this description? Provide at least two specific examples of how the language suggests something about the author's background, knowledge, or frame of reference.
- What can you determine about the observation schedule that the author—the researcher—followed to write this description?
- What kinds of details must the researcher have noted when observing to write this description?
- Did you find any language that seems to reveal bias on the part of the researcher? If so, make a note of this language.
- Based on your answers to the previous questions, what kind of plan for systematic observation would you recommend for the topic you chose in the previous Inside Work activity? ❱

MOVING FROM DESCRIPTION TO SPECULATION

The distinction between description and speculation is a subtle but important one to understand as it relates to scientific inquiry. As we've seen, descriptive writing in the sciences is based on observations. Of course, descriptive writing in the sciences isn't only applicable to a physical space or a stored energy device. A researcher could use similar observational methods to describe, say, the movements of an ant crawling along a sidewalk or tidal erosion along a section of a beach. **Descriptive writing**, then, is the action outcome associated with the first step of the scientific method—observation.

Speculative writing, in contrast, seeks to explain *how* or *why* something behaves the way that it does, and it is most commonly associated with asking a research question and formulating a hypothesis—the second and third steps of the scientific method. In order to speculate about how or why something exists or behaves as it does, a researcher must first observe and describe. Developing a thorough observational strategy and completing a descriptive writing process will help you to lay a solid foundation for speculating about your object of study so that you can later develop a clear research question and formulate a credible hypothesis worthy of testing through experimentation.

To understand the difference between description and speculation, compare the following two zoo memos written by middle school students.*Which one is the better example of descriptive writing? Which one engages more fully in speculative writing?

*From Carolyn W. Keys. "Revitalizing Instruction in Scientific Genres: Connecting Knowledge Production with Writing to Learn in Science." *Science Education*, vol. 83, no. 2 (1999), pp. 115–30.

Middle School Students' Science Memo #1 (12-year-old girls)

On Monday, July 17, DC and I observed the Muntjac. We learned that this animal comes from Asia. And that they eat the bottom part of the grass because it is fresher. We also learned that Muntjacs are very secretive animals. We also observed the difference between a male and female. The male has a [*sic*] earring in his left ear and he has horns. To urinate they stand on three legs. They like to disappear into the bushes. Their habbitat [*sic*] is bushy land.

Another behavior that we observed was the adult Muntjac often moved toward the fence and sniffed. We believe he was sniffing for food. He also rolled back his ears and stuck out his neck. We think he is always alert to protect his family from danger. On one occasion, the male Muntjac came toward the fence. KT [another student] held her shirt toward him. He ran away quickly.

In conclusion, we can say that the Muntjac constantly hunts for food, but is always alert to protect itself and its family.

Middle School Students' Science Memo #2 (13-year-old boys)

Today we went to the Atlanta zoo, where we looked at different animals such as zebras, giraffes, gorilas [*sic*], monkeys, and orangatangs [*sic*]. From my observations of the giraffe I found out that they are rather slow and are always eating. They do many strange things, such as wagging their tails, wiggling their ears, and poking out their tounges [*sic*]. They are very large and I read that they weigh more than a rhinoserous [*sic*], which is close to 2 or 2½ tons, and their necks extend out 7 ft. long. Their tails are 3 ft. long and are sometimes used for swating [*sic*] flies. At times the giraffes will stand completely motionless.

Discussion Questions

1. What similarities and differences do you notice between the two samples?
2. Which sample engages in speculative writing more fully, and which one adheres to mostly descriptive writing?

The process of articulating an explanation for an observed phenomenon and speculating about its meaning is an integral part of scientific discovery. By collecting data on your own and then interpreting it, you're engaging in the production of knowledge even before you begin testing a proposed hypothesis. In this respect, scientific discovery is similar to writing in the humanities and the social sciences. Scientists interpret data gained through observation, modeling, or experimentation much in the same way that humanists interpret data collected through observation of texts. The ability to *observe systematically* and *make meaning* is the common thread that runs through all academic research.

Descriptive writing seeks to define an object of study, and it functions like a photograph. Speculative writing engages by asking *how* or *why* something behaves the way that it does, and in this sense it triggers a kind of knowledge production that is essential to scientific discovery. Following a writing process that moves a researcher from describing a phenomenon to considering *how* or *why* something does what it does is a great strategy for supporting scientific inquiry.

To this end, we encourage you to collect original data as modeled in the writing projects presented at the end of this chapter—the observation logbook (p. 258), the research proposal (p. 271), and the lab report (p. 279). Your view on the natural world is your own, and the data you collect and how you interpret that data are yours to decide. The arguments you form based on your data and your interpretation of that data can impact your world in small or very large ways.

INSIDE WORK **Practicing Description and Speculation**

For this activity, you should go outdoors and locate any type of animal (a squirrel, bird, butterfly, frog, etc.) as an object of study. Decide beforehand the amount of time you'll spend observing your subject (five minutes may be enough), and write down in a notebook as many observable facts as possible about your subject and its behavior. Consider elements of size, color, weight, distance traveled, and interaction with other animals or physical objects. If you're able to make a video or take a picture (e.g., with a cell phone camera), please do so.

After you've collected your notes and/or video, return to your classroom and write two paragraphs about your subject. Label the first paragraph "Description" and the second paragraph "Speculation," and use the following writing prompt.

Writing Prompt: The director of your local wildlife management agency needs a written report detailing the behaviors that you observed while watching your animal. Be sure to use your notes or video for accuracy. In the first paragraph, write a *description* of the subject and its behavior. Limit your description to observable facts; resist explaining why the subject appears the way it does or behaves the way it does. In the second paragraph, *speculate* about why the animal appears or behaves the way it does. Limit your speculation to the subject's behavior (or appearance) based on the observable data you wrote in your description. Finally, consider writing questions at the end of the second paragraph that might be answered in future research but that cannot be answered on the basis of your observations alone. ❱

Once you've conducted observations and collected data, you can move on to formalize your speculation by writing research questions and formulating a hypothesis, consistent with the second and third steps of the scientific method. Writing research questions and hypotheses in the natural sciences is a similar process to those activities in the social sciences (see Chapter 8). Devoting time to several days of focused observation, collecting data, and writing and reflecting on your object of study should trigger questions about what you're observing.

As you write research questions, you might consider the difference between open-ended and closed-ended research questions. A **closed-ended question** can be answered by *yes* or *no*. By contrast, an **open-ended question** provokes a fuller response. Here are two examples:

Closed-Ended Question: Is acid rain killing off the Fraser fir population near Mount Mitchell in North Carolina?

Open-Ended Question: What factors contribute to killing off the Fraser fir population near Mount Mitchell in North Carolina?

Scientists use both open-ended and closed-ended questions. Open-ended questions usually begin with *What, How,* or *Why*. Closed-ended questions can be appropriate in certain instances, but they can also be quite polarizing. They often begin with *Is* or *Does*. Consider the following two questions:

Closed-Ended Question: Is global warming real?

Open-Ended Question: What factors contribute to global warming?

Rhetorically, the closed-ended question divides responses into *yes* or *no* answers, whereas the open-ended question provokes a more thoughtful response. Neither form of question is better per se, but the forms do function differently. If you're engaging in a controversial subject, a closed-ended research question might serve your purpose. If you're looking for a more complete answer to a complex issue, an open-ended question might serve you better.

Once you've established a focused research question, informed by or derived on the basis of your observation and speculation about a natural science phenomenon, then you're ready to formulate a hypothesis. This will be a testable proposition that provides an answer or that predicts an outcome in response to the research question(s) at hand.

INSIDE WORK   **Developing Research Questions and a Hypothesis**

Review the observation notes and the descriptions and explanations you produced in the Inside Work activity on page 247. What potential research questions emerged? For example, in an observation logbook about house finches and nesting practices written by one of the authors of this textbook, a question that remained unanswered was why two eggs from the initial brood of five were removed from the nest. Potential research questions for a study might include the one shown here.

> Research Question: **Do female house finches remove eggs from their own nests?**

From such a question, we can formulate a hypothesis.

> Hypothesis: **Our hypothesis is that female house finches do remove eggs from their own nests. Furthermore, our observational data supports other scholars' claims that female house finches cannibalize their brood on occasion.**

Now you try it. Write down at least two research questions that emerged from your observations, and then attempt to answer each question in the form of a hypothesis. Finally, discuss your hypotheses with a classmate or small group, and make the case for which one most warrants further study. Freewrite for five minutes about the evidence you have or additional evidence you could collect that would support your chosen hypothesis. ▶

DESIGNING A RESEARCH STUDY IN THE NATURAL SCIENCES

As we've noted, research in the natural sciences most often relies on quantitative data to answer research questions. While there are many ways to collect and analyze quantitative data, most professional scientists rely on complex statistical procedures to test hypotheses and generate results.

We interviewed Michelle LaRue, a research fellow at the Polar Geospatial Center, a research group based at the University of Minnesota. Her doctorate is in conservation biology, and her research has focused mainly on large-mammal habitat selection and movement—in particular, the phenomenon of potential recolonization of cougars in the American Midwest. In her Insider's View excerpt, LaRue describes the kinds of questions she asks as a scientist and the kinds of data collection and analysis she typically undertakes as part of her efforts to answer her research questions.

In the previous two sections, we discussed how to conduct systematic observation that leads to description of a phenomenon, and then we explored processes for speculating about what you observed in order to construct a research question and a hypothesis. One way to test a hypothesis is to engage in a systematic observation of the target of your research phenomenon. Imagine that you're interested in discovering factors that affect the migration patterns of bluefin tuna, and you've hypothesized that water temperature has some effect on those patterns. You could then conduct a focused observation to test your hypothesis. You might, for instance, observe bluefin tuna in their migration patterns and measure water temperatures along the routes.

Another way to test a hypothesis, of course, is to design an experiment. Experiments come in all shapes and sizes, and one way to learn about the experimental methods common to your discipline is by reading the Methods sections of peer-reviewed scholarly articles in your field. Every discipline has slightly different approaches to experimental design. Some disciplines, such as astronomy, rely almost exclusively on non-experimental systematic observation, while others rely on highly controlled experiments. Chemistry is a good example of the latter.

One of the most common forms of experimental design is the **comparative experiment**, in which a researcher tests two or more types of objects and assesses the results. For example, an engineering student may want to test different types of skateboard ball bearings. She may design an experiment that compares a skateboard's distance rolled when using steel versus ceramic bearings. She could measure distances rolled, speed, or the time it takes to cover a preset distance when the skateboard has steel bearings and when it has ceramic bearings.

In some disciplines of the natural sciences, it's common practice to test different objects against a control group. A **control group** is used in a comparative experimental design to act as a baseline with which to compare other objects. For example, a student researcher might compare how subjects score on a memorization test after having consumed (a) no coffee, (b) two cups of decaf coffee, or (c) two cups of caffeinated coffee. In this example, the group of subjects consuming no coffee would function as a control group.

LaunchPad

Hear more about the prewriting process from a professional mathematician.

Regardless of a study's design, it is important to realize that academic institutions have very clear policies regarding experimental designs that involve human subjects, whether that research is being conducted by individuals in the humanities, the social sciences, or the natural sciences. Both professional and student researchers are required to submit proposals through an institutional review board, or IRB. In the United States, *institutional review boards* operate under federal law to ensure that any experiment involving humans is ethical. This is often something entirely new to undergraduate students, and it should be taken seriously. No matter how harmless a test involving human subjects may seem, you should determine if you must submit your research plans through an IRB. This can often be done online. Depending on the nature and scope of your research, though, the processes of outlining the parameters of your research for review may be quite labor-intensive and time-consuming. You should familiarize yourself with the protocol for your particular academic institution. An online search for "institutional review board" and the name of your school should get you started. (For more on the role of institutional review boards, see Chapter 8.)

INSIDE WORK   **Freewriting about an Experiment**

Start this activity by writing, in one sentence, what your initial research goal was when you began an observation about a phenomenon that interested you. You might draw on your writing from earlier Inside Work activities to start.

Example: **My goal was to study a bird's nest I discovered on my front porch.**

For many students beginning their inquiry in the sciences, learning about a topic may be the extent of their initial objective. For more advanced students, however, starting an observation from a strong knowledge base may sharpen the objective. The example below draws on prior knowledge of the object of study.

Example: **My goal was to determine whether a female house finch eats her own eggs.**

Once you've written down what your initial objective was, then freewrite for five minutes about what you now know. What are the most important things you learned about your object of study?

Most important, what hypothesis can you make about your object of study?

Hypothesis: **My observational data suggest that female house finches often remove eggs from their nest and may occasionally cannibalize their brood.**

After developing a hypothesis, the next step in the scientific method is to test the hypothesis. Keep in mind that data in the sciences to support a hypothesis come from either a systematic observation or an experiment.

Freewrite for five minutes about how you could collect data that would test your hypothesis. As you write, consider feasible methods that you could follow soon, as well as methods that might extend beyond the current semester but that you could develop into a larger project for later use in your undergraduate studies. Consider whether an experiment or a systematic observation would be more useful. Most important, use your imagination and have fun. ▶

After observing and describing, speculating and hypothesizing, and conducting an experimental study or systematic observation, scientists move toward publishing the results of their research. This is the final step of the scientific method and the final stage of the scientific writing process that we introduced at the beginning of the chapter: scientists explain their results by reporting their data and discussing its implications. There are multiple forms through which scientists report their findings, and these often depend on the target audience. For instance, a scientist presenting his research results at an academic conference for the consideration of his peers might report results in the form of a poster presentation. Research results can also be presented in the form of an academic journal article. A scientist who wants to present her results to a more general audience, though, might issue a press release. In the next two sections of this chapter, we discuss conventions for reporting results in the natural sciences and provide examples of common genres that researchers in the natural sciences produce as a means of reporting their results.

Conventions of Writing in the Natural Sciences

Although the different fields of study that make up the natural sciences have characteristics that distinguish them from one another, a set of core values and conventions connects these areas of inquiry. The values shared among members of the scientific community have an impact on the communication practices and writing conventions of professionals in natural science fields:

- objectivity
- replicability

- recency
- cooperation and collaboration

In this section, we examine each of these commonly held values in more detail. And we suggest that these values are directly linked to many of the conventions that scientists follow when they write, or to the ways scientists communicate with one another more generally.

Insider's View
I also learned the KISS principle during my undergraduate career
MICHELLE LaRUE, CONSERVATION BIOLOGY

COURTESY OF MICHELLE LaRUE

"I learned the conventions of science writing through literature review, imitation, and a lot of practice: this often included pages and pages of feedback from advisors and colleagues. Further, reading wildlife and modeling articles helped me focus on the tone, writing style, and format expected for each journal. After that, it was all about practicing my writing skills.

"I also learned the KISS principle during my undergraduate career: Keep It Simple, Stupid. This mantra reminds me to revise my writing so it's clear, concise, and informative. It is my opinion that science writing can be inherently difficult to understand, so it's important to keep the message clear and straightforward.

"I find that as I progress and hone my writing and research skills, sitting down to write gets easier, and I have been able to move up in the caliber of journal in which I publish papers. Writing is a skill that is never perfected; striving for the next best journal keeps me focused on improvement."

OBJECTIVITY

In her Insider's View, Michelle LaRue notes the importance of maintaining clarity in the presentation of ideas in science writing. Of course, clarity is a general expectation for all writing, but the desire for clarity in science writing can also be linked to the community's shared value of objectivity. As we noted earlier, *objectivity* (or neutrality) in observation and experimentation is essential to the research that scientists do. Most researchers in the natural sciences believe that bias undermines the reliability of research results. When scientists report their results, therefore, they often use rhetorical strategies that bolster the appearance of objectivity in their work. (Note that our marginal annotations below indicate which parts of the SLR model apply—structure, language, and reference; see Chapter 6.)

Rhetorical Features That Convey Objectivity

- **Titles** Scientists tend to give their reports very clear titles. Rarely will you find a "creative" or rhetorical title in science writing. Instead, scientists prefer non-rhetorical, descriptive titles, or titles that say exactly what the reports are about.

Titles may be considered a language and/or a structural feature of a text.

- **IMRaD**   Researchers in the sciences generally expect research reports to appear in the IMRaD format (for more detail, see Chapters 6 and 8):

(for more detail, see Chapters 6 and 8)

> Introduction
>
> Methods
>
> Results
>
> Discussion

Notice how the structure of IMRaD parallels the ordered processes of the scientific writing process (observe and describe, speculate, experiment, and report). This reporting structure underscores the importance of objectivity because it reflects the prescribed steps of the scientific method, which is itself a research process that scientists follow to reduce or eliminate bias.

- **Jargon**   Scientists often communicate in highly complex systems of words and symbols that hold specific meaning for other members of the scientific community. These words and symbols enable scientists to communicate their ideas as clearly as possible. For example, a scientific researcher might refer to a rose as *Rosa spinosissima*. By using the Latin name, she communicates that the specific type of rose being referenced is actually the one commonly referred to as the Scotch rose. The use of jargon, in this instance, is actually clarifying for the intended audience. Using jargon is a means of communicating with precision, and precision in language is fundamental to objective expression.

- **Numbers**   Scientific reports are often filled with charts and figures, and these are often filled with numbers. Scientists prefer to communicate in numbers because unlike words, which can inadvertently convey the wrong meaning, numbers are more fixed in terms of their ability to communicate specific meaning. Consider the difference between describing a tree as "tall" and giving a tree's height in feet and inches. This represents the difference between communicating somewhat qualitatively and entirely quantitatively. The preference for communicating in numbers, or quantitatively, enables members of the scientific community to reduce, as much as possible, the use of words. As writers use fewer words and more numbers in scientific reports, the reports appear to be more objective.

INSIDE WORK   **Looking for Conventions of Objectivity**

Although we've discussed a number of writing expectations related to objectivity in the sciences, we need to stress again that these expectations are conventional. As such, you'll likely encounter numerous studies in the sciences that rely on only a few of these features or that alter the conventional expectations in light of a study's particular aims.

- Choose a scientific topic of interest to you, and locate a research article on some aspect of that topic in a peer-reviewed academic journal article.

- Once you've found an appropriate article, look at the features of the article that reflect the writers' desire for objectivity in science reporting. Note evidence of the following in particular:
  - straightforward, descriptive titles
  - IMRaD
  - jargon
  - numbers

- Take notes on instances where the article follows conventional expectations for science reporting as explained in this chapter, as well as instances where the article alters or diverges from these expectations. Speculate as to the authors' reasoning for their decisions to follow the conventional expectations or to diverge from them. ▶

REPLICABILITY

Like objectivity, the **replicability** of research methods and findings is important to the production and continuation of scientific inquiry. Imagine that a scientific report reveals the discovery that eating an orange every day could help prevent the onset of Alzheimer's disease. This sounds great, right? But how would the larger scientific community go about verifying such a finding? Multiple studies would likely be undertaken in an attempt to replicate the original study's finding. If the finding couldn't be replicated by carefully following the research procedures outlined in the original study, then that discovery wouldn't contribute much, if anything at all, to ongoing research on Alzheimer's disease precisely because the finding's veracity couldn't be confirmed.

Several conventional aspects of writing in the natural sciences help ensure the replicability of a study's findings and underscore replicability as an important value shared by members of the scientific community:

- **Detail** One of the conventional expectations for scientific writing involves the level of detail and specificity, particularly in certain areas of research reporting (e.g., Methods sections). Scientists report their research methods in meticulous detail to ensure that others can replicate their results. This is how scientific knowledge builds. Verification through repeated testing and retesting of results establishes the relative value of particular research findings. It's not surprising, then, that the Methods sections of scientific research reports are typically highly detailed and specific.

  > Detail may be considered a **language** or a **structural** feature.

- **Hypotheses** Hypothesis statements predict the outcome of a research study, but the very nature of a prediction leaves open the possibility of

  > Hypotheses are a **structural** feature.

other outcomes. By opening this "space" of possibility, scientists acknowledge that other researchers could potentially find results that differ from their own. In this way, scientists confirm the importance of replicability to their inquiry process.

- **Precision**   Scientific communication must be precise. Just as researchers must choose words and numbers with attention to accuracy and exactness, so too must they present their findings and other elements of scientific communication with absolute precision. As you engage with scientific discourse, you should be able to develop a sense of the precise nature of scientific description and explanation.

Precision is a language feature of scientific writing.

LaunchPad

Learn about putting your research in context.

RECENCY

Scientific research is an ongoing process wherein individual studies or research projects contribute bits of information that help fill in a larger picture or research question. As research builds, earlier studies and projects become the bases for additional questioning and research. As in other fields, like the social sciences, it's important that scientific researchers remain current on the developments in research in their respective fields of study. To ensure that their work demonstrates **recency**—that is, it is current and draws on knowledge of other recent work—researchers in the sciences may follow numerous conventions in their writing, including those listed here:

The purposeful selection of resources is a reference feature.

- **Reference Selection**   Scientific writers typically reference work that has been published recently on their topic. One way to observe the importance of recency is to examine the dates of studies and other materials referenced in a recent scientific publication. If you do this, then you'll likely discover that many studies referenced are relatively recent. By emphasizing recent research in their reports, scientists convey the importance of remaining on top of the current state of research in their areas of expertise. Knowledge production in the natural sciences is highly methodical and builds slowly over time. It's not surprising, then, that the recency of research is important to members of this community.

Scientific documentation systems of reference are often APA or CSE, but they are frequently also specific to the journal in which an article is published.

- **Documentation**   The importance of recency is also evident in the methods of documentation most often employed in the fields of the natural sciences, like APA (American Psychological Association), CSE (Council of Science Editors), and others. Unlike MLA, for instance, where only page numbers appear next to authors' names in parenthetical citations—as in (Jacobs 1109)—the APA system requires a date next to authors' names, both for in-text references to research and, often, in parenthetical remarks when this is not provided in text—as in (Jacobs, 2012, pp. 198–199). The fact that the APA method generally requires a date highlights scientists' concern for the recency of the research they reference and on which they build their own research.

Start with the same article that you used in the previous Inside Work activity to search for writing conventions that demonstrate objectivity. If you don't already have an article selected, search for an academic article published in a peer-reviewed journal on a scientific topic of interest to you.

- Look for at least one example of the researchers' use of the following conventions that might demonstrate how much they value replicability and recency. Note evidence of the following:
  - details
  - precision
  - timely reference selection
  - choice of documentation style

- Take notes on instances where the article follows conventional expectations for science reporting as explained in this chapter and instances where the article alters or diverges from these expectations. Speculate as to the authors' reasoning for their decisions to follow the conventional expectations or to diverge from them. ❱

COOPERATION AND COLLABORATION

Unlike the clichéd image of the solitary scientist spending hours alone in a laboratory, most scientists would probably tell you that research in their fields takes place in a highly cooperative and collaborative manner. In fact, large networks of researchers in any particular area often comprise smaller networks of scholars who are similarly focused on certain aspects of a larger research question. These networks may work together to refine their research goals in light of the work of others in the network, and researchers are constantly sharing—through publication of reports, team researching, and scholarly conferences—the results of their work. Several common elements in scientific writing demonstrate this value:

- **Presentation of Researchers' Names** As you examine published research reports, you'll find that very often they provide a list, prominently, of the names of individuals who contributed to the research and to the reporting of that research. This information usually appears at the top of reports just after the title, and it may also identify the researchers' institutional and/or organizational affiliations. Names typically appear in an order that identifies principal researchers first. Naming all the members of a research team acknowledges the highly cooperative nature of the researching processes that many scientists undertake.

  > The presentation of researchers' names is a **structural** feature.

- **Treatment of Other Researchers** Another feature you might notice is the way science professionals treat one another's work. In the humanities,

  > How researchers in the natural sciences treat one another is a feature of **reference**.

where ideas are a reflection of the individuals who present them, research-ers and writers often direct commentary toward individuals for their ideas when there's cause for disagreement or dissatisfaction with other research-ers' ideas. Conventionally, however, science researchers treat others in their field more indirectly when objections to their research or findings come up. Instead of linking research problems to individuals, scientists generally direct their dissatisfaction with others' work at problems in the research process or design. This approach highlights the importance of cooperation and collaboration as shared values of members of the scientific community.

Genres of Writing in the Natural Sciences

Once again we interviewed Paige Geiger, whom you met earlier in this chapter. She teaches in the Department of Molecular and Integrative Physiology at the University of Kansas Medical Center. In the following Insider's View, she describes two important genres of writing in her discipline.

In this section, we provide descriptions of, and steps for producing, three of the most common genres that writers in the natural sciences produce: an observation logbook, a research proposal, and a lab report. The observation logbook provides a location for carefully recording systematic observations at the beginning of a research process. The research proposal forms the basis for the important grant proposals that Geiger describes, and it might draw on information gathered during initial observations. It also incorporates other elements such as a careful review of the literature on a subject. Lab reports are the final results of research, and they reflect the form in which a scientist might ultimately publish a scholarly journal article.

AN OBSERVATION LOGBOOK

Systematic and carefully recorded observations can lay a solid foundation for further exploration of a subject. These observations might take place as an initial step in the scientific writing process, or they might be part of the data collection that occurs when testing a hypothesis.

The tools that we discuss over the next few pages parallel the kind of systematic observation that's needed to undertake scientific inquiry. One way to focus and record your observations of a phenomenon is to keep an **obser-vation logbook,** which functions as both a data collection tool and a reflective strategy that becomes useful later in research writing and reporting stages. The observation logbook is a foundational part of the research process that pre-cedes the construction of a formal lab report.

Sometimes observation logbooks include speculation in addition to description, but the two types of writing should be clearly separated from each other to ensure that the more objective observations are not confused with any speculation. Speculation, you'll remember, occurs at the stage of formulating research questions and a hypothesis.

Two different forms serve very different purposes

PAIGE GEIGER, MOLECULAR AND INTEGRATIVE PHYSIOLOGY

COURTESY OF PAIGE GEIGER

"There are two kinds of writing in my discipline—writing manuscripts for publication and writing grant applications. The two different forms serve very different purposes. We must write grant applications to obtain funding to perform our research. The applications are usually for three to five years of funding and are very broad in scope. These applications describe what you plan to do and the results you expect to see. This requires a comprehensive assessment of the literature, an explanation of what is known and what is unknown regarding the specific research question. You must describe how you will design the studies, how you will collect and analyze data, and how you will handle problems or unexpected results. This kind of writing is considered an art form. It is something that you improve upon throughout your career.

"Writing manuscripts for publication is quite different. A manuscript deals with a very specific research question, and you report the direct results of your investigation. There is some background information to place the study in a greater context, but the focus is on the data and the interpretation of the data from this one study. This form of writing is very direct, and overinterpretation of the data is frowned upon. In addition to these two forms of writing, scientists also write review articles and textbook chapters on their area of expertise."

Keeping an Observation Logbook

WRITING PROJECT

For this project, you'll need to decide on a particular object of study and collect at least five days of observations about it. We encourage you to develop a multi-modal data collection process that includes digital photos and videorecorded evidence. For each daily entry, begin with description before moving into speculation. A natural outgrowth of descriptive writing should include brainstormed research questions that could be answered with further experiments, research, or observation.

For each day, you should do the following.

1. Collect and include photographic evidence.

2. Write a description of your object of study.

3. Generate questions for future research.

At the conclusion of five days, answer the following questions.

1. What did I learn about my object of study?

2. What claims can I now make regarding my object of study?

3. What evidence could I use from my observational logbook to support those claims?

Finally, write a one- to two-page paper that includes two sections.

1. Description
2. Speculation

For the **Description** section, write a description of your object of study. Refrain from explaining or speculating about behavior in this section; simply write the observations that are most important to give a clear picture of what you studied and how you studied it. Make use of time measurements and physical measurements such as weight, size, and distance. For the **Speculation** section, assert suggestions as to why certain behaviors emerged in your object of study. You might begin by deciding which behaviors most surprised you or seem most interesting to you.

You might also use the Speculation section as a place to begin thinking about future questions that could be explored as a follow-up to your observations.

Insider Example
Student Observation Logbook

In the following observation logbook, written using APA style conventions, student Kedric Lemon catalogs his observations concerning the efficiency of several types of batteries over a five-day period. His observations form the basis for his experimental study, which appears later on pages 280–90. You'll notice that he carefully separates his observations and description from any speculation about why he observed what he did.

Comparing the Efficiency of Various Batteries

Being Used over Time

Kedric Lemon

North Carolina State University

Comparing the Efficiency of Various Batteries
Being Used over Time

Logbook

Introduction

> Establishes the purpose of the study, and outlines an observational protocol

The purpose of this study is to see if some batteries can hold their charge for longer periods of time than others. Also, this observational study will determine if there is an overwhelming difference between generic brand and the top name-brand batteries, or if people are really just paying for the name. I will perform this study by first recording all of the batteries' initial voltages, and then each day I will allow each of the batteries to go on for an hour and a half and then again check the voltage. It is important that I test the voltage immediately after the batteries come out of the flashlight. Otherwise, results could vary. Before putting in the second set of batteries, I will allow the flashlight to cool down for an hour because after being in use for an hour and a half they are likely hot, and I am unsure if this can affect how fast the other batteries will be consumed. I will look first at how much charge was lost over the duration that they were used in the flashlight. Then I will compare them to one another to determine which one has lost the most over a day, and second, which of the batteries still holds the highest voltage. I hypothesize that the Duracell battery will decrease at the slowest rate and that it will have the highest initial voltage.

> Outlines methods

> Establishes a hypothesis

Friday, October 11, 2013

Today was the first day that I observed results from my batteries. I believe that the first thing is to state the initial voltages of all three types of batteries. (Also, it is important to note that these are the averages of the batteries, as the flashlight demands two AA batteries.)

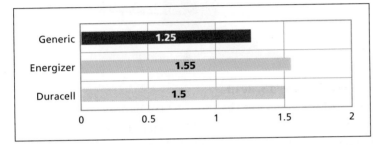

So from these initial observations the Energizer battery has the highest initial voltage.

After allowing all of the batteries to run for an hour and a half, I again took the voltages of the batteries and found this:

Energizer and Duracell both appear to be decreasing at approximately the same rates thus far in the observation, whereas the generic brand has already dropped much faster than the other two types of batteries. From this observation I have raised the question: What is the composition of the

Begins a report on systematic observation of the phenomenon

Observations leading to questions

Duracell and Energizer batteries that allows them to hold a better initial charge than the generic brand of batteries?

Sunday, October 13, 2013

Today I again put the three sets of batteries into the flashlight, in the same order as the trial prior, to allow them all to have close to the same time between usages, again to try and avoid any variables. Today my data showed similar results after allowing all of the batteries to run in the flashlight for an hour and a half:

After this day of observing the results I found that the generic brand of batteries did not decrease as significantly as it did after the first trial. This day the generic brand lost close to the same voltage as the other two types of batteries. Another interesting observation I found was that Energizer and Duracell had the same voltages.

> Provides evidence of the researcher's attempt to remain systematic in his observations

Tuesday, October 15, 2013

On this day of observation I again put the batteries into the flashlights for the trial time. The data I found for this day was as follows:

On this day I found that again the generic brand decreased by an amount similar to the other two batteries. Also I found that the generic brand's intensity has begun to decrease. However, both the other two batteries still give off a strong light intensity. This observation raises the question: At what voltage does the light intensity begin to waver? Another question is: Will the other two batteries begin to have lower light intensity at approximately the same voltage as the generic, or will they continue to have a stronger light intensity for longer? The figures below show the change of light intensity of the generic brand of batteries from the beginning until this day's observation.

Student's observations continue to raise questions

Figure 1. Before

Figure 2. After

Thursday, October 17, 2013

Today is my fourth day of observation. The readings for the voltages for this day were:

The generic brand is losing even more intensity when it is in the flashlight. It is obvious that it is getting near the end of its battery charge. Today was also the biggest decrease in charge for the generic brand of batteries. This is interesting because it is actually producing less light than before, so why does it lose more voltage toward the end of its life? Also, another thing I observed for this day was that again the Energizer brand holds more voltages than the Duracell, like before. There is still no change in light intensity for the two name brands.

Saturday, October 19, 2013

Today is my final day of observation. This is the data I collected for this day:

Today the generic battery hardly produced any light out of the flashlight by the end of the time period, although it still didn't drop to 0 voltage, so there are clearly still some electrons flowing in the current throughout the battery. Also, I observed that the Duracell battery has clearly dropped well below the Energizer now. The Duracell has shown a slight decrease in the light intensity compared to when the observational study first started. So what is the composition of the Energizer battery that makes it outlast the Duracell battery?

Narrative

Description

Five days of observations were conducted over an eight-day period. It did not matter what day of the week I took these observations nor the conditions of the environment around my object of study at the time of the observations. The only thing that I made sure that was constant environmentally for all of the batteries in the study was the temperature because more heat results in higher kinetic energy, which causes electrons to move faster. I had to decide on the types of batteries that I wanted to study for the observational study. The batteries I decided on were: Duracell, Energizer, and a generic brand from Wal-Mart. Before I took my first observation I tested each of the batteries that were to be used with the voltmeter to know the initial charge of the battery. Doing this gave me an idea from the beginning of which battery is typically the most powerful and also how much the batteries would be losing in comparison to their initial charge.

Each of these battery types was tested for the same amount of time for each day that they were observed. Since the flashlight took two batteries to run properly I was planning on taking the average of the two batteries, but I found them to be very similar in all of the trials. I believe that this occurrence

The narrative description provides a summary of the student's systematic observation.

is a result of the entire circuit acting at the same time, causing equal electron transfer between the two batteries to occur, thus causing them to have equal voltages.

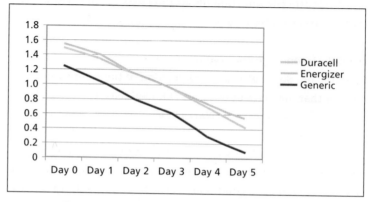

Final Graph from Five Days of Observations

The graph above shows the change in voltage over the five-day period that I took the observations. As you can see, Duracell and Energizer are very similar to one another, with Energizer performing slightly higher than the Duracell brand. The generic has a lower initial voltage than the other two batteries and continues to decrease at a faster rate than the other two batteries. Another thing you can see from this graph is how quickly the generic brand lost its voltage toward the end of its life, whereas the other two batteries seemed to continue to decrease at approximately the same rate throughout.

Speculation

My initial hypothesis that the Duracell battery would decrease at the slowest rate was not supported by this data. I have done a little bit of research on the composition of the cathodes of the Duracell and Energizer batteries. I found that

Evaluates initial hypothesis (speculation) in light of the data the Duracell battery uses a copper tip on the cathode, whereas the Energizer uses a combination of lithium with the copper tip to allow longer battery life. This would explain why the Energizer battery decreases at a slightly lower rate than the Duracell battery does. Also, the generic brand of batteries uses a carbon and copper tip. This would explain why it decreases at a higher rate than the other two name-brand batteries. Also, the cathodes and anodes of the generic batteries may not be as professionally manufactured as the other two types of batteries. All of these reasons could explain why there is a higher voltage density in the Energizer battery than in the other two batteries.

Further speculates about factors that contributed to rejection of the hypothesis

Also, my initial hypothesis that the Duracell battery would have the highest initial voltage was incorrect. From the research that I have gathered, the only explanation for the higher initial voltage in the Energizer battery would be the presence of the alkaline metals that the manufacturer puts into its batteries, whereas the Duracell manufacturer does no such thing. However, there is little information on the Internet about the generic brand of batteries that I used for the experiment, but I was able to find that the reason it has such a lower initial voltage than the other two types of batteries is because it is not packed as well. It takes special equipment to make all the electrons store properly, and the equipment used is not as powerful as the ones that Duracell and Energizer use for their batteries. These ideas all make up my understanding of why there is such a major difference in the rates at which the batteries lose their charge.

For further research into this topic I would recommend using a larger sample, because I used only two batteries for each type of battery. Also, I would recommend looking into the new rechargeable batteries, as that is what a lot of people

Provides suggestions for future research on the subject

are turning to more recently. Another thing that I would try is leaving the batteries on longer because from some of the research that I have done, Duracell does better than Energizer over continuous usage. This means that maybe there is something in the Energizer batteries that causes them to speed up reactions over long periods of use that will cause them to decrease faster over this period. A study like that would be very interesting to compare to my own.

Another interesting topic to follow up on would be the cost of each of the batteries and which battery would be the most cost-effective for users. A lot of people today are buying the generic brand of batteries because they think that this is saving them money. Yes, the generic brand is sold at a lower price, but it is also being used up faster than the other two types of batteries.

RESEARCH PROPOSAL

The research proposal is one of the most common genres of academic writing in the natural sciences. Professional scholars use the **research proposal** to plan out complex studies, to formulate their thoughts, and to submit their research designs to institutional review boards or to grant-funding agencies. The ability to secure grant funding (i.e., to write an effective research proposal and connect it to a realistic, clear budget) is a highly sought-after skill in a job candidate for many academic, government, and private industry positions. In many cases, an effective proposal results from practice with and knowledge of the conventions expected for the genre. No doubt, much of the work of science could not get done without the research proposal, because it is such an important vehicle for securing the funding and materials necessary to conduct research.

Most research proposals include the following sections:

- Title page
- Introduction (and literature review)
- Methods
- References

The *title page* should include (1) the title of your proposal, (2) your name and the names of any co-authors/researchers, and (3) the name of your academic institution. Your instructor may require additional information such as a running header, date, or author's note. Be sure to ask your instructor what documentation and formatting style to use and what information is required in any specific writing context.

The *introduction* of a research proposal explains the topic and purpose of the proposed research. Be sure to include your research question and/or your proposed hypothesis. Additionally, your introduction should contextualize your research by reviewing scholarly articles related to your topic and showing how your proposed research fills a gap in what is already known about the topic. Specifically, the introduction should explain how other researchers have approached your topic (or a closely related one) in the past, with attention to the major overlapping findings in that research. An effective introduction incorporates a literature review that demonstrates your knowledge of other scholars' research. As such, it builds your credibility to conduct your proposed research. (See Chapter 8, pp. 211–26, for more information about writing a literature review.)

The *Methods section* of a research proposal explains exactly what you will do to test your hypothesis (or answer your research question) and how you will do it. It differs from the Methods section of a lab report in several ways: (1) it should be written in future tense, and (2) it should include more detail about your plans. Further, the Methods section should address how long your study will take and should specify how you will collect data (in a step-by-step descriptive manner).

The *references list* for a research proposal is essentially the same as the references list for a lab report or any other academic project. You'll need to include the full citation information for any work you used in your literature review or in planning or researching your topic.

WRITING PROJECT

Developing a Research Proposal

Drawing on a topic of interest to you, develop a research proposal that outlines a specific research question and/or hypothesis, and describe how you would go about answering the question or testing the hypothesis. Keep in mind that successful research proposals include the elements listed below.

- Title page
- Introduction (and literature review)
- Methods
- References

You might try drawing on the observations you collected while completing an observation logbook to develop your research question and/or hypothesis.

Insider Example
Research Proposal

In the following example of a professional research proposal by Gary Ritchison, a biologist at Eastern Kentucky University, note how the Introduction section begins with a brief introduction to the topic (par. 1) and then proceeds to review the relevant literature on the topic (pars. 1 and 2). As you read, consider how a potential funding entity would likely view both the content and the form in which that content is presented. Also note that the references list is titled "Literature Cited." Minor variations like this are common from discipline to discipline and in various contexts. Here, Ritchison has followed CSE style conventions in his proposal.

Hunting Behavior, Territory Quality, and Individual
Quality of American Kestrels (*Falco sparverius*)

Gary Ritchison

Department of Biological Sciences
Eastern Kentucky University

Introduction

American Kestrels (*Falco sparverius*) are widely distributed throughout North America. In Kentucky, these falcons are permanent residents and are most abundant in rural farmland, where they hunt over fields and pastures (Palmer-Ball 1996). Although primarily sit-and-wait predators, hunting from elevated perches and scanning the surrounding areas for prey, kestrels also hunt while hovering (Balgooyen 1976). Kellner (1985) reported that nearly 20% of all attacks observed in central Kentucky were made while kestrels were hovering. Habitats used by hunting kestrels in central Kentucky include mowed and unmowed fields, cropland, pastures, and plowed fields (Kellner 1985).

Several investigators have suggested that male and female American Kestrels may exhibit differences in habitat use during the non-breeding period, with males typically found in areas with greater numbers of trees, such as wooded pastures, and females in open fields and pastures (Stinson et al. 1981; Bohall-Wood and Collopy 1986). However, Smallwood (1988) suggested that, when available, male and female kestrels in south-central Florida established winter territories in the same type of habitat. Differential habitat use occurred only because migratory female kestrels usually arrived on wintering areas before males and, therefore, were more likely to establish territories in the better-quality, more open habitats before males arrived (Smallwood 1988).

In central Kentucky, many American Kestrels are residents. As a result, male and female kestrels would likely have equal opportunity to establish winter territories in the higher-quality, open habitats. If so, habitat segregation should be less apparent in central Kentucky than in areas further south, where wintering populations of kestrels are largely migratory. In addition, territory quality should be correlated

---

Establishes the topic and provides background information on American Kestrels

Reveals evidence of a review of previous scholarship

Establishes a local context for research

with individual quality because higher-quality resident kestrels should be able to defend higher-quality territories.

The objectives of my proposed study of American Kestrels will be to examine possible relationships among and between hunting behavior, territory quality, and individual quality in male and female American Kestrels. The results of this study will provide important information about habitat and perch selection by American Kestrels in central Kentucky in addition to the possible role of individual quality on hunting behavior and habitat use.

Reveals research purposes and identifies significance of the proposed research

Methods

Field work will take place from 15 October 2000 through 15 May 2001 at the Blue Grass Army Depot, Madison Co., Kentucky. During the study period, I will search for American Kestrels throughout accessible portions of the depot. Searches will be conducted on foot as well by automobile.

An attempt will be made to capture all kestrels observed using bal-chatri traps baited with mice. Once captured, kestrels will be banded with a numbered aluminum band plus a unique combination of colored plastic bands to permit individual identification. For each captured individual, I will take standard morphological measurements (wing chord, tarsus length, tail length, and mass). In addition, 8 to 10 feathers will be plucked from the head, breast, back, and wing, respectively. Plumage in these areas is either reddish or bluish, and the quality of such colors is known to be correlated with individual quality (Hill 1991, 1992; Keyser 1998). Variation in the color and intensity of plumage will be determined using a reflectance spectrometer (Ocean Optics S2000 fiber optic spectrometer, Dunedin, FL), and these values will be used as a measure of individual quality. To confirm that plumage color and intensity are dependent on condition, we will use

This section provides a highly detailed description of proposed research procedures, or methods.

References established methods, or those used by other researchers, to support his own method design

tail feather growth rates as a measure of nutritional condition during molt. At the time of capture, the outermost tail feathers will be removed and the mean width of daily growth bars, which is correlated with nutritional condition (Hill and Montgomerie 1994), will be determined.

Each focal American Kestrel ($N =$ at least 14; 7 males and 7 females) will be observed at least once a week. Observations will be made at various times during the day, with observation periods typically 1 to 3 hours in duration. During focal bird observations, individuals will be monitored using binoculars and spotting scopes. Information will be recorded on a portable tape recorder for later transcription. During each observation, I will record all attacks and whether attacks were initiated from a perch or while hovering. For perches, I will note the time a kestrel lands on a perch and the time until the kestrel either initiates an attack or leaves for another perch (giving up time). If an attack is made, I will note attack distances (the distance from a perch to the point where a prey item was attacked) and outcome (successful or not). If successful, an attempt will be made to identify the prey (to the lowest taxonomic category possible).

The activity budgets of kestrels will also be determined by observing the frequency and duration of kestrel behaviors during randomly selected 20-min observation periods (i.e., a randomly selected period during the 1- to 3-hour observation period). During these 20-minute periods, the frequency of occurrence of each of the following behaviors will be recorded: capturing prey, preening, engaging in nonpreening comfort movements (including scratching, stretching wing or tail, shaking body plumage, cleaning foot with bill, and yawning), vocalizing, and flying. The context in which flight occurs, including pounces on prey, and the duration of flights and of preening bouts will also be recorded.

Territories will be delineated by noting the locations of focal kestrels, and the vegetation in each kestrel's winter territory will be characterized following the methods of Smallwood (1987). Possible relationships among hunting behavior (mode of attack, perch time, attack distance and outcome [successful or unsuccessful], and type of prey attacked), territory vegetation, time budgets, sex, and individual quality will be examined. All analyses will be conducted using the Statistical Analysis System (SAS Institute 1989).

Literature Cited

Balgooyen TG. 1976. Behavior and ecology of the American Kestrel in the Sierra Nevada of California. Univ Calif Publ Zool 103:1-83.

Bohall-Wood P, Collopy MW. 1986. Abundance and habitat selection of two American Kestrel subspecies in north-central Florida. Auk 103:557-563.

Craighead JJ, Craighead FC Jr. 1956. Hawks, owls, and wildlife. Harrisburg (PA): Stackpole.

Hill GE. 1991. Plumage coloration is a sexually selected indicator of male quality. Nature 350:337-339.

Hill GE. 1992. Proximate basis of variation in carotenoid pigmentation in male House Finches. Auk 109:1-12.

Hill GE, Montgomerie R. 1994. Plumage colour signals nutritional condition in the House Finch. Proc R Soc Lond B Biol Sci 258:47-52.

Kellner CJ. 1985. A comparative analysis of the foraging behavior of male and female American Kestrels in central Kentucky [master's thesis]. [Richmond (KY)]: Eastern Kentucky University.

Keyser AJ. 1998. Is structural color a reliable signal of quality in Blue Grosbeaks? [master's thesis]. [Auburn (AL)]: Auburn University.

Mengel RM. 1965. The birds of Kentucky. Lawrence (KS): Allen Press. (American Ornithologists' Union monograph; 3).

Palmer-Ball B. 1996. The Kentucky breeding bird atlas. Lexington (KY): Univ. Press of Kentucky.

SAS Institute. 1989. SAS user's guide: statistics. Cary (NC): SAS Institute.

Smallwood JA. 1987. Sexual segregation by habitat in American Kestrels wintering in southcentral Florida: vegetative structure and responses of differential prey availability. Condor 89:842-849.

Smallwood JA. 1988. The relationship of vegetative cover to daily rhythms of prey consumption by American Kestrels wintering in southcentral Florida. J Raptor Res 22:77-80.

Stinson CH, Crawford DL, Lauthner J. 1981. Sex differences in winter habitat of American Kestrels in Georgia. J. Field Ornithol 52:29-35.

LAB REPORT

Lab reports are the formal reporting mechanism for research in the sciences. When a scientist publishes an article that reports the results of a research study, it is generally in the form of a lab report. Lab reports include information reported in IMRaD format, and the sections of the lab report are often listed exactly in that order:

- Introduction
- Methods
- Results
- Discussion

Be sure to read through the section on pages 197–204 of Chapter 8 that describes the different kinds of information typically presented in each of these sections.

If a group of researchers writes a research proposal before writing a lab report, they've already completed the first two sections of the lab report and only need to revise the report to reflect what they actually accomplished in the study (instead of what they planned to do). The Results and Discussion sections report new information about the data they gathered and what they offer as explanations and interpretations of what those results might mean. The Discussion section might also include suggestions for future research, demonstrating how research in the sciences is always building upon prior research.

Composing a Lab Report

The final writing project for this chapter is a lab report. You might report results from either experimentation or systematic observation. Your research could take place in an actual laboratory setting, or it could just as easily take place in the wider environment around you. Regardless, be sure to check with your instructor about whether your lab report should be based on formal observation or experimentation.

Since lab reports use IMRaD organizational format, your report should include the following sections:

- Introduction
- Methods
- Results
- Discussion

As you report your results and discuss their significance, you might include elements of visual design to help communicate the results to your audience. These might include tables or figures. Also, you might include an abstract, and you'll need to include a reference list that cites all sources used in your report. (See Chapter 8 for more information on writing tables and figures, and more information on abstracts.)

Insider Example
Student Lab Report

In the following sample lab report, Kedric Lemon revisits the question of which battery type is most effective. He draws on the information gathered in his observation logbook (pp. 260–70) to design a research study that allows him to conduct further investigation to answer his research question.

Which Type of Battery Is the Most Effective

When Energy Is Drawn Rapidly?

Kedric Lemon

North Carolina State University

The researcher provides a descriptive, non-rhetorical title.

Which Type of Battery Is the Most Effective
When Energy Is Drawn Rapidly?

Introduction

The report follows the conventional IMRaD format.

The researcher establishes a focus for his research by positing a research question.

Today batteries are used in many of the products that we use every day, from the TV remote to the car we drive to work. AA batteries are one of the most widely used battery types, but which of these AA batteries is the most effective? Almeida, Xará, Delgado, and Costa (2006) tested five different types of batteries in a study similar to mine. They allowed each of the batteries to run the product for an hour. The product they were powering alternated from open to closed circuit, so the batteries went from not giving off energy to giving off energy very quickly. The researchers then measured the pulse of the battery to determine the charge. The pulse test is a very effective way of reading the battery because it is closed circuit, meaning it doesn't run the battery to find the voltage, and it is highly accurate. They found that the Energizer battery had the largest amount of pulses after the experiment. The energizer had on average 20 more pulses than the Duracell battery, giving the Energizer battery approximately a half hour longer in battery life when being used rapidly. Booth (1999) also performed his experiment using the pulse test. However, this experiment involved allowing the batteries to constantly give off energy for two hours, and then Booth measured the pulse. So his experiment is more comparable to my observational study because it was constantly drawing energy from the battery. In this experiment he found that the Duracell battery was the most effective. The Duracell battery had over 40 more pulses per minute than the Energizer battery, which means that the battery could last for an hour longer than the Energizer battery would.

Reviews previous research, and connects that research to the current research project

However, in today's market, rechargeable batteries are becoming increasing popular. Zucker (2005) compared 16 different types of rechargeable batteries. Most of these batteries were Nickel Metal Hydride, but a couple of them were the more traditional rechargeable AA battery, the Nickel Cadmium. In his study Zucker was testing how these batteries faired on their second charge after being discharged as closely as they could; rechargeable batteries are not allowed to go to 0 volts because then they cannot be recharged. In the end Zucker found that all but four of the batteries came back up to at least 70% of their initial charge, two of which did not even recharge at all. He found that, not surprisingly, the two most effective rechargeable batteries were Duracell and Energizer, which both came back to 86% of the first charge. However, the Energizer rechargeable battery had the higher initial charge, so Zucker concluded that the Energizer battery was the most effective rechargeable battery. Yu, Lai, Yan, and Wu (1999) looked at the capacity of three different Nickel Metal Hydride (NiMH) rechargeable batteries. They first took three different types of NiMH batteries and found the electrical capacity through a voltmeter. After, they measured the volume of each of the batteries to discover where it fell in the AA battery range of 600 to 660 mAh/cm3. They used this to test the efficiency of the NiMH batteries, as there are slightly different chemical compositions inside the batteries. In the end they concluded that the NiMH battery from the Duracell brand was the most efficient.

Li, Daniel, and Wood (2011) looked at the improvements being made to lithium ion AA batteries. The lithium ion AA batteries are extremely powerful, but in recent years they have become increasingly more popular for studying by many researchers. Li et al. tested the voltage of the lithium ion AA rechargeable battery and found that the starting voltage was

> Prominence of dates points to the researcher's concern for the recency of source materials

> Continues review of previous scholarship on this topic

on average 3.2 volts. That is more than the average onetime-use AA battery. They further found that what makes modern lithium ion batteries so much more powerful is the cathodes. Research into cathode materials has significantly increased the rate of reactions for lithium ion batteries.

The objective of this study is to determine which brand of batteries is the most efficient and to compare a generic rechargeable battery to these regular AA batteries. My original research question for my logbook was Which brand of AA batteries is the most effective over extended usage? However, for my final study I wanted to look at how batteries reacted when they were being used very quickly, so I formed two research questions for this study: Which type of battery is the most effective for rapid uses? How do regular AA batteries compare to a generic AA rechargeable battery? My hypothesis for this experiment is that the Energizer battery will be the most effective battery when energy is being taken from the battery rapidly.

Method

Observation Logbook

In my observation logbook I looked at how different types of batteries compared when they were being tested through a flashlight. The batteries I observed were Duracell, Energizer, and a generic brand. I allowed the flashlight to run for an hour with the set of batteries inside. I did this step for all three types of batteries that I observed in that study. After the hour was up I tested the voltage with a voltmeter. I continued to do this for five consecutive days. For each of the tests I made sure that the temperature was the same for each of the batteries while they were being tested. I also allowed the flashlight to remain off for an hour to let it cool down. These steps were taken to avoid any unknown variables.

Establishes specific research questions on the basis of previous observations

Hypothesis

Reports on research previously conducted

For my follow-up study, I decided to look at how batteries compare when they are being used in quick bursts, meaning that they quickly change from using no energy to using a lot of energy rapidly. In order to test the battery this way I had to change the flashlight to a strobe light so that it quickly turns on and off automatically. I also decided to add a rechargeable battery to my tests since this is an increasingly popular item today. I found my data by attaching the batteries to a voltmeter immediately after they were taken out of the strobe light. Each of the set of batteries was in the strobe light for 20 minutes.

Variables that I made sure remained constant for this experiment were the temperature of the room as well as the temperature of the strobe light. For this reason I allowed the strobe light a 30-minute cooldown before I put the next set of batteries into it.

Limitations

One of the limitations that I faced in this study was an inability to get the thermocouple that I wanted to measure the temperature of the battery. Also I had a small sample size, so if I had taken more samples, then my results would have been more valid. I could improve on these by getting a thermocouple that would measure the temperature. This would allow me to compare the expected voltage of the battery through the

Provides a detailed account of research procedures

The researcher uses technical language, or jargon.

thermocouple and the voltmeter. After the battery got out of the strobe light I would hook it up to the thermocouple and then measure the voltage by looking at the voltmeter. I could tell what the voltage of the battery is through the thermocouple using a graph that one of my secondary sources provided. Another limitation that I faced in this experiment was that I lacked better equipment that could have made my results more accurate—like a pulse reader or a better voltmeter, as I was using a fairly inexpensive one.

Results

My results from my logbook provided me with primarily quantitative data. For each of the types of batteries I found these results.

For the Energizer battery I found that it started off with the largest initial charge of 1.55 volts. On average the Energizer battery lost .16 volts for every hour. The Duracell battery had an initial charge of 1.5 volts and lost an average of .18 volts per hour. Last, the generic brand of battery had an initial voltage of 1.25 volts and lost on average .23 volts every hour.

In this experiment I found that the Energizer battery again had the highest starting charge and highest ending charge. The Duracell AA battery was close behind the

The researcher notes limitations he encountered with the methods.

Outlines the major findings of the study. A number of results are also presented visually, in the form of graphs and figures.

The researcher frequently presents results in tables and charts.

Energizer. The generic brand of batteries came next, followed by the rechargeable battery.

This experiment showed similar results to what I had found in my logbook. The Duracell and Energizer batteries were both very similar, while the generic brand lagged behind.

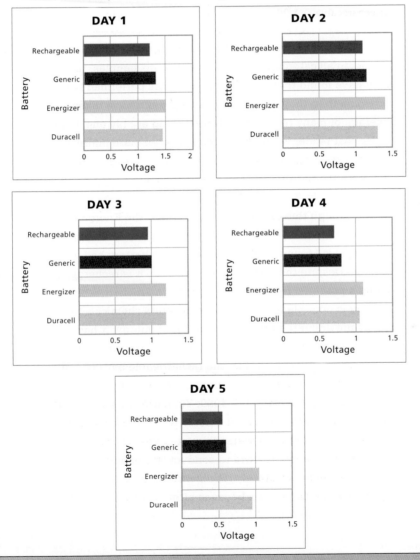

Battery	Initial voltage (volts)	Final voltage (volts)	Average volts lost (volts/20 min)
Energizer	1.60	1.10	0.10
Duracell	1.55	0.95	0.12
Generic	1.40	0.60	0.16
Rechargeable	1.20	0.55	0.13

The table shows that the Energizer battery had the best results in all categories. If I had taken more samples, then I may have found that some of the batteries performed better or worse than they did here, because I could have taken the average of many tests rather than looking at only one. Using a pulse test reader would have been an even more informative way of exploring this experiment because that instrument can estimate the battery life with high precision.

Discussion

Through this experiment I found that the Energizer battery is the most effective battery when used in rapid bursts. Also I found that the rechargeable battery had very bad ratings. Despite the poor ratings, however, it is rechargeable, being a potential reason for its failure. The rechargeable battery is not able to commit as many of its chemicals to solely providing the maximum amount of energy; it has to provide some of the chemicals to the battery's capabilities of recharging. Based on this, the rechargeable battery could be the most effective battery. I found that other studies with similar methods (Booth 1999; Yu, Lai, Yan, & Wu 1999) determined that the Duracell battery was the most effective. However, these studies were conducted years ago.

If I had had more days to conduct this experiment, I could have more accurately represented the usefulness of the rechargeable battery, because after it exhausted its first

Provides an overview of the implications of major findings in light of previous scholarship charge it came back completely recharged for the next day. Another limitation that I faced in this experiment was that I overestimated how fast the battery voltages would decrease in the strobe light, so I was unable to see how the batteries acted near the end of their charge. An area of study for further research would be to compare different types of rechargeable batteries. For instance, I already know that the lithium ion AA rechargeable batteries carry more volts than regular AA batteries, and they are rechargeable.

If I had had more time to perform this experiment or had allowed the batteries to be in the strobe light for a longer time, I think that I would have found that the rechargeable battery would be ahead of the generic battery in terms of the average voltage lost. Also I think that the gap would have been larger between the Duracell battery and the Energizer battery because looking at my results from the observation logbook shows that the Energizer battery does a lot better than the Duracell battery toward the end of its life. This being said, I think that the Duracell battery does not handle the rapid uses as well as the extended uses.

These results show that the Energizer battery is the most effective battery for rapid use and, from my observation logbook, the most effective for extended use. The rechargeable battery used in this experiment is hard to compare to these regular AA batteries because I wasn't able to exploit its sole advantage, recharging. However, this was just a generic brand of rechargeable batteries, so it would be interesting to see how the Duracell and Energizer rechargeable batteries compare to their regular batteries.

> Discusses limitations of the study overall

Provides a list of sources used in the construction of the lab report.

References

Almeida, M. F., Xará, S. M., Delgado, J., & Costa, C. A. (2006). Characterization of spent AA household alkaline batteries. *Waste Management, 26*(5), 466-476. doi:10.1016/j.wasman.2005.04.005

Booth, S. A. (1999). High-drain alkaline AA-batteries. *Popular Electronics, 16*(1), 5.

Li, J., Daniel, C., & Wood, D. (2011). Materials processing for lithium-ion batteries. *Journal of Power Sources, 196*(5), 2452-2460. doi:10.1016/j.jpowsour.2010.11.001

Yu, C. Z., Lai, W. H., Yan, G. J., & Wu, J. Y. (1999). Study of preparation technology for high performance AA size Ni–MH batteries. *Journal of Alloys and Compounds, 293*(1-2), 784-787. doi:10.1016/S0925-8388(99)00463-6

Zucker, P. (2005). AA batteries tested: Rechargeable batteries. *Australian PC User, 17*(6), 51.

tip sheet

- **Systematic observation plays a critical role in the natural sciences.** The disciplines of the natural sciences rely on methods of observation to generate and answer research questions about how and why natural phenomena act as they do.

- **Many natural scientists work in interdisciplinary fields of study.** These fields, such as biochemistry and biophysics, combine subject matter and methods from more than one field to address research questions.

- **Scientists typically conduct research according to the steps of the scientific method:** observe, ask a research question, formulate a hypothesis, test the hypothesis through experimentation, and explain results.

- **The scientific writing process follows logically from the steps of the scientific method:** observe and describe, speculate, experiment, and report.

- **To test their hypotheses, or their proposed answers to research questions, natural scientists may use multiple methods.** Two common methods are systematic observation and experimentation.

- **Scientific research proposals are typically vetted by institutional review boards (IRB).** Committees that review research proposals are charged with the task of examining all elements of a scientific study to ensure that it treats subjects equitably and ethically.

- **Conventional rhetorical features of the scientific community reflect the shared values of the community's members.** Some of these values are objectivity, replicability, recency, and cooperation and collaboration.

- **Members of the scientific community frequently produce a number of genres.** These include the observation logbook, the research proposal, and the lab report.

10

Reading and Writing in the Applied Fields

Introduction to the Applied Fields

In this chapter, we explore some of the applied fields that students often encounter or choose to study as part of their college experience. In some cases, one or more of these applied fields may correspond to your intended major or to your selected area of focus for your career. Throughout the chapter, we also examine some of the common genres through which professionals in these fields communicate to various audiences.

WHAT ARE APPLIED FIELDS?

Applied fields are areas of academic study that focus on the production of practical knowledge and that share a core mission of preparing students for specific careers. Often, such preparation includes hands-on training. Examples of applied fields that prepare students for particular careers include nursing, business, law, education, and engineering, just to name a few. A list of some additional applied fields appears below.

Some Applied Fields

Sports psychology	Counseling
Business	Statistics
Law	Engineering
Education	Speech pathology
Nursing	Public administration
Applied physics	Architecture
Applied linguistics	Broadcast journalism
Social work	

As you might expect, research that occurs in the applied fields is quite varied. These variations among the fields are often reflected in the kinds of questions each field asks and attempts to answer, the forms of evidence it relies on, the data-collection methods it employs, and the ways it reports findings from research to differing audiences. Nevertheless, research in the applied fields typically attempts to solve problems. An automotive engineering team, for example, might start with a problem like consumers' reluctance to buy an all-electric vehicle. To address the issue, the engineering team would first attempt to define the scope of the problem. Why does the problem exist? What are the factors contributing to consumers' reluctance to buy an all-electric vehicle? Once the problem has been identified and clearly defined, the team of researchers can then begin to explore possible solutions.

Examples of large-scale problems that require practical applications of research include issues such as racial inequality in the American criminal justice system, the lack of clean drinking water in some nonindustrialized nations, obesity and heart disease, and ways to provide outstanding public education to children with behavioral problems. These are all real-world problems scholars and practitioners in the applied fields are working to solve this very moment.

INSIDE WORK **Defining and Solving Problems**

Describe a time when you conducted research to solve a problem. Start by defining the problem and explaining why you needed to solve it. When did you first identify the problem? What caused you to seek solutions to it? How did you research and understand the problem? What methods did you use to solve it? Finally, make a list of applied field professionals (e.g., engineer, lawyer, nutritionist) who might have some interest in helping to solve the kind of problem you identified. What do you think each of these fields could contribute to an understanding of or solution to the problem? ▶

Professionals in applied fields often work in collaboration with one another, or in teams, to complete research and other projects, and professors who teach in these areas frequently assign tasks that require interaction and cooperation among a group of students to create a product or to solve a problem. In the field of business management, for example, teams of professionals often must work together to market a new product. Solid communication and interpersonal skills are necessary for a team to manage a budget, design a marketing or advertising campaign, and engage with a client successfully all at the same time. As such, the ability to work cooperatively—to demonstrate effective interpersonal and team communication skills—is highly valued among professionals in the applied fields. You shouldn't be surprised, then, if you're one day applying for a job in an applied field and an interviewer asks you to share a little about your previous experiences working in teams to successfully complete a project. As you learn more about the applied fields examined in this chapter, take care to note those writing tasks completed by teams, or those moments when cooperation among professionals working in a particular field are highlighted by the content of the genres we explore.

Our purpose in this chapter is to offer a basic introduction to a few of the many applied fields of study and to explore some of the kinds of writing that typically occur in these fields. Because the applied fields vary so much, and since it would be impossible to generalize conventional expectations for communication across these diverse fields, we've chosen to focus on specific fields as examples. The rest of the chapter, then, explores specific applied fields and provides examples of the kinds of writing routinely produced by professionals in these fields. Our aim here is to highlight a rhetorical approach to these fields that would be helpful for any student attempting to acclimate to one or more of these communities.

INSIDE WORK **Considering Additional Applied Fields**

Visit your college or university's website, and locate a listing of the majors or concentrations offered in any academic department. In light of the definition of an *applied field* proposed above, consider whether any of the majors or concentrations identified for that particular discipline could be described as applied fields. Additionally, spend some time considering your own major or potential area of concentration: Are you studying an applied field? Are there areas of study within your major or concentration that could be considered applied fields? If so, what are they, and why would you consider them applied fields? ▶

Rhetoric and the Applied Fields

Because applied fields are centrally focused on preparing professionals who will work in those fields, students are often asked to engage audiences associated with the work they'll do in those fields after graduation. Imagine that you've just graduated from college with a degree in business management and have secured a job as a marketing director for a business. What kinds of writing do you expect to encounter in this new position? What audiences do you expect to be writing for? You may well be asked to prepare business analyses or market reports. You may be asked to involve yourself in new product management or even the advertising campaign for a product. All these activities, which call for different kinds of writing, will require you to manage information and to shape your communication of that information into texts that are designed specifically for other professionals in your field—such as boards of directors, financial officers, or advertising executives. As a student in the applied field of business management, you therefore need to become familiar with the audiences, genres, conventions, and other expectations for writing specific to your career path that extend beyond academic audiences. Being mindful of the rhetorical situation in which you must communicate with other professionals is essential to your potential success as a writer in an applied field.

As with more traditional academic writing, we recommend that you analyze carefully any writing situation you encounter in an applied field. You might begin by responding to the following questions:

LaunchPad

Criminal justice instructor Michelle Richter discusses the role of audience.

1. **Who is my audience?** Unlike the audience for a lab report for a chemistry class or the audience for an interpretation of a poem in a literature class, your audience for writing in an applied field is just as likely to be non-academic as academic. Certainly, the writing most students will do in their actual careers will be aimed at other professionals in their field, not researchers or professors in a university. In addition to understanding exactly who your audience is, you'll want to be sure to consider the specific needs of your target audience.

2. **In light of my purpose and my audience's needs, is there an appropriate genre I should rely on to communicate my information?** As in the more traditional academic disciplines, there are many genres through which professionals in applied fields communicate. Based on an analysis of your rhetorical situation, and keeping your purpose for writing in mind, you'll want to consider whether the information you have to share should be reported in a specific genre: Should you write a memorandum, a marketing proposal, or an executive summary, for instance? Answering this question can help you determine if there is an appropriate form, or genre, through which to communicate your information.

3. **Are there additional conventional expectations I should consider for the kind of writing task I need to complete?** Beyond simply identifying an appropriate genre, answering this question can help you determine how to shape the information you need to communicate to your target audience. If the writing task requires a particular genre, then you're likely to rely on features that conventionally appear as part of that genre. Of course, there are many good reasons to communicate information in other ways. In these situations, we recommend that you carefully consider the appropriateness of the structural, language, and reference features you employ.

Genres in Selected Applied Fields

In the sections that follow, we offer brief introductions to some applied fields of study and provide examples of genres that students and professionals working in these fields often produce. We explore expectations for these genres by highlighting conventional structure, language, and reference features that writers in these fields frequently employ.

STEVE DEBENPORT/GETTY IMAGES

HEALTH FIELDS

One of the fastest-growing segments of the U.S. economy is related to health services. As the population of the country ages, and as science and medicine come together to lengthen average life spans, it's not surprising that health professionals of all sorts, including those with various levels of training and expertise in providing emotional, mental, and physical health services, are in high demand.

Allied Health Professions

Along with this increased demand and the continued development of the medical arts as a result of scientific discoveries and technological advances, it's also not surprising that the allied health fields are constantly expanding and evolving to meet the needs of patients. The Association of Schools of Allied Health Professionals defines "allied health" as "those health professions that are distinct from medicine and nursing." Allied health professionals typically work in a highly cooperative manner with other professionals, including medical doctors and nurses, to provide various forms of direct and indirect care to patients. In fact, allied health professionals regularly have a role to play in the prevention, diagnosis, treatment, and recovery from illness for most patients. A small sampling of the many diverse allied health fields includes:

- Medical Assistant
- Nutritionist
- Occupational Therapist
- Phlebotomist
- Physical Therapist
- Physician Assistant
- Radiographer
- Respiratory Therapist
- Speech Pathologist

Nursing

Most of us have had experiences with nurses, who, along with physicians and other health professionals, serve on the front lines of preventing and treating illness in our society. In addition to their hands-on engagement with individuals in clinical and community settings, nurses spend a good deal of their time writing—whether documenting their observations about patients in medical charts, preparing orders for medical procedures, designing care plans, or communicating with patients. A student of nursing might encounter any number of additional forms of writing tasks, including nursing care plans for individuals, reviews of literature, and community or public health assessment papers, just to name a few. Each of these forms of communication requires that nurses be especially attuned to the needs of various audiences. A nurse communicating with a patient, for example, might have to translate medical jargon so that the individual can fully understand his or her treatment. Alternatively, a nurse who is producing a care plan for a patient would likely need to craft the document such that other nurses and medical professionals could follow methodically the assessments and recommendations for care. Some nurses, especially those who undertake advanced study or who prepare others to become nurses, often design, implement, or participate in research studies.

We interviewed Janna Dieckmann, a registered nurse and clinical associate professor in the School of Nursing at the University of North Carolina at Chapel Hill. In her Insider's View, she offers valuable insights into the writing and researching practices of the nursing community.

As Dieckmann notes, many nurses, especially those working to prepare other nurses, may also participate in various kinds of scholarly research endeavors. In the section that follows, we provide an excerpted look at a 2005 research study published in the nursing journal *Newborn and Infant Nursing Reviews*, along with an example of discharge instructions. The former is a genre of writing common across health professions, and the latter is a genre of writing that nurses who work in a clinical setting often produce for patients.

Scholarly Research Report Some professionals in health fields are both practitioners and scholars. As practitioners, they assess and care for patients in cooperation with other medical professionals. As scholars, they may, as Dieckmann indicates, conduct research on a host of issues, including the history and best practices of nursing, the best therapy for healing repetitive stress injuries, or the benefits of food tracking apps in maintaining a balanced diet. In addition to producing scholarship that advances the health fields, these professionals typically work in colleges or universities with programs that prepare individuals for careers in nursing or the allied health fields. Such professionals, then, may assume multiple roles as researchers and educators, and as practitioners.

Insider Example
Professional Research Report

As you read the following research report, pay particular attention to the structure, language, and reference parallels between the form of the report and those you've encountered already in the fields of the natural sciences and the social sciences. Keep in mind that the text presented here is made up of a series of excerpts from a much lengthier and more substantial research report.

Rural African-American Mothers Parenting Prematurely Born Infants: An Ecological Systems Perspective

MARGARET SHANDOR MILES, PhD, FAAN; DIANE HOLDITCH-DAVIS, PhD, FAAN; SUZANNE THOYRE, PhD; LINDA BEEBER, PhD

The abstract provides an overview of the report, including a description of the study's purpose, its methods, and its central findings.

— ABSTRACT

This qualitative descriptive study describes the concerns and issues of rural African-American mothers with prematurely born infants. Mothers were part of a larger nurse-parent support intervention. The 18 mothers lived in rural areas in the Southeast, and their infants were younger than 35 weeks gestational age at birth and at high risk for developmental problems because they either weighed less than 1500 grams at birth or required mechanical ventilation. Field notes written by the intervention nurses providing support to the mothers after discharge from the hospital were analyzed using methods of content analysis. Concerns of the mothers related to the infant's health and development, the maternal role in parenting the infant, personal aspects of their lives, and relationship issues particularly with the fathers. Findings support the importance of an ecological systems perspective when designing research and caring for rural African-American mothers with prematurely born children.

The review of the literature begins with a synthesis point: mothers experience a period of transitioning. Both McHaffie and May confirm this conclusion.

REVIEW OF THE LITERATURE

Although mothers are excited about taking the preterm infant home, a number of studies have noted that they are also anxious during this important transition. McHaffie[1] found mothers insecure and lacking in confidence at first, followed by a period of accommodation as they learned about the infant's behavioral cues and needs. During this period, mothers became overwhelmed with responsibilities, and fatigue resulted. As the infants settled into their new surroundings and the mothers felt the rewards of caregiving, they became confident in their maternal role. May[2] also found that mothers went through a process of learning about the added responsibilities of caregiving, and this resulted in strains on their time and energy. Mothers were vigilant about looking for changes in the infant's status and for signs of progress through improved physical health and development. During this process, they looked for signs that their child was normal and sought support from others. . . .

METHOD

This study used a qualitative descriptive design[3] to identify the concerns and issues of the mothers based on field notes written by the intervention nurses providing support to the mothers after discharge from the hospital.[4] The Nursing Support Intervention was an 18-month in-person and telephone intervention provided by master's-prepared nurses starting around the time of discharge of the infant and ending when the infants were around 18 months old corrected for prematurity. The nurses helped the mothers to process the mothering experience and resolve emotional distress that is caused by prematurity, identify and reduce parenting and other life stresses, develop relationships with their infants, and identify and use acceptable resources to meet needs of the infant and the mother. . . .

Qualitative research methods are explained.

RESULTS

The concerns and issues raised by the mothers with the intervention nurses fell into four major categories: infant health and development, parenting, personal concerns, and relationship issues (Table 1). ──────────────

Results of the study, or categories of concerns identified among mothers, are presented in the form of a summary table. The researchers explore these results in more detail in a number of additional paragraphs.

Table 1.
Maternal concerns of rural African-American mothers in parenting prematurely born infants

Infant health and development	Establishing feeding and managing gastrointestinal tract distress
	Managing medical technologies
	Preventing and managing infections
	Establishing sleep patterning
	Learning developmental expectations
Parenting	Learning the infant's needs
	Establishing daily patterns
	Balancing roles
Personal concerns	Coping with financial problems
	Managing stressful jobs while securing appropriate childcare
	Losing and trying to regain educational opportunities toward a better life
	Working toward securing a home of one's own
	Managing depressive symptoms
Relationship issues	Working through relationship with infant's father

DISCUSSION

Findings from this study provide insight into the needs of mothers of prematurely born infants after discharge from the hospital. In the early months after discharge, support is needed related to caring for the infant. As their infants grow, mothers may need help in identifying and getting resources for developmental problems. Agencies that provide services to mothers need to consider the complex lives of the mothers, especially those who are single and living in poverty. Of utmost importance is helping the mothers to manage issues related to finding a job, managing work, and care of their infant. Finding acceptable day care is a particularly important need. Furthermore, community programs are needed to help the mothers achieve their dreams of furthering their education and finding acceptable homes for themselves and their children.

REFERENCES

1. McHaffie HE. Mothers of very low birthweight babies: how do they adjust? *J Adv Nurs.* 1990;15:6–11.

2. May KM. Searching for normalcy: mothers' caregiving for low birthweight infants. *Pediatr Nurs.* 1997;23:17–20.

3. Sandelowski M. Whatever happened to qualitative description? *Res Nurs Health.* 2000;23:334–340.

4. Holditch-Davis D. A nursing support intervention for mothers of preterm infants. Grant funded by the National Institute of Nursing Research (NR05263). 2001.

Discharge Instructions   If you've ever been hospitalized, then you probably remember the experience quite vividly. It's likely that you interacted with a nurse, who perhaps assessed your health upon arrival. You were also likely cared for by a nurse, or a particular group of nurses, during your stay. Nurses also often play an integral role in a patient's discharge from a hospital. Typically, before a patient is released from a hospital, a nurse explains to the patient (and perhaps a family member or two, or another intended primary caregiver) and provides in written form a set of instructions for aftercare. This constitutes the **discharge instructions**.

This document, or series of documents, includes instructions for how to care for oneself at home. The instructions may focus on managing diet and medications, as well as caring for other needs, such as post-operative bandaging procedures. They may also include exercise or diet management plans recommended for long-term recovery and health maintenance. These plans may include seeing an allied health professional such as a physical or occupational therapist. Often presented in a series of bulleted items or statements, these lists are usually highly generic; that is, the same instructions frequently apply for patients with the same or similar health conditions. For this reason, discharge instruction forms may include spaces for nurses or other healthcare professionals to write in more specific information relating to a patient's individual circumstances. As well, discharge instructions frequently include information about a patient's follow-up care with his or her doctor or primary caregiver. This could take the form of a future appointment time or directions to call for a follow-up appointment or to consult with another physician. An additional conventional element of discharge instructions is a list of signs of a medical emergency and directions concerning when and how to seek medical attention immediately, should certain signs or symptoms appear in the patient. Finally, discharge instructions are typically signed and dated by a physician or nurse, and they are sometimes signed by the patient as well.

Many patients are in unclear states of mind or are extremely vulnerable at the time of release from a hospital, so nurses who provide and explain discharge instructions to patients are highly skilled at assessing patients' understanding of these instructions.

Insider Example
Discharge Instructions

The following text is an example of a typical set of discharge instructions. As you read the document, consider areas in the instructions that you think a nurse would be more likely to stress to a patient in a discharge meeting: What would a nurse cover quickly? What would he or she want to communicate most clearly to a patient?

FIRST HOSPITAL
Where Care Comes First

Patient's Name: John Q. Patient
Healthcare Provider's Name: First Hospital
Department: Cardiology
Phone: 617-555-1212
Date: Thursday, May 8, 2014
Notes: **Nurses can write personalized notes to the patient here.**

Discharge Instructions for Heart Attack

A heart attack occurs when blood flow to the heart muscle is interrupted. This deprives the heart muscle of oxygen, causing tissue damage or tissue death. Common treatments include lifestyle changes, oxygen, medicines, and surgery.

Steps to Take

Home Care

- Rest until your doctor says it is okay to return to work or other activities.
- Take all medicines as prescribed by your doctor. Beta-blockers, ACE inhibitors, and antiplatelet therapy are often recommended.
- Attend a cardiac rehabilitation program if recommended by your doctor.

Diet

Eat a heart-healthy diet:

- Limit your intake of fat, cholesterol, and sodium. Foods such as ice cream, cheese, baked goods, and red meat are not the best choices.
- Increase your intake of whole grains, fish, fruits, vegetables, and nuts.
- Discuss supplements with your doctor.

Your doctor may refer you to a dietician to advise you on meal planning.

Physical Activity

The American Heart Association recommends at least 30 minutes of exercise daily, or at least 3–4 times per week, for patients who have had a heart attack. Your doctor will let you know when you are ready to begin regular exercise.

- Ask your doctor when you will be able to return to work.
- Ask your doctor when you may resume sexual activity.
- Do not drive unless your doctor has given you permission to do so.

Medications

The following medicines may be prescribed to prevent you from having another heart attack:

- Aspirin, which has been shown to decrease the risk of heart attacks
  - Certain painkillers, such as ibuprofen, when taken together with aspirin, may put you at high risk for gastrointestinal bleeding and also reduce the effectiveness of aspirin.
- Clopidogrel or prasugrel
  - Avoid omeprazole or esomeprazole if you take clopidogrel. They may make clopidogrel not work. Ask your doctor for other drug choices.
- ACE inhibitors
- Nitroglycerin
- Beta-blockers or calcium channel blockers

- Cholesterol-lowering medicines
- Blood pressure medicines
- Pain medicines
- Anti-anxiety or antidepressant medicines

If you are taking medicines, follow these general guidelines:

- Take your medicine as directed. Do not change the amount or the schedule.
- Do not stop taking them without talking to your doctor.
- Do not share them.
- Ask what the results and side effects are. Report them to your doctor.
- Some drugs can be dangerous when mixed. Talk to a doctor or pharmacist if you are taking more than one drug. This includes over-the-counter medicine and herbal or dietary supplements.
- Plan ahead for refills so you do not run out.

Lifestyle Changes and Prevention

Together, you and your doctor will plan proper lifestyle changes that will aid in your recovery. Some things to keep in mind to recover and prevent another heart attack include:

- If you smoke, talk to your doctor about ways to help you quit. There are many options to choose from, like using nicotine replacement products, taking prescription medicines to ease cravings and withdrawal symptoms, participating in smoking cessation classes, or doing an online self-help program.
- Have your cholesterol checked regularly.
- Get regular medical check-ups.
- Control your blood pressure.
- Eat a healthful diet, one that is low in saturated fat and rich in whole grains, fruits, and vegetables.
- Have a regular, low-impact exercise program.
- Maintain a healthy weight.
- Manage stress through activities such as yoga, meditation, and counseling.
- If you have diabetes, maintain good control of your condition.

Follow-Up

Since your recovery needs to be monitored, be sure to keep all appointments and have exams done regularly as directed by your doctor. In addition, some people have feelings of depression or anxiety after a heart attack. To get the help you need, be sure to discuss these feelings with your doctor.

Schedule a follow-up appointment as directed by your doctor.

Call for Medical Help Right Away If Any of the Following Occurs

Call for medical help right away if you have symptoms of another heart attack, including:

- Chest pain, which may feel like a crushing weight on your chest
- A sense of fullness, squeezing, or pressure in the chest
- Anxiety, especially feeling a sense of doom or panic without apparent reason
- Rapid, irregular heartbeat
- Pain, tingling, or numbness in the left shoulder and arm, the neck or jaw, or the right arm
- Sweating
- Nausea or vomiting
- Indigestion or heartburn
- Lightheadedness, weakness, or fainting
- Shortness of breath
- Abdominal pain

If you think you have an emergency, call for medical help right away.

Directions are provided in as few words as possible.

Provides directions for how to "follow up" with medical provider(s)

Identifies emergency indicators

Nurse for a Day

In Table 1 on page 299, the authors of the qualitative research report "Rural African-American Mothers Parenting Prematurely Born Infants: An Ecological Systems Perspective" identify a number of "concerns and issues" among rural mothers with premature infants. Choose one of these "concerns and issues," and develop a discharge plan for a mother and child in response. Using "Discharge Instructions for Heart Attack" as a model for your own set of discharge instructions, complete the following.

- Provide a brief introduction in which you offer a quick overview of the concern or issue.

- Provide supporting instructions for patients in three central areas: Steps to Take, Follow-Up, and Emergency Response. Note that many, or all, of the directives or recommendations that make up your instructions may be non-medical treatments, interventions, or therapies. You may consult additional sources for support, as needed.

- Authorize the discharge orders by signing and dating your document.

Once you've completed the discharge instructions, spend some time reflecting on the challenges you faced in the process of devising your instructions: What were the least and most challenging parts of writing the instructions? ❱

EDUCATION

When your teachers tell you that writing is important, they're probably conveying a belief based on their own experiences. Professional educators do a lot of writing. As students, you're aware of many contexts in which teachers write on a daily basis. They have project assignment sheets to design, papers to comment on and grade, websites to design, and e-mails to answer, just to name a few. However, educators also spend a great deal of time planning classes

and designing lesson plans. Though students rarely see these written products, they are essential, if challenging and time-consuming, endeavors for teachers. We provide examples and discussion of two forms of writing frequently produced by professionals in the various fields of education: the lesson plan and the Individualized Education Program (IEP).

Lesson Plan

When designing a **lesson plan**, teachers must consider many factors, including their goals and objectives for student learning, the materials needed to execute a lesson, the activities students will participate in as part of a lesson, and the methods they'll use to assess student learning. Among other considerations, teachers must also make sure their lesson plans help them meet prescribed curricular mandates.

Insider Example
Student Lesson Plan

The following lesson plan for a tenth-grade English class was designed by Myra Moses, who at the time of writing the plan was a doctoral candidate in education. In this plan, Moses begins by identifying the state-mandated curricular standards the lesson addresses. She then identifies the broader goals of her lesson plan before establishing the more specific objectives, or exactly what students will do to reach the broader learning goals. As you read, notice that all the plan's statements of objectives begin with a verb, as they identify actions students will take to demonstrate their learning. The plan ends by explaining the classroom activities the teacher will use to facilitate learning and by identifying the methods the instructor will use to assess student learning. These structural moves are conventional for the genre of a lesson plan.

Educational Standard → Goals → Objectives → Materials → Classroom Activities → Assessment

Lesson Plan

Overview and Purpose

This lesson is part of a unit on Homer's *Odyssey*. Prior to this lesson students will have had a lesson on Greek cultural and social values during the time of Homer, and they will have read the *Odyssey*. In the lesson, students will analyze passages from the *Odyssey* to examine the author's and characters' points of view. Students will participate in whole class discussion, work in small groups, and work individually to identify and evaluate point of view.

Education Standards Addressed

This lesson addresses the following objectives from the NC Standard Course of Study for Language Arts: English II:

1.02 Respond reflectively (through small group discussion, class discussion, journal entry, essay, letter, dialogue) to written and visual texts by:

- relating personal knowledge to textual information or class discussion.
- showing an awareness of one's own culture as well as the cultures of others.
- exhibiting an awareness of culture in which text is set or in which text was written.

> Identifies the state-mandated curricular elements, or the educational objectives, the lesson addresses. Notice that these are quite broad in scope.

1.03 Demonstrate the ability to read, listen to, and view a variety of increasingly complex print and non-print expressive texts appropriate to grade level and course literary focus, by:

- identifying and analyzing text components (such as organizational structures, story elements, organizational features) and evaluating their impact on the text.
- providing textual evidence to support understanding of and reader's response to text.
- making inferences, predicting, and drawing conclusions based on text.
- identifying and analyzing personal, social, historical, or cultural influences, contexts, or biases.

5.01 Read and analyze selected works of world literature by:

- understanding the importance of cultural and historical impact on literary texts.

Teacher identifies specific goals for the lesson. These goals fit well within the broader state-mandated curricular standards.

Goals

1. To teach students how to identify and evaluate an author's point of view and purpose by examining the characters' point of view.
2. To teach students to critically examine alternate points of view.

Objectives identify what students will do as part of the lesson. Notice that the statements of objectives begin with verbs.

Objectives

Students will:

1. Identify point of view in a story by examining the text and evaluating how the main character views his/her world at different points in the story.
2. Demonstrate that they understand point of view by using examples and evidence from the text to support what they state is the character's point of view.
3. Apply their knowledge and understanding of point of view by taking a passage from the text and rewriting it from a supporting character's point of view.
4. Evaluate the rationality of a character's point of view by measuring it against additional information gathered from the text, or their own life experience.

Materials, Resources

Identifies materials needed for the lesson

- Copies of *The Odyssey*
- DVD with video clips from television and/or movies
- Flip chart paper
- Markers
- Directions and rubric for individual assignment

Activities

Outlines classroom procedures for the two-day lesson plan

Session 1

1. Review information from previous lesson about popular cultural and social views held during Homer's time (e.g., Greek law of hospitality). This would be a combination of a quiz and whole class discussion.
2. Teacher-led class discussion defining and examining point of view by viewing clips from popular television shows and movies.
3. Teacher-led discussion of 1 example from *The Odyssey*. E.g., examine Odysseus's point of view when he violates Greek law of hospitality during his encounter with the Cyclops, Polyphemus. Examine this encounter through the lens of what Homer might be saying about the value Greeks placed on hospitality.
4. In small groups the students will choose 3 places in the epic and evaluate Odysseus's point of view. Students will then determine what Odysseus's point of view might reflect about Homer's point of view and purpose for that part of the epic.
5. Groups will begin to create a visual using flip chart paper and markers to represent their interpretations of Odysseus's point of view to reflect about Homer's point of view and purpose.

Session 2

1. Groups will complete visual.
2. Groups will present their work to the rest of the class.
3. The class will discuss possible alternate interpretations of Homer's point of view and purpose.
4. Class will review aspects of point of view based on information teacher provided at the beginning of the class.
5. Beginning during class and finishing for homework, students will individually take one passage from the epic that was not discussed by their groups and do the following:
    - write a brief description of a main character's point of view

- write a response to prompts that guide students in evaluating the rationality of the main character's point of view based on information gathered from the text, or the students' own life experience
- rewrite the passage from a supporting character's point of view

Identifies how the teacher will assess students' mastery of the concepts and material covered in the lesson

Assessment

- Evaluate students' understanding of Greek cultural/social values from Homer's time through the quiz.
- Evaluate group's understanding of point of view by examining the visual product—this artifact will not be graded, but oral feedback will be provided that should help the students in completing the independent assignment.
- Evaluate the written, individual assignment.

Individualized Education Program (IEP)

Professional educators are often required to design education plans that address the specific needs of individual students who, according to federal definitions, are identified with a disability. These are examples of an **individualized education program (IEP)**. IEP development most often results from cooperation among educational professionals (teachers, school administrators, guidance counselors, etc.) and parents as they plan a student's educational course in light of his or her individual disability and needs. IEPs, like general lesson plans, are guided by the identification of goals and objectives for individual students, taking into account the student's disability or disabilities.

Insider Example
Student IEP

The sample IEP that follows indicates both an academic goal and a functional goal for the student. The academic goal relates to the student's desired academic achievement, while the functional goal specifies a desired behavioral outcome. These goals are followed by statements of objectives that represent steps the student will take to achieve the specified goals. Both sections end with descriptions of how the student's progress toward the desired goals will be measured or assessed.

Student Description for IEP

Joey Smith is a 16-year-old 11th grader. He has a learning disability in reading, and he also has attention deficit hyperactivity disorder.

Joey generally works well with others and has a good sense of humor. He likes to be helpful and is good at encouraging others. He tries hard when assigned tasks, but gets extremely frustrated and gives up quickly when he has difficulty completing a task as easily or quickly as he thinks he should. He responds well to being asked to try again if someone can work with him individually to get him started on the task again. Sometimes he acts up in class, usually in a joking manner. This tends to result in him frequently being off-task, as well as affecting the students around him. He displays the classic characteristics of a student with attention deficit hyperactivity disorder, including losing focus easily, needing to move around frequently, exhibiting difficulty paying attention to details, and continually blurting out inappropriate comments, or talking at inappropriate times.

Check Purpose: ☐ Initial

☒ Annual Review

☐ Reevaluation

☐ Addendum

☐ Transition Part C to B

INDIVIDUALIZED EDUCATION PROGRAM (IEP)

Duration of Special Education and Related Services: From: 06/05/2008 To: 06/04/2009

Student: Joey Smith

DOB: 08/21/1992

School: ABC High School

Grade: 10

Primary Area of Eligibility* Learning Disability
Secondary Area(s) of Eligibility (if applicable): Other Health Impairment
(*Reported on Child Count)

Student Profile

Student's overall strengths:
Joey works hard to complete assignments and accomplish his goals. He interacts well with others, including his peers. He is very helpful and often encourages his peers when they are trying to accomplish their own goals. Joey has a good sense of humor and is good at entertaining others.

Summarize assessment information (e.g., from early intervention providers, child outcome measures, curriculum based measures, state and district assessments results, etc.), and review of progress on current IEP/IFSP goals:
Overall, Joey is making significant progress on his IEP goals. He continues to do well with improving his reading skills. He still struggles with implementing strategies consistently to help him remain focused and committed to completing his tasks; however, he continues to make progress.

Parent's concerns, if any, for enhancing the student's education:
Parent had no concerns at this time.

Parent's/Student's vision for student's future:
Joey will learn to motivate himself to complete tasks and learn to rely less on external motivation from others. He will complete high school and then attend community college.

INDIVIDUALIZED EDUCATION PROGRAM (IEP)

**Duration of Special Education and Related Services: From: 06/05/2008
To: 06/04/2009**

Student: Joey Smith   DOB: 08/21/1992

School: ABC High School   Grade: 10

Consideration of Transitions

If a transition (e.g., new school, family circumstances, etc.) is anticipated during the life of this IEP/IFSP, what information is known about the student that will assist in facilitating a smooth process? ☒ N/A

The student is age 14 or older or will be during the duration of the IEP.
☒ Yes ☐ No

Consideration of Special Factors (Note: If you check yes, you must address in the IEP.)

Does the student have behavior(s) that impede his/her learning or that of others? ☒ Yes ☐ No

Does the student have Limited English Proficiency? ☐ Yes ☒ No

If the student is blind or partially sighted, will the instruction in or use of Braille be needed? ☐ Yes ☐ No ☒ N/A

Does the student have any special communication needs? ☐ Yes ☒ No

Is the student deaf or hard of hearing? ☐ Yes ☒ No
☐ The child's language and communication needs.
☐ Opportunities for direct communications with peers and professional personnel in the child's language and communication mode.
☐ Academic level.
☐ Full range of needs, including opportunities for direct instruction in the child's language, and
☐ Communication mode.
(Communication Plan Worksheet available at www.ncpublicschools.org/ec/policy/forms.)

Does the student require specially designed physical education?
☐ Yes ☒ No

Present Level(s) of Academic and Functional Performance
Include specific descriptions of what the student can and cannot do in relationship to this area. Include current academic and functional performance, behaviors, social/emotional development, other relevant information, and how the student's disability affects his/her involvement and progress in the general curriculum.

Joey consistently reads at grade level. He can answer comprehension questions accurately if given additional time. He does well on tests and assignments that require reading if given additional time and if allowed to be in a separate setting with minimized distractions during longer tests.

INDIVIDUALIZED EDUCATION PROGRAM (IEP)

**Duration of Special Education and Related Services: From: 06/05/2008
To: 06/04/2009**

Student: Joey Smith   DOB: 08/21/1992

School: ABC High School   Grade: 10

Annual Goal

☒ Academic Goal   ☐ Functional Goal

> Joey will continue to learn and demonstrate functional reading skill at grade level.

The academic goal for the student is identified here.

Does the student require assistive technology devices and/or services?
☐ Yes   ☒ No

If yes, describe needs:

(Address after determination of related services.) Is this goal integrated with related service(s)?   ☐ Yes*   ☒ No
*If yes, list the related service area(s) of integration:

Competency Goal

> **Required for areas (if any) where student participates in state assessments using modified achievement standards.**
> **Select Subject Area:**   ☐ Language Arts   ☐ Mathematics   ☐ Science
> **List Competency Goal from the NC Standard Course of Study:**
> *(Standard must match the student's assigned grade.)*
>
> *Note: Selected Grade Standard Competency Goals listed are those identified for specially designed instruction. In addition to those listed, the student has access to grade-level content standards through general education requirements.*

Benchmarks or Short-Term Objectives (if applicable)
(Required for students participating in state alternate assessments aligned to alternate achievement standards)

> 1) Joey will recognize and use vocabulary appropriate for grade level with 90% accuracy.
> 2) Joey will recognize the author's point of view and purpose with 85% accuracy.
> 3) Joey will apply decoding strategies to comprehend grade-level text with 85% accuracy.

The IEP identifies specific objectives the student will achieve toward reaching the academic goal.

Describe how progress toward the annual goal will be measured

> Progress toward this annual goal will be measured by work samples and tests or quizzes.

The IEP identifies ways the student's progress will be measured.

INDIVIDUALIZED EDUCATION PROGRAM (IEP)

Duration of Special Education and Related Services: From: 06/05/2008 To: 06/04/2009

Student: Joey Smith   DOB: 08/21/1992

School: ABC High School   Grade: 10

Present Level(s) of Academic and Functional Performance

Include specific descriptions of what the student can and cannot do in relationship to this area. Include current academic and functional performance, behaviors, social/emotional development, other relevant information, and how the student's disability affects his/her involvement and progress in the general curriculum.

> Joey does well getting back on task with assistance and when he implements attention-focusing strategies. He needs to improve working on his ability to self-monitor and keep himself on task.

Annual Goal

☐ Academic Goal   ☒ Functional Goal

> Joey will continue learning to identify situations where he is more likely to lose focus. He will learn to identify and apply appropriate attention-focusing strategies in a variety of situations.

The functional goal for the student is identified here.

Does the student require assistive technology devices and/or services?

☐ Yes   ☒ No

If yes, describe needs:

(Address after determination of related services.) Is this goal integrated with related service(s)?   ☐ Yes*   ☒ No

*If yes, list the related service area(s) of integration:

Competency Goal

Required for areas (if any) where student participates in state assessments using modified achievement standards.
Select Subject Area: ☐ Language Arts ☐ Mathematics ☐ Science
List Competency Goal from the NC Standard Course of Study:
(Standard must match the student's assigned grade.)

Note: Selected Grade Standard Competency Goals listed are those identified for specially designed instruction. In addition to those listed, the student has access to grade-level content standards through general education requirements.

INDIVIDUALIZED EDUCATION PROGRAM (IEP)

Duration of Special Education and Related Services: From: 06/05/2008 To: 06/04/2009

Student: Joey Smith   DOB: 08/21/1992

School: ABC High School   Grade: 10

Benchmarks or Short-Term Objectives (if applicable)
(Required for students participating in state alternate assessments aligned to alternate achievement standards)

> 1) Joey will be able to articulate how he feels when he becomes frustrated when work gets difficult on 4 trials over a 2-week period as evaluated by structured observations every 6 weeks.
> 2) By January, Joey will independently request a break from work when he needs it to prevent class disruptions and allow himself to refocus.

Describe how progress toward the annual goal will be measured

> Progress will be monitored through documented teacher observation, student self-monitoring checklist, and anecdotal logs.

The IEP identifies specific objectives the student will achieve toward reaching the functional goal.

The IEP identifies ways that the student's progress will be measured.

Teacher for a Day

For this exercise, imagine that you've just taken a job teaching in your major area of study. Identify a specific concept or skill you can see yourself teaching to a group of students. Consider the background and previous knowledge of your target audience. Then, with the concept or skill in mind, design a single-day lesson plan that addresses each of the following elements of a typical lesson plan.

- **Goal(s)**   State the specific goal(s) for the skill you want to teach.

- **Objectives**   Identify what students will do to better understand the concept or learn the target skill.

- **Materials**   Identify the materials needed to carry out the lesson plan successfully.

- **Classroom Activities**   Outline the procedures, in chronological order, for the day's lesson.

- **Assessment**   Explain how you will assess your students' mastery of the concept or skill. ▶

BUSINESS

Communication in businesses takes many forms, and professionals writing in business settings may spend substantial amounts of time drafting e-mails and memos, or writing letters and proposals. In some instances, businesses may hire individuals solely for their expertise in business communication practices. Such individuals are highly skilled in the analysis and practice of business communication, and their education and training are often aimed at these purposes. Still, if your experiences lead you to employment in a business setting, you're likely to face the task of communicating in one or more of the genres frequently used in those settings. It's no surprise, then, that schools of business, which prepare students to work in companies and corporations, often require their students to take classes that foster an understanding of the vehicles of communication common to the business setting. In the following section, we provide some introductory context and annotated examples of a couple of the more common forms of communication you're likely to encounter in a business setting: the memorandum and the business plan.

Memorandum

The **memorandum**, or memo, is a specialized form of communication used within businesses to make announcements and to share information among colleagues and employees. Although memos serve a range of purposes, like sharing information, providing directives, or even arguing a particular position, they are not generally used to communicate with outside parties, like other companies or clients. While they may range in length from a couple of

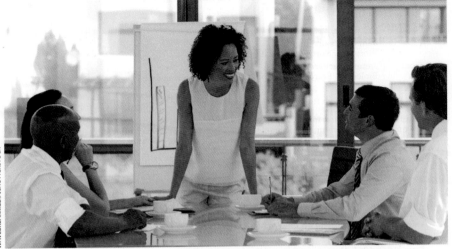

paragraphs to multiple pages, they're typically highly structured according to conventional expectations. In fact, you'd be hard-pressed to find an example of a professional memo that didn't follow the conventional format for identifying the writer, the audience, the central subject matter, and the date of production in the header. Also, information in memos typically appears in a block format, and the content is often developed from a clear, centralized purpose that is revealed early on in the memo itself.

Insider Example
Student Memorandum

The following is an example of a memo produced by a student in a professional writing class. His purpose for writing was to share his assessment of the advantages and drawbacks of a particular company he's interested in working for in the future. As you read, notice how the information in the opening paragraphs forecasts the memo's content and how the memo summarizes its contents in the concluding passages. We've highlighted a number of the other conventional expectations for the memo that you'll want to notice.

MEMO

To: Jamie Larsen
        Professor, North Carolina State University

From: James Blackwell
        Biological Engineering, North Carolina State University

Date: September 2, 2014

Subject: Investigative Report on Hazen and Sawyer

I plan on one day using my knowledge gained in biological engineering to help alleviate the growing environmental problems that our society faces. Hazen and Sawyer is a well-known environmental engineering firm. However, I need to research the firm's background in order to decide if it would be a suitable place for me to work. Consequently, I decided to research the following areas of Hazen and Sawyer engineering firm:

- Current and Past Projects
- Opportunities for Employment and Advancement
- Work Environment

The purpose of this report is to present you with my findings on Hazen and Sawyer, so that you may assist me in writing an application letter that proves my skills and knowledge are worthy of an employment opportunity.

Current and Past Projects

Founded in 1951, Hazen and Sawyer has had a long history of providing clean drinking water and minimizing the effects of water pollution. The company has undertaken many projects in the United States as well as internationally. One of its first projects was improving the infrastructure of Monrovia, Liberia, in 1952. I am interested in using my knowledge of environmental problems to promote sustainability. Designing sustainable solutions for its clients is one of the firm's main goals. Hazen and Sawyer is currently engaged in a project to provide water infrastructure to over one million people in Jordan. Supplying clean drinking water is a problem that is continuously growing, and I hope to work on a similar project someday.

Opportunities for Employment and Advancement

Hazen and Sawyer has over forty offices worldwide, with regional offices in Raleigh, NC, Cincinnati, OH, Dallas, TX, Hollywood, FL, Los Angeles, CA, and its headquarters in New York City. The company currently has over thirty job openings at offices across the United States. I would like to live in the Raleigh area following graduation, so having a regional office here in Raleigh greatly helps my chances of finding a local job with the company. Hazen and Sawyer also has offices in Greensboro and Charlotte, which also helps my chances of finding a job in North Carolina. I am interested in finding a job dealing with stream restoration, and the Raleigh office currently has an opening for a Stream Restoration Designer. The position requires experience with AutoCAD and GIS, and I have used both of these programs in my Biological Engineering courses.

In addition to numerous job openings, Hazen and Sawyer also offers opportunities for professional development within the company. The Pathway Program for Professional Development is designed to keep employees up-to-date on topics in their fields and also stay educated to meet license requirements in different states. Even if I found a job at the Raleigh office, I would most likely have to travel out of state to work on projects, so this program could be very beneficial. I am seeking to work with a company that promotes continuous professional growth, so this program makes me very interested in Hazen and Sawyer.

Work Environment

Hazen and Sawyer supports innovation and creativity, and at the same time tries to limit bureaucracy. I am seeking a company that will allow me to be creative and assist with projects while not being in charge initially. As I gain experience and learn on the job, I hope to move into positions with greater responsibility. The firm offers a mentoring program that places newly hired engineers with someone more experienced. This program would help me adapt to the company and provide guidance as I gain professional experience. I hope to eventually receive my Professional Engineering license, so working under a professional engineer with years of experience would be a great opportunity for me. Hazen and Sawyer supports positive relationships among its employees, by engaging them in social outings such as sporting events, parties, picnics, and other activities.

References

Hazen and Sawyer—Environmental Engineers and Scientists. Web. 2 Sept. 2014.
<http://www.hazenandsawyer.com/home/>.

Business Plan

Many people dream of being their own bosses. One avenue for achieving this dream is to create a successful business, or to own and operate a service or company. Anyone undertaking such a task in the economy today will need a solid business background that includes knowledge of the many forms of written communication required to start and continue the operation of a successful business. Two very important genres for these purposes are the business plan and the business proposal. If you're a business owner looking to raise capital, or if you've got a good idea or product that you want to sell to potential investors, then you're going to need a solid **business plan**, a document that clearly and efficiently describes your business and its essential operations, analyzes your market competition, and assesses the expected expenses and potential for profit. Let's say that you've got a great idea for a new lawn care service, but you need capital to purchase the necessary equipment and to advertise your services to potential customers. To obtain that capital, you're likely going to need a business plan that others can read when deciding whether to invest in your business.

By contrast, the **business proposal** is a form of communication through which a company proposes a relationship of some sort with another entity— often another company. Companies frequently receive unsolicited business proposals. A photocopying company, for instance, may design a proposal to begin a relationship that involves installing and maintaining all the photocopiers owned by a particular city or municipality. At other times, companies request business proposals. Imagine that you're the president of a landscaping service, for example, and you've decided to outsource all work that involves tree removal. To determine whom you want to hire for those jobs, you call for proposals from those companies or individuals to determine whose services best match your needs. In the world of business, effective communication means making money.

Insider Example
Student Business Plan

The following business plan was produced by a student in a writing class that addressed the communication needs of his major. As you read, notice how the student shapes the plan to satisfy the needs of the target audience, a bank, as a potential source of funding.

The Electricity Monitor Company

Daniel Chase Mills

The Electricity Monitor Company

This document is a request for a start-up business loan for a company that will design, manufacture, and sell an electricity-monitoring product that will answer customers' demands for a solution to high power bills.

To: Ms. Jane Harmon Bausch, President
First National Bank
10 Money Street
Raleigh, North Carolina 27695

Prepared By:
Daniel Chase Mills
The Electricity Monitor Company
100 Satellite Lane
City, North Carolina 20000
Email: dcmills@ncsu.edu
Phone: (919) 555-2233

November 21, 2014

Executive Summary

The Electricity Monitor Company
Prepared by Daniel Chase Mills, November 21, 2014

This document is a start-up business proposal for the Electricity Monitor Company and a request for an investment from First National Bank of Raleigh, North Carolina. The Company will design, manufacture, and sell the Electricity Monitor. Families with a traditional circuit-breaker box often struggle with high power bills, due to their inability to monitor their electricity usage. The Electricity Monitor is a device that will answer this pain point. This device is an adapter that attaches to any existing breaker box with installation simple enough for consumers to perform on their own. The device monitors current electricity usage and determines ways to reduce energy consumption. The device is superior to alternatives in the market in that it is cheaper, easier to install, and more effectively solves the problem of not knowing how much electricity is being used. The overall purpose of the Electricity Monitor Company is to develop a high-quality

The cover page for the plan highlights the name of the proposed company, along with the author of the plan.

The author identifies a specific audience for the plan—in this case a potential source of funding. More than a generic plan, then, this document is crafted specifically for the purpose of seeking start-up capital.

Identifies the writer/company submitting the plan for consideration, along with appropriate contact information

In the executive summary, the writer provides a general overview of the plan: identifies a problem, briefly describes the company's unique product and market, and highlights potential customers. The section ends by noting the dollar amount requested from the bank.

In what way is an executive summary like an abstract?

product that can generate excitement in the electricity monitor market and turn a profit for its business owners and investors. The total loan request from First National Bank is three hundred and fifty-four thousand dollars ($354,000.00).

Table of Contents

Title Page	ii
Executive Summary	iii
Table of Contents	iv
List of Tables and Figures	iv
Introduction to the Electricity Monitor Company	1
A. Purpose	1
B. Problem: High Power Bills	2
C. Current Alternatives to High Power Bills	2
D. The Electricity Monitor	2
E. Market for This Product	3
Plan of Business	4
A. Overview	4
B. Cost Analysis	4
C. Summary	6
Conclusion	6
Bibliography	6
Attachments	7
A. Cost Breakdown	7

> Notice the ordering of elements of the plan. How would you describe the order of these elements?

List of Tables and Figures

Figure 1, Price Comparison	3
Figure 2, Market Breakdown	4
Table 1, Design Expense	4
Table 2, Manufacturing Expense	5
Table 3, Marketing Expense	5
Table 4, Total Cost Analysis	5

Introduction to the Electricity Monitor Company _____

A. Purpose

The purpose of this document is to request funding from First National Bank for a start-up business called the Electricity Monitor Company. This

> Briefly identifies the general purpose of the document and offers a preview of the document's contents

document will contain an overview of the problem that the company will address in the market, how the Electricity Monitor will solve this problem, and a plan for this business.

Explains a problem that consumers face

— B. *Problem: High Power Bills*

In twenty-first century America, and in most first world countries, electricity is a necessity. In the home, electricity is used for a variety of devices. Due to the vast number of devices that use electricity, and no good way of knowing how much power they are consuming on a daily basis, families with a traditional circuit-breaker box often struggle with using too much electricity. The problem is high power bills.

Provides a brief market analysis, and identifies a gap in the market

— C. *Current Alternatives to High Power Bills*

There are three currently available solutions to measuring home energy usage in an attempt to lower power bills: Plug-in Meters, Energy Meter Monitors, and Home Energy Monitors. Plug-in Meters are devices that plug in to individual outlets to measure energy usage of a single device. An Energy Meter Monitor attaches to an electricity meter, measures total energy consumption of a home, and estimates what the power bill will be for the month. Neither device is effective in determining energy usage of the entire home across multiple devices. The Home Energy Monitors contain multiple channels to measure energy usage across multiple devices in the home, but these devices are extremely expensive and require detailed installation that increases the cost of the products. Three Home Energy Monitoring Devices are the TED 5000, eGuage, and EnviR, with respective prices of $239, $494, and $129. I have determined that the current solutions in this market are too expensive and do not adequately provide families with an affordable way to monitor their electricity usage. I have developed a better solution to this pain point.

How is this section of the report similar to or different from a review of scholarship?

Stresses reasons that support the business's potential for success

— D. *The Electricity Monitor*

The Electricity Monitor is a device that can solve the pain point of high power bills by measuring the electricity usage of each device in the home. This device can easily attach to any existing breaker box. Installation of the device can be performed by any customer with the instructions provided with the device. At a price of $75, this device will be much cheaper than current solutions to monitoring power usage. A price comparison is shown in Figure 1 below. By measuring electricity usage of each device in the home, the Electricity Monitor will be able to accurately estimate the power bill for the month (within 1% error) and update daily with changes to electricity usage trends in the home. All data will be transmitted to a monitoring display. This device is also superior to the competition in that it makes suggestions as to how to decrease energy consumption and provides information on which devices in the home are using the most energy. Using the data from the Electricity Monitor, families will finally have the tool they need to save money on their power bill.

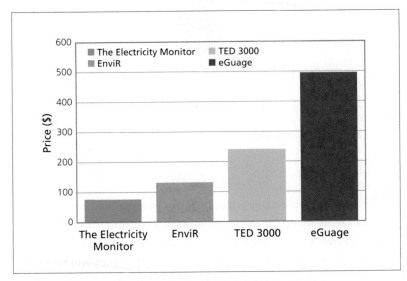

Fig. 1. Price comparison

Charts and figures appear commonly in business documents for clarification of ideas or to explain relationships between variables.

E. Market for This Product

Performs a more detailed market analysis

Industry market research from the IBIS World database shows small household appliance manufacturing to have $3.1 billion in annual revenue with $77.9 million in annual profit. This number alone shows the vastness of this market. In addition, IBIS World estimates 38.4% of this market to account for small household devices similar to the Electricity Monitor. Figure 2 below from IBIS World shows the market breakdown. The main demographic for this product will be families of three or more who are unhappy with their current power bill. The United States Census Bureau estimated there to be 4.4 million households with families of three or more people, accounting for 39% of all households in 2011. IBIS World describes the technology change in this market to be "Medium." This leads me to believe that a new product in this market could really shake the market and attract interest from consumers. Assuming that the current trend for revenue and profit in the small household appliance industry performs as predicted, the market for the Electricity Monitor will be large.

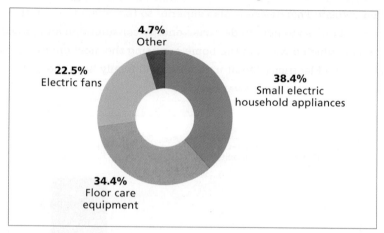

Fig. 2. Market breakdown

Explains governance and operating procedures of the proposed company

Plan of Business

A. Overview

I plan to construct the Electricity Monitor Company to hold complete ownership of all business sectors for the Electricity Monitor product. The Company will have an engineering department responsible for the design of the product, a manufacturing facility where the product will be built, and a marketing department responsible for the marketing and selling of the product. The overall cost for the start-up is analyzed below. This breakdown of cost can also be found in the Attachments section of this document.

Offers a detailed analysis of costs associated with the business start-up

B. Cost Analysis

Table 1
Design Expense

Design Expense	Description	Total Cost
Building	Rented office space	$ 5,000.00
Software	CAD modeling and FEA software license	$ 4,000.00
Total		$ 9,000.00

Table 1 is an analysis of the cost for designing the product. The requested loan will need to cover the first month of rent for an office and also a license for software that will be used to design the product. The labor is not included in the cost here because I will be designing the product myself.

Table 2
Manufacturing Expense

Manufacturing Expense (First 500 Products)	Description	Total Cost
Building	Small manufacturing facility	$ 100,000.00
Manufacturing equipment	Laser cutting machine, etc.	$ 200,000.00
Tools	Screwdrivers, socket wrenches, Allen wrenches, etc.	$ 5,000.00
Materials	First 500 monitors (avg cost $20/ monitor)	$ 10,000.00
Labor	$25/hr with five employees @ 40 hours a week	$ 20,000.00
Total		$ 335,000.00

Table 2 is an analysis of the cost for manufacturing the product. The building and manufacturing equipment are one-time costs for the initial start-up. The materials and labor will be ongoing costs, but the loan request is only enough to cover the first 500 products manufactured. Five hundred products have been estimated as enough to cover the first month of sales and will allow my company to be self-sufficient after selling the first 500 products.

Table 3
Marketing Expense

Marketing Expense	Description	Total Cost
Commercial	Television ad	$ 5,000.00
Web search	Google AdWords	$ 5,000.00
Total		$ 10,000.00

Table 3 is an analysis of the total marketing expense. I will additionally market this product to retail stores that could also sell this product, but cost for labor of this marketing is not included here because I will do it myself.

Table 4
Total Cost Analysis

Business Sector	Total Cost
Design	$ 9,000.00
Manufacturing	$ 335,000.00
Marketing	$ 10,000.00
Total	$ 354,000.00

Table 4 is a summary of the total cost analysis for this product. The highlighted cell in Table 4 represents the total start-up cost for the Electricity Monitor Company. This is also the total requested loan amount from First National Bank.

C. Summary

The total cost for this start-up was analyzed in Tables 1 through 4 above. The cost of materials was estimated from current market cost of materials and is subject to change with the market. However, my request for the bottom-line loan amount for this start-up is three hundred and fifty-four thousand dollars ($354,000.00), and this request will not change with cost of materials. A sound business plan has been constructed that will allow the Electricity Monitor Company to become self-sufficient after one month. In order for this business plan to work, the product must be successful in attracting customers quickly as projected by the market research.

The conclusion reiterates the proposed product's unique characteristics and potential for success in hopes of securing the capital investment.

Conclusion

The overall purpose of the Electricity Monitor start-up business is to develop a high-quality product that can generate excitement in the electricity monitor market and turn a profit for its business owners and investors. This product will benefit not only its investors, but also its consumers in that it will solve their pain point of not being able to affordably measure their current energy consumption. In comparison to other products in the market that attempt to solve the problem of high power bills, the Electricity Monitor is superior in price, ease of installation, and overall ability to solve the problem. There is nothing quite like this product currently in the market, and this is why it will be successful. The market research has proven that there is a large potential market and that current technology change is not very high. I am excited about starting the Electricity Monitor Company, the potential of this product, and the benefits for all parties involved. Please grant the requested loan amount of three hundred and fifty-four thousand dollars ($354,000.00) and help me make unnecessarily high power bills a thing of the past.

Documents sources consulted in the preparation of the business document

Bibliography

Entrepreneur. "TV Ads." Web. <http://www.entrepreneur.com/article/83108>.

IBIS World. "Vacuum, Fan, & Small Household Appliance Manufacturing in the US." Web. <http://clients1.ibisworld.com.prox.lib.ncsu.edu/reports/us/industry/ataglance.aspx?indid=786>.

Kreider, Rose M. "America's Families and Living Arrangements: 2012."
    United States Census Bureau. Web. <https://www.census.gov/prod
    /2013pubs/p20-570.pdf>.

Thornton Oliver Keller Commercial Real Estate. "Rental Rate Calculations."
    Web. <http://tokcommercial.com/MarketInformation/LearningCenter
    /RentalRateCalculations.aspx>.

Attachments

A. Cost Breakdown

Compiles the costs associated with the business start-up. See the reference to the attachment on page 322.

Design Expense	Description	Total Cost
Building	Rented office space	$ 5,000.00
Software	CAD modeling and FEA software license	$ 4,000.00
Total		**$ 9,000.00**

Manufacturing Expense (First 500 Products)	Description	Total Cost
Building	Small manufacturing facility	$ 100,000.00
Manufacturing equipment	Laser cutting machine, etc.	$ 200,000.00
Tools	Screwdrivers, socket wrenches, Allen wrenches, etc.	$ 5,000.00
Materials	First 500 monitors (avg cost $20/monitor)	$ 10,000.00
Labor	$25/hr with five employees @ 40 hours a week	$ 20,000.00
Total		**$ 335,000.00**

Marketing Expense	Description	Total Cost
Commercial	Television ad	$ 5,000.00
Web search	Google AdWords	$ 5,000.00
Total		**$ 10,000.00**

Business Sector	Total Cost	
Design	$ 9,000.00	
Manufacturing	$ 335,000.00	
Marketing	$ 10,000.00	
Total	**$ 354,000.00**	

INSIDE WORK   CFO for a Day

For this exercise, imagine that you're the chief financial officer for a company, Music Studio Emporium. Your company has twenty employees, and you've been charged with the task of notifying ten of them that they'll be receiving a 2 percent annual pay increase, effective immediately, based on their sales records. Unfortunately, you must also notify your other ten employees that they will not be receiving raises. Draft a brief memo to each group of employees—one for those receiving raises and one for those who aren't—in which you explain the company's decisions regarding your employees' compensation. Feel free to provide additional reasoning for those decisions, as you see fit.

Refer to the memo on page 316 as a model of the structural features you'll want to employ in constructing your memo. Once you're done, consider how the nature of the news you had to convey to each audience influenced the way you delivered that news. What did you do the same for each of your audiences? What did you do differently in constructing the two memos? ▶

CRIMINAL JUSTICE AND LAW

Millions of people are employed in the areas of law and criminal justice in the United States. When we encounter the terms "law" and "criminal justice," the image of a lawyer, or attorney, often comes to mind first. No doubt, attorneys make vital contributions to almost every aspect of our lives; their work helps us to understand, to enforce, and even to change our policies, procedures, and laws, whether they are civil or criminal in nature. Though attorneys make a significant contribution to our system of governance, they actually represent only a fraction of the vast number of professionals who work in the U.S. criminal justice system.

Criminal Justice

If you've ever watched a crime show on television, then you've likely been exposed to some of the many areas of training and expertise that make up the U.S. criminal justice system. Professionals who work in the fields of criminal justice are responsible for enforcing our laws and ensuring the safety of our communities. They are also responsible for such jobs as investigating crime scenes, staffing our jails and prisons, and providing essential services to victims of crimes and to those charged with or convicted of a crime. Careers in the fields of criminal justice range from forensic technician to parole officer to corrections counselor. While each of these career paths requires a different level of training and expertise, and many colleges and universities offer specific plans of study that culminate in certification or licensure in these diverse areas, they are unified by a commitment to the just treatment of all individuals under the law.

As criminologist Michelle Richter notes in her "Insider's View," there are various reasons that might compel an individual to choose a career in criminal justice, and there are various constituencies to whom differing careers in the fields of criminal justice must deliver support and services. Here's a small sampling of the many career paths available to those interested in the field of criminal justice:

- Bailiff
- Correctional Officer
- Corrections Counselor
- Court Reporter
- Emergency Management Director
- Fire Inspector
- Forensic Science Technician
- Legal Secretary
- Paralegal
- Police Detective
- Sheriff and Deputy Sheriff

Law

Most of us probably have clichéd understandings of the law at work. Many of these likely originated from television shows and movies. In these scenarios, there's almost always lots of drama as the lawyers battle in court, parse witnesses' words, and attempt to sway a judge or jury to their side of a case.

In real life, the practice of law may not always be quite as dramatic or enthralling as it appears on the screen. In fact, many lawyers rarely, or maybe never, appear in court. A criminal defense attorney may regularly appear before a judge or jury in a courtroom setting, but a corporate lawyer may spend the majority of her time drafting and analyzing business contracts. This difference is directly related to the field of law an individual specializes in, be it criminal law, family law, tax law, or environmental law, just to name a few.

Regardless of an attorney's chosen specialization, though, the study of law remains fundamentally concerned with debates over the interpretation of language. This is because the various rules that govern our lives—statutes, ordinances, regulations, and laws, for example—are all constructed in language. As you surely recognize, language can be quite slippery, and rules can often be interpreted in many different ways. We need only briefly to consider current

Insider's View
There's a wide variety of reasons for being here
MICHELLE RICHTER, CRIMINAL JUSTICE

"Motivation can be really critical.... If you want to work with people, it gets really complex. Do you want to work with law-abiding citizens or folks who have not been convicted of anything? Or do you want to work with the offender population? Do you want to work with the victim population? If you're looking at offenders, do you want to work with adults? Juveniles? Men, women, the elderly, the disabled, the mentally disabled? Most of the time students go into criminal justice, criminology, and forensics to understand a particular type of behavior, or to make the world a better place, or to make it safer, or something has happened to them in the past, and they want to make sure nobody ever has to go through that again. So there's a wide variety of reasons for being here."

debates over free speech issues or the "right to bear arms" or marriage equality to understand how complicated the business of interpreting laws can become. In the United States, the U.S. Supreme Court holds the authority to provide the final interpretation on the meaning of disputed laws. However, there are lots of legal interpretations and arguments that lower courts must make on a daily basis, and only a tiny portion of cases are ever heard by the U.S. Supreme Court.

As in the other applied fields, there are many common forms of communication in the various fields of law, as lawyers must regularly communicate with different kinds of stakeholders, including clients, other lawyers, judges, and law enforcement officials. For this reason, individuals working in the legal professions are generally expert at composing e-mail messages, memos, letters to clients, and legal briefs, among other genres. The following examples provide a glimpse into two types of writing through which lawyers frequently communicate.

Legal Brief   One of the first forms of writing students of law are likely to encounter in their academic study is the **legal brief**. Briefs can serve any number of functions, but their primary purpose is to outline the critical components of a legal argument to a specified audience. They may be descriptive or argumentative. A typical assignment for a student in law school might include writing a legal brief that describes a particular court's decision and explains how the court reached that decision. Cases that appear before the U.S. Supreme Court are usually accompanied by numerous legal briefs that are written and filed with the Court by parties who are interested in the outcomes of those cases. Many of these briefs are argumentative. Students of law, then, must be familiar with the basic structural components, or the structural conventions, of the legal brief. And law schools regularly instruct their students to produce legal briefs using the generalized form known as **IRAC**—an acronym for **Introduction, Rule, Application, and Conclusion**—as a means to describe past court decisions and/or to present written arguments to a court:

- **Introduction: Identify the Legal Issue(s) in the Case**   Legal cases can be very complicated. It is a lawyer's task to explore the facts of a case, along with its legal history, to determine which facts are actually relevant and which are irrelevant as they pertain to a legal question or dispute.

- **Rule: Identify and Explain the Relevant Law(s) to the Case**   Often, many different statutes, regulations, laws, or other court precedents are applicable and need exploration as part of a legal dispute. A lawyer must identify the applicable rules of law and explain their relevance to the legal question or dispute at hand.
- **Application: Apply the Relevant Rules to the Facts of the Case**   The facts of the case are explored through the lens of relevant rules. Arguments are presented in these sections of a brief.
- **Conclusion: Argue for a Particular Decision or Outcome**   Based on the application of relevant rules to the facts of the case, a lawyer makes a recommendation that the judge or court should reach a particular conclusion.

Insider Example
Professional Legal Brief

The following excerpts are from a 55-page legal brief that was filed with the U.S. Supreme Court on behalf of the University of Texas at Austin, et al., which was sued by an applicant after being denied admission to the university. In arguing their case, attorneys writing on behalf of the respondents, or the university, defended its decision to deny admission to the complainant, or the petitioner, Abigail Fisher. As you read the excerpted sections below, try to identify parts of the brief that correspond to the elements of the IRAC structure for presenting legal arguments: Introduction, Rule, Application, and Conclusion.

No. 11-345

In the
Supreme Court of the United States

ABIGAIL NOEL FISHER,
Petitioner,

v.

UNIVERSITY OF TEXAS AT AUSTIN, ET AL.,
Respondents.

ON WRIT OF CERTIORARI TO THE
UNITED STATES COURT OF APPEALS
FOR THE FIFTH CIRCUIT

BRIEF FOR RESPONDENTS

PATRICIA C. OHLENDORF
*Vice President for
Legal Affairs*

GREGORY G. GARRE
Counsel of Record
MAUREEN E. MAHONEY

THE UNIVERSITY OF
TEXAS AT AUSTIN
Flawn Academic Center
2304 Whitis Avenue
Stop G4800
Austin, TX 78712

DOUGLAS LAYCOCK
UNIVERSITY OF VIRGINIA
SCHOOL OF LAW
580 Massie Road
Charlottesville, VA 22903

J. SCOTT BALLENGER
LORI ALVINO MCGILL
KATYA S. GEORGIEVA
LATHAM & WATKINS LLP
555 11th Street, NW
Suite 1000
Washington, DC 20004
(202) 637-2207
gregory.garre@lw.com

JAMES C. HO
GIBSON, DUNN &
CRUTCHER LLP
2100 McKinney Avenue
Suite 1110
Dallas, TX 75201-6912

Counsel for Respondents

INTRODUCTION

Identifies the critical issue at stake, and lays out the respondents' position

After considering largely the same objections raised by petitioner and her amici here, this Court strongly embraced Justice Powell's controlling opinion in *Regents of the University of California v. Bakke*, 438 U.S. 265 (1978), and refused to prohibit the consideration of race as a factor in admissions at the Nation's universities and graduate schools. *Grutter v. Bollinger*, 539 U.S. 306 (2003); *see id.* at 387 (Kennedy, J., dissenting). And although the Court has made clear that any consideration of race in this context must be limited, it has been understood for decades that "a university admissions program may take account of race as one, non-predominant factor in a system designed to consider each applicant as an individual, provided the program can meet the test of strict scrutiny by the judiciary." *Id.* at 387 (Kennedy, J., dissenting) (citing *Bakke*, 438 U.S. at 289-91, 315-18 (Powell, J.)); *see id.* at 322-23. The University of Texas at Austin (UT)'s highly individualized consideration of race for applicants not admitted under the State's top 10% law satisfies that demand, and meets strict scrutiny under any conception of that test not designed simply to bar the consideration of race altogether.

Reviews relevant precedents, or earlier conclusions reached by the Court

That conclusion follows *a fortiori* from existing precedent. UT's admissions plan was modeled on the type of plan upheld in *Grutter* and commended by Justice Powell in *Bakke*. Moreover, UT's plan lacks the features criticized in *Grutter* by Justice Kennedy—who agreed with the majority that *Bakke* is the "correct rule." *Id.* at 387 (dissenting). Justice Kennedy concluded that Michigan Law School's admissions plan used race "to achieve numerical goals indistinguishable from quotas." *Id.* at 389. Here, it is undisputed that UT has not set any "target" or "goal" for minority admissions. JA 131a. Justice Kennedy stressed that Michigan's "admissions officers consulted . . . daily reports which indicated the composition of the incoming class along racial lines." *Grutter*, 539 U.S. at 391 (dissenting). Here, it is undeniable that no such monitoring occurs. JA 398a. And Justice Kennedy believed that race was "a predominant factor" under Michigan's plan. *Grutter*, 539 U.S. at 393 (dissenting). Here, petitioner argues (at 20) that UT's consideration of race is too "minimal" to be constitutional. That paradoxical contention not only overlooks the indisputably meaningful impact that UT's plan has on diversity, *infra* at 36-38, it turns on its head Justice Powell's conception of the appropriately nuanced and modest consideration of race in this special context.

Because petitioner cannot dispute that UT's consideration of race is both highly individualized and modest, she is forced to take positions directly at odds with the record and existing precedent. Her headline claim that UT is engaged in "racial balancing" (Pet. Br. 6-7, 19, 27-28, 45-46) is refuted by her own concession that UT has *not* set any "target" for minority admissions. JA 131a. Her argument that the State's top 10% law bars UT from considering race in its holistic review of applicants not eligible under that law is foreclosed by *Grutter*'s holding that percentage plans are not a complete, workable alternative to the individualized consideration of race in full-file review. 539 U.S. at 340. And her argument that, in 2004, UT had already achieved all the diversity that the Constitution allowed is based on "a limited notion of diversity" (*Parents Involved in Cmty. Schs. v. Seattle Sch. Dist. No. 1*, 551 U.S. 701, 723 (2007)) rejected by this Court—one that crudely lumps together distinct racial groups and ignores the importance of diversity among individuals *within* racial groups.

Presents the complainant's central claims, and offers response

In the end, petitioner really is just asking this Court to move the goal posts on higher education in America—and overrule its precedent going back 35 years to *Bakke*. Pet. Br. 53-57. *Stare decisis* alone counsels decisively against doing so. Petitioner has provided no persuasive justification for the Court to reexamine, much less overrule, its precedent, just nine years after this Court decided *Grutter* and eliminated any doubt about the controlling force of Justice Powell's opinion in *Bakke*. And overruling *Grutter* and *Bakke* (or effectively gutting them by adopting petitioner's conception of strict scrutiny) would jeopardize the Nation's paramount interest in educating its future leaders in an environment that best prepares them for the society and workforce they will encounter. Moreover, the question that petitioner herself asked this Court to decide is the constitutionality of UT's policy under *existing* precedent, including *Grutter*. *See* Pet. i; Pet. Br. i. Because the court of appeals correctly answered that question, the judgment below should be affirmed.

Identifies stakes for the outcome of the decision, and reasserts the respondents' position

STATEMENT OF THE CASE

. . .

E. Petitioner's Application for Admission

Petitioner, a Texas resident, applied for admission to UT's Fall 2008 freshman class in Business Administration or Liberal Arts, with a combined SAT score of 1180 out of 1600 and a cumulative 3.59 GPA. JA 40a-41a. Because petitioner was not in the top 10% of her high school class, her application was considered pursuant to the holistic review process described above. JA 40a. Petitioner scored an AI of 3.1, JA 415a, and received a PAI score of less than 6 (the actual score is contained in a sealed brief, ECF No. 52). The summary judgment record is uncontradicted that—due to the stiff competition in 2008 and petitioner's relatively low AI score—petitioner would not have been admitted to the Fall 2008 freshman class even if she had received "a 'perfect' PAI score of 6." JA 416a.

Petitioner also was denied admission to the summer program, which offered provisional admission to some applicants who were denied admission to the fall class, subject to completing certain academic requirements over the summer. JA 413a-14a. (UT discontinued this program in 2009.) Although one African-American and four Hispanic applicants with lower combined AI/PAI scores than petitioner's were offered admission to the summer program, so were 42 Caucasian applicants with combined AI/PAI scores identical to or lower than petitioner's. In addition, 168 African-American and Hispanic applicants in this pool who had combined AI/PAI scores identical to or *higher* than petitioner's were *denied* admission to the summer program.[1]

---

[1]These figures are drawn from UT's admissions data and are provided in response to petitioner's unsupported assertion (at 2) that her "academic credentials exceeded those of many admitted minority applicants." Petitioner presented a subset of this data (admitted minority students) to the district court as Plaintiffs' Exhibits 26 and 27 at the preliminary injunction hearing (the court later returned the exhibits). *See* W.D. Tex. Record Transmittal Letter (July 27, 2012), ECF No. 136. UT summarized additional data in a sealed letter brief after the hearing. ECF No. 52; JA 20a (discussing data and explaining that petitioner had not requested data regarding the applicants "who were *not* admitted to UT"). In denying a preliminary injunction, the district court stated (without citation) that 64 minority applicants with lower AI scores than petitioner were *admitted* to Liberal Arts. *Fisher v. Texas*, 556 F. Supp. 2d 603, 607 & n.2 (W.D. Tex. 2008). That statement is not binding at the merits stage. *University of Texas v. Camenisch*, 451 U.S. 390, 395 (1981). Although the district court did not specify whether it was referring to admissions to the fall class or the summer program, that figure can only encompass admits to the summer program. As explained in the unrebutted summary judgment record, with her AI score, petitioner could not "have gained admission through the fall review process," even with a "perfect" PAI score. JA 415a-16a. Petitioner has submitted no contrary evidence (and UT is aware of none). That leaves the now-defunct summer program. The district court's statement that minority applicants with lower AI scores than petitioner were admitted does not establish that race was a factor in petitioner's

UT did offer petitioner admission to the Coordinated Admissions Program, which allows Texas residents to gain admission to UT for their sophomore year by completing 30 credits at a participating UT System campus and maintaining a 3.2 GPA. JA 414a. Petitioner declined that offer and enrolled at Louisiana State University, from which she graduated in May.

F. Procedural History

Petitioner and another applicant—"no longer involved in this case," Pet. Br. ii—filed suit in the Western District of Texas against UT and various University officials under 42 U.S.C. § 1983, alleging, *inter alia*, that UT's 2008 full-file admissions procedures violate the Equal Protection Clause. JA 38a. They sued only on their own behalf (not on behalf of any class of applicants) and sought a declaratory judgment and injunctive relief barring UT's consideration of race and requiring UT to reconsider their own applications in a race-blind process. JA 39a. They also sought a "refund of [their] application fees and all associated expenses incurred . . . in connection with applying to UT." *Id.*; *see* App. 3a-4a.

The district court denied petitioner's request for a preliminary injunction. The parties filed cross-motions for summary judgment and supporting statements of fact (JA 103a-51a, 363a-403a). Applying strict scrutiny (App. 139a), the court granted judgment to UT, holding that UT has a compelling interest in attaining a diverse student body and the educational benefits flowing from such diversity, and that UT's individualized and holistic review process is narrowly tailored to further that interest. App. 168-69a.

The Fifth Circuit affirmed. Like the district court, the court of appeals found that "it would be difficult for UT to construct an admissions policy that more closely resembles the policy approved by the Supreme Court in *Grutter*." App. 5a. And the court likewise took it as "a given" that UT's policy "is subject to strict scrutiny with its requirement of narrow tailoring." App. 35a. While acknowledging that *Bakke* and *Grutter* call for some deference to a university's "educational judgment," the court emphasized that "the scrutiny triggered by

> Provides a brief history of the case in the courts, explaining decisions by lower courts

---

denial from the summer program, because (as noted above) many more minority applicants (168) with identical or *higher* AI/PAI scores were *denied* admission to the summer program. It is thus hard to see how petitioner could establish any cognizable injury for her § 1983 damages claim—the only claim still alive in this case—or, for that matter, standing to maintain that claim. *See Texas v. Lesage*, 528 U.S. 18, 19, 21 (1999) (per curiam); *Lujan v. Defenders of Wildlife*, 504 U.S. 555, 562 (1992). (Petitioner's claims for injunctive relief dropped out of the case at least once she graduated from a different university in May 2012, making this issue pertinent now.) And that is just one apparent vehicle—if not jurisdictional—defect with this case. *See* Br. in Opp. 6-22; *see also* Adam D. Chandler, *How (Not) to Bring an Affirmative-Action Challenge*, 122 Yale L. J. Online (forthcoming Sept. 2012), *available at* http://ssrn.com/abstract_id=2122956 (discussing vehicle defects stemming from, among other things, the unusual manner in which this case was framed).

racial classification 'is no less strict for taking into account' the special circumstances of higher education." App. 34a, 36a. Applying strict scrutiny, the court upheld UT's admissions policy. App. 71a.

Judge Garza concurred. He recognized that the court's opinion was "faithful" to *Grutter*, but argued that *Grutter* was wrongly decided. App. 72a-73a.

SUMMARY OF ARGUMENT

UT's individualized consideration of race in holistic admissions did not subject petitioner to unequal treatment in violation of the Fourteenth Amendment.

I. Racial classifications are subject to strict scrutiny, including in the higher education context. But ever since Justice Powell's opinion in *Bakke*, this Court has recognized that universities have a compelling interest in promoting student body diversity, and that a university may consider the race of applicants in an individualized and modest manner—such that race is just one of many characteristics that form the mosaic presented by an applicant's file.

UT's holistic admissions policy exemplifies the type of plan this Court has allowed: race is only one modest factor among many others weighed; it is considered only in an individualized and contextual way that "examine[s] the student in 'their totality,'" JA 129a; and admissions officers do not know an applicant's race when they decide which "cells" to admit in UT's process. At the same time, UT's policy *lacks* the features that Justice Kennedy found disqualifying in *Grutter*: it is undisputed that UT has not established any race-based target; race is not assigned any automatic value; and the racial or ethnic composition of admits is not monitored during the admissions cycle.

II. Petitioner's arguments that she was nevertheless subjected to unequal treatment in violation of the Fourteenth Amendment are refuted by both the record and existing precedent.

. . .

III. The Court should decline petitioner's far-reaching request to reopen and overrule *Bakke* and *Grutter*. That request is outside the scope of the question presented, which asks the Court to review UT's policy under *existing* precedent, including *Grutter*. In any event, petitioner has failed to identify any special justification for taking the extraordinary step of overruling *Grutter*, just nine years after this Court decided *Grutter* and unequivocally answered any doubt about the validity of Justice Powell's opinion in *Bakke*. Abruptly reversing course here would upset legitimate expectations in the rule of law—not to mention the profoundly important societal interests in ensuring that the future leaders of America are trained in a campus environment in which they are exposed to the full educational benefits of diversity.

. . .

Presents a summary of arguments in defense of the respondents' position in light of the facts of the case

CONCLUSION

The judgment of the court of appeals should be affirmed.

Respectfully submitted,

PATRICIA C. OHLENDORF
*Vice President for
Legal Affairs*
THE UNIVERSITY OF
TEXAS AT AUSTIN
Flawn Academic Center
2304 Whitis Avenue
Stop G4800
Austin, TX 78712

DOUGLAS LAYCOCK
UNIVERSITY OF VIRGINIA
SCHOOL OF LAW
580 Massie Road
Charlottesville, VA 22903

GREGORY G. GARRE
Counsel of Record
MAUREEN E. MAHONEY
J. SCOTT BALLENGER
LORI ALVINO MCGILL
KATYA S. GEORGIEVA
LATHAM & WATKINS LLP
555 11th Street, NW
Suite 1000
Washington, DC 20004
(202) 637-2207
gregory.garre@lw.com

JAMES C. HO
GIBSON, DUNN &
CRUTCHER LLP
2100 McKinney Avenue
Suite 1110
Dallas, TX 75201-6912

AUGUST 2012
Counsel for Respondents

Concludes by asserting the decision that respondents believe the Court should reach

E-Mail Correspondence As you might expect, technological advances can have a profound impact on the communication practices of professionals. There may always be a place for hard copies of documents, but e-mail communication has no doubt replaced many of the letters that used to pass between parties via the U.S. Postal Service. Like most professionals these days, those employed in the legal fields often spend a lot of time communicating with stakeholders via e-mail. These professionals carefully assess each rhetorical situation for which an e-mail communication is necessary, both (1) to make sure the ideas they share with stakeholders (the explanations of legal procedures, or legal options, or applicable precedents, etc.) are accurate, and (2) to make sure they communicate those ideas in an appropriate fashion (with the appropriate tone, clarity, precision, etc.).

Insider Example
E-Mail Correspondence from Attorney

The following example is an e-mail sent from a practicing lawyer to a client. In this instance, the lawyer offers legal advice concerning a possible donation from a party to a foundation. As you read the lawyer's description of the documents attached to his e-mail correspondence with the client, pay attention to the ways the attorney demonstrates an acute awareness of his audience, both in terms of the actual legal advice he provides and in terms of the structure and language of his message.

Establishes the level of familiarity and tone

Provides transactional advice, explaining what procedure needs to occur between the two parties involved: a donor and a receiving foundation

Provides additional advice to protect the interests of the parties in the event that either party decides to back out of the transaction

Explains more specific details included in the attached legal documents to protect the interests of the Foundation

Communicates a willingness to continue the relationship with the client

Provides standard identification and contact information for communication between and among professionals

---

Dear _____

As promised, here are two documents related to the proposed gift of the ABC property to the XYZ Foundation (the "Foundation"). The first document summarizes the recommended due diligence steps (including the creation of a limited liability company) that should take place prior to the acceptance of the property, accompanied by estimated costs associated with each such step. The second document contains a draft "pre-acceptance" agreement that the Foundation could use to recover its documented costs in the event that either the donor or the Foundation backs out of a gift agreement following the due diligence process.

You will note that we have limited the Foundation's ability to recover costs in the event that the Foundation is the party that "pulls the plug." In such a scenario, the Foundation could recover costs only if it reasonably determines that either (i) the property would create a risk of material exposure to environmentally related liabilities or (ii) the remediation of environmental issues would impose material costs on the Foundation. We realize that even in light of this limiting language, the agreement represents a fairly aggressive approach with the donor, and we will be glad to work with you if you wish to take a softer stance.

Please don't hesitate to call me with any questions, concerns, or critiques. As always, we appreciate the opportunity to serve you in furthering the Foundation's good work.

Best regards,

Joe

Joseph E. Miller, Jr.
Partner
joe.miller@FaegreBD.com
Direct: +1 317 237 1415
FaegreBD.com Download vCard
FAEGRE BAKER DANIELS LLP
300 N. Meridian Street
Suite 2700
Indianapolis, IN 46204, USA

INSIDE WORK · **Lawyer for a Day**

Imagine that you're an attorney, and you've just been hired as a consultant by the Board of Governors of a local college that's in the process of designing new guidelines for student admissions. As part of that process, the Board has asked you to review legal briefs presented on behalf of various stakeholders in *Fisher v. University of Texas at Austin,* et al. Additionally, the Board wants you to provide a summary of UT–Austin's response to the charge that its admissions procedures violated the petitioner's rights under the Fourteenth Amendment to the U.S. Constitution.

Read again the section of the legal brief filed with the U.S. Supreme Court entitled "Summary of Argument" (on p. 334), and then draft an e-mail to your client (the Board of Governors) in which you offer an overview of UT–Austin's response to its possible violation of a prospective student's constitutional rights. As part of your summary, offer your client an assessment of the likely effectiveness of UT–Austin's argument. Be clear and precise in your presentation of UT–Austin's argument in defense of its position. Keep your audience and your relationship to that audience in mind as you compose your e-mail. ◗

Discovering Genres of Writing in an Applied Field

WRITING PROJECT

In this chapter, you've read about some of the conventions of writing in the applied fields of health, education, business, criminal justice, and law. You might be interested in a field that's not represented in this chapter, though. For this assignment, you will conduct research to discover more about the kinds of writing that are common within a particular applied field—ideally, one you're interested in. You might conduct either primary or secondary research to respond to this assignment. However, you should focus on collecting examples of the kinds of writing done in the field. Consider following the steps below to complete this assignment.

1. Collect examples of the kinds of writing done in the field.

2. Describe the different genres and how they relate to the work of that applied field.

3. Look for comparisons and contrasts across those genres. Do any commonalities point to conventions shared across genres? Are there differences that are important to notice? What do the patterns across the genres tell you about the work and values of that applied field?

Variation: Imagine that your audience is a group of incoming students interested in the same field of study you've researched for this project. Your task is to write a guide for those students about the conventions of writing expected in this applied field. Depending on what you have found, you may need to identify what conventions are appropriate for specific genres of writing.

tip sheet

Reading and Writing in the Applied Fields

- **The applied fields focus on the practical application of knowledge and career preparation.** Many applied fields also focus on problem-solving as part of the practical application of knowledge.

- **When beginning a writing task in applied fields, carefully analyze the rhetorical situation.** Consider your purpose and your audience carefully, and assess the appropriateness of responding in a particular genre.

- **Much of the writing in applied fields follows conventional expectations for structure, language, and reference appropriate to the fields.** Regardless of your writing task, you should be aware of these conventional expectations.

- **Students and professionals in applied fields often communicate information through field-specific genres.** Nurses, for example, often construct discharge directions, just as students and professionals in the fields of law often compose legal briefs.

Introduction to Documentation Styles

You've likely had some experience with citing sources in academic writing, both as a reader and as a writer. Many students come to writing classes in college with experience only in MLA format, the citation style of the Modern Language Association. The student research paper at the end of Chapter 5 is written in MLA style, which is the most commonly required citation style in English classes. Although MLA is the citation style with which English and writing teachers are usually most familiar, it is not the only one used in academic writing—not by a long shot.

Some students don't realize that other citation styles exist, and they're often surprised when they encounter different styles in other classes. Our goal in this appendix is to help you understand (1) why and when academic writers cite sources and (2) how different citation styles represent the values and conventions of different academic disciplines. This appendix also provides brief guides to MLA, APA (American Psychological Association), and CSE (Council of Science Editors) styles—three styles that are commonly used in the first three chapters in Part Two of this book. These citation styles are discussed in some detail in Chapter 5 as well. Near the end of this appendix, you'll find a table with other citation styles commonly used in different disciplines, including some of the applied fields discussed in Chapter 10.

Why Cite?

There are several reasons why academic writers cite sources that they draw upon. The first is an ethical reason: academic research and writing privilege the discovery of new knowledge, and it is important to give credit to scholars who discover new ideas and establish important claims in their fields of study. Additionally, academic writers cite sources to provide a "breadcrumb trail" to show how they developed their current research projects. Source citations show what prior work writers are building on and how their research contributes to that body of knowledge. If some of the sources are well respected, that ethos helps to support the writers' research as well. It demonstrates that the writers have done their homework; they know what has already been discovered, and they are contributing to an ongoing conversation.

These two values of academic writing—the necessity of crediting the person or persons who discover new knowledge, and the importance of understanding prior work that has led to a specific research project—shape the choices that academic writers make when citing sources. Anytime you quote, summarize, or paraphrase the work of someone else in academic writing, you must give credit to that person's work. *How* academic writers cite those sources, though, differs according to their academic discipline and writing situation.

Disciplinary Documentation Styles

Citation styles reflect the values of specific disciplines, just like other conventions of academic writing that we've discussed in this book. When you compare the similarities and differences in citation styles, you might notice that some conventions of particular citation styles that seemed random before suddenly have meaning. For example, if we compare the ways that authors and publication dates are listed in MLA, APA, and CSE styles, we'll notice some distinctions that reflect the values of those disciplines:

MLA

Author's full name

Year of publication listed near the end

Greenwell, Amanda M. "Rhetorical Reading Guides, Readerly Experiences, and WID in the Writing Center." *WLN: A Journal of Writing Center Scholarship,* vol. 41, no. 7-8, Mar.-Apr. 2017, pp. 9-16.

APA

Only author's last name included in full

Year included toward the beginning, in a place of importance

Greenwell, A. (March-April 2017). Rhetorical reading guides, readerly experiences, and WID in the writing center. *WLN: A Journal of Writing Center Scholarship, 41*(7–8), 9–16.

CSE

Only last name given in full, and first and middle initials are not separated from last name by any punctuation.

Year also has a place of prominence and isn't distinguished from the name at all, emphasizing that timeliness is as important as the name of the author

Greenwell A. 2017 Mar-Apr. Rhetorical reading guides, readerly experiences, and WID in the writing center. WLN. 41(7-8):9-16.

MLA lists the author's full name at the beginning of the citation, emphasizing the importance of the author. Date of publication is one of the last items in the citation, reflecting that a publication's currency is often not as important in the humanities as it is in other disciplines. By contrast, APA and CSE list the date of publication near the beginning of the citation in a place of prominence. Interestingly, CSE does not use any unique punctuation to distinguish the author from the date other than separating them by a period, reflecting that they are of almost equal importance.

Citation styles reflect the values of the respective disciplines. In a very real sense, citation styles are rhetorically constructed: they are developed, revised, updated, and used in ways that reflect the purpose and audience for citing sources in different disciplines. Some rules in documentation styles don't seem to have a clear reason, though, and this is why it's important to know how to verify the rules of a certain system. Our goal is to help you understand, on a rhetorical level, the way three common citation styles work. Memorizing these styles is not always the most productive endeavor, as the styles change over time. Really understanding how they work will be much more useful to you long term.

Modern Language Association (MLA) Style

WHAT IS UNIQUE ABOUT MLA STYLE?

MLA style is generally followed by researchers in the disciplines of the humanities such as foreign languages and English. One of the unique aspects of MLA style, when compared with other styles, is that the page numbers of quoted, summarized, or paraphrased information are included in in-text citations. While other styles sometimes also include page numbers (especially for exact quotations), the use of page numbers in MLA allows readers to go back to find the original language of the referenced passage. In the disciplines that follow MLA style, the way in which something is phrased is often quite important, and readers might want to review the original source to assess how you are using evidence to support your argument.

We offer some basic guidelines here for using MLA style, but you can learn more about the style guides published by the Modern Language Association, including the *MLA Handbook*, at www.mla.org.

IN-TEXT CITATIONS IN MLA STYLE

When sources are cited in the text, MLA style calls for a parenthetical reference at the end of a sentence or at the end of the information being cited (if in the middle of a sentence). The author's name and the page number(s) of the reference appear in parentheses with no other punctuation, and then the end-of-sentence punctuation appears after the parenthetical reference.

> The frequency with which customers ordered dessert at restaurants can be correlated with the BMI of the waitstaff (Döring and Wansink 198).

1. Paraphrase from article
2. Last name of author
3. Page number where paraphrased material can be found

WORKS CITED CITATIONS IN MLA STYLE

The citations list at the end of an academic paper in MLA style is called a Works Cited page. Citations are listed on the Works Cited page in alphabetical order by the authors' last names.

> Döring, Tim, and Brian Wansink. "The Waiter's Weight." *Environment and Behavior*, vol. 49, no. 2, 2017, pp. 192-214.

1. **Author.**   Author's name is listed first, with the last name preceding the first name and any middle initials. The first name is spelled out and followed by a comma, and then the other authors are listed with the first name preceding the last name.

2. **Title of source.**   Article titles and book chapters are given in quotation marks. All words in the title are capitalized except for articles and prepositions (unless they are the first words). Include a period after the title, inside the last quotation mark.

3. **Title of container where the source was found.**   Book, journal, magazine, and newspaper titles appear in italics. A comma follows the title.

4. **Other contributors.**   If the container has editors, translators, or other contributors, those would be listed directly after the title of the container.

5. **Version.**   If the source is an edition or specific version of a text, that information would be listed next.

6. **Number.**   For a journal, the volume number follows the title of the journal, preceded by the abbreviation "vol." If the journal has an issue number, that would then be listed after the volume number, preceded by the abbreviation "no." Use commas to separate the volume, issue number, and any information that follows.

7. **Publisher.**   If a specific publisher is listed, give the name of the publisher next.

8. **Publication date.**   The year of publication is listed next, followed by a comma. For journals, include the month and/or season before the year.

9. **Location.**   Inclusive page numbers are provided in the MLA citation of a journal article, preceded by "pp." and followed by a period. If you are citing an online source, list the URL as the location.

Citing Different Types of Sources in MLA Style

Comparison of different kinds of sources in MLA style

Type of Source	Example of Works Cited Entry	Notes
Book	Davies, Alice, and Kathryn Tollervey. *The Style of Coworking: Contemporary Shared Workspaces.* Prestel Verlag, 2013.	When more than one author is listed, only the first author's name is reversed in MLA style.
Book chapter	Ludvigsen, Sten, and Hans Christian Arnseth. "Computer-Supported Collaborative Learning." *Technology Enhanced Learning,* edited by Erik Duval, Mike Sharples, and Rosamund Sutherland, Springer International, 2017, pp. 47-58.	Be sure to list both the book chapter and the title of the book when citing a chapter from an edited collection.
Scholarly journal article	Waldock, Jeff, et al. "The Role of Informal Learning Spaces in Enhancing Student Engagement with Mathematical Sciences." *The Journal of Mathematical Education in Science and Technology,* vol. 48, no. 4, 2017, pp. 587-602. *Taylor Francis Online,* www.tandfonline.com/pp/waldock_rowlett_7.pdf.	If more than two authors are listed, write *et al.* after the first author's name. If the source was found in an online database, list the database or website as a second, external, container.
Magazine or newspaper article	Goel, Vindu. "Office Space Is Hard to Find for Newcomers." *The New York Times,* 2 Apr. 2015, p. F2.	Periodical articles can differ in print and online, so be sure to cite the correct version of the article.
Website	Goodloe, Amy. "TIPS—Composing and Framing Video Interviews." *Digital Writing 101,* 2017, digitalwriting101.net/content/composing-and-framing-video-interviews/.	For online sources, include the exact URL for the source as the location, excluding http:// or https://.
Website with no individual author listed	Sage One. "Eight Ideas for Designing a More Collaborative Workspace." *Microsoft for Work,* Microsoft Corporation, 10 Jul. 2014, blogs.microsoft.com/work/2014/07/10/eight-ideas-for-designing-a-more-collaborative-workspace.	When no author is listed, you can begin the citation with the title of the article or site. If an organization or some other entity is sponsoring the article (as in this case), that can be listed as the author.

SAMPLE MLA WORKS CITED PAGE

Works Cited

Davies, Alice, and Kathryn Tollervey. *The Style of Coworking: Contemporary Shared Workspaces*. Prestel Verlag, 2013.

Goel, Vindu. "Office Space Is Hard to Find for Newcomers." *The New York Times*, 2 Apr. 2015, p. F2.

Goodloe, Amy. "TIPS — Composing and Framing Video Interviews." *Digital Writing 101*, 2017, digitalwriting101 .net/content/composing-and-framing-video-interviews/.

Ludvigsen, Sten, and Hans Christian Arnseth. "Computer-Supported Collaborative Learning." *Technology Enhanced Learning*, edited by Erik Duval, Mike Sharples, and Rosamund Sutherland, Springer International, 2017, pp. 47-58.

Sage One. "Eight Ideas for Designing a More Collaborative Workspace." *Microsoft for Work*, Microsoft Corporation, 10 Jul. 2014, blogs.microsoft.com/work/2014/07/10/ eight-ideas-for-designing-a-more-collaborative-workspace.

Waldock, Jeff, et al. "The Role of Informal Learning Spaces in Enhancing Student Engagement with Mathematical Sciences." *The Journal of Mathematical Education in Science and Technology*, vol. 48, no. 4, 2017, pp. 587-602. *Taylor Francis Online*, www.tandfonline.com/pp/waldock _rowlett_7.pdf.

American Psychological Association (APA) Style

WHAT IS UNIQUE ABOUT APA STYLE?

Researchers in many areas of the social sciences and related fields generally follow APA documentation procedures. Although you'll encounter page numbers in the in-text citations for direct quotations in APA documents, you're less likely to find direct quotations overall. Generally, researchers in the social sciences are less interested in the specific language or words used to report research findings than they are in the results or conclusions. Therefore, social science researchers are more likely to paraphrase information from sources than to quote information.

Additionally, in-text documentation in the APA system requires that you include the date of publication for research. This is a striking distinction from the MLA system. Social science research that was conducted fifty years ago may not be as useful as research conducted two years ago, so it's important to cite the date of the source in the text of your argument. Imagine how different the results would be for a study of the effects of violence in video games on youth twenty years ago versus a study conducted last year. Findings from twenty years ago probably have very little bearing on the world of today and would not reflect the same video game content as today's games. Including the date of research publication as part of the in-text citation allows readers to quickly evaluate the currency, and therefore the appropriateness, of the research you reference. Learn more about the *Publication Manual of the American Psychological Association* at www.apastyle.org.

IN-TEXT CITATIONS IN APA STYLE

When sources are cited in the text, APA style calls for a parenthetical reference at the end of a sentence or at the end of the information being cited (if in the middle of a sentence). The author's name and the year of publication are included in parentheses, separated by a comma, and then the end-of-sentence punctuation appears after the parenthetical reference. Page numbers are only included for direct quotations.

> The frequency with which customers ordered dessert at restaurants can be correlated with the BMI of the waitstaff (Döring & Wansink, 2017).

1. Paraphrase from article
2. Last name of author(s)
3. Year of publication

Often, the author's name is mentioned in the sentence, and then the year is listed in parentheses right after the author's name.

> According to Döring and Wansink (2017), the frequency with which customers ordered dessert at restaurants can be correlated with the BMI of the waitstaff.

1. Name of author(s) mentioned in the sentence
2. Year of publication listed in parentheses directly following author's name
3. Paraphrase from article

REFERENCE PAGE CITATIONS IN APA STYLE

The citations list at the end of an academic paper in APA style is called a References page. Citations are listed on the References page in alphabetical order by the authors' last names.

> Döring, T., & Wansink, B. (2017). The waiter's weight. *Environment and Behavior, 49*(2), 192–214.

1. The author's name is listed first, with the last name preceding first and middle initials. Only the last name is spelled out, and the initials are followed by periods.
2. The year directly follows the name, listed in parentheses and followed by a period outside the parentheses.
3. Article titles and book chapters are listed with no punctuation other than a period at the end. Only the first word in the title and any proper nouns are capitalized. If there is a colon in the title, the first word after the colon should also be capitalized.
4. Journal titles appear in italics, and all words are capitalized except articles and prepositions (unless they are the first words). A comma follows a journal title.
5. The volume number follows the title, also in italics. If there is an issue number, it is listed in parentheses immediately following the volume number, but not in italics. This is followed by a comma.
6. Inclusive page numbers appear at the end, followed by a period.

Citing Different Types of Sources in APA Style

Comparison of different kinds of sources in APA style

Type of Source	Example of Reference Page Entry	Notes
Book	Davies, A., & Tollervey, K. (2013). *The style of coworking: Contemporary shared workspaces*. Munich, Germany: Prestel Verlag.	In APA, multiple authors are linked with an ampersand (&).
Book chapter	Ludvigsen, S., & Arnseth, H. C. (2017). Computer-supported collaborative learning. In E. Duval, M. Sharples, & R. Sutherland (Eds.), *Technology enhanced learning* (pp. 47–58). Gewerbestrasse, Switzerland: Springer International Publishing.	Be sure to list both the book chapter and the title of the book when citing a chapter from an edited collection.
Scholarly journal article	Waldock, J., Rowlett, P., Cornock, C., Robinson, M., & Bartholomew, H. (2017). The role of informal learning spaces in enhancing student engagement with mathematical sciences. *The Journal of Mathematical Education in Science and Technology, 48*(4), 587–602.	In APA, the journal number is italicized with the journal title, but the issue number (in parentheses) is not.
Magazine or newspaper article	Goel, V. (2015, April 2). Office space is hard to find for newcomers. *The New York Times*, p. F2.	Periodical articles can differ in print and online, so be sure to cite where you found your version of the article.
Website	Goodloe, A. (2017). TIPS—composing and framing video interviews. *Digital Writing 101*. Retrieved from digitalwriting101.net /content/composing-and-framing-video -interviews/	
Website with no individual author listed	Sage One. (2014, July 10). Eight ideas for designing a more collaborative workspace [Web log post]. Retrieved from http:// blogs.microsoft.com/	When no author is listed for a web-based source, you can begin the citation with the title of the article or site. If an organization or some other entity is sponsoring the article (as in this case), that can be listed as author.

SAMPLE APA REFERENCE PAGE

References

Davies, A., & Tollervey, K. (2013). *The style of coworking: Contemporary shared workspaces*. Munich, Germany: Prestel Verlag.

Goel, V. (2015, April 2). Office space is hard to find for newcomers. *The New York Times*, p. F2.

Goodloe, A. (2017). TIPS—composing and framing video interviews. *Digital Writing 101*. Retrieved from digitalwriting101.net/content/composing-and-framing -video-interviews/

Ludvigsen, S., & Arnseth, H. C. (2017). Computer-supported collaborative learning. In E. Duval, M. Sharples, & R. Sutherland (Eds.), *Technology enhanced learning* (pp. 47–58). Gewerbestrasse, Switzerland: Springer International Publishing.

Sage One. (2014, July 10). Eight ideas for designing a more collaborative workspace [Web log post]. Retrieved from http://blogs.microsoft.com/

Waldock, J., Rowlett, P., Cornock, C., Robinson, M., & Bartholomew, H. (2017). The role of informal learning spaces in enhancing student engagement with mathematical sciences. *The Journal of Mathematical Education in Science and Technology, 48*(4), 587–602.

Council of Science Editors (CSE) Style

WHAT IS UNIQUE ABOUT CSE STYLE?

As the name suggests, the CSE documentation system is most prevalent among disciplines of the natural sciences, although many of the applied fields of the sciences, like engineering and medicine, rely on their own documentation systems. As with the other systems described here, CSE requires writers to document all materials derived from sources. Unlike MLA or APA, however, CSE allows multiple methods for in-text citations, corresponding to alternative forms of the reference page at the end of research reports. The three styles—**Citation-Sequence**, **Citation-Name**, and **Name-Year**—are used by different publications. In this book, we introduce you to the Name-Year system.

For more detailed information on CSE documentation, you can consult the latest edition of *Scientific Style and Format: The CSE Manual for Authors, Editors, and Publishers*, and you can learn more about the Council of Science Editors at its website: http://www.councilscienceeditors.org.

IN-TEXT CITATIONS IN CSE STYLE

When sources are cited in the text, CSE style calls for a parenthetical reference directly following the relevant information. The author's name and the year of publication are included in parentheses with no other punctuation.

> The frequency with which customers ordered dessert at restaurants can be correlated with the BMI of the waitstaff (Döring and Wansink 2017).

1. Paraphrase from article
2. Last name of author(s)
3. Year of publication

REFERENCE PAGE CITATIONS IN CSE STYLE

The citations list at the end of an academic paper in CSE style is called a References page. Citations are listed on the References page in alphabetical order by the authors' last names.

> Döring T, Wansink B. 2017. The waiter's weight. Envir and Behav. 49:192-214.

1. The author's name is listed first, with the full last name preceding the first and middle initials. No punctuation separates elements of the name.
2. The year directly follows the name, followed by a period.

3. Article titles and book chapters are listed with no punctuation other than a period at the end. Only the first word in the title and any proper nouns are capitalized. If there is a colon in the title, the first word after the colon should not be capitalized.

4. Journal titles are often abbreviated, and all words are capitalized. A period follows the journal title.

5. The volume number follows the title. If there is an issue number, it is listed in parentheses following the volume number, but not in italics. This is followed by a colon. No space appears after the colon.

6. Inclusive page numbers appear at the end, followed by a period.

Citing Different Types of Sources in CSE Style
Comparison of different kinds of sources in CSE style

Type of Source	Example of Reference Page Entry	Notes
Book	Davies A, Tollervey K. 2013. The style of coworking: contemporary shared workspaces. Munich (Germany): Prestel Verlag. 159 p.	Listing the number of pages is optional in CSE, but useful.
Book chapter	Ludvigsen S, Arnseth HC. 2017. Computer-supported collaborative learning. In: Duval E, Sharples M, Sutherland R, editors. Technology enhanced learning. Gewerbestrasse (Switzerland): Springer International Publishing. p. 47-58.	
Scholarly journal article	Waldock J, Rowlett P, Cornock C, Robinson M, Bartholomew, H. 2017. The role of informal learning spaces in enhancing student engagement with mathematical sciences. Journ of Math Ed in Sci and Tech. 48(4):587-602.	Some journal titles in CSE are abbreviated.
Magazine or newspaper article	Goel V. 2015 Apr 2. Office space is hard to find for newcomers. New York Times (National Ed.). Sect. F:2 (col. 1).	
Website	Goodloe A. 2017. Tips—composing and framing video interviews. Digital Writing 101; [accessed 2018 Jan 10]. http://digitalwriting101.net/content /composing-and-framing-video-interviews/.	CSE calls for the exact URL and an access date for web-based sources.
Website with no individual author listed	Sage One. 2014. Eight ideas for designing a more collaborative workspace [blog]. Microsoft at Work. [accessed 2015 Apr 2]. Available from http://blogs.microsoft.com/work/2014/07/10 /eight-ideas-for-designing-a-more -collaborative-workspace/.	

SAMPLE CSE REFERENCE PAGE

References

Davies A, Tollervey K. 2013. The style of coworking:
    contemporary shared workspaces. Munich (Germany):
    Prestel Verlag. 159 p.

Goel V. 2015 Apr 2. Office space is hard to find for newcomers.
    New York Times (National Ed.). Sect. F:2 (col. 1).

Goodloe A. 2017. Tips—composing and framing video
    interviews. Digital Writing 101; [accessed 2018 Jan 10].
    http://digitalwriting101.net/content/composing-and-framing
    -video-interviews/.

Ludvigsen S, Arnseth HC. 2017. Computer-supported
    collaborative learning. In: Duval E, Sharples M, Sutherland
    R, editors. Technology enhanced learning. Gewerbestrasse
    (Switzerland): Springer International Publishing. p. 47-58.

Sage One. 2014. Eight ideas for designing a more collaborative
    workspace [blog]. Microsoft at Work. [accessed 2015 Apr 2].
    Available from http://blogs.microsoft.com/work/2014/07/10
    /eight-ideas-for-designing-a-more-collaborative-workspace/.

Waldock J, Rowlett P, Cornock C, Robinson M, Bartholomew
    H. 2017. The role of informal learning spaces in enhancing
    student engagement with mathematical sciences. Journ of
    Math Ed in Sci and Tech. 48(4):587-602.

Other Common Documentation Styles

Many disciplines have their own documentation styles, and some are used more commonly than others. The following chart lists a few of the most popular.

Name of Citation Style	Disciplines	Website
American Chemical Society (ACS)	Chemistry and Physical Sciences	http://pubs.acs.org/series/styleguide
American Institute of Physics (AIP)	Physics	http://publishing.aip.org/authors
American Mathematical Society (AMS)	Mathematics	http://www.ams.org/publications/authors
American Medical Association (AMA)	Medicine	http://www.amamanualofstyle.com/
American Political Science Association (APSA)	Political Science	http://www.apsanet.org/Portals/54/files/APSAStyleManual2006.pdf
American Sociological Association (ASA)	Sociology	http://www.asanet.org/documents/teaching/pdfs/Quick_Tips_for_ASA_Style.pdf
Associated Press Stylebook (AP Style)	Journalism	https://www.apstylebook.com/
Bluebook style	Law, Legal Studies	https://www.legalbluebook.com/
Chicago Manual of Style (CMoS)	History and other humanities disciplines	http://www.chicagomanualofstyle.org/
Institute of Electrical and Electronics Engineers (IEEE)	Engineering	https://www.ieee.org/documents/style_manual.pdf
Linguistic Society of America (LSA)	Linguistics	http://www.linguisticsociety.org/files/style-sheet.pdf
Modern Humanities Research Association (MHRA)	Humanities	http://www.mhra.org.uk/Publications/Books/StyleGuide/StyleGuideV3.pdf

TRACKING RESEARCH

There are many useful, free digital tools online that can help you track your research and sources. Three of the best are personalized research-tracking tools and social applications that enable you to find additional resources through other users of the application:

- **Diigo (https://www.diigo.com/)**   Diigo is a social bookmarking application that solves two dilemmas faced by many writers. First, you can access all of the bookmarks that you save in a browser on multiple devices. Additionally, you can tag your sources and share them with others. That means you can search using tags (not very different from searching with key words in a database) and find other sources that users of Diigo have tagged with the same words and phrases that you have chosen.

- **Zotero (https://www.zotero.org/)**   Zotero is a robust research tool that helps you organize, cite, and share sources with others. You can install Zotero into your web browser and quickly save and annotate sources that you're looking at online. Zotero can help you generate citations, annotated bibliographies, and reference lists from the sources that you have saved.
- **Mendeley (http://www.mendeley.com/)**   Similar to Zotero, Mendeley is a free reference manager and academic social network that allows you to read and annotate PDFs on any device.

Your school may also have licenses for proprietary tools such as RefWorks and EndNote, which are also very useful research-tracking applications. Most of these applications can help you generate citations and reference lists as well. However, you need to understand how a documentation style works in order to check what is generated from any citation builder. For example, if you save the title of a journal article as "Increased pizza consumption leads to temporary euphoria but higher long-term cholesterol levels," a citation builder will not automatically change the capitalization if you need to generate a citation in MLA format. You have to be smarter than the application you use.

ACKNOWLEDGMENTS

Text Credits

Barbara L. Allen. "Environmental Justice, Local Knowledge, and After-Disaster Planning in New Orleans." From *Technology in Society*, Volume 29, Issue 2, April 2007, pp. 153–59. Copyright © 2007 Elsevier. Republished with the permission of Elsevier Science and Technology Journals; permission conveyed through Copyright Clearance Center, Inc.

Mike Brotherton. Excerpt from "Hubble Space Telescope Spies Galaxy/Black Hole Evolution in Action." From press release on mikebrotherton.com, June 2, 2008. Reproduced with the permission of the author.

Mike Brotherton, Wil van Breugel, S. A. Stanford, R. J. Smith, B. J. Boyle, Lance Miller, T. Shanks, S. M. Croom, and Alexei V. Filippenko. Excerpt from "A Spectacular Poststarburst Quasar." From *Astrophysical Journal*, August 1, 1999. Copyright © 1999 The American Astronomical Society. Reproduced with the permission of the authors.

Wanda Cassidy, Karen Brown, and Margaret Jackson. "'Under the Radar': Educators and Cyberbullying in Schools." From *School Psychology International*, Volume 33, Issue 5, October 2012, pp. 520–32. Copyright © 2012 by the Authors. Reprinted by permission of SAGE Publications, Ltd.

EBSCO Health. "Sample Discharge Orders." From www.ebscohost.com. Reproduced with permission from EBSCO Information Services.

Arthur L. Greil, Kathleen Slauson-Blevins, and Julia McQuillan. "The Experience of Infertility: A Review of Recent Literature." From *Sociology of Health & Illness*, Volume 32, Issue 1. © 2010 by Blackwell Publishing Ltd. Reproduced with permission of John Wiley and Sons Inc.; permission conveyed through Copyright Clearance Center, Inc.

Dale Jacobs. "More Than Words: Comics as a Means of Teaching Multiple Literacies." From *English Journal*, Volume 96, Issue 3, January 2007. Copyright © 2007 by the National Council of Teachers of English. Reprinted with permission.

Charles Kerns and Kenneth Ko. "Exploring Happiness and Performance at Work." From *Leadership & Organizational Management Journal*. Copyright © 2009. Reproduced with the permission of the authors.

Aimee C. Mapes. "Two Vowels Together: On the Wonderfully Insufferable Experiences of Literacy." From *College Composition and Communication*, Volume 67, No. 4, June 2016, pp. 686–92. Copyright © 2016 by the National Council of Teachers of English. Reprinted with permission.

Margaret Shandor Miles, Diane Holditch-Davis, Suzanne Thoyre, and Linda Beeber. "Rural African-American Mothers Parenting Prematurely Born Infants: An Ecological Systems Perspective." From *Newborn and Infant Nursing Reviews*, Volume 5, Issue 3, September 2005, pp. 142–48. Copyright © 2005 Elsevier. Republished with the permission of Elsevier Science and Technology Journals; permission conveyed through Copyright Clearance Center, Inc.

Myra Moses. "IEP" class materials and "Lesson Plan" class materials. Reproduced with permission of the author.

Kalervo Oberg. Excerpt from "Cultural Shock: Adjustment to New Cultural Environments." From *Practical Anthropology*, 1960, Volume 7. Copyright © 1960 American Association of Missiology. Reproduced with permission.

Kevin Rathunde and Mihaly Csikszentmihalyi. "Middle School Students' Motivation and Quality of Experience: A Comparison of Montessori and Traditional School Environments." From *American Journal of Education*, Volume 111, Issue 3, May 2005. Copyright © 2005 University of Chicago Press. Reproduced with permission.

Kevin Rathunde and Mihaly Csikszentmihalyi. "The Social Context of Middle Schools: Teachers, Friends, and Activities in Montessori and Traditional School Environments." From *Elementary School Journal*, Volume 106, No. 1, September 2005, pp. 59–79. Copyright © 2005 by the University of Chicago. Reproduced with permission.

Gary Ritchison. "Hunting Behavior, Territory Quality, and Individual Quality of American Kestrels (*Falco sparverius*)." From Eastern Kentucky University web page. Reproduced by permission of the author.

Jack Solomon. "Masters of Desire: The Culture of American Advertising." From *The Signs of Our Time: Semiotics, the Hidden Messages of Environments, Objects, and Cultural Images* by Jack Solomon. Copyright © 1988 by Jack Solomon. Reprinted by permission of Tarcher, an imprint of Penguin Publishing Group, a division of Penguin Random House LLC. All rights reserved. Any third-party use of this material, outside of this publication, is prohibited. Interested third parties must apply directly to Penguin Random House LLC for permission.

WPA Outcomes Statement. Ratified in July 2014. Reproduced with permission by The Council of Writing Program Administrators.

Index

LaunchPad Additional video material may be found online in LaunchPad when the ⊙ icon appears.

A

abstracts, in social sciences, 205, 214
academic disciplines
   categories of, four, 8–10, 119
   conventions of writing in, 15–16, 120
   defined, 8
   genres in, 120
   number of, 8–10
   research in, 119–20
academic journals, 88–92
academic literacy, 14
academic presses as sources, 93
academic research
   bibliography, annotated, 101–2
   choosing primary and secondary sources, 82–84
   databases of journals, using, 88–91
   documentation systems, 99–101
   evaluating sources, 92–94
   paraphrasing in, 94–98
   plagiarism, avoiding, 98–99
   PsycINFO database, 89–90
   questions, developing, 81
   quoting in, 94–98
   scholarly sources for, 92–93
   searching for journal articles, 89–91
   sources, searching for, 84–92
   summarizing in, 94–98
academic text, analysis of, 127
academic writers

audience for, 10–11
   reasons for citing sources, 339–40
   reasons for writing, 11
academic writing
   in college compared to other contexts, 12–14
   Council of Writing Program Administrators (CWPA), 13–14
   goals of writing course, 14
   profile of a writer, 15–18
   writing in different contexts, 15
acknowledgments, in social sciences writing, 206
advertisement, analysis of, 70–78
Allen, Barbara, excerpts from "Environmental Justice, Local Knowledge, and After-Disaster Planning in New Orleans," 193–94, 206
American Chemical Society (ACS), 352
American Council of Learned Societies, 139
American Institute of Physics (AIP), 352
American Mathematical Society (AMS), 352
American Medical Association (AMA), 352
American Political Science Association (APSA), 352
American Psychological Association (APA), 100, 128, 170, 206, 256
   citing different types of sources in, 347
   in-text citations in, 345–46
   reference page citations in, 346
   sample reference page, 348
   unique features of, 345
American Sociological Association (ASA), 352

analyzing rhetorical context, 47
appeals, rhetorical, 60–61
appendices, in social sciences writing, 206–7
applied fields
  business
    memorandum, 314–16
    plan, 317–26
  communication, importance of, 293
  cooperation and collaboration in, 293–94
  criminal justice and law as, 326–38
    e-mail correspondence, 335–36
    Introduction, Rule, Application, and Conclusion
      (IRAC), 328–29
    legal brief, 328–35
  defined, 292
  education
    individualized education program (IEP), 308
    lesson plan, 304–8
  health fields
    allied health fields, 296
    discharge instructions, 300–303
    nursing, 296–97
    scholarly research report, 297–300
  identifying problems, 293
  problem solving, 293
  research, varied, 293
  rhetoric and, 294–95
  scholarly research report, 297–300
  scholars in, 10
  writing situation, analysis of, 295
argument
  analyzing advertisements, 70–78
  appeals to ethos, logos, and pathos, 60–61
  assumptions, understanding, 67–68
  claims, making, 59–62
  controversial issue, example of, 103–14
  counterarguments, anticipating, 68–69
  defined, 59
  evidence to support reasons, 65–67
  position, qualifying, 69
  proofs and appeals, 60–61
  reasons, developing, 63–64
  simple and complex thesis statements, 63–64
  statistical data and research findings, 66
  thesis-driven, in the humanities, 161
  thesis statement, forming, 61–62
Aristotle, 60–61
artistic proofs, 60
artistic texts, 167, 180–81
assumptions, understanding, 67–68
audience
  in the applied fields, 295
  as element of rhetorical contexts, 51–53

for press release, 124–26
primary and secondary, 46
and reading rhetorically, 49
rhetorical contexts and, 52
author
  as element of rhetorical contexts, 51–53
  reading rhetorically, 49
  and rhetorical context, 46

B

Bahls, Patrick (mathematics), on genres, 27 ○
Baumgartner, Jody (political science), on the writing
  process, 26 ○
Beeber, Linda. *See* "Rural African-American Mothers
  Parenting Prematurely Born Infants: An Ecological
  Systems Perspective" (Miles et al.)
bias, avoiding, 195, 244
bibliography, annotated
  in academic research, 101–2
  in literature review, 214
Bieda, Michaela (student), "My Journey to Writing,"
  40–43
Bluebook style, 352
Brotherton, Mike (astronomy)
  on argument and choosing the "right" side, 69 ○
  on audience for a press release, 126
  on how accuracy trumps strong writing, 130
  "Hubble Space Telescope Spies Galaxy/Black Hole
    Evolution in Action," from, 125–26
  "Spectacular Poststarburst Quasar, A" (Brotherton
    et al.), 129–30
  on writing for different audiences, 123
  on writing in the sciences, 123
Bush, George H. W., "Letter to Saddam Hussein,"
  53–55
business writing
  business plan, 317–25
  memorandum, 314–16
  plans and proposals, 317

C

Cassidy, K., K. Brown, and M. Jackson, excerpts from
  "Under the Radar: Educators and Cyberbullying in
  Schools," 189–90, 199, 201
characters, in student essay, 41
charts, tables, and figures, 202–4, 254
Chicago Manual of Style (CMS), 170–71, 352
Chopin, Kate, "The Story of an Hour," 155, 157–59
citations, reasons for making, 339–40

claims
  hedging, 168–69, 208
  making, 61–62
close reading
  content/form-response grid, 154–56
  in the humanities, 144–45
  responding to others' interpretations,
    159–60
  strategies for, 154–59
college, three stages of transition to, 7
colleges and universities
  different kinds, 4–5
  expectations of writing skills, 3
  mission or values statements, 6
  purpose of, 5–6
  resources at your school, 7
communication skills, 19–20, 49, 293
community colleges, 4
composing, discovering ideas through, 25–27
comprehensive colleges/universities, 4
content/form-response grid, 154–56
control group, 250
conventions
  language
    active and passive voice, 167–68, 207–8
    in different disciplines, 127–28
    in the humanities, 167–69
    in the natural sciences, 254
    in the social sciences, 207–8
  references
    in the humanities, 169–72
    in the natural sciences, 254
    in the social sciences, 256, 272
  structural
    in the humanities, 161, 166–67
    in the natural sciences, 254
    in the social sciences, 197–204
  writing, 11
    in the humanities, 160–72
    in the natural sciences, 253–58
    in the social sciences, 196–207
    varied, in the applied fields, 294–95
cooperation and collaboration
  in the applied fields, 293–94
  other researchers, treatment of, 257–58
Council of Science Editors (CSE), 101, 256
  citing different types of sources in, 350
  in-text citations, 349
  reference page citations in, 349–50
  sample references page, 351
  unique features of, 349
Council of Writing Program Administrators
    (CWPA)

outcomes, common, of first-year writing course,
    13–14
  selected goals for writing process, 20
counterarguments, anticipating, 68–69
criminal justice and law
  careers in, 326–27
  e-mail correspondence, 335–36
  Introduction, Rule, Application, and Conclusion
    (IRAC) for legal briefs, 328–29
  professional legal brief, 328–35
Csikszentmihalyi, Mihaly, 184
  excerpts from "Happiness in Everyday Life: The Uses
    of Experience Sampling" (with Jeremy Hunter),
    205–6, 212–13, 216
"Cultural Shock: Adjustment to New Cultural
  Environments" (Oberg), 186–89

D

data
  academic journal databases, searching, 88–91
  collection, 191–93, 242
  for research in the humanities, 142–43
debatable subject in academic research, 82
debate. *See* argument
Deconstruction theory, 144
descriptive and rhetorical language
  in the humanities, 167
  in the natural sciences, 245–46
detail, sensory, 43
dialogue, 42
Dieckmann, Janna (nursing), on areas of research in
    nursing, 297
Diigo, online bookmarking tool, 353
discourse communities, 120
doctoral-granting/research-intensive universities, 4
documentation
  American Psychological Association (APA),
    340–41
  Chicago Manual of Style, 170–71, 352
  Council of Science Editors, 340–41
  in the humanities, 170–72
  Modern Language Association (MLA), 340–44
  in the natural sciences, 256
  in the social sciences, 196, 206, 209
  systems for research, 99–101
drafting, to develop writing project, 21, 23–26

E

EbscoHOST, 90–91
editing/proofreading, in idea mapping stage, 27

education
    individualized education plan (IEP), 308–13
    lesson plan, 304–8
    written products of educators, 304
"Effects of Sleep Deprivation: A Literature Review"
        (O'Brien), 218–26
"Electricity Monitor Company, The" (Mills), 317–25
e-mail correspondence, 17, 335–36
EndNote, research-tracking application, 353
entertainment and reading rhetorically, 49
"Environmental Justice, Local Knowledge, and After-
        Disaster Planning in New Orleans," excerpts from
        (Allen), 193–94, 206
essays, five-paragraph, 165–66
ethos, appeals to, 60–61, 65, 75–76
"Evaluating Hydration Levels in High School Athletes"
        (Gomperts), 104–13
"Evaluation of the Attribution Theory" (Kapadia),
        229–38
evidence to support reasons, 65–67
"Experience of Infertility: A Review of Recent
        Literature," abstract from (*Society of Health and
        Illness*), 215–16
expert testimony, 65–66
"Exploring Happiness and Performance at Work,"
        excerpt from (Kerns and Ko), 190

F

feasibility issue in academic research, 82
feedback, giving and acting on, 22–25
Feminist Theory, 144
field of study and rhetorical context, 46–47
five-paragraph essay, 165–66
focus/stance, establishing, 169–70
Formalism (New Criticism) theory, 144
for-profit schools, 5
freewriting, 26

G

Garrigan, Shelley (Spanish language and literature)
    on peer-mentoring, 160
    on writing for other academics, 172
Geiger, Paige (molecular and integrative physiology)
    on manuscripts versus grant writing, 259
    on research study design and scientific integrity, 243
genres
    in the academic disciplines, 120
    analyzing, 121
    choosing, in the applied fields, 295–98

in the humanities, 172–80
memoir, 29
in the natural sciences, 254–79
of reflective writing, 29
in the social sciences, 211–38
understanding, 48–49
Gomperts, Jack (student), "Evaluating Hydration Levels
        in High School Athletes," 104–13
Google and identifying search terms, 85–88

H

"Happiness in Everyday Life: The Uses of Experience
        Sampling," excerpts from (Csikszentmihalyi and
        Hunter), 205–6, 212–13, 216
health fields
    allied health professions, 296
    in the applied fields, 296–98
    discharge instructions, 300–303
    nursing, 296–97
    scholarly research report, 297–300
    writing for, in the applied fields, 296–98
hedging claims, 168–69, 208
Hemingway, Ernest, *Death in the Afternoon*, 140
higher education, choices of schools, 4–5
Holditch-Davis, Diane. *See* "Rural African-American
        Mothers Parenting Prematurely Born Infants: An
        Ecological Systems Perspective" (Miles et al.)
Holtzhauser, Timothy, "Rhetoric of a 1943 War Bonds
        Ad," 74–78
"Hubble Space Telescope Spies Galaxy/Black Hole
        Evolution in Action," from (Brotherton), 125–26
humanities
    American Council of Learned Societies, 139
    asking "why," 162
    conventions of writing
        essays, five-paragraph, 165–66
        learning from peer and others' writings, 160–61
        open-ended questions, 163
        paragraphs and transitions, 167
        research questions, developing, 161–63
        thesis statements, 161–65
        titles and subtitles, 166
        why, what, and *how* questions, 163
    documentation of sources, 170–72
    genres of writing in
        artistic texts, 180–82
        textual interpretation, 172–80
    language conventions
        active voice versus passive voice, 167–68
        descriptive and rhetorical language, 167
        hedging of claims, 168–69

references conventions
  Chicago Manual of Style (CMS), 170–71
  focus/stance, establishing, 169–70
  introduction and citations in, 169–70
  Modern Language Association (MLA), 170
  other scholars, incorporating works of, 169
  scholarly writing, analyzing, 171–72
research in
  close reading, 144–59
  content/form-response grid, 154
  images, observing and interpreting, 143–44
  interpretations, responding to, 159–60
  role of theory in, 144
  texts as primary source for, 142–43
scholars in, 9, 11
structural conventions, 161, 166–67
texts and meaning, 140–41
"Hunting Behavior, Territory Quality, and Individual
    Quality of American Kestrels (*Falco sparverius*)"
    (Ritchison), 272–79
hypotheses
  defined, 62
  in the natural sciences, 246–47, 255–56
  in the social sciences, 189–90

I

ideas
  discovering through composing, 25–27
  main idea, 31
  mapping, 26
  tools for composing/invention, 25–26
images, observing and interpreting, 143
inartistic proofs in argument, 60, 61
individualized education plan (IEP), 308–13
Institute of Electrical and Electronics Engineers (IEEE),
    352
institutional review boards (IRB), 196, 251
interdisciplinary fields, 242
in-text documentation
  American Psychological Association (APA) style, 209,
    345–46
  Council of Science Editors, 349
  documentation in the social sciences, 209
Introduction, Methods, Results, and Discussion
    (IMRaD) format, 122, 197–204, 254, 279
Introduction, Rule, Application, and Conclusion (IRAC)
    format, 328–29
"I" point of view, 30, 32, 40
issues or topics
  controversial, developing a supported,
    102–13

as element of rhetorical writing, 51–53
and rhetorical context, 46
IT industry, writing for, 17–18

J

Jackson, Karen Keaton (writing studies)
  on accidental plagiarism, 99 **O**
  on considering purpose and audience, 46 **O**
  on different kinds of texts, 120 **O**
  on incorporating research to support ideas, 161 **O**
  on transition into college writing, 13 **O**
Jacobs, Dale, "More Than Words: Comics as a Means of
    Teaching Multiple Literacies," 145–53
jargon, in the natural sciences, 254
journals databases, using, 88–91

K

Kapadia, Matt (student), "Evaluation of the Attribution
    Theory," 229–38
Kerns, C., and K. Ko, excerpt from "Exploring
    Happiness and Performance at Work," 190
Kish, Zenia (American studies), statement of claim,
    example of, 164
Kumar, Rubbal (student), "Profile of a Writer: Benu
    Badhan," 16–18

L

lab reports
  IMRaD format, 279–90
  in the natural sciences, 258
Lambrecht, Gena (student), on academic writing,
    12 **O**
language, or word choice
  active and passive voices, 167–68
  conventions in different disciplines, 127–28
  descriptive and rhetorical, in the humanities, 167
  humanist views on, 210
  jargon in the natural sciences, 254
language conventions
  in the humanities, 167–69
  in the natural sciences, 254
  in the social sciences, 207–8
LaRue, Michelle (conservation biology), on forming
    study questions, 249–50
law, writing for, 327–28
learning skills and reading rhetorically, 49
legal brief, 329–35

Lemon, Kedric (student)
    "Comparing the Efficiency of Various Batteries Being Used over Time," 260–70
    "Which Type of Battery Is the Most Effective When Energy Is Drawn Rapidly?," 280–90
liberal arts colleges/universities, 4
"Life May Be Possible on Other Planets" (Natasi), 133–36
Linguistic Society of America (LSA), 352
literacy, defined, 29
literacy narrative, 30–43
literary analysis, 62
literature as prompts for writing, 12
literature review, 211–26
logos, appeals to, 60, 61
Lopez, Sofia (student), "The Multiple Audiences of George H. W. Bush's Letter to Saddam Hussein," 55–57

M

magazines as popular sources, 93
main claim
    developing, 163–65
    in structure of writing, 127
main idea, 30, 31, 43
Mapes, Aimee C., "Two Vowels Together: On the Wonderfully Insufferable Experiences of Literacy," 32–38
Marxism theory, 144
"Masters of Desire: The Culture of American Advertising" (Solomon), 70–73
Matsuda, Aya (linguistics), 196–97
    on kinds of writing in applied linguists, 211
    on reading, in order to learn conventions, 196–97
McCracken, Moriah (writing studies)
    on entering academic conversations, 66 ●
    on methods for primary research, 83 ●
    on thinking about audience, purpose, and form, 122 ●
McCurdy, John (history), 139, 140
Mendeley, online resource manager, 353
metacognition, defined, 28
"Middle School Students' Motivation and Quality of Experience: A Comparison of Montessori and Traditional School Environments," excerpts from (Rathunde and Csikszentmihalyi), 183–84, 193, 194, 195, 200–203, 204, 205–6
Miles, Margaret Shandor, et al., "Rural African-American Mothers Parenting Prematurely Born Infants: An Ecological Systems Perspective," 298–300

Mills, Daniel Chase (student), "The Electricity Monitor Company," 317–25
mission statements of colleges/universities, 6–7
Modern Humanities Research Association (MHRA), 352
Modern Language Association (MLA), 99–100, 128, 170, 209
    citing different types of sources in, 342
    compared to APA and CSE styles, 340–41
    in-text citations, 341
    sample works cited page, 344
    unique features of, 341
    works cited citations in, 342
"More Than Words: Comics as a Means of Teaching Multiple Literacies" (Jacobs), 145–53
Morris, Jonathan (political science)
    on finding scholarly sources, 92 ●
    on the writing process, 26 ●
Moses, Myra (educator), lesson plan, 305–8
"Multiple Audiences of George H. W. Bush's Letter to Saddam Hussein, The" (Lopez), 55–57
"My Journey to Writing" (Bieda), 40–43

N

narrative, literacy, 30–32
Natasi, Jonathan (student, translator), "Life May Be Possible on Other Planets," 133–36
natural sciences
    bias, eliminating, 244
    conventions of writing in
        charts and figures, 254
        cooperation and collaboration, 257–58
        detail in writing, 255
        documentation, 256
        jargon in research writing, 254
        objectivity, 253–55
        precision in writing, 256
        recency, 256–57
        replicability, 255–56
    descriptive writing, 245–46
    designing a research study, 249–52
    genres of writing
        Introduction, Methods, Results and Discussion (IMRaD) format, 254
        lab report, 279–90
        observation notebook, 258–70
        research proposal, 271–79
    institutional review board (IRB), 251
    interdisciplinary fields, 242
    language, or word choice, in research papers, 254
    open-ended questions, 248
    other researchers' work, treatment of, 257–58

references in, 256, 272
research in
    closed-ended questions, 248
    comparative experiment, 250
    control group, 250
    from description to speculation, 245–49
    designing a research study, 249–52
    hard and soft sciences, 243
    hypotheses, forming, 246–47, 255–56
    institutional review board (IRB), 251
    observation and description, 243–45
    open-ended questions, 248
    publishing, 252
    qualitative data, 244
    replicable and quantifiable methods, 243–44
        results, presenting, 252
    speculative writing, 245–46
    statistical procedures, 249
scholars in, 9
scientific method, 241–42
scientific writing process, 241–42
structural conventions of research papers, 254
titles of research papers, 253–54
neutrality, in the social sciences, 195
New Criticism (Formalism) theory, 144
New Historicism theory, 144
newspapers as popular sources, 93
nursing field, writing for, 296–97

O

Oberg, Kalervo, from "Cultural Shock: Adjustment to
    New Cultural Environments," 186–89
objectivity, 195, 253–54
O'Brien, William (student), "Effects of Sleep
    Deprivation: A Literature Review," 218–26
observation
    in academic disciplines 121–22
    and description, 244
    and interpretation, 142
    in natural sciences 244–45
    notebook, 258–70
open-ended questions, 163, 248
Oquendo, Nichelle (student), peer review feedback of
    sample rough draft, 23–25
organization of writing, 127
others' experiences, writing about, 228

P

paragraphs and transitions, 167
paraphrasing, 96–97, 210

passive voice, 47, 207–8
pathos, appeals to, 60
peer review
    in idea mapping stage, 26
    of student's literacy narrative, 22–25
peer-reviewed articles, 88
personal experiences, writing about, 65, 227–28
personal investment, in academic research, 82
plagiarism, avoiding, 98–99
position, qualifying, in argument, 69
Postcolonialism theory, 144
press releases, 125–26
prewriting/invention, 25
primary audience, 46
primary sources for academic research, 83
problems
    identifying, in applied fields, 293
    posed in an essay, 41
Proctor, Sian (geology), on the different specialties of
    geological studies, 240–41
"Profile of a Writer: Benu Badhan" (Kumar), 16–18
programming code, 17
proofs in argument, inartistic and artistic, 60
PsycINFO database, 89–90
Publication Manual of the American Psychological Association
    (APA), 100, 128, 170, 206, 209, 256, 345–48

Q

qualitative research methods, 193–94, 243–44
quantitative research methods, 191–93, 243–44
Queer Theory, 144
questions
    developing, 293
    why, what, and *how* questions, 163
quoting
    in academic research, 97–98
    others' interpretations of texts, 160
    in the social sciences, 210
    summarizing and paraphrasing others' writing, 210

R

Rathunde, Kevin (social sciences), 183
    on conditions for well-being and connection, 184
    on having multiple perspectives on a question, 192
    "Middle School Students' Motivation and Quality
        of Experience: A Comparison of Montessori and
        Traditional School Environments," excerpts from
        (with Csikszentmihalyi), 183–84, 193, 194, 195,
        200–203, 204, 205–6

ement, 164

art: An Analysis of Kate Chopin's
or an Hour,'" 174–80

sponse theory, 144

ing and writing rhetorically, 46–50

rebuttal, in argument, 68

recency of research, 256–57

reference conventions

American Psychological Association (APA),
170, 206

Chicago Manual of Style (CMS), 170–71

in different disciplines, 128

in the humanities, 169–72

Modern Language Association (MLA), 170–71

in the natural sciences, 254

for a research proposal, 272

in the social sciences, 206, 256, 272

summarizing and paraphrasing others' writing, 210

reflective writing, 28–29

RefWorks, research-tracking application, 353

replicable and quantifiable research methods,
243–44

reports

lab, 258, 279–90

scholarly research, 297–300

research

developing questions, in the humanities, 161–62

in the humanities, 161–62

in idea mapping stage, 26

issues, researchable, 82

in the natural sciences, 186–92

primary and secondary, 82–84, 119–20

tracking, 321

research methods

institutional review boards (IRBs) format, 196

mixed-methodology studies, 194–95

qualitative, 193–94

quantitative, 191–93

research papers, structure of, 254

research process

designing a research study, 249–51

hypotheses, 242–43, 245–46, 248

methods section, 271–72

observation, 243–45, 258–70

scholarly report, 297–300

sections in, 271–72

speculation, 245

statistical data and findings, 66

study, designing, 249–51

research proposal, 271–72

research questions

content/form-response grid, 162

developing, 81–82

in the humanities, 161–62

natural sciences, 246–47, 255–56

open-ended questions, 163

popular sources, 92–94

in the social sciences, 189–90

revising, in idea mapping stage, 26

rhetoric

in the applied fields, 294–95

principles of, for college writing, 12–13

"Rhetoric of a 1943 War Bonds Ad" (Holtzhauser),
74–78

rhetorical analysis, 50, 52–57

rhetorical appeals, 60–61

rhetorical contexts, 52–53, 95, 123

Richter, Michelle (criminologist), on motivations for
working in criminal justice, 327

Ritchison, Gary, "Hunting Behavior, Territory Quality,
and Individual Quality of American Kestrels (*Falco
sparverius*)," 272–79

"Rural African-American Mothers Parenting
Prematurely Born Infants: An Ecological Systems
Perspective" (Miles et al.), 298–300

S

scene writing, 30, 31, 38–39, 41

scholarly articles and engaging with other scholars, 169

scholarly research report, 297–300

scholarly sources, 92–94

schools with specific vocational focus, 4–5

science memos, examples of, 246

scientific writing process, 241–42

search terms, identifying, 85–88

social sciences

charts and figures, 202–4

conventions of writing

abstracts, 205

acknowledgments, 206

appendices, 206–7

conclusion, 205

Introduction, Methods, Results and Discussion
(IMRaD) format, 197–204

references, 206

structural, other, 205–7

titles, 205

Discussion section, 204

genres of writing

literature review, 211–26

source synthesis chart, 214

theory response essay, 227–38

introduction to, 183–84
language conventions
    active and passive voices, 207–8
    hedging, 208
observing behavior, 184–85
others' experiences, 228
personal experience, 227–28
reference conventions
    in-text documentation, 209
    Publication Manual of the American Psychological Association (APA), 206, 209
    summary and paraphrase, 210
research in
    bias, addressing, 195
    institutional review board (IRB) policies, 196
    methods, 191–95
    mixed-methodology studies, 194–95
    neutrality, 195
    qualitative research methods, 193–94
    quantitative research methods, 191–93
    questions and hypotheses, 189–91
    statisticians, role in, 191–93
    theories of human behavior and human systems, 186
    theory, development of, 189
    theory, role of, 185–89
results, 200–204
scholars in, 9
structural conventions, 197–204
synthesizing sources, in the social sciences, 214–15
titles, for articles, 205
visual representations of data, 202–4
writing about others' experiences, 228
writing about personal experiences, 227–28
Society of Health and Illness, abstract from "Experience of Infertility: A Review of Recent Literature," 215–16
Solomon, Jack, "Masters of Desire: The Culture of American Advertising," 70–73, 95
sources
    evaluating, 92–94
    journal databases, 88–92
    peer-reviewed articles, 88
    primary and secondary, 82–84
    scholarly versus popular, distinguishing between, 92–94
    searching for, 85–94
    summarizing, paraphrasing, and quoting, 94–98
    synthesizing, in the social sciences, 214–15
    why to cite, 339–40
source synthesis chart, 214

"Spectacular Poststarburst Quasar, A" (Brotherton et al.), 129–30
speculative writing, 245–46
statistics
    data and research findings, 66
    procedures, 191–93
    role in social sciences, 191–93
Stegner, Jack (student), draft of literacy narrative, 23–25
"Story of an Hour, The" (Chopin), 155, 157–59
Stout, Sam (student), on academic writing, 12 ○
structure
    conventions in social sciences, 197–204
    in the humanities, 161, 166–67
    in the natural sciences, 254
    of research papers, 254
    in social sciences, 205–7
structure, language, and reference (SLR), 127–29

T

technology, to assist writing, 27–28
theories of human behavior and human systems, 186
theory response essay, 227–38
thesis statement
    claims, making, 61–62
    constructing, 64
    content/form-response grid, 162
    developing, in the humanities, 161–65
    ending of essay, 78
    versus hypothesis, 62–63, 190
    research questions, 162
    simple and complex, 63–64
    in student essay, 74
Thoyre, Suzanne. *See* "Rural African-American Mothers Parenting Prematurely Born Infants: An Ecological Systems Perspective" (Miles et al.)
"Till Death Do Us Part: An Analysis of Kate Chopin's 'The Story of an Hour'" (Ray), 174–80
Tinto, Vincent, 7
title, choosing, 166, 205, 253–54
translation methods, for scholarly article, 138–39
"Two Vowels Together: On the Wonderfully Insufferable Experiences of Literacy" (Mapes), 32–38

U

"Under the Radar: Educators and Cyberbullying in Schools," excerpts from (Cassidy, Brown, and Jackson), 189–90, 199, 201

...ions of data, 202–4
...ng rhetorically, 50

W

"Which Type of Battery Is the Most Effective When Energy Is Drawn Rapidly?" (Lemon), 280–90
why, *what*, and *how* questions, 163
Woods, Alexandria (student), on academic writing, 12 ▶
workplace, writing in, 17–18
writing
    author's purpose in, 50
    college, compared to other contexts, 12–14
    conventions, 11
    five-paragraph essay, 165–66
    metacognition of thought processes, 28
    process, 20–28
    reflective, 29
    rhetorically, 50–53
    in the workplace, 17–18
writing process and reflection
    Council of Writing Administrators' Selected Goals for Writing Processes, 20
    defined, 20

drafts, multiple, to develop project, 21
feedback, giving and acting on, 22–25
flexible strategies, 21–22
goals for, 20
ideas, discovering, 25–26
literacy narrative, 29–43
metacognition and writing, 28
reflective writing, 28–29
sample rough draft with feedback, 23–25
strategies, flexible, 21–22
writing projects
    annotated bibliography, writing a, 101–2
    composing a literacy narrative, 39–40
    developing a supported argument on a controversial issue, 102
    profile of a writer, 15–18
    rhetorical analysis, 57
    rhetorical analysis of an advertisement, 79
    translating a scholarly article, 136–37
    writing a comparative genre analysis, 131–32
    writing a literature review, 216
    writing an artistic text, 181–82

Z

Zotero, online research tool, 353